MAJOR WRITERS
of the
WORLD

I. A. LANGNAS *and* J. S. LIST

About the Book

Original in concept and encyclopedic in scope, this literary reference work provides a comprehensive catalog of nearly fourteen hundred significant writers of all ages and nations—from Homer to Sandburg, from Sappho to Sagan, from Aesop to Arthur Miller.

It includes pertinent biographical information, a listing of each author's major and/or best-known works, and a critical evaluation of his writings and their significance. No era or area has been overlooked in the selection, which includes Europeans, Asians, Africans, North- and South-Americans, and writers of every period and school.

LITTLEFIELD, ADAMS & CO.
PATERSON, NEW JERSEY

MAJOR
WRITERS
of the
WORLD

I. A. LANGNAS *and* J. S. LIST

1 9 6 3

LITTLEFIELD, ADAMS & CO.

PATERSON, NEW JERSEY

PREFACE

The purpose of this Dictionary is to provide a readily accessible source of basic information about the major writers of the world from earliest times up to the present day. Where space is limited selection is bound to present difficulties, and must inevitably be to some extent a subjective expression of the Editors' personal opinions. There can be little argument about the outstanding names that take their place at the top of the hierarchy of writers. Among those of the second rank, however, agreement on those who ought to be included is far less likely. Every writer has his importance; it is in assessing his relative importance that the difficulty lies. If any reader feels very strongly about the absence of a particular author from this volume, he is urged to inform the Editors so that appropriate action may be taken when the Dictionary comes up for revision.

In regard to the writers of antiquity and of foreign countries, our policy has been to favor those whose works are at least partly available in English. Up to the time of the Renaissance the branches of learning were so intertwined that we have necessarily admitted the claims of many writers who were primarily philosophers and historians; after that time, however, far more specialization became apparent, and sheer weight of numbers has forced us to confine our choice (with very few exceptions) to those who contributed to the field that we now call literature, that is to say, poets, dramatists, novelists and essayists.

In preparing this volume every care has been taken to check the information against the most reliable sources.

No work of this kind, however, has ever reached the public without containing a few errors that have eluded the most vigilant scrutiny of its editors; it is unlikely that this volume will prove to be any exception. We should be grateful if readers would draw to our attention any errors they may detect, so that these may in due course be corrected.

We should like to thank the editors of the Philosophical Library, especially Dr. Joseph T. Shipley, for permission to use material from their publications *Encyclopedia of Literature, Dictionary of French Literature,* and *Dictionary of Russian Literature.*

The Editors

A

Aanrud, Hans

Norwegian writer and critic (1863-1953).

Born in Gausdal. Wrote stories about Norwegian peasant life, books for children, and theatrical criticism. Chief work: "Tales" (1905).

Aasen, Ivar

Norwegian philologist and poet (1813-1896).

Born on his father's farm in Volda, died in Oslo. Self-taught son of a small farmer, he became the leading Norwegian philologist and a staunch defender of peasant values. His philological studies led to the creation of the "landsmaal" (country language, now called "new Norwegian") based on the peasant speech to compete against the Danish prevailing in the Norwegian cities. Aasen wrote poems and plays in the new language and made a valuable collection of peasant tales.

Abd-ul-Hakk Hamid

Turkish poet (1852-1938).

Born and died in Istanbul. A politician and statesman now remembered as founder of the new Turkish poetry. He was the first Turk to write on Western models. Wrote erotic verse and descriptive poems like "Sahara" and "History."

Abelard, Peter

French philosopher (1079-1142).

Born near Nantes in Brittany. Studied theology and

1

philosophy in Paris, rose to become master of a philosophical school, which inaugurated what Charles Haskins has called "the Renaissance of the Twelfth Century." His philosophy, known as conceptualism, was condemned by the Church as heretical (1121). Meanwhile, he had secretly married Heloise, whose uncle, Fulbert, had him castrated. He then led a wandering life from monastery to monastery and died on his way to Rome to present his defense. His body was given to Heloise, then prioress of a convent, and after her death their bodies were buried together. Their tomb, at the Pere Lachaise cemetery in Paris, is still visited by lovers. Chief philosophical work: "Yes and No," in which Abelard gives both positive and negative answers to a number of questions. Also famous is his correspondence with Heloise.

About, Edmond

French novelist and journalist (1828-1885).

Born in Dieuze; died in Paris. Educated in Paris and Athens. His first novel, "Tolla Ferdi" (1853), caused a great stir. He followed it up with "The Marriage of Paris" (1856), "Germaine" (1857), "The King of the Mountains" (1857), "The Man With the Broken Ear" (1862). His political writings were successful, but not his plays. He was a monarchist until the Franco-Prussian War of 1870-71, later a Republican. From 1875, he was editor-in-chief of the newspaper "Le XIXe Siècle."

Abraham a Santa Clara

German preacher (1644-1709).

Real name: Ulrich Megerle. Born in Kreenheinstetten (Baden); died in Vienna. Augustinian monk, became in 1677 preacher at the Vienna Imperial Court. His sermons are a mixture of baroque and popular. The sermon warning against the Turkish peril to Vienna was taken by Schiller as a model of his Capuchin sermon in "Wallenstein."

Abrahams, Peter

South African novelist (born 1919).

Born in Vrededorp, a native suburb of Johannesburg. Son of an Abyssinian father and a mother of mixed European and African origin. Managed to acquire an education at missionary schools and to leave South Africa as a ship's stoker at the beginning of the war. Settled in England. He had started writing in South Africa but it was only from London that he was able to become the first writer to tell to the outside world the story of his native land from the point of view of its silenced majority. Wrote: "Dark Testament" (1942); "Song of the City" (1943); "Mine Boy" (1946); "The Path of Thunder" (1948); etc.

Abu'l Fazl

Indian Moslem writer (1550-1602).

Prime Minister of the Mughal emperor Akbar, prominent in the creation of the synthetic religion, "Din Ilahi," with which Akbar tried to replace the ever-clashing creeds of Islam, Hinduism and Christianity. He wrote a biography of Akbar and the "Institutes," a survey of the Empire and its government. Though marred by a servile flattery of the Emperor, they are valuable documents and breathe an admirable spirit of religious toleration. Abu'l Fazl was murdered at the instigation of Akbar's son, the future emperor Jahangir.

Abu Nuwas

Arab poet (762-812).

Born at Ahwas. Poet of love, wine, and other sensual pleasures. One of the great writers of Baghdad during the Abbassid period, when Arab poetry became courtly and elegant under Persian influence. He wrote drinking and hunting songs, love poems, and diatribes in polished verse. He died of a beating he received as a result of one of his satirical poems.

Abu Tammam

Arab poet and critic (about 800-about 845).

His collection "Hamasa" (courage) gathered songs and poems of over 500 Arab poets. It consists of fighting songs, elegies, and didactic verse.

Accolti, Bernardo

Italian poet (1458-1535).

Born in Arezzo; died in Rome. Became a favorite of Leo X and was named to high offices in the Vatican. He wrote dramas and lyrical verse, but is best known for his "Strambotti," epigrams in stanza form.

Acevedo Diaz, Eduardo

Uruguayan novelist (1851-1924).

Took a prominent part in his country's politics at a time when they were marked by savage violence. All the more remarkable is the ruthless impartiality of his three novels of gaucho life, "Ishmael" (1888); "The Native Girl" (1890) and "The Cry of Glory" (1894), perhaps the best introduction for anyone who tries to understand a kind of man that is gone, but certainly not forgotten.

Achilles Tatius

Greek writer (3rd century A.D.).

An Alexandrian rhetorician, wrote "The Romance of Leucippe and Clitophon," a melodramatic and romantic tale that was much read in the Byzantine Empire, was translated into a number of European languages during the Renaissance and influenced the development of the European novel.

Acuna, Hernando de

Spanish poet (about 1520-about 1580).

Born in Valladolid, died in Granada. Served as soldier of Charles V in Italian and African campaigns. Re-wrote in Spanish verse the emperor's prose translation of "The Deliberate Knight" by Olivier de la Marché. His own poetry glorifies Charles and the imperial idea, with touches of modern totalitarianism, especially in the famous lines: "One shepherd and one flock only in the field; one king, one throne and one sword," reminiscent of the Nazi "One People, One Reich, One Fuehrer."

Adamnan

Irish writer (about 625-704).

Born in Donegal, died on the island of Iona in Scotland. Became abbot of Iona in 679, advocated the adoption of Roman regulations on Easter and tonsure, thus breaking the isolation of the Irish church. Wrote a famous life of Saint Columba, a mystical "Vision" in Irish, and a Latin account of his pilgrimage to Jerusalem, "On the Holy Places."

Adams, Andy

American Western novelist (1859-1935).

He was one of the few to write cowboy stories of high literary merit, including "The Log of a Cowboy" (1903), "The Outlet" (1905), "Reed Anthony, Cowman: An Autobiography." The locale of his stories is mostly Texas.

Adams, Henry

American historian and novelist (1838-1918).

Born in Boston, died in Washington. Member of the most prominent family in Boston, if not the United States. His great-grandfather and grandfather were presidents, his father ambassador to London in the crucial Civil War days. Henry turned to writing as consolation for what he bitterly regarded as rejection by his countrymen, who refused him political office. In addition to writing a history of the United States, he interpreted the rise and fall of the West in "Mont Saint Michel and Chartres" (1904), contrasting the cults of the Virgin and the Dynamo, and settled his personal account with his age in "The Education of Henry Adams" (1907), one of the great autobiographies of all times. A less-known side of his writing are his novels—largely because he permitted them to be published in private and limited editions only. The American reader was the loser, as the recent re-publication of his "Democracy" (1879), a withering account of Washington under Grant, proved.

Addison, Joseph
English essayist (1672-1719).

Born in Amesbury; died in London. Whig politician and diplomat. Traveled on the continent on diplomatic missions, connected with the War of the Spanish Succession, 1699-1703. Married the Countess of Warwick and settled in London. His play, "The Dying Cato" (1713), was written according to French classicist models. It was acclaimed in Europe and translated into various languages. However, Addison's chief title to fame today is his essays, published in the "moral weeklies": "Tatler" (1709-11), "Spectator" (1709), and "Guardian" (1713).

Ade, George
American writer (1866-1944).

Born at Kentland, Indiana. His "Fables in Slang" (1899) are written in the American vernacular. He also wrote stories collected in "People You Know" (1903) and "Handmade Fables" (1920).

Ady, Endre
Hungarian poet (1877-1919).

Born in Ermindszent; died in Budapest. Started as a journalist. Became leader of a group of young poets with radical political tendencies. Spent many years in Paris and was deeply influenced by French symbolists. His chief aim was to open up Hungary to Western European influences; the movement he headed was called simply "Nyugat" (The West). Wrote lyrical verse and short stories, including "New Poems" (1905), "Blood and Gold" (1906), "On Elijah's Chariot" (1909), "The Poem of All Secrets" (1911), "Before the Dead" (1918). Many of his works were published only posthumously. They include a volume of translations, "On the Left Hand of God," published in 1942.

Aeschines

Greek orator (about 389-about 330 B.C.).

Born in Athens; died on Samos. Political opponent of Demosthenes, partisan of Philip of Macedon. Accused of high treason, he saved himself—but only just —by a brilliant speech to the citizens' court. Later, he had to leave Athens and went to Rhodes where he started a school for orators. The only speeches of his that are preserved are three which he made against Demosthenes.

Aeschylus

Greek dramatist (525/24-456 B.C.).

Born in Athens, died at Gela in Sicily. Fought against the Persians in the battle of Marathon (490 B.C.). Professional actor. By adding a second actor to the Dionysian monologues, he became the founder of Greek and thus of Western tragedy. His plays are mostly dramatizations of Greek legends, with emphasis on the inexorability of fate. Only seven of his seventy-nine plays are preserved: "The Persians" (dealing with the Greek-Persian War), "Seven Against Thebes" "The Suppliants," "Prometheus," "Agamemnon," "Choephorei," and "The Eumenides" forming the Orestes trilogy.

Aesop

Greek fabulist (Sixth Century B.C.).

Lived on the island of Samos as a slave. His fables, written down about 550 B.C., are preserved only in the Latin verse versions of Phaedrus (First Century A.D.). They introduced the ever-popular device of talking animals which express social criticism.

Agnon

Israeli novelist (born 1888).

Pen name of Shmuel Joseph Tchatsky. Born in Buchach, Western Ukraine, then under Austrian rule. Went to Palestine in 1908, became the most prominent writer of the state of Israel. His trilogy of novels, spread over 25 years (1922-1957), is an epic tale of Eastern European Jewry. It describes the fate of a Jewish community not unlike that of Buchach.

Agustini, Delmira

Uruguayan poetess (1886-1914).

Born and died in Montevideo, murdered by her jealous husband. Her poetry is erotic, obscure and decadent in its content, modernist and symbolist in its form. It has had a great and not altogether happy influence on other women writing in Spanish.

Ahad ha-'Am

Hebrew philosopher (1856-1927).

Was the most influential and important of modern Hebrew writers. He advocated the concentration of all efforts toward a spiritual rebirth of Judaism, and minimized Herzel's endeavors in behalf of political Zionism. He contended that Jews were destined in greater majority to remain in the Diaspora, and envisaged Palestine only as a cultural center from which the Hebraic spirit will emanate to inspire Jewry all over the world. He established the monthly *Hashiloah,* which for over a generation served as a platform for the most serious Hebrew writers, followers or opponents, and developed a large group of young talented authors.

Ahmad Khan, Sir Syed

Indian Muslim writer (1817-1898).

Born in Delhi, died in Aligarh near Delhi. Member of a family which held high positions at the Mughal court. After the defeat of the 1857 rising, he was the first to rouse the Indian Muslims from the apathy and despair into which they had sunk. Visited England in 1869, was much impressed by its progress, met Carlyle and other distinguished people. After his return to India, started a magazine in Urdu to promote his ideas and in 1877 founded the Anglo-Oriental College at Aligarh, now Aligarh University. His "Essays on the Life of Mohammed" (1870) and "Commentaries on the Koran" maintained that the Koran was not verbally inspired and that it must be interpreted in the light of reason. Sir Syed was known to his fellow-Muslims of India as *Nacheri*, i.e. the naturalist philosopher. Though he paid occasional tribute to the unity of India and said that Hindus and Muslims were India's two eyes, Pakistan is fully justified in claiming him as one of her spiritual founders. By an irony of history, however, his greatest creation, Aligarh, remained in India after the partition.

Ahmedi

Turkish poet (1334-1413).

Real name: Taceddin Ibrahim. Birthplace unknown, died in Amasia. Studied in Egypt, became court poet of Anatolian princes and Ottoman sultans. Wrote some fresh and colorful lyrical poems and an epic of Alexander the Great which includes the first known chronicle of the Ottoman Empire.

Aho, Juhani

Finnish novelist (1861-1921).

Real name: Johannes Brofelt. Born in Jisalmi; died in Helsinki. Influenced at first by French and Scandinavian naturalism, later by a popular and romantic Finnish naturalism. His writings include: "The Pastor's Daughter" (1885); "Panu" (1897), an historical novel describing the end of paganism in Finland; "Heavy Blood" (1911).

Ailly, Pierre d'

French medieval theologian (1350-1420).

Chancellor of the University of Paris, became bishop of Cambrai and Cardinal. A strong character, he became known as "the Hammer of Heretics." But late in life his main concern became the reform of the Church. He was a prominent member of the Conciliar Movement, helped to convoke the Council of Constance and presided over its third session. His Latin "Booklet on the Correction of the Church," written for the Council in 1411, was not published until 1631. It contains strong attacks on corrupt church dignitaries and grasping mendicant orders.

Ainsworth, William Harrison

English novelist (1805-1882).

Born in Manchester, died in Reigate, Surrey. Became a journalist and edited several magazines. Wrote many historical novels, including "The Tower of London" (1840) and "Old Saint Paul's" (1841), mostly in the Victorian three-decker format. Popular in his day; but the most likely reason why a modern reader should open one of his books is to look at Cruikshank's illustrations.

Akhmatova, Anna

Russian poetess (born 1888).

Real name: Gorenko. Born in Kiev. Wrote her first

poems under the influence of the Russian symbolist school; later became more realistic. But her poems never lost their feminine tenderness and sensitivity. Her poetry is quite nonpolitical, but she was unable to avoid political trouble. Her husband, the poet Gumilov, was executed by the Communists. She herself was under a cloud in the Stalinist era and it is only now that she has been "rehabilitated." Wrote: "The Evening" (1912), "The White Swarm" (1917), and "Anno Domini MCMXXI."

Aksakov, Sergei Timofeyevich
Russian writer (1791-1859).

Born in Ufa, died in Moscow. Civil servant in Moscow, active in literary circles and friend of Gogol, of whom he wrote some reminiscences. Best-known for his "Family Chronicle" (1840-1856), which gives a charming picture of life on the confines of European and Asian Russia. Its style is realistic, and the book is one of the fountainheads of the "Russian novel." Aksakov defends the old-fashioned Russian life and its values. Both he and his two writer sons, Ivan and Konstantin, were ardent Slavophiles and opposed the Westernization of Russia.

Akutagawa, Ryunosuke
Japanese writer (1892-1927).

Born and died in Tokyo. Wrote essays and short stories. The latter had often weird and fantastic themes but were written in an impeccable language and showed great psychological penetration. One of them, "Rashomon," written in 1915, was turned into the film that had a worldwide success.

Alain de Lille
French philosopher and poet (1114-about 1203).

Also called Alanus de or ab Insulis. A scholastic thinker of Platonic persuasion who was called Doctor universalis because of his versatility who defended with logical acumen Christianity against pagan, Jewish and heretical thought. His "Anticlaudianus" is one of the most famous poems of the Middle Ages.

Alarcon, Pedro Antonio de
Spanish writer (1833-1891).

Born in Guadix, died in Madrid. Educated by Jesuits, volunteered for the Moroccan campaign of 1859, in which he was badly wounded. His "Eyewitness Account of the War in Africa" (1859), a very realistic and outspoken book, made him famous. He became a violent and radical anti-clerical and ended up as an equally violent and conservative clerical. More important than his controversial writings are his brilliant tales, including "The Three-Cornered Hat" (1874), which Falla turned into an opera.

Alas, Leopoldo
Spanish writer and critic (1852-1901).

Born in Zamora, died in Oviedo. Professor of law at Oviedo University, was fascinated and repelled by the bourgeoisie of that city, considered the most vulgar and snobbish of Spain. His "La Regenta" (1884-85) is a novel which gives a masterly portrayal of the society against the story of one of its members, slowly crushed by her environment. Under the pen name of "Clarin," Alas wrote some of Spain's best literary criticisms. Fakes and phonies were the targets of his dreaded darts; but he was the first to encourage many unknown writers who later became famous, like Unamuno.

Alberti, Leon Battista
Italian writer (1400-1472).

Was the Quattrocento's best representative of the typical 'universal scholar' of Renaissance humanism. Thoroughly educated in the classics, he wrote extensively in both Latin and Italian. In Latin, Alberti wrote theoretical works on painting, sculpture, architecture (*De re aedificatoriâ*), mathematics and physics (*Ludi mathematici, Mathematical Diversions*), as well as literary works: the comedy *Philodoxus* and the dialogues known as *Intercenales*. In Italian, his best known work is the treatise *On the Family*, a theoretical and practical discussion of the basis of family life. Other of his vernacular works are the dialogues *Il Teogenio; The Tranquillity of the Spirit; On Household Management*. In 1440, Alberti held the famous 'certame coronario' for a meritorious work in Italian; the contest was a failure, but significant in showing Alberti's interest in Italian literature.

Albertus Magnus

German medieval theologian (1206-1280).

Born in Lauingen (Southwest Germany), died in Cologne. Studied at Padua, became a Dominican in 1223. Taught at Paris and Cologne Universities. A universal mind, he had an encyclopedic knowledge that made his contemporaries attribute magical powers to him. His rediscovery of Aristotle through the Arab translations made him a predecessor of Saint Thomas Aquinas. Like Thomas, he wrote two "Summas," one on the creatures, and one on theology. But Albert had a mystical as well as a rational side. He is not only the official patron saint of chemistry but also the father of German mysticism, through his influence on Eckhart (q.v.).

Albo, Joseph

Spanish Jewish philosopher (about 1380-1444).

Birthplace unknown, died in Monreale. Last of the great medieval Jewish philosophers, pupil of Hasdai Crescas, whose ideas he tried to popularize. His masterpiece is the "Sefer ha-iqqarim," which tried to reduce Judaism to three basic dogmas.

Alcaeus

Greek poet (7th and 6th centuries B.C.).

Member of an aristocratic family on the island of Lesbos. Took a prominent part in the politics of his native land and was twice exiled for his opposition to the tyrants Myrsilus and Pittacus. Wrote hymns, political poems and drinking songs in the Aeolian dialect; invented the Alcaic meter. Important as predecessor of Sappho, who learned a good deal from him, though their personal relations were none too happy.

Alcman

Greek poet (Seventh Century B.C.)

Born a slave in Sardis in Asia Minor; later freed in Sparta. First Greek choral lyricist and head of the Dorian school of poets. He is said to have introduced the erotic motive into Greek lyric poetry. Especially famous were his choral songs for girls ("Parthenia").

Alcoforado, Mariana

Portuguese writer (1640-1723).

A Franciscan nun at a convent in Beja. Deserted by her lover, Noel Bouton, later Count of Chamilly, a French officer stationed in the neighborhood, she wrote him five letters, published anonymously in Paris (1669) in French translation. The Portuguese original has disappeared and it is impossible to determine the extent to which the translation was a matter of editing as well as translating. In any case, "The Portuguese Letters," as they were called, took the French literary world of the time by storm. They became a model of the literary expression of unrestrained emotion. They inspired the psychological novels of Madame de La Fayette (q.v.), and were used as models of style by Stendhal.

Alcott, Bronson

American writer and educationist (1799-1888).

Born in Wolcott, Conn., died in Concord, Mass.

After five years (1818-23) as itinerant peddler in Virginia and the Carolinas, he turned to education that was to provide him with a lifetime, though checkered career. Started a number of educational institutions, including the Concord Summer School of Philosophy and Literature (1874) and acted as superintendent of schools. His educational theories are expounded in "Observations on the Principles and Methods of Infant Instruction" (1830) and "The Doctrine and Discipline of Human Culture" (1836). An ardent transcendentalist and disciple of Emerson, about whom he wrote a book.

Alcott, Louisa May
American writer (1832-1888).

Born in Germantown, Pa., died in Boston. Daughter of the transcendentalist Bronson Alcott (q.v.). Nurse in a Union hospital at Georgetown during the Civil War, an experience which made her write "Hospital Sketches" (1863), with which she embarked on her literary career. Achieved a great and lasting success with "Little Women" (1868), a book to which she wrote a number of sequels. The tone of the book is set by its title.

Alcuin
Anglo-Saxon scholar (735-804).

Original name "Ealhwine," latinized into "Alcuinus Flaccus." Born in York, died in Tours (France). The most prominent scholar of Western Europe in his day, he was invited in 781 by Charlemagne to lead the revival of learning at his court. Became abbot of Tours in 796. Alcuin became the most prominent figure of the Carolingian revival. He wrote a number of school manuals, theological works and annals in verse.

Aldhelm
Anglo-Saxon scholar (about 650-709).

Died at Sherborne, of which he was bishop. Studied

under Irish and Roman teachers, wrote in a corrupt and tortuous Latin a treatise "On Virginity," in a prose and a verse version.

Aldrich, Thomas Bailey

American writer (1836-1907).

Born in Portsmouth, N. H., died in Boston. Poet and short story writer. As editor of the "Atlantic Monthly" defended the "genteel tradition." As author of the autobiographical "Story of a Bad Boy" (1870), the only book by which he lives, he wrote in the tradition of "Huckleberry Finn."

Alecsandri, Vasile

Rumanian poet (1821-1890).

Born in Bacau in Moldavia; died in Mircesti. Politician and romantic poet. Wrote popular songs, plays, and verse. Collected in "Pastels" (1867) and "Legend" (1871). Pioneered in gathering and publishing Roumanian folk songs (1852-56).

Alegria, Ciro

Peruvian novelist (born 1909).

Born in Trujillo. Devoted himself to telling to the world the plight of the Peruvian Indian. His "Broad and Alien is the World" (1941) won an international prize and was translated into several languages. It is more than a social document; it is a work of art which makes its reader feel that Peru is one of the saddest and most tragic countries in the world.

Aleman, Mateo

Spanish novelist (1547-after 1615).

Born in Seville, died in Mexico City. Adventurer, professional soldier, and minor official. Wrote the picaresque novel, "Guzman de Alfarache" (1599) with moralizing views. The novel was largely based on autobiographical experiences. After an embezzlement, he had to emigrate to Mexico, where he worked as a printer.

Alembert, Jean Le Rond d'
French writer (1717-1783).

Born and died in Paris. Mathematician and philosopher, member of the Academy of Science after 1741. Edited together with Diderot (q.v.) the French Encyclopedia in twenty-eight volumes (1751-1780). He wrote the philosophical and mathematical articles as well as the Introduction ("Discours Preliminaire").

Alencar, Jose de
Brazilian novelist (1829-1877).

Born in Fortaleza, Ceara, died in Rio de Janeiro. One of the first stylists of Brazilian letters, he took as his main subject the Brazilian Indian whom he romanticized in the manner of his time. Accused of imitating Cooper, he claimed Chateaubriand as his model. Chief works: "The Guarani" (1852, turned into an opera); "Luciola" (1862); "Iracema" (1865).

Alfieri, Vittorio Count
Italian dramatist (1749-1803).

Born in Asti, died in Florence. Started under the influence of French classicism, later influenced by Italian nationalism, of which he became leading spokesman. His tragedies, marked by an austere language and a heroic tone and content, include "Saul," "Merope," "Philip II," "Antigone," "Misogallo" (against the French conquest of Italy by Napoleon), and "Rosamund." His "Life of Vittorio Alfieri," written by himself, is a classic.

Alfonso X of Castile
Spanish king and writer (1221-1284).

Born in Toledo, died in Seville. Was a far greater success as an intellectual than as a king. Known as

"Alfonso the Learned" or "the Wise"; but, as the English historian Martin Hume put it, "Alfonso the Learned was, unfortunately, not wise," and his reign was punctuated by wars and family squabbles culminating in a rebellion of his son. Alfonso gathered scholars in Toledo to make translations from Arabic and Latin works. He himself wrote poetry in Galician, the chief poetic language in Spain at that time, including the "Songs to Our Lady." His prose works are in Castilian, and he is regarded as the chief creator of Castilian prose. They include the legal code "The Seven Parts," a universal and a Spanish history. The latter is remarkable for using poetry as historical evidence.

Alfred the Great
Anglo-Saxon king and translator (849-899).

Born at Wantage, became king of Wessex and defended it against the Danes. His cultural activities included translation, with the help of native and foreign scholars, of Latin books on religion, history, geography, philosophy etc. In some cases original material was added, e.g. when Alfred wrote prefaces to the travel reports of the Saxon Wulfstan and the Norwegian Ohthere. Some scholars think that he inspired the writing of the earliest version of the Anglo-Saxon Chronicle.

Alger, Horatio
American clergyman and writer (1832-1899).

An unhappy youth spent in Puritanical surroundings drove him to Bohemianism in Paris after running away from Harvard at graduation. Became a Unitarian minister in 1864 but only for two years. Wrote some 130 success novels for boys yet never produced the masterpiece he wanted to write. His uncle William Rounseville Alger (1822-1905) also was a theologian and writer who wrote "The Poetry of the

Orient," "The Genius of Solitude" and "Friendships of Women."

Al Ghazali

Persian philosopher (1058-1111).

Born and died in Tus. Wrote in Arabic. Travelled and taught in Iraq, Syria, Egypt and Arabia, with interludes in which he withdrew into a life of ascetic contemplation. Wrote "The Alchemy of Happiness," in which he rejected intellectual scholasticism in favor of a mystical vision of God. Greatest opponent of Aristotelian trends among the Muslims.

Ali Sher Neva'i

Turkish poet of Central Asia (1444-1501).

Born and died in Herat (Afghanistan). His patrons included the rulers of Khorasan and Herat, the latter a school friend. After occupying high offices, retired to devote himself to writing. He left four books of poems, written in childhood, youth, middle age and old age in a poetic language that he made classical for Eastern Turks and is still called "the language of Navoi." His prose works include a defense of the Turkish language against Persian, a collection of biographies of Turkish poets and a book on the art of Turkish poetry.

Almeida-Garrett

Portuguese writer (1799-1854).

Full name: Joao Baptista da Silva Leitao, Viscount Almeida-Garrett. Took prominent part in Portuguese politics as a liberal, fought in civil wars and suffered exile in England. His clashes with the powers that be started when he was accused of blasphemy by the Inquisition, because in his poem "The Portrait of Venus," he made Venus and not Jupiter create the world. His English exile acquainted him with romanticism, which he introduced to Portugal with his heroic poems "Camoes" (1825) and "Dona Branca" (1826). His "Fallen Leaves" (1853) are personal poems; his "Romanceiro" (1842) tried to restore the tradition of popular balladry. His dramas include his masterpiece "Frei Luiz de Sousa" (1844). He was a romantic nationalist who asked that Portuguese literature be written "in Portuguese, about Portugal and in a Portuguese way." He practiced what he preached.

Almquist, Carl Jonas Love
Swedish poet (1793-1866).

Born in Stockholm; died in Bremen (Germany). Romantic poet and story writer. Influenced by German romanticism. His masterpiece was "The Book of the Sleeping Beauty" (1832-51), a collection of stories which made him famous and included "The Hunting Lodge," "The Palace," "The Chapel," and "The Queen's Jewels."

Al Mutanabbi
Arab poet (915-965).

Born in Kufa, Iraq, killed by Bedouins on his way home from Egypt. Nicknamed "Al Mutanabbi" i.e. "He who pretends to be a prophet." Made an unsuccessful attempt to lead a Bedouin rebellion. Found princely patrons in Aleppo and Cairo. Called the greatest Arab poet by the Orientalist Hammer-Purgstall. His verses are widely quoted to this day. He stands for the old Arab virtues, especially personal pride. His style tends towards the rhetorical.

Altamirano, Ignacio
Mexican novelist (1834-1893).

Born in Tixtla, died in San Remo, Italy. Of purely Indian origin, he wrote a simple and vivid language on Mexican subjects. He took a prominent part in politics, fighting at the side of Juarez against Maximilian. His best-known novel, "El Zarco" (1900), contains realistic descriptions of life in Mexico in the story of a bandit.

Amaru

Indian poet (Seventh Century A.D.).

His chief work, "Amaru Shataka," or "One Hundred Stanzas of Amaru," describes, in each stanza, the erotic experiences of a woman, whom he claims to have been in a previous incarnation.

Ambrose, Saint

Medieval Latin writer (337-397).

Became bishop of Milan in 374 and defended the rights of the Church against Arian heretics and the Emperor Theodosius, whom he forced to do penance publicly for ordering the massacre of Thessalonica (390). Wrote biblical commentaries and theological treatises; but is more important for his hymns, some of which are still sung. They were an important factor in creating medieval Latin prosody.

Amicis, Edmondo de

Italian novelist (1824-1889).

Born in Oneglia; died in Bordighera. Started with descriptions of experiences as a soldier. Wrote many travel books, including "Spain" (1872), "Morocco" (1876), and "Constantinople" (1877). But he is remembered today as the writer of "The Heart" (1886), a classic children's book.

Amiel, Henri Frederic

Swiss writer (1821-1881).

Born and died in Geneva, of Jewish origin. Professor at Geneva Academy. Left behind a Journal of 16,900 pages which he kept from 1847 to 1881. It was published posthumously (1882-84) and created a great sensation with its harrowing self-analysis and psychological penetrations. Amiel was an introspective idealist who derived his deep pessimism from his personal failures.

Ammianus Marcellinus

Roman historian (about 330-about 395 A.D.).

Born in Antioch, of Greek origin; died in Rome. As historian, he modelled himself on Tacitus. He wrote a history of Rome, ranging from Nerva (First Century A.D.) to Valens (Fourth Century A.D.) in thirty-one books of which only eighteen are preserved.

Amyot, Jacques

French translator (1513-1593).

Born in Melun near Paris, died in Auxerre in Burgundy. Tutor to the future kings Charles IX and Henri III, became Grand Almoner of France in 1560 and bishop of Auxerre in 1570. A Greek and Latin scholar. Among his more important translations are the "Parallel Lives" of Plutarch (1559) which was the original of North's English Plutarch and thus of Shakespeare; the "Ethiopian History" of Heliodorus (1548) and the "Daphnis and Chloe" of Longus (1559), important sources of the French drama and a pastoral novel.

Anacreon

Greek poet (about 572-about 488 B.C.).

Born in Teos in Ionia (Asia Minor). Said to have served in Greek forces resisting the invasion of Cyprus by Cyrus of Persia. Spent some time on Samos and in Athens at the courts of the tyrants Polycrates and Hipparchos. His poems in praise of love and wine have given rise to the phrase "Anacreontic verse." But only three of them are preserved in full.

Andersen, Hans Christian

Danish writer (1805-1875).

Born in Odense (Fyn); died in Copenhagen. Son of

a cobbler, lived for a long time in great poverty but was helped by a number of patrons who enabled him to get a good education and to travel extensively in Europe and the East. He tried his hand unsuccessfully at many literary genres until he discovered his true vocation with his tales for children that made him world-famous. Published from 1835 through 1872, they include "The Emperor's New Clothes," "The Princess and the Pea," "The Little Mermaid," "The Match Seller," etc. His autobiography, "The Tale of My Life," was published in 1857.

Andersen-Nexö, Martin

Danish novelist (1869-1954).

Born in Copenhagen; died in Hellerau near Dresden (East Germany). Born in poverty, he had a very difficult and unhappy childhood and youth, spent partly in Copenhagen and partly on the island of Bornholm. Became a best-selling novelist and won both the Nobel and the Stalin prizes, but never forgot his origin. His tetralogy "Pelle the Conqueror" (1906-10) is largely autobiographical. He described his early years in "Childhood Memories" (1911). Also wrote "Ditte, Child of Man," the story of a girl born out of wedlock (1918-23).

Anderson, Sherwood

American novelist, poet, and story writer (1876-1941).

Born in Camden, Ohio, died in Colon, Panama. Started working at 12, fought in the Spanish-American War (1898), became manager of a paint-factory in Illinois. In his late thirties, he suddenly left his job and his family, feigning madness. He made his way to Chicago with the intention of becoming a writer. After a spell in advertising, he became a professional writer and died as a newspaper editor. Wrote "Windy McPherson's Son" (1916), "Winesburg, Ohio" (1919), which made him famous, "Poor White" (1920), "A

Story Teller's Story" (1923), "Dark Laughter" (1925),
"Puzzled America" (1935), "Hometown" (1940),
"Memoirs" (1942), etc. His work deals mostly with
the impact of industrialization on his native Middle
West. Race relations—and a pioneering understand-
ing of the Negro—also play an important part.

Andreas Capellanus
French writer (about 1220).

Was chaplain of the King of France and wrote in
Latin a "Treatise on Love" which was very popular
at the time, but has been preserved in a single Fourteenth Century manuscript.

Andreyev, Leonid Nicolayevich
Russian writer (1871-1919).

Born in Orel, died in Finland. Member of the symbolist movement, his writing abounds in mystical and
decadent overtones. Was much read at one time in
Europe and America as well as Russia, especially
"Seven Who Were Hanged" (1908). Is all but forgotten today. An ardent anti-Communist, he died in
exile.

Andrewes, Lancelot
English divine (1555-1626).

Born and died in London. Educated at Cambridge
where he taught for a while. Whitgift, Elizabeth's
Archbishop of Canterbury, acted as his patron. He became Whitgift's chaplain and Dean of Westminster
(1601). James I continued the patronage and made
him in succession Bishop of Chichester, Ely and Winchester. His views were typical of the "middle way" of
the Church of England, with some leanings towards
the high church. His "sermons" were very popular;
but Andrewes is far more important as the leader and
organizer of the scholars who translated the "King

James' Bible." He himself translated parts of the Old Testament.

Aneirin
Welsh poet (about 600).

His poem "Gododdin," preserved in a 13th century manuscript, is one of the classics of Welsh literature and has had great influence on Welsh writers, of succeeding centuries. It is a tale of heroic defeat of a band of warriors fighting against overwhelming odds.

Angelus Silesius
German poet (1624-1677).

Real name: Johann Scheffler. Born in Breslau. Converted to Catholicism in 1655; became the great poet of the Catholic baroque. Wrote a number of hymns, still in use, and the mystical volume "The Cherubinic Wanderer" (1674).

Angiolieri, Cecco
Italian poet (about 1260-about 1312).

Born in Siena, and poet of a typically Sienese discontent. His sonnets attack in a violently bitter language everybody with whom he came in contact, beginning with his parents, who kept him short of money and whom he wishes dead, continuing with his wife and mistress, and ending with Dante, whom he addresses with a complete absence of respect. Boccaccio makes him appear in one of his "Decameron" tales.

Anker-Larsen, Johannes
Danish novelist (born 1874).

Born on the island of Langeland. Professional actor, started writing under the influence of Kierkegaard and English religious writers. He tries to capture the religious and metaphysical anxieties of modern man. His first book, "A Dream" (1904), was highly successful. He also wrote "The Stone of Wisdom" (1923),

"Martha and Mary" (1925), "With an Open Door" (1926), "Olsen's Stupidity" (1943), etc.

Anna Comnena
Byzantine writer (1083-1148) .

Daughter of Emperor Alexius I. Was disappointed when her husband Nicephorus Bryennius did not succeed to the throne after her father's death in 1118, and wrote the "Alexiad," a history of her father's reign, and an important source-book. Anna defended the traditions of the Greek classics and the Orthodox faith; she was appalled by the uncouth barbarism of the Latin crusaders and by their military successes, due to superior technical equipment. Her style is vigorous and her prejudices help to make her book readable.

Anouilh, Jean
French dramatist (born 1910).

Born in Bordeaux. Won a first success with "The Traveller Without Luggage" (1936) but it was his wartime adaptation of "Antigone" (1942), with very modern overtones, that made him famous. After the war, his plays conquered the world's stages by their bitter pessimism and excellent stagecraft. Recent successes include "Poor Bitot" and "The Waltz of the Toreadors."

Anselm of Canterbury
Italian philosopher and theologian (1033-1109).

Born in Aosta; became Archbishop of Canterbury, where he died after a bitter and victorious conflict with King William Rufus. One of the founders of scholasticism. Chief works: "Monologue," "Why God Became Man," "Prologion." The latter gave Anselm's famous ontological proof of the existence of God, which Kant refuted.

Ansky, Sh. A.

Russian Jewish writer (1863-1920).

Pen name of Solomon Samuel Rappaport. Born in Vitebsk, Byelorussia, died in Warsaw. Wrote in Yiddish. A prominent member of the Jewish Socialist Bund Party, wrote "The Oath," that became its hymn. His plays are still performed, and his "Dybbuk" (1916) has conquered the world's stages—and film studios—for one of the great Jewish legends.

Antar

Arab poet (6th century A.D.)

Antar was the son of an Arab and a Negro slave woman, who became a famous poet and a representative figure of the virtues of Arab chivalry. His importance in literature lies less in his own writings than in the "Story of Antar" that gathered around his exploits. The 9th century philologist al Asmi wrote it down from the mouths of popular story tellers. It has been popular not only in Arab lands but also in 19th century France, which admired its chivalrous tones, and among 20th century Negroes who are attracted by the hero's mixed ancestry and the misadventures arising therefrom.

Apollinaire, Guillaume

French poet (1880-1918).

Real name Wilhelm Apollinaris de Kostrowitski. Born in Rome of Polish noble family; died in Paris, where he established himself at the age of 20. He became a leader of the literary and artistic avant garde which included Picasso, Matisse, Modigliani, Alfred Jarry, etc. One of the first to proclaim Cubism and to experiment in surrealism. His works mark the beginning of a new era in French poetry. Wrote "The Rotting Enchanter" (1909), "Alcohols" and "The Cubist Painter" (1913), "Calligrams" (1918) and "The

New Spirit and the Poets" (1918). He died of war wounds shortly before the Armistice.

Apollinaris Sidonius
Roman poet (about 430 to 480).

Full name: Gajus Sollius Modestus. Hailed from a prominent Christian family of Lyon. Went to Rome and attained high honors under the Emperor who became his son-in-law, but suddenly retired and became Bishop of Clermont in 472. His panegyric poems and his volumes of letters are of little literary value, but furnish much information about his period.

Apollonius of Rhodes
Greek poet (295-215 B.C.).

Upheld the tradition of epic poetry among the Alexandrians. In his poem, the *Argonautica,* which has as its theme the quest for the golden fleece and the love of Jason and Medea, Apollonius attempted to establish his literary views against those of Callimachus. The epic, however, lacks unity of composition, and is at its best in single episodes, such as the love scenes between Jason and Medea. It is Homeric in diction, but Alexandrian in the romantic treatment of the love theme (on which Vergil drew for his story of Dido and Aeneas), in a feeling for nature, and, unfortunately, in its recondite geographical details.

Apuleius, Lucius
Roman writer (about 125 A.D.-after 180 A.D.).

Born at Madaurus in Numidia (North Africa). Philosopher, rhetorician, and novelist. His masterpiece "Metamorphoses or the Golden Ass" is a picaresque story of the adventures of a man transformed into an ass, and returned to human form by the grace of the goddess Isis. It includes the famous tale of Cupid and Psyche.

28

Aragon, Louis

French poet and novelist (born 1897).

Born in Paris, son of a police prefect. Started as a surrealist, with "Fire of Joy" (1920), became a militant Communist in the early thirties and has hewed to the party line ever since. But his grief over France's fall transcended party lines and his "Broken Heart" (1941) and "Elsa's Eyes" (1942, dedicated to his wife Elsa Triollet) appealed not only to the French ground by the Nazi heel but also to the friends of France abroad. After the war, his work became stereotyped, but his literary criticism is full of useful insights and he has written lately a historical novel on the Restoration that is far above his previous party-line novels.

Arai, Hakuseki

Japanese historian (1657-1725).

Real name: Arai Kimiyoshi. Born and died in Tokyo. Tutor and later adviser of Shogun Ienobu and his successor Ietsugu. A Confucian scholar of wide talents, he concerned himself with many spheres of government. Wrote a history of the Japanese feudal houses and the first methodical and analytical history of Japan, the "Readings of History." Also left an important autobiography and an account of his conversations with Father Sidotti, whom he questioned about his missionary activities, which were prohibited by the Japanese exclusion of all Europeans except for a handful of Dutch traders. His interest in the West made him compile the "Notes on the Western World," from which the Japanese learned a good deal.

Arany, John

Hungarian poet (1817-1882).

Born in Nagyszalonta, died in Budapest. Professor

at a secondary school, later secretary of the Hungarian Academy. Best-known for his folk epic in three parts, "Toldi" (1847-1874), whose writing covered the Hungarian rising against the Hapsburgs, its repression with the aid of Russia and Hungary's achievement of political economy. The epic made him Hungary's national poet. Its language, for all its popular borrowings, is of a classical purity. Arany wrote studies of Hungarian prosody and translated Western classics, including Shakespeare.

Arbuthnot, John
English writer (1667-1735).

Born in Bervie (Scotland), died in London. A Scottish physician, moved to London to become a professional writer. Became a prominent member of the coterie of Swift and Pope, and was the principal contributor to the "Scriblerus Memoirs" which they produced in 1741. His "History of John Bull" (1712), duly publicized by Swift and Pope, created the British national stereotype.

Archpoet
German poet (Twelfth Century).

Real name unknown. The "Archpoet," as he came down to us, was a courtier and personal friend of the emperor Frederick I. His poems praise the emperor's deeds in Italy.

Aretino, Pietro
Italian writer (1492-1556).

Born in Arezzo; died in Venice. Went to Perugia to study literature and painting, then to Rome where he acquired as his patrons Popes Leo X and Clement VII, and Giovanni de Medici. In 1527 he moved to Venice where he became friend and business agent of Titian, who painted him. Vigorous satirist, good stylist, and complete amoralist, his writings are an important testimony of the Renaissance. Known to his contemporaries as "The Divine" and "The Scourge of Princes." Chief works: the verse tragedy "Orazia" (1546), the comedies "La Cortegiana" and "La Talanta" (1534, 1550), dialogues and letters.

Aribau, Bonaventura Carles
Catalan poet (1798-1862).

Born and died in Barcelona. His "Ode to the Fatherland" (1833) marks the start of the Catalan cultural renaissance called "Renaixenca." His varied activities also included editing modern editions of Spanish classics and publicity work in Madrid in favor of Catalan industries.

Arion
Greek poet (Seventh-Sixth Century B.C.).

Born at Methymna on Lesbos; died in Corinth. Is said to have been the first to use dithyrambic verse. Became court poet of the tyrant Periander of Corinth, became famous by his much represented adventure. Thrown into the sea by greedy sailors on the way to Corinth, he reached the shore on the back of a dolphin, whom his songs had charmed. Only fragments of his poetry remain.

Ariosto, Ludovico
Italian poet (1474-1533).

Born at Reggio nell' Emilia; died at Ferrara. In 1503 entered the diplomatic and military service of Ippolito, Cardinal d'Este, and later that of his brother, Duke Alfonso. To glorify the house of Este, rulers of Ferrara, he continued the chivalrous epic of Boiardo (q.v.) about Roland. Ariosto's "L'Orlando Furioso" (Furious Roland: 40 cantos edition in 1516, 46 cantos edition in 1532) is one of the glories of the Italian Renaissance. He also wrote satires, sonnets, odes, Latin poems, and comedies for the ducal theatre.

These include "La Cassaria" (1508), "Il Nigromante" (1520), and "La Lena" (1519), landmarks in the history of the Renaissance drama.

Aristophanes

Greek dramatist (450-385 B.C.).

Born and died in Athens. Chief representative of the "old Comedy" and the only one of whom more than fragments are preserved. His biting satire attacked, among others, Cleon (the demagogue who ruled Athens after the death of Pericles) and Socrates. Eleven of his forty comedies are preserved in full: "The Acharnians" (425), "The Knights" (424), "The Clouds" (423), "The Wasps" (422), "The Birds" (414), "Lysistrata" (411), "Thesmophoriazousae" (411), "The Frogs" (405), "Ecclesiazousae" (about 395), and "Plutos" (388).

Aristotle

Greek philosopher (384-322/21 B.C.)

Born in Stagira, a Greek colony in Macedonia (hence called the Stagyrite); died at Chalcis in Euboea. Became court physician of Amyntos II of Macedon. Studied (367-347) under Plato at the Athens Academy; returned to the Macedonian court under Philip II to become tutor to Alexander, heir to the throne (about 342-355). For the rest of his life he taught in Athens as head of the Peripatetic School. His numerous treatises are largely lecture notes. They are traditionally divided into five classes: (1) "Organon" i.e. Logic: Prior Analytics (two books), Posterior Analytics (two books) Sophisms. (2) Philosophy: Metaphysics (thirteen books). (3) Natural Science: Physics (eight books), On the Heavens, On Beginning and Perishing, On the Anatomy of Animals, On Generation, On the Winds, and On Plants. (4) Ethics and Politics: Nicomachean Ethics (ten books), Politics (eight books).

(5) Literature: Rhetorics and Poetics (only the parts on tragedy and epic poetry have remained).

Arjun

Indian religious writer (1581-1606).

Fifth guru (religious leader) of the Sikh sect, compiled the "Adi Granth," still the Sikh Bible. It includes hymns written by his four predecessors and extracts from writings of saints and holy men, both Hindu and Muslim. He was put to death by the Mogul emperor Jahangir for participating in a conspiracy against him.

Arndt, Ernst Moritz

German poet (1769-1860).

Born at Schoritz on Rugen Island; died in Bonn. Son of a freed serf who had belonged to a Swedish nobleman. Educated at Greifswald and Jena Universities. His "Essay on the History of Serfdom in Pomerania and Rugen" (1803) made the Swedish king abolish serfdom. Taught history and philosophy at Greifswald. His patriotic poems and songs led the German resistance to Napoleon and, later, to the princes of the Holy Alliances. Some of their titles became proverbial: "The God That Let Iron Grow," "What is the German's Fatherland?" and "The Rhine, Germany's River, Not Germany's Frontier." He had to flee to Stockholm and later to Russia to escape Napoleon's wrath. In his later years he championed German democracy and was a deputy to the German National Assembly in 1848-49. Wrote "The Spirit of the Times" (1807), "Songs for the Germans" (1813), "Poems" (1818), "Stories and Memories of Youth" (1818).

Arnim, Achim von

German writer (1781-1831).

Real name, Ludwig Joachim Von Arnim. Born in

Berlin; died at Wiepersdorf in Brandenburg. Friend of Clemens Brentano (q.v.) whose sister he married and with whom he published "The Boy's Wonder Horn" (1806-08), a pioneering collection of German folk songs. A leading figure of German Romanticism. Wrote fantastic novels and stories. Best known is his unfinished two-volume novel "Guardians of the Crown" (1817/1854).

Arnim, Bettina Von
German writer (1785-1859).

Born Elizabeth Brentano at Frankfurt am Main; died in Berlin. Sister of Clemens Brentano (q.v.); married Achim Von Arnim (q.v.) in 1811. In Frankfurt was friendly with Goethe and his mother; her book "Goethe's Exchange of Letters With a Child" (1835) tells in semi-fictionalized form of her childish passion. Also wrote "Die Gunderode" (letters and poems, two volumes, (1840).

Arnold, Sir Edwin
English poet (1832-1904).

Born in Gravesend, Kent, died in London. Journalist, became editor of the London "Daily Telegraph" in 1873. His five years in India (1856-1861), where he was principal of Deccan College in Bombay bore their poetic fruit in "The Light of Asia," a long and once popular poem on the life and teachings of Buddha. His interest in the Orient continued, and he married a Japanese lady at the age of 65.

Arnold, Matthew
English writer (1822-1888).

Born in Laleham, died in Liverpool. Educated at Rugby School where his father, Thomas Arnold, was headmaster and started a reform of the English public school system, and at Oxford. Inspector of schools from 1851-1886, with a spell of ten years (1857-1867) as professor of poetry at Oxford. His lifelong interest in education also took him abroad, especially to France. He was deeply concerned about the growing materialism and philistinism of Victorian England. His "Culture and Anarchy" (1869) made the famous classification of men into "barbarians, philistines and populace." Arnold was also an important literary critic who stressed the value of literary classics and the ideas they embodied and a poet, whose poetry is unjustly neglected today.

Ascasubi, Hilario
Argentine writer (1807-1875).

Born in Fraile Muerto. Originator of gaucho poetry which culminated in the folk epic of Jose Hernandez (q.v.). Ascasubi opposed the dictatorship of Rosas and attacked it in polemical writings, later gathered in "Paulino Lucero" (1839-1851) and "Aniceto the Rooster," the former written in Montevideo. After the fall of Rosas in 1852, he returned to Buenos Aires and wrote a three-volume epic, "Santos Vega" (1872) about an 18th century gaucho who had become a legend.

Asch, Sholem
Jewish novelist and playwright (1880-1956).

Born in Kutno, Poland, died in New York. Wrote in Yiddish and Hebrew, came to America in 1909. First gained fame with realistic pictures of small-town Jewish life in Poland, e.g. "Motke the Thief." Then wrote "panoramic" novels of cosmopolitan Jewish life in the "Three Cities." Finally, with "The Nazarene" (1939), he embarked on a series of books which claimed to revindicate for Judaism the figures of Christ and his circle. This produced accusations of apostasy; but the books themselves do not have enough merit for a serious controversy.

Ascham, Roger
English pedagogue (about 1515-1568).

Born in Kirby Wiske. A great Greek and Latin scholar who served as English ambassador to Emperor Charles V and as tutor and secretary to Princess Elizabeth, later Queen. He wrote two treatises, in Latin, on archery (1545) and school-mastering (published 1570).

Ashkenazi, Yankev ben Yitskhok
Yiddish writer (1550-1628).

Compiler of the *Tseno Ureno,* the most popular book in old Yiddish literature. He devoted his life to popularizing the Bible and the teachings of the Jewish moralists. To that end he published in 1576 his *Seyfer Hamaggid,* a paraphrase of the Prophets and the Hagiographa with a commentary; it has been reprinted many times. Eng. trans., *Tseno Ureno,* by P. T. Hirshow (London), 1885.

Attar
(Farid ud-Din, Persian, 1119-1230).

One of the three main Persian mystic poets (with Sanai and Rumi). A physician who traveled widely in the East. Said to have been killed during Mongol invasion. His copious works, devoted to teachings of the Sufis, generally written in couplets, include: *Pand-Namah, Mantiq ut-Tayr, Elahi-Namah.*

Aubanel, Theodore
Provencal poet (1829-1886).

Born and died in Avignon. A leader of the Provencal renaissance and friend of Mistral (q.v.). One of the founders of the "Felibrige" society that sparked the renaissance. His poetry, especially "The Half-opened Pomegranate" (1860) and "The Daughter of Avignon" (1885), deals mostly with love, in a mixture of Christian sentiment and pagan sensuality.

Auden, Wystan Hugh

Anglo-American Poet (born 1907).

Educated at Oxford. His life and work fall into two very different parts. In the thirties, he was appalled at the march of fascism, moved considerably towards the left and wrote verse and drama marked by hard language and social passions e.g. "The Orators" (1932) and "The Dance of Death" (1933). In 1939 he crossed the Atlantic, became an American citizen, and adopted the language, religion and politics of the 17th rather than 20th century, e.g. in "Nones" (1952).

Augier, Emile Guillaume

French playwright (1820-1889).

Born in Valence, died in Croissy. Writer of popular and well-constructed plays on social topics like divorce, prostitution, illegitimacy and class distinctions. The latter theme inspired his masterpiece, "The Son-in-Law of M. Poirier" (1854), which contains, among others, the immortal line: "Art must be encouraged, but not artists."

Augustine, Saint

Latin philosopher and theologian (354-430).

Real name: Aurelius Augustinus. Born at Tagaste (North Africa); died at Hippo (North Africa). Son of a pagan Roman and of Monica, who became a Christian Saint. Taught rhetoric at Carthage, Rome, and Milan. Originally a Manichaean, became a Christian in 287 after a spiritual crisis and under the influence of Bishop Ambrose of Milan. Returned to Tagaste and was ordained priest in 391, consecrated bishop in 395, and bishop of Hippo from 396 till his death. He became a champion of orthodoxy against Manichaeism and Donatist and Pelagian heresies. Was greatly concerned with the menace of the fall of the Roman Empire and with the survival of Christianity. His two most famous works are "The City of God" (twenty-

two books) and his autobiographical "Confessions."
Also wrote "On the Trinity" and "On Christian
Doctrine."

Aurelius, Marcus

Roman philosopher (121-180).

Born in Rome, became emperor in 161, and died
near the present site of Vienna. Was a Stoic philosopher, and gentle and tolerant man, but opposed and
persecuted Christianity. His "Meditations," books
written in Greek, are a treatise of practical morality as
well as a self-revelation.

Aurobindo, Sri

(Sri Aurobindo Ghose, Indian, 1872-1950).

Philosopher-poet of modern India. Son of Bengalese
physician, educated in England. Anticipated Gandhi
in organizing passive resistance as a political weapon
in Bengal. After imprisonment by British, went to
live in French Pondicherry. Author of 3 volumes of
poetry and 2 major philosophic works: *The Life
Divine* and *The Synthesis of Yoga.*

Ausonius

Roman poet (310-395).

Full name: Decimus Magnus Ausonius. Born and
died in Bordeaux. Became tutor to Gratian, son of
emperor Valentinian, and emperor after his father's
death. Gratian made him consul for 379. After his
patron's murder in 383, retired to his home. Wrote
prose summaries of the Iliad and the Odyssey, and a
good deal of miscellaneous verse. Best-known for
idyllic descriptions of the countryside near Bordeaux
and of the Moselle valley, where he lived while teaching Gratian. Ausonius is the last great poet of classical
Rome.

Austen, Jane

English novelist (1775-1817).

Born in Steventon, Hampshire, died in Winchester.

After her father's death lived an uneventful life with her mother and sisters. Started writing in 1798 but gave it up because of discouragement through inability to find publisher until 1811, when "Sense and Sensibility" at last found a publisher. It was followed by "Pride and Prejudice" (1813); "Mansfield Park" (1814) and "Emma" (1816). "Northanger Abbey" and "Persuasion" were published posthumously in 1818. Jane Austen started writing as a reaction against the absurdities and extravagances of contemporary women writers like Mrs. Radcliffe. She created a small world of her own, within the limitations of the life of a provincial Englishwoman of her time but with remarkable psychological insights and penetrations. Her style is in the best polished tradition of the 18th century, spiced with feminine wit and sparkle. Much admired in her native land—Somerset Maugham put her among the world's ten greatest novelists—her fame has not traveled much beyond its borders for reasons which fanatical "Janeites" find difficult to explain.

Austin, Mary

(American, 1868-1934).

A spirited student of anthropological and social problems. Investigated American Indian and early Spanish cultures in the Southwest. Her novels and plays also dealt with social injustices and problems of machine age. Important works: *The Land of Little Rain, A Woman of Genius, No. 26 Jayne Street.*

Avvakum

Russian writer (1620-1682).

Full name: Avvakum Petrovich. Born in Grigorovo, died in Moscow. Arch-priest of the Russian Orthodox church, become a leader of the "raskolniki," the schismatics who opposed the church reforms sponsored by Patriarch Nikon and Tsar Alexei. He spent a number of years in exile in Siberia and in the Arctic but his defiance remained unabated and he was finally burned on the stake. His "Life of the Archpriest Avvakum, Written by Himself" (1672-73) is a classic of early Russian literature. It mirrors the author's proud and turbulent personality and is written in spoken Russian, not in the artificial Church Slavonic that served as the literary language of his time.

Azuela, Mariano
Mexican novelist (1873-1952).

Born in Lagos de Moreno, died in Mexico City. A physician who dabbled in politics. Became an army doctor during the Revolution and wrote "Those Below" (1916) a novel that has become a classic account of the revolutionary struggle. Azuela performed the remarkable feat of viewing the Revolution through the eyes and mind of a man of the people—his bandit-hero. His own intellectual vision of the Revolution is entirely subordinated to that purpose.

B

Babel, Isaac

Russian writer (1894 to late 1930's).

Born in Odessa, of Jewish origin. Fought in Budyenny's cavalry in the Revolution and the war against Poland. His "Red Cavalry" (1926) and "Jewish Tales" (1927) are written with an implacable realism that made the Stalinist version of the Revolution look like the literary fairy tale that it was. Babel was arrested and murdered at Stalin's orders. He was posthumously re-habilitated under Khrushchev.

Bacon, Francis

English scientist, essayist, and philosopher (1561-1626).

Born and died in London. Educated at Cambridge; elected to Parliament in 1584. Became attached to Earl of Essex, when he was the Queen's favorite; helped to convict him, when Essex lost the Queen's favor. Served James I, rose to be Lord Chancellor and was raised to the peerage (1618) as Baron Bacon of Verulam. Lost his offices after confessing to acts of bribery and corruption in 1621, but was soon pardoned by the king. Chief works: "Essays" (1597 ff.), "The Advancement of Learning" (1605), "Novum Organum" (1620), and "New Atlantis" (1626).

Bahr, Hermann

Austrian writer (1863-1934).

Born in Linz; died in Munich. Journalist, playwright, theatre critic and manager. Good stylist, with deep psychological insights. Works include "The New Men" (1887), "The Overcoming of Naturalism" (1891), "Viennese Women" (1900), "The Concert" (1910), "Expressionism" (1914), "Diaries" (1920-23).

Bahya ibn Pakuda
Spanish Jewish writer (died about 1080).

Said to have died in Saragossa. Poet and philosopher, best known for his treatise on "The Duties of the Heart," an analysis of man's inner life that includes some remarkable prefigurations of Freud's theory of the subconscious.

Baif, Jean Antoine de
French writer (1532-1589).

Born in Venice, died in Paris. A humanist who became a prominent member of the group of seven poets called the Pléiade and led by Ronsard (q.v.). Wrote a play, "The Brave One," modeled on Plautus and lyrical verse. Specially interested in prosody and the musical qualities of poetry. Used the Alexandrine line before Ronsard and invented his own 15 syllable line. Neither this nor his system of phonetic spelling caught on.

Baki, Mahmud Abdul
Turkish poet (about 1526-1600).

Born and died in Constantinople. Lyric poet, master of the classical style, strongly influenced by Persia. Called "The King of Poets." His language is polished and his feelings are exquisite. Considered the greatest Turkish classical poet.

Bakin, Kyokutei
Japanese novelist (1767-1848).

Real name Takizawa Tokuru. Born and died in Tokyo. Left home at 13 and led an adventurous life until he settled down to write. Studied Japanese poetry, Confucian poetry and medicine in a desultory way. Became a novelist under the influence of Santo Kyoden who took him into his home. Bakin used traditional Chinese and Japanese themes and his own experiences to write his novels, of which the most famous is "The Story of Eight Dogs" (1814-41) in 106 volumes. It is disjointed and full of improbabilities, romantic and idealistic and opposed to the degenerate tendencies of his time—which did not prevent the Japanese government from banning it in 1842. Bakin's interminable novels are not much to the taste of a contemporary reader, even a Japanese one.

Balzac, Honoré de
French novelist (1799-1850).

Born in Tours; died in Paris. Educated by the Oratorians at Vendome. His father sent him to Paris to become a notary public, but he turned to literature instead, earning his livelihood as editor, printer, typefounder, etc. After a series of mediocre novels, published under the name of "H. de Saint Aubin" and other pseudonyms, failed to attract the reading public, he had his first success with "The Chouans," a historical novel about Brittany in the style of Walter Scott. He followed it quickly with "The Psychology of Marriage," which made him famous. He became a friend and associate of a circle that included Hugo, Vigny, Lamartine, and George Sand. He conceived and carried out the design of presenting the society of his time in a series of interconnected novels published under the general title of "The Human Comedy" (first series published in 1842; the whole—unfinished—published posthumously in forty-seven novels). Over 2,000 characters were created by Balzac who realistically described them within their environment. Chief works include, in addition to those mentioned above: "Louis

Lambert" (1832), "Eugenie Grandet" (1832), "Le Père Goriot" (1834), "The Lily in the Valley" (1835), "The Village Priest" (1837), "Splendors and Misery of Courtesans" (1834), "Cousin Pons" (1847), as well as the collection of "Droll Stories" (1832-37).

Bandello, Matteo
Italian story writer (1485-1562).

Born in Castelnuovo (Lombardy); died in Agen (France). Dominican monk. Had to flee to France where he became bishop of Agen. His "Novelle" (four volumes, 1510-1560) are comparable to those of Boccaccio. They were soon translated and widely used as source material, e.g. by Shakespeare for his "Romeo and Juliet" plot, Lope de Vega and Byron.

Banville, Theodore de
French poet (1823-1891).

Born in Moulins, died in Paris. Started under the romantic influence of Hugo and Gautier, became a classicist and a leader of the Parnassian school with its ideal of a rather cold perfection. Wrote: "The Cariatides" (1842); "The Stalactites" (1846); "Funambulesque Odes" (1857). Also active as journalist and society columnist.

Barbey d'Aurevilly, Jules
French writer and critic (1808-1889).

Born in Saint-Sauveur-le-Vicomte, died in Paris. Member of aristocratic Norman family, was driven to writing by the decline and ruin of his family's fortune. Poverty bred in him a haughty and aristocratic aloofness and a razor-sharp wit which he did not hesitate to apply to writers he disapproved of. His novels, still read in France for literary quality and sense of bizarre, include "The Old Mistress" (1849); "A Married Priest" (1865) and "The Diaboliques" (1874).

Barbour, John
Scottish poet (about 1320-1395).

Believed to be born in Aberdeen. Became archdeacon of Aberdeen and a household officer of King Robert II. Travelled in England and France. Wrote in 1375 "Brus," a national epic of over 13,000 lines on Robert Bruce, his war of independence against the English, and his victory at Bannockburn.

Barbusse, Henri
French novelist (1873-1935).

Born in Asnieres, died in Moscow. Had a degree in philosophy but worked as a journalist. Started writing symbolist poetry and became a naturalist novelist after his shattering experiences in World War I, in which he served. His "Fire" (1916) was the first great anti-war novel. He became an ardent Communist and died on a visit to Russia.

Barham, Richard
English poet (1788-1845).

Born in Canterbury, died in London. Known as the author of the "Ingoldsby Legends," gentle burlesques of medieval monkish tales which he published from 1837 in "Bentley's Magazine" under the pen name of "Thomas Ingoldsby."

Baroja, Pio
Spanish novelist (1872-1958).

Born in Vera de Bidasoa, in the Basque Country, died in Madrid. Did not turn to writing until the age of 30. Before that he practiced medicine and managed his brother's bakery. After the business failed, he published nearly 100 novels which critics find almost impossible to classify—they are as shapeless as life itself. Hemingway visited Baroja on his deathbed and stated that he learned all about writing from him—but the statement is not to be taken too literally. Baroja is at his best in a picaresque vein and when he presents the paradoxes of human existence without trying to solve them. Novels include: "The Inquietudes of Shanti Andia" (1911); "Zalacain the Adventurer" (1909); "The Tree of Science" (1911) and "The Adventures, Inventions and Mixtifications of Sylvester Paradox" (1901), one of his earliest—and best. His violent anti-clericalism—most patent in "The Priest of Monleon"—did not prevent him from returning to Franco Spain after the Civil War.

Barrès, Maurice

French writer (1862-1923).

Born in Charmes (Lorraine); died in Paris. Took part in politics as right-wing ultra-patriot; elected deputy in 1889 as adherent of the would-be dictator of France, General Boulanger. Was elected to the French Academy in 1906. His writings are inspired by a romantic naturalism and include: "The Cult of the Ego" (1888-91); "The Uprooted" (1897), "The Bastions of the East" (1905-09).

Barrie, Sir James

Scottish dramatist and novelist (1860-1937).

Born in Kirriemuir, died in London. Went to London as a free-lance journalist in 1885, after studying at Dumfries and Edinburgh. His novels, including the nostalgic "A Window in Thrums" (1889) were fairly popular, but it was his plays and notably "Peter Pan" (1904) that made him a perennial public favorite and earned him a baronetcy in 1913. Barrie's patent sentimentality could not disguise the shrewd and practical master of stagecraft who played on the feelings of his public.

Basho

Japanese poet (1644-1694).

Pen name of Matsuo Munefusa. Born in Ueno, died in Osaka. A samurai, he left the service of his feudal lord at 23. Travelled in Japan and learned in Kyoto the twin arts of the haiku, a 17 syllable poem, and haibun or prose interspersed with haiku, in which he became a master. Worked for a time constructing waterworks in Tokyo, but was able to retire with the aid of disciples and friends. He became a Zen Buddhist hermit and took the name of "Hermit of the Banana Grove Hut." He left his retreat to go on several journeys of which he wrote travel diaries in haibun style. His haiku verse became so popular that it overshadowed the very different kind of poetry that Japanese wrote before he spread his gospel of an aesthetic and sentimental nature mysticism. He is still the Japanese poet *par excellence* both to his countrymen and to foreigners, both because of his intrinsic merits and because he suits the mood of our time.

Baudelaire, Charles

French writer (1821-1867).

Born and died in Paris. He was primarily concerned with aesthetic problems and led an unconventional life, brought to an early end by overindulgence in drugs, alcohol, and sex. Became, with Edgar Allan Poe (q.v.), whose tales he translated, a leader of the literary revolution which produced modern poetry. He was a forerunner of the symbolist and neoromantic schools; his neurotic sensibilities expressed themselves in an exquisite language. His desire "to shock the bourgeois" is shown in the title of his most famous book, "The Flowers of Evil" (1857). Also published "Little Prose Poems," "Aesthetic Curiosities," etc. Baudelaire was also a front-rank art critic who sponsored what is now generally accepted as modern art, but was almost universally rejected at the time.

Beaumarchais, Pierre Augustin Caron de

French playwright (1732-1799).

Born and died in Paris. A watchmaker who followed his father's trade, he added the aristocratic name "de Beaumarchais" to his bourgeois name of "Caron" after marrying the widow of a court official. Became a speculator and engaged in all kinds of business, not all legitimate. Supplied arms to American colonists fighting for independence, travelled over most of Europe. Attacked the corruption and hereditary privileges of the nobility, was jailed for his outspoken criticism. His two plays, "The Barber of Seville" and "The Marriage of Figaro" helped to start the French Revolution, though they are mostly known now as the inspiration of operas of Mozart and Rossini. Beaumarchais welcomed the Revolution, but emigrated in 1792 and returned only after the end of the Terror, in 1796.

Beaumont, Francis

English playwright (1584-1616).

Studied at Oxford, came to London where he became a friend of Drayton, Jonson and John Fletcher (q.v.). He wrote most of his plays in collaboration with the latter. Since they shared bed, board and pleasures at their house in Southwark it is not surprising that scholars have a hard job disentangling the respective shares of the two in such plays as "The Knight of the Burning Pestle," "The Woman Hater" and "Cupid's Revenge." They specialized in tragi-comedies suitable for courtly spectators of private theaters, showing strong Spanish influences.

Beauvoir, Simone de

French philosopher and novelist (born 1909).

Born in Paris, taught philosophy, began writing during World War II. One of the chief exponents of Sartre's (q.v.) existentialist philosophy. Main works include "The Mandarins," a novel; "The Second Sex," (1949) a study of femininity; and travel books on the

United States ("America, Day by Day") and China ("The Long March").

Bebel, Heinrich
German humanist (about 1472-1518).

Born near Justingen and died at Tübingen where he was a professor. While travelling and frequenting the inns on the way he collected the jokes and tall stories he overheard and translated them into impeccable Latin as Facetiae.

Beckett, Samuel
Irish playwright (born about 1900).

Emigrated to Paris where he worked as secretary to James Joyce. Writes in French. His books on Proust (1931) and his novels failed to cause any stir, but his plays, especially "Waiting for Godot" and "End Game," with their nihilistic message that life is utterly pointless, conquered the world's stages.

Beckford, William
English novelist (1760-1844).

Born in Fonthill, died in Bath. A millionaire with odd and macabre tastes he built himself a fantastic mansion at Fonthill and wrote a "Gothic" novel, "Vathek" (1782) in French. An unauthorized English translation proved a great success.

Becque, Henri
French playwright (1837-1899).

Born and died in Paris. Wrote plays on social subjects which shocked his contemporaries by mentioning such tabooed themes as syphilis. Best known is "La Parisienne" (1885).

Bécquer, Gustavo Adolfo
Spanish poet (1836-1870).

Born in Seville, died in Madrid. Son of a painter of German origin, orphaned early and brought up by his grandmother. Went to Madrid at 18 to seek glory but found only hack journalism and translation. Unfortunate in his great love, he died of tuberculosis, unknown beyond a circle of friends. His "Poems" were published posthumously in 1872 and it took some time for literary critics to recognize their great literary worth. They were read and appreciated by the people, who were moved by its themes of broken hopes, unhappy love and welcome death long before the critics pointed out the austere economy of their language, the delicacy of their expression and the innovations of their prosody.

Beddoes, Thomas

English poet (1803-1849).

Born in Clifton, died in Basle, Switzerland. Spent most of his life on the Continent. Was obsessed by death and ended a suicide. His "Death Jestbook" was published anonymously in 1850. It is a macabre and incoherent drama, a favorite of Dorothy Sayers, who quotes it in her detective stories.

Bede the Venerable

Latin writer (670-735).

One of the most charming figures of the Middle Ages, was early an orphan; raised at the Northumbrian monastery of Jarrow, a foundation of Benedict Biscop who provided it with books and treasures from the Continent. His "life-long pleasure was to devote himself to learning, teaching, and writing," producing works on theology, scripture, metrics, rhetoric, astronomy, biography and history. His Latin *Ecclesiastical History of the English People* tells the story of his native land from the earliest times down to his own day. He is calm, deliberate, detached, meticulous in his use of sources. His limpid prose (strongly colored by the *Vulgate* of St. Jerome) is a mirror of

the man, containing unforgettable stories and character sketches.

Beecher Stowe, Harriet
American novelist (1811-1896).

Born in Litchfield, Conn.; died in Hartford, Conn.;
married in 1836 the theologian Calvin Ellis Stowe.
Had a world-wide success with her abolitionist novel
"Uncle Tom's Cabin" (1852), which further abolitionist and feminist novels failed to follow up. She gained
notoriety with an article in the September 1869 issue
of "Atlantic Monthly" entitled "The True Story of
Lady Byron's Life." On the basis of information provided by Lady Byron, Mrs. Stowe accused Byron of
incest with his sister Augusta. She also rose to the defense of Scottish landlords who expelled their tenants
wholesale in the Highlands.

Behn, Mrs. Aphra
English woman writer (1640-1689).

Born Aphra Johnson in Wye, died in London. Spent
her youth in Surinam in the Dutch West Indies, served
as British spy in the Netherlands. Wrote plays, novels
and verse and became the first Englishwoman to make
a living out of writing. Her best comedy is "Forced
Marriage " (1671). Her novel "Oroonoko" (1688) forecast Rousseau's "noble savage." On the whole, her
writing is more notable for her pioneering than her
literary qualities.

Belinsky, Vissarion Grigorievich
Russian critic (1811-1848).

Born in Sveaborg (Finland, then Russia), died in
Saint Petersburg. Studied at Moscow University, expelled for writing a revolutionary play, became free-
lance critic. His "Literary Thoughts" (1834), written
under the influence of Schelling at 23, made his reputation. Later, he came under the influence of Hegel

and Feuerbach and veered from idealism to materialism. Belinsky defended realism in literature and democracy in politics and did much to form the opinions of the great literary generation that succeeded him. His judgments of his contemporaries have acquired a classical quality. Particularly famous is the letter to Gogol (1847), once his idol, chiding him for his apostasy from the cause of freedom.

Bellamy, Edward
American novelist (1850-1898).

Born and died in Chicopee Falls, Mass. Remembered for his novel of a Socialist Utopia, "Looking Backward" (1888), widely read on both sides of the Atlantic. A dull sequel, "Equality" (1897) was an equally pronounced failure.

Belli, Gioacchino Giuseppe
Italian poet (1791-1863).

Born and died in Rome. Wrote sonnets in Roman dialect (published only 1886-89) which satirize all elements of Roman society and do not spare the Pope, the secular ruler of the city in Belli's day. Frightened by the Roman Revolution of 1848-9, Belli abandoned his radicalism and became a stanch defender of the powers that be.

Bellman, Karl Michael
Swedish poet (1741-1795).

Born and died in Stockholm. Occupied several modest government posts until King Gustavus III gave him a sinecure office of "court secretary." Had a free and bohemian life, and after the assassination of his patron died in direst poverty. Generally considered Sweden's greatest lyric poet. Wrote psalms, satires, drinking and love songs. Chief works: "Temple of Bacchus" (1783), "Fredman's Epistles" (1790), "Fredman's Songs" (1791), "Scaldic Pieces" (1814).

Bello, Andres
Venezuelan writer and critic (1781-1865).

Born in Caracas, died in Santiago de Chile. Went to Santiago in 1829 at invitation of the Chilean government. He taught and created a university. His Spanish grammar was for long a standard work. His poetry is in the classical Spanish tradition, but not without feeling. Bello became involved in a controversy with the Argentine Sarmiento (q.v.) on the possibility of creating a Spanish American language and literature independent of Spain. When Sarmiento proclaimed that "the only way to create an American literature is to burn the works of Cervantes, Lope de Vega and Calderon," Bello replied in the only possible way—by a dignified silence.

Bely, Andrei
Russian writer (1880-1934).

Pen name of Boris Nikolayevich Bugayev. Born in Moscow, died in Tiflis. Started as a symbolist poet (1904-09), turned to writing novels like "The Silver Dove" (1910) and "Petersburg" (1913), in which symbolist influences merged with those of Gogol and Dostoyevski. A friend of Alexander Blok (q.v.), of whom he wrote a "Memoir" (1922), he welcomed the Revolution in the same messianic spirit, but his last years were marked by a significant literary silence.

Bembo, Pietro
Italian writer (1470-1547).

Was the leading spirit in the establishment of academic humanism as the dominating trend in Italian Cinquecento literature. At first the leading Latin poet of the times, he turned to Italian, and in so doing set the literary model for the rest of the century. His *The Italian Language* (ca. 1502-25) is at the same time a defense of the vernacular as a literary medium, a prescription of models (Petrarch for verse, Boccaccio for prose) and a brief Italian grammar. In his own work, Bembo furnished examples of his precepts in the carefully polished and perfected lyrics of his *Canzoniere,* and in his neo-Platonic dialogues *The Asolani* (1502-5).

Benavente, Jacinto
Spanish playwright (1866-1956).

Born and died in Madrid. Son of a doctor, studied law but gave it up to devote himself to writing. Started with poems and short stories but found his true vocation as dramatist with the success of "The Other's Nest" (1893). His first plays were pioneering and reformed the Madrid stage of his day. He excelled in dialogue, satire and the presentation of the unexpected reality that lies behind solid appearances. His later plays showed a distinct falling-off in creativity. Won Nobel Prize in 1922. Plays include: "People We Know" (1896); "Saturday Night" (1903) and his masterpiece, "Vested Interests" (1907).

Benet, Stephen Vincent
American poet (1898-1943).

Born in Bethlehem, Pa., died in New York. His long narrative poem, "John Brown's Body" (1928) could have only been written by a man who understood both North and South because they were both an intimate part of his family and upbringings. His "The Devil and Daniel Webster" (1937) showed him as one of the masters of the modern short story.

Benn, Gottfried
German poet and writer (1886-1958).

Born in Mannsfeldt (East Germany, now Poland); died in Berlin. A doctor, specializing in skin and venereal diseases, he became a leading poet of the Expressionist school. After flirting with the Nazis, whose coming to power he hailed, he became disillusioned with them. The army, which he called "aristocratic refuge," offered him shelter during World War II. The postwar years made him known outside Germany. Nihilism is the prevailing mood of his writings, which include "Morgue" (1912), "Sons" (1914), "Brains" (1916), "Flesh" (1917), "The Modern Ego" (1919), "After Nihilism" (1932), "The New State and Intellectuals" (1933), "Static Poems" (1947), "The Ptolemaean" (1947), "Double Life" (1950), "The Voice Behind the Curtain" (1952).

Bennett, Arnold
English novelist (1867-1931).

Born in Hanley, Staffordshire, died in London. Went to London in 1888 and earned a living as hack journalist. Wrote novels about his native Potteries area in a realistic vein: "The Old Wives' Tale" (1908); "Clayhanger" (1910); "Hilda Lessways" (1911); and "These Twain" (1916). In these he created a new literary world of the "Five Towns." These novels were immensely popular in their day, but even before his death, his reputation was in eclipse. Attempts are being made now to rescue him from unjustified oblivion.

Beranger, Pierre Jean de
French poet (1780-1857).

Born and died in Paris. He was born in humble circumstances and, before becoming a professional writer, was successively waiter, print-setter, and secretary at the Sorbonne. His "Chansons" (Songs) contained attacks on the Bourbon monarchy. Following their publication in 1821, he was removed from his Sorbonne post and jailed several times. After the fall of the Bourbons (1830) he was hailed as a national hero. But, with a poem "To my Friends, the Ministers," he refused all honors and rewards. He spent the rest of his life in relative retirement. In 1858 he published "My Biography." The two main themes of his very popular poetry are given in two of his "Chansons": "The Old Flag," with his nostalgia for Napoleon allied to a hatred of his Bourbon successors, and "The King of Yvetot," attacking the inglorious reign of Louis-Philippe.

Berdiajew, Nicolai
Russian philosopher (1874-1948).

Was born in Kiev and expelled from Russia in 1922 as opponent of Communism although as early as 1898 he had been arrested because of his revolutionary activities. He had, however, disavowed Marxism as early as 1902 and turned to a deeply Christian conception of history, believing firmly in the messianic mission of the Russian people. Mysticism of a Gnostic type is evident in all his writings, e.g., "Sub specie aeternitatis" (1907), "The Philosophy of Freedom" (1911), "Russia's Destiny" (1918), "The Meaning of History" (1923), "The Truth and Falseness of Communism" (1934), "Human Personality and the Superpersonal Values" (1937), "Spirit and Reality" (1949). He died at Clamart near Paris.

Berg, Bengt
Swedish writer (born 1885).

Born in Kalmar; writer of books about animals, including "With Migratory Birds in Africa" (1922) and "Tiger" (1934).

Bergelson, David
Yiddish writer (born 1884).

Outstanding Yiddish novelist in the U.S.S.R. He was born in the Ukraine into a well-to-do merchant family. In an atmosphere of growing impoverishment, the writer spent his youth; it marks writings of his first period, refined impressionistic stories and a novel, the heroine of which is an aristocratic woman pervaded by autumn moods *(Nokh Alemen, After All)*. After the Revolution, he was for a while a political émigré but he submitted to the *Yoke* (the name of a magazine that he published), began to see in the Revolution *The Quality of Justice* (the title of his novel dealing with that period), and was finally reconciled to it. He then portrays the newly emerging or coordinated figures and narrates his childhood and youth in his work, *Bam Dnyepr (On The Dnieper)*. As with Mendele, portrayal, not narration, is foremost. He is one of the finest stylists of the new Yiddish literature.

Bergengruen, Werner
German novelist (born 1892).

Born in Riga (Latvia). Translator from Russian and writer of novels and short stories including "The Sign of Fire" (1949) and "The Last Master of the Horse" (1955).

Bergson, Henri
French philosopher (1859-1941).

Born and died in Paris. Of Jewish origin, refused an exemption from disabilities imposed on Jews by the Vichy regime. Professor of philosophy at the College de France. Elected to the French Academy in 1914 and awarded the Nobel Prize in 1927. Works include "Matter and Memory" (1897), "Laughter" (1900), "Spiritual Energy" (1925), "Duration and Simultaneity" (1922), "The Two Sources of Morality and Religion" (1932).

Bernanos, Georges
French novelist (1888-1948).

Born and died in Paris. Studied law and literature, fought in World War I, worked for an insurance company. Turned to writing after a serious illness. A serious Catholic, he found the hypocritical religiosity of the French middle class too much to bear. He opposed Franco, moved with his family to Brazil as a protest against the Munich agreement and gave his whole-hearted support to the Free French cause. One of the deepest probers into the present crisis of humanity, he is at his best in "The Diary of a Country Priest" (1936).

Bernard of Clairvaux, Saint

Latin writer (1090-1153).

Doctor Mellifluus, was famous for his eloquent Latin writing and preaching; was active in all the outstanding events of the 12th c. He was the standard bearer of the Cistercian Order; preached the Second Crusade; his gigantic figure looms large in both secular and religious life. His sermons on the *Cantica Canticorum* (*Song of Songs*) were admired for their charm of style and spiritual content. He wrote famous treatises on *Contemplation* and on the *Love of God,* and at least inspired the *Jesu dulcis memoria,* one of the most beautiful rhythmical hymns of the Middle Ages. He was more of a mystic than a speculative theologian, and was a strong opponent of the theological novelties of Abailard and Gilbert of Porrée.

Bernardin de Saint-Pierre, Jacques-Henri

French novelist (1737-1814).

Born in Le Havre, died in Eragny. A naturalist scientist and engineer, was government engineer on the island of Mauritius (1768-1771). Tropical nature inspired him to become a disciple of Rousseau and to write an idyll of two children stranded on a desert island, "Paul and Virginia" (1788), immensely popular in his time.

Bertran de Born

Provencal poet (about 1170-1200).

Born at the family castle of Hautefort on the Dordogne. Of quarrelsome disposition and great bravery, fought against his own brother and took active part in any local war within his reach. Died a Cistercian monk. Famous for his love songs, addressed among others to Mathilda, daughter of Henry II of England, and his satirical "sirventes" that taunted the nobles of Southern France and drove them to fights. For this Dante put his severed head in Hell; but Bertran was much admired by the 19th century romanticists.

Bhartrihari

(Sanskrit,——651).

Distinguished Sanskrit grammarian and lyric poet, compared with Horace. His three *satakas* or "centuries" of verse are *Sringāra Sataka* (*Century of Love*), *Nīti Sataka* (*Century of Worldly Life*), and *Vairāgyra Sataka* (*Century of Renunciation*).

Bhasa

(Sanskrit, *ca.* A.D. 350).

Legendary dramatist, author of thirteen Sanskrit plays discovered in Malabar in 1912. The most important is *Svapnavāsavadatta* (*The Dream of Vāsavadattā*).

Bhavabhuti

(Sanskrit, *ca.* A.D. 730).

Leading Sanskrit dramatist, of the 8th century. Author of three dramas: *Mālatī Mādhava* (*Stolen Marriage*), *Mahāvīracharita* (*Story of the Great Hero*), and *Uttara Rāmacharita* (*Later Story of Rama*).

Bialik, Chaim Nachman

Hebrew poet (1873-1934).

Born in Rady in the Ukraine, died in Tel Aviv. Educated in the traditional Jewish way, was then influenced by the ideas of the "Haskala," the Jewish En-

lightenment in Eastern Europe. His poem "El Hazi-
por," published at the age of 18 established his stature
as the greatest modern Hebrew poet. The rest of his
work merely confirmed this judgment. Bialik was
deeply concerned with the fate of Russian Jews, menaced by the officially-sponsored pogroms and discri-
mination. His "Songs of Wrath and Retribution,"
especially those written after the massacre of Kishinev
Jews, were a call to self-defense. Went to Palestine in
1924. There he wrote stories, tales and essays rather
than poetry. Together with J. C. Ravnicki published
a collection of talmudic and Midrashic (Jewish traditional) legends.

Bierce, Ambrose
American writer (1842-1914?).

Born in Meigs County, Ohio, died in Mexico. Fought
in Civil War, became journalist in San Francisco. His
short stories, e.g. "Tales of Soldiers and Civilians"
(1891) are full of brutality, horror and irony. Went to
Mexico in 1913 and disappeared as mysteriously as a
hero of any of his stories.

Bjoernson, Bjoernstjerne
Norwegian poet and dramatist (1832-1910).

Born in Kuikne; died in Paris. Earned his first fame
with stories of Norwegian peasant life, written in his
student days: "Symnoeve Solbakken" (1857), and
"Arne" (1858). As dramatic critic and theater director,
fought to emancipate the Norwegian drama from
Danish influence. Wrote dramas: "Mary Stuart in
Scotland" (1864), "King Sverre" (1861), the trilogy
"Sigurd the Bastard" (1862), "A Bankruptcy" (1875),
"Beyond Human Power" (1883), etc. His poems were
collected in "Poems and Lays" (1870). A strong champion of nationalism and democracy, he wrote "Yes, we
love this land," which became the Norwegian national

anthem. In 1903, he became the first Scandinavian to be awarded the Nobel Prize.

Blake, William
English poet and painter (1757-1827).

Born and died in London. Apprenticed to an engraver, became an illustrator of books of Dante, Vergil, Chaucer and contemporaries like Mary Wollstonecraft. He rejected all academic standards fashionable in his day and bitterly denounced their upholder, Sir Joshua Reynolds. His poems are visionary and mystical, use popular rather than academic language. They include: "Songs of Innocence" (1789), "Book of Thel" (1789), "Songs of Experience" (1794), "The Book of Urizen" (1794), "Jerusalem" (1804) and "Milton" (1804). Often ridiculed by his contemporaries, he has been one of the most influential poets in the years that followed, both in England and in America—but remains hardly known outside the Anglo-Saxon world.

Blanco Fombona, Rufino
Venezuelan writer (1874-1944).

Born in Caracas, died in Buenos Aires. Took prominent part in Venezuelan politics, was exiled under the Gomez dictatorship. Published letters of Bolivar and other important Latin American texts. His novels are marred by tendentiousness, e.g. the anti-clerical "Mitre in Hand" (1927). But his two earlier novels, "The Man of Iron" (1907) and "The Man of Gold" (1916) are powerful and still relevant delineations of the personality of tropical America.

Blasco Ibanez, Vicente
Spanish novelist (1867-1928).

Born in Valencia, died in Menton, France. His life is divided into two distinct parts by the international success of his later novels. In the first half he was deeply involved in Spanish politics as an anarchist kind of Republican. He was 7 times in the Spanish Parliament—and 30 times in Spanish jails. His early novels are powerful descriptions of regional life in Valencia and the surrounding "huerta" (agricultural plain). They include: "Flower of May" (1895), "The Hut" (1898) and "Reeds and Clay" (1902). His later novels, e.g. "Blood and Sand" and "The Four Horsemen of the Apocalypse" (a strongly anti-German novel of World War I) gave him a world success, but Spanish critics deplore them as commercial and trashy.

Blok, Alexander Alexandrovich

Russian poet (1880-1921).

Born and died in Saint Petersburg. Was much influenced in his youth by German romanticism, the Russian poet Zhukovski and the historian Solovyev. Started as a symbolist, wrote verse with sexual and mystical overtones. The Revolution of 1905 hardened him and turned him into a realist. He was bitterly disappointed by its failure, tried to drown his despair in alcohol. World War I and the Revolution inspired him to write two apocalyptic poems that make him, in the opinion of many, the greatest Russian poet since Pushkin: "The Scythians"—a cry of defiance to the West to respect Russia—and "The Twelve"—in which Lenin and his men are merged in Christ and his apostles. But this faith, too, gave way to despair and his death was hastened by starvation.

Bloy, Leon

French writer (1846-1917).

Born in Perigueux, died in Bourg-la-Reine. An ardent Catholic, he lived a life of bitter but self-chosen poverty. He had a vitriolic style which he used in the fulness of its resources in his attacks against the enemies of France and of the Church. He was, in fact, a Christian existentialist, and his influence has been considerable in post-war France. Wrote: "The Desperate" (1886), "Salvation Through the Jews" (1892), and "The Woman Who Was Poor" (1897).

Boccaccio, Giovanni
Italian writer (1313-1375).

Born in Paris; died in Certaldo near Florence. His father was a Florentine merchant, his mother a Frenchwoman. Was sent to Naples in 1328 to study accounting. Frequented the court of King Robert of Anjou, whose illegitimate child Maria d'Aquino (whom he immortalized as "Fiametta") inspired him to become a writer. He then moved to Florence where, except for short intervals, he stayed to the end of his life. It was here that he became acquainted with Petrarch (q.v.). His collection of 100 novelle (short stories) which he makes Florentine refugees from the Great Plague tell each other in the "Decameron" (1353) made him the father of Italian classical prose, as Dante was the father of Italian classical poetry. The "Decameron" is moreover, a landmark of the Renaissance and of the development of European literature. Later in his life, Boccaccio, who had carried out a number of diplomatic missions for Florence, was appointed by the city as official lecturer on Dante, and his critical life of Dante inaugurated modern literary criticism. Of Boccaccio's other writings, his "Corbaccio" (Raven), a satire on women written in Italian, and his Latin "Lives of Famous Men," should be mentioned.

Bodmer, Johann Jacob
Swiss literary critic (1698-1783).

Born in Greifensee; died in Schoenenberg near Zurich. Professor of history at Zurich. Edited, with Breitinger (q.v.), "The Discourses of Painters," a literary journal modelled on Addison's "Spectator." He advocated in it English and national tendencies against the then-prevailing French classicism. Edited Milton's "Paradise Lost," and part of the "Niebelungenlied"; and made a critical study of German medieval poetry.

Boehme, Jacob

German mystic (1575-1624).

Born in Altseidenberg; died in Goerlitz. Known as the "Teutonic philosopher." His mysticism, based on the hypothesis of the duality of God—who is both Good and Evil—strongly attracted German romanticists and such contemporary writers as Rilke and Kolbenheyer (q.v.). It also had adherents in England, where Mrs. Jane Lead founded the Philadelphians, a Boehmian sect. Boehme was condemned as heretic by the ecclesiastical authorities of his time. Chief works: "Aurora" (written 1612, published 1634), "Description of the Three Principles of the Divine Being and Careful Description of the Threefold Life of Man" (1619), and "Mysterium Magnum" (Great Mystery, 1633).

Boethius

Roman Scholar (480-524).

Held all the highest civil offices in Rome under the Gothic emperor, Theodoric. Wrote treatises on *Arithmetic, Geometry,* and *Music;* planned a complete translation of Plato and Aristotle and a reconciliation of their divergencies. Early death (executed by Theodoric for religio-political reasons) prevented all but translation and commentary on some of Aristotle's logic. Wrote five theological tractates, applications of Aristotelian terminology to Christian revelation. In prison wrote his Latin *Consolation of Philosophy,* a study of the problem of evil in the light of the concept of an orderly universe, translated by Alfred the Great, Chaucer, Jean de Meun, Notker Labeo, and Queen Elizabeth. He rivals St. Augustine in the depth of his influence on the Middle Ages and is the bridge between the Ancient and Medieval worlds.

Boiardo, Matteo
Italian poet (1441-1494).

Born and died in Reggio Emilia. A gentleman who served the Este family and was their governor of Modena and Reggio. Famous for the great Arthurian and Carolingian epic "Orlando, i.e. Roland, in Love" (1487). It was re-written in the 16th century according to the new canons of style, and the original text was not recovered until the 19th century. Ariosto (q.v.) wrote a continuation of Boiardo's romantic epic which breaks off dramatically with a reference to the invasion of Italy by Charles VIII of France.

Boileau, Nicolas
French critic and poet (1636-1711).

Full name: Nicolas Boileau Despreaux. Born and died in Paris. Wrote "Satires" (1669-71) and "Epistles" (1674-98), as well as occasional verse in praise of Louis XIV and his court. But he earned his position as one of the chief glories of the "Age of Louis XIV" by his "Art of Poetry" (1674), based largely on Horace's (q.v.) work of the same name, in which Boileau laid down the rules of poetry for France and the entire Western civilization for almost two centuries.

Borges, Jorge Luis
Argentine writer (1900-1959).

Born in Buenos Aires, of Jewish origin. Started under the influence of the Spanish "ultraista" school, a movement parallel to imagism. But as his talents matured, his verse became more personal and intense, e.g. "Fervor of Buenos Aires" (1923), "The Moon in Front" (1925), "Fictions" (1944). Borges also wrote critical essays of considerable power. Deeply moved by World War II, he wrote "German Requiem" as an epitaph for Nazi Germany.

Borrow, George
English traveler and writer (1803-1881).

Born in East Dereham, died in Oulton Broad. Tried law and publishing as professions and found them wanting. Traveled in Russia, North Africa and Spain for the British and Foreign Bible Society. Interested in languages—he knew 36—and gypsies. Books include: "The Bible in Spain" (1843), "Lavengro" (1851), "Romany Rye" (1857) and "Wild Wales" (1862).

Boscan, Juan
Spanish poet (1490-1542).

Born and died in Barcelona. Fought in the wars of Charles V against the Turks. The Duke of Alba was his patron. In 1526, the Venetian envoy, Andrea Navagiero, persuaded him to write Spanish poems in Italian rhythms, a landmark in the story of Spanish letters. Boscan himself failed, as his sonnets, tercets and blank-verse version of the legend of Hero and Leander are poetic exercises rather than poetry, but his friend Garcilaso (q.v.) succeeded. Boscan's widow, Ana Giron de Rebolledo, published the poems of both men in 1543. Boscan was more successful as the translator of Castiglione's "Book of the Courtier."

Bossuet, Jacques Benigne
French preacher and historian (1627-1704).

Born in Dijon; died in Paris. Became bishop of Meaux in 1681, after serving eleven years as tutor to the Dauphin, son of Louis XIV. Had strong influence on king, whom he helped persuade to abolish the toleration of Protestants granted by Louis' grandfather Henry IV. Bossuet wrote a history of the Protestant churches, whose multiplicity he contrasted with Catholic unity; and a "Discourse on Universal History" (1681) in which history is presented as the working out of the Will of God. But his chief masterpiece is his "Funeral Orations," which still models as an example of classical French prose.

Boswell, James
Scottish writer (1740-1795).

Born in Edinburgh, son of a Lord Justiciary. Trained as a lawyer, traveled widely in Europe, met Voltaire, Rousseau, and Pasquale Paoli, hero of the Corsican war of independence. Met Samuel Johnson (q.v.) in London in 1763, and became a member of his circle and his biographer. In addition to the "Life of Johnson" (1791), wrote "Account of Corsica" (1768) and "Journal of a Tour to the Hebrides" (1786). A number of his European journals have been recently discovered and published.

Bourget, Paul
French novelist (1852-1935).

Born in Amiens. His novels deal with social and religious problems, treated from a strongly conservative point of view. They include "The Irreparable" (1884), "A Woman's Heart" (1890), "Cosmopolis" (1893) and "A Divorce" (1904).

Braak, Menno ter
Dutch writer (1902-1940).

Born in Eibergen, died at The Hague. Intended originally for the Church, became writer and critic. Was strongly concerned with the decline of ethical values among the Dutch, e.g. in "Politician Without a Party" (1934), and with the menace of Nazi Germany and its Dutch accomplices. He was one of the first victims of the Nazi invaders of Holland. His writings, especially his letters, were among the chief inspirations of the Dutch Resistance movement.

Bradstreet, Anne
American poetess (1612-1672).

Born Anne Dudley in Northampton, England, died

in Andover, Mass. Lived a pioneering life in the wilderness. Bore her husband eight children. Her "The Tenth Muse Lately Sprung Up in America," published in London in 1650, is the first significant poetry written in the United States.

Brainin, Reuben

Hebrew writer (1862-1939).

Born in Liady, Russia, was educated in the universities of Vienna and Berlin. A talented novelist and critic, his main achievement is the introduction of progressive European literary ideas in Hebrew literature. He waged a war upon the hackneyed ideas that cluttered Hebrew literature, founding the periodical *Memizrah Umimarab* (*From East and West*) wherein he promulgated liberal European ideas. As critic he lashed unmercifully at long established literary personalities, exposing their artistic faults and weaknesses in style and form. He recognized and encouraged new writers of ability and talent. He was a great traveler and lecturer. For a time he edited a Yiddish paper in Canada, and at one time a Hebrew monthly and then a Hebrew weekly in New York. In his last years he rallied to the Bolshevik cause, and contributed to radical Yiddish papers.

Brandes, Georg

Danish literary critic (1842-1927).

Real name: Morris Kohn. Born in Copenhagen of Jewish middle-class family. Studied at Copenhagen University, became disciple of Comte, Taine, Spencer, and Mill, and a fervent champion of materialism in life and literature. None the less, was one of the first to appreciate the greatness of Kierkegaard (q.v.), to whom he devoted a book in 1877. Taught at Copenhagen University from 1872, with an interval of five years (1877-82) which he had to spend in Berlin because of his radical views. Professor of aesthetics after

1902. Brandes' reputation as literary critic far transcended Denmark or even Scandinavia; he was a European figure. Wrote "Main Currents in Nineteenth Century Literature" (six volumes, 1872-90), "Aesthetic Studies" (1868), "The Jesus Myth" (1925), and biographies of Disraeli, Lassalle, Goethe, Voltaire, and Shakespeare.

Brant, Sebastian
German satirist (1457-1521).

Born and died in Strasbourg. Councilor of Emperor Maximilian I of Germany. His "Ship of Fools" (1494), a satire describing the various kinds of fools, was widely read and imitated all over Europe.

Brecht, Bert(old)
German poet and dramatist (1898-1957).

Born in Augsburg; died in East Berlin. Started writing under the shock of his experiences as hospital attendant in World War I. After a brief anarchist interlude, became staunch Communist and remained one to the end of his life. Theatrical director in Munich, invited by Max Reinhardt to come to Berlin where he remained until Hitler drove him into exile in Denmark, Russia, U.S.A. (Hollywood), and Switzerland. After the war, Brecht settled in East Berlin, where he and his wife, the actress Helene Weigel, directed a theatre largely devoted to staging his plays. Brecht also developed some original and widely-discussed views on the nature of drama and the functions of the theatre. His chief contribution is the "alienation effect." His fame, first confined to Germany, became international after World War II. Chief works: "Drums in the Night" (1922). "Baal" (1922), "Threepenny Opera" (1928) (a libretto to which Kurt Weill wrote the music), "Mother Courage and Her Children" (1941), "The Good Woman of Szechuan"

(1942), "The Affairs of Mr. Julius Caesar" (1949),
"The Condemnation of Lucullus" (1951).

Breitinger, Johann Jacob

Swiss literary critic (1701-1776).

Born and died in Zurich, where he taught classics.
Edited "The Discourses of Painters" with Bodmer
(q.v.), and published a number of books of literary
criticism.

Brentano, Clemens Von

German writer (1778-1842).

Born in Ehrenbreitstein; died in Aschaffenburg.
Brother of Bettina Von Arnim (q.v.), published the
pioneering collection of folk-songs, "The Boy's Enchanted Horn" (1806-08). Became an ardent Roman
Catholic and after the death of his wife Sophie (1806),
retired to a monastery at Duelmen, where he recorded
the revelations of the stigmatic nun Katherina Em-
merich. Most popular of his writings are his stories for
children, which include "The Story of the Brave
Kasperl and Beautiful Annerl" (1816), and "Gockel,
Hinkel, and Gackeleia" (1838).

Breton, André

French poet (born 1896).

Born in Tinchebray, Normandy. Was introduced
to Freud's teachings as a medical student and they
strongly influenced his poetry, even after it veered
from Dadaism to Surrealism, of which Breton became
the "literary Pope." His politics shifted from Communism through Trotskyism to anarchism. Was leader
of a group of poets of the 1920's who then moved into
all kinds of directions—Cocteau, Aragon, Eluard and
others. Wrote: "The Surrealist Manifestos" (1924-42);
"Nadia" (1928); "The White-haired Pistol" (1932).

Bridges, Robert

English poet (1844-1930).

Born in Walmer, Kent, died in Chilswell. Was a

70

leading figure in English literary life, Poet Laureate and respected critic. His own poetic talents culminated, quite late in life, in "The Testament of Beauty." He was a pre-modernist, but encouraged some of the makers of modernism.

Brillat-Savarin, Anthelme

French gastronomist and writer (1755-1826).

Born in Belley, died in Paris. A jurist by profession, a gourmet by avocation he lived up to his birth in a part of France that is the Mecca of French cooking. Exiled to the United States during the terror, he enjoyed such local specialties as wild turkey. His "Physiology of Taste" (1826) contains many penetrating observations like "Animals feed, men eat, only the wise men know how to eat"; "The man who discovers a new dish has done more for mankind than the man who discovered a new star" and "The destiny of peoples depends on the manner in which they eat."

Brod, Max

German novelist and critic (born 1884).

Born in Prague, emigrated to Palestine in 1939, now lives in Tel Aviv. Treats religious and Zionist themes in "Jewesses" (1911), "Tycho Brahe's Way to God" (1916), "Galileo in Prison" (1948), etc., written in a rich, expressionist German prose. Friend and literary executor of Franz Kafka (q.v.) whose fame he greatly helped to establish by publishing Kafka's best books after his death. Published a Kafka biography in 1936.

Bronte, Anne

English writer (1820-1849).

Born in Thornton, died in Scarborough. Youngest of the three Bronte sisters, daughters of the eccentric Patrick Bronte, brought up in the Haworth parsonage in the wilds of the Yorkshire Moors. The sisters wrote about imaginary countries called Gondal and Angria and chose the male pen names of Acton, Currer and Ellis Bell. Anne, who wrote "Agnes Gray" (1848) and "The Tenant of Wildfell Hall" (1848), was the least talented of the three, but still a respectable writer.

Bronte, Charlotte
English writer (1816-1854).

Born in Thornton, died in Haworth. Oldest of the three Bronte sisters (see Anne Bronte). Charlotte was teacher and governess in England and Belgium, won a resounding success with "Jane Eyre" (1847), a novel whose emotional vitality pleasantly shocked its Victorian readers, married her father's curate, Arthur Bell Nicholls, and settled at Haworth. Her "Shirley" (1849) and "Villette" (1853) did not match "Jane Eyre."

Bronte, Emily
English writer (1818-1848).

Born in Thornton, died in Haworth. Second of the three Bronte sisters (see Anne Bronte). Wrote a single novel, "Wuthering Heights" (1848), whose dark and passionate intensity made it a romantic masterpiece, and poetry. Generally considered the most talented of the three, though her sisters are by no means lacking in champions, especially Charlotte.

Brooke, Rupert
English poet (1887-1915).

Born in Rugby, died on the Greek island of Scyros. A precocious talent, wrote at school and as student at Cambridge. His "Poems" (1911) gave him immediate fame. Travelled to remote parts of the world as London "Times" correspondent in 1913-14. Joined up immediately after outbreak of World War I and was killed and buried in "a corner of a foreign field that is forever England." He became the symbol of an entire generation of young Englishmen who sacrificed themselves for their country and whose loss the country could ill afford.

Brooks, Van Wyck

American writer (1886-   ).

Was born in Plainfield, N. J., graduated from Harvard and worked editorially in England. Known best for his criticism of the Puritans and his original estimates of American literature. "The Ordeal of Mark Twain" (1920), "The Pilgrimage of Henry James" (1925), "The Flowering of New England" won him the Pulitzer Prize in 1937, "The Writer in America" (1953).

Brown, Charles Brockden

American writer (1771-1810).

The first professional author of the U. S., wrote within a few feverish years a group of unpolished but powerful Gothic romances which, by intentionally uniting popular interest, philosophic ideas, local subject matter, and a psychological method, practically originated the genuine American novel. Beneath their hasty, overwrought plots and the machinery of terror lies Brown's expressed moral concern for social reform and rational triumph over superstition, as well as a frequent intense realism of scene, heightened by a superb command of suspense. Four basically rationalistic novels, *Wieland* (1798), *Ormond* (1799), *Arthur Mervyn* (1799-1800) and *Edgar Huntly* (1799), were followed in 1801 by two showing increasing sentimentality and conservatism. After these Brown did only hack writing and editing.

Browne, Sir Thomas

English scientist and writer (1605-1682).

Born and died in London. A physician by profession. Travelled in Ireland, France and Italy before he settled at Shipden Hall in Yorkshire. There he wrote

"The Doctor's Religion" sometime before 1637, when he moved to Norwich. It not only gives his personal views on religion but also includes essays on various subjects. Also wrote letters in a vivid and colloquial style.

Browning, Elizabeth Barrett

English poetess (1806-1861).

Born in Durham, died in Florence. Semi-invalid through injury by a horse, she lived in her father's Wimpole Street mansion in London, until Robert Browning (1846) braved the wrath of her paternal dragon and eloped with her to Italy. In gratitude, she wrote for him "Sonnets from the Portuguese" (1850), her best work. Rilke, who did not know that Browning called her "my dear Portuguese," thought the sonnets were translated from the Portuguese language and published what he thought to be a German re-translation.

Browning, Robert

English poet (1812-1889).

Born in Camberwell, London, died in Venice. Son of a clerk in the Bank of England who encouraged his talents. His first long poem, "Pauline" came out when he was 21 (1833) and was, as was to be expected, autobiographical. Browning then vowed to write only impersonal poetry and produced "Sordello" (1840), with allusions so deeply impersonal that he himself could not explain them after a while. Went to live in Italy with Barrett (q.v.) and continued to write, mostly on Italian subjects. His long poem "The Ring and the Book," about a Roman murder case viewed by 12 participants, is considered his masterpiece (1864-69) but many people prefer his short lyrics like "Oh to be in England." Browning's reputation, which rests chiefly on his long philosophical poems is at a rather low ebb right now. The poets who dominate English poetry have a low opinion of Browning, although they share at least two qualities with him: obscurity and pedestrianism.

Bruno, Giordano

Italian philosopher (1548-1600).

Real name: Filippo Bruno. Born in Nola; died in Rome. A Dominican monk, was forced to leave the order because of his unorthodox pantheist views. Defended the opinions of Luther and Copernicus and developed philosophical views foreshadowing those of Leibnitz, Spinoza, and Hegel. Wandered many years in various European countries. Upon returning to Italy, was arrested by the Inquisition. Was tried for breaking his monastic vows and for apostasy from the church. Condemned to death and publicly burned at the stake.

Bryant, William Cullen

American poet (1794-1878).

Born in Cummington, Mass., died in New York. A liberal journalist, edited the New York "Post" for almost 50 years (1829-1878). Best known for his two early poems, "Thanatopsis" and "To a Waterfowl" (1817). Much quoted but little read.

Buber, Martin

Austrian writer and philosopher (1878-   ).

Born in Vienna he grew up in Lemberg. Was professor of the Religion of Judaism at Frankfort a/M., and has been teaching at the Hebrew University of Jerusalem since 1938. In his works he endeavors to renew Judaism through Polish Chassidism and manifests great affinity with German mysticism although he disavows mysticism as such. His books are widely read and tranlated, among them "I and Thou" (1923), "The Books of Chassidism" (1928), "Dialogical Life" (1947, a collection of philosophical and pedagogical writings), "The Problem Man" (1948), "Israel and Palestine" (1950), and autobiographical fragments entitled "Encounters" (1961).

Buck, Pearl

American novelist (born 1892).

Born Pearl Sydenstricker in Hillsboro, West Virginia; daughter of American missionaries to China. Spent childhood and youth in China, which provided the scene of her best novels. Won Nobel Prize in 1938. Novels include "East Wind—West Wind" (1930), "The Good Earth" (1931), "Sons" (1932), "Mother" (1934), "A House Divided" (1936), "Dragon Seed" (1942).

Buechner, Georg

German dramatist (1813-1837).

Born in Goddelau near Darmstadt; died in Zurich. Studied medicine and natural science; professor at Zurich in 1836. Man of advanced views; founded a "Society for the Rights of Man" and the first German Socialist newspaper. After his early death, his works remained unpublished except for the drama "Danton's Death" (published in 1835), and he was forgotten for almost a century. It was only in the Expressionist era that he was discovered as one of Germany's leading dramatists. Other works were published: "Leonce and Lena," a comedy; "Lenz"; and "Woyzeck," a tragedy which became the leading modernist opera.

Buerger, Gottfried August

German poet (1747-1794).

Born at Molmerswende in the Harz Mountains; died in Goettingen. Member of the poets' circle known as the "Goettingen Grove," which included the Stolberg brothers and Voss. Romantic poet of the "Storm and Stress" tendency; wrote ballads of which "Lenore," "The Song of the Brave Man," and "The

Wild Huntsman" became most famous. Fostered the new poetry as editor of the "Almanack of the Muses." Translated Homer (in part) and Shakespeare; edited the Baron Muenchhausen story with additions of his own. His "Poems" were published in 1778.

Bulwer-Lytton, Edward
English novelist (1803-1873).

Born in London; died in Torquay. Became Lord Lytton in 1843. Wrote poems and plays, but is remembered for his historical novels: "The Last Days of Pompeii" (1834), and "Rienzi, The Last of the Tribunes" (1835) which provided the libretto for Wagner's opera.

Bunin, Ivan
Russian writer (1870-1953).

Born in Voronezh; exiled in France after 1918. Poet of nature and love, novelist of declining Russian nobility. Impressionist in style, perfectionist in language. Obtained the 1933 Nobel Prize for his autobiographical novel "Arsenyev's Life." Other works: "The Rose of Jericho" (1924), "Mitya's Love" (1925), "The Grammar of Love" (1935), "The Village" (1936), "The Lord of San Francisco" (1942).

Bunyan, John
English religious writer (1628-1688).

Born in Elstow near Bedford; died in London. Tinsmith by profession, spent two years in Parliamentary army (1644-46). In 1653, moved by two devotional books of his wife, gave up amusements and swearings and became a Baptist preacher. Published his first writings—against Quakers—in 1656-57. Under Charles II, imprisoned for twelve years (1660-1672) for preaching without license, until released by that monarch's "Declaration of Indulgence." In prison, preached to his fellow-prisoners and wrote nine books, including

"Grace Abounding" (1666). Imprisoned again for a short period in 1675, is said to have written in prison his "The Pilgrim's Progress From This World to That Which Is to Come" (published 1678). Later works include "The Life and Death of Mr. Badman" (1680) and "The Holy War" (1682).

Buonarroti, Michelangelo
Italian artist and writer (1475-1564).

Born in Caprese; died in Rome. Michelangelo has a place in the history of Italian letters through his voluminous poetry, especially through his sonnets, on both love and religious topics. Best known of these are a series written to his friend Vittoria Colonna.

Burckhardt, Jacob
German art historian (1818-1897).

He was born in Basel and died there. A fine writer especially in the field of the Italian Renaissance in which he produced his masterwork.

Burns, Robert
Scottish poet (1759-1796).

Born in Alloway near Ayr, died in Dumfries. Grew up in poverty but obtained a sound literary education. Tried farming, without making a go of it and was about to emigrate to the West Indies when the success of his "Poems Chiefly in the Scottish Dialect" (1786) made him stay. In 1789 he became an exciseman. His marriage to Jean Armour did not prove a success, and he was plagued by poor health, addiction to alcohol and sneers from people who thought themselves his superiors. He collected folk songs and wrote poems that became folk songs like "The Auld Lang Syne." The main sources of his strength are a passionate and emotional lyricism that pervades his love poetry, and a hard-hitting genius for satire that made him write "Holy Willie's Prayer," whose savage irony explains why he has been so hated by religious hypocrites. Burns is at his best when closest to the people from which he sprung; he fails most when he tries to write a cultivated style that is not his own. The annual celebration of "Burns' Night" by Scotsmen the world over is but one indication of his status as Scotland's national poet.

Burton, Robert
English writer (1577-1640).

Born in Lindley, died in Oxford. A clergyman who was vicar of Saint Thomas, Oxford, from 1616. Wrote under the pen name of "Democritus Junior." His best and only remembered book is the "Anatomy of Melancholy" (1621) which not only diagnoses and offers cures for various varieties of melancholy, including religious and amorous, but also presents a general utopia.

Busch, Wilhelm
German poet and artist (1832-1908).

Born in Wiedensahl near Hanover, died in Mechtshausen. His humorous poems, illustrated by his own drawings, satirized the foibles of the German bourgeoisie, e.g. "Max and Moritz"; "Fipps the Ape"; "The Painter Klecksel"; "The Pious Helen." They also made him, without his knowledge, the artistic father of the American comic strip. His satire was sharp and sometimes offended against the canons of good taste, especially in his attacks on Roman Catholicism. When the Austrian government banned his "Saint Anthony of Padua," a socialist deputy to the Austrian parliament, Adler, read the poem in a parliamentary session and secured for it free printing and free distribution in the Austrian equivalent of the "Congressional Record."

Butler, Samuel
English poet (1612-1680).

Born in Strensham. Served in the Civil War under the Puritan Sir Samuel Lake, but welcomed the Restoration and became steward of Ludlow Castle under Charles II (1661). His burlesque epic "Hudibras" (in three parts, 1663-78) is a witty satire on the Puritans written in "Hudibrastic" verse, i.e. four-foot couplets with double and triple rhyme.

Butler, Samuel
English writer (1835-1902).

Born in Bingham, died in London. Born of a family of Church of England clergymen, he refused ordination and became a sheep farmer in New Zealand. Returned to London in 1865 and devoted himself to music, painting and literature. His two utopian novels, "Erewhon" (1872) and "Erewhon Revisited" (1901) attacked the conventional morality. His autobiography, published posthumously in 1903 under the title of "The Way of All Flesh" was a settlement of accounts not only with his tyrannical father but also with Victorian hypocrisy generally.

Byron, George Gordon Lord
English poet (1788-1824).

Born in London, died at Missolonghi (Greece). Child of an unhappy marriage; spent his childhood at Aberdeen until at the age of 10 he became Lord Byron through the death of a great-uncle. Published a collection of poems, "Hours of Idleness," while a student at Cambridge (1807). Answered an unfavorable review in the "Edinburgh Review" with a biting satire, "English Bards and Scotch Reviewers," published two years later. Travelled through southern Europe and in 1810 swam the Hellespont. He used his experiences to write "Childe Harolde's Pilgrimage," a thinly-disguised autobiographical poem that brought him fame (1813-14). He followed it up with poems of the Eastern Mediterranean, "The Giaour," "The Corsair," "Lara," "The Bride of Abydos." Married in 1815, but his marriage turned out to be as disastrous as that of his parents. His poems and behavior had made him many enemies in England. In 1816 he left England, never to return. For eight years, lived in Italy, where he continued "Childe Harolde," wrote "Don Juan" and a number of dramas, including "Marino Falieri," "Sardanapalus," and "Cain." Among his English friends in Italy were Leigh Hunt and Shelley (q.v.). He continued to live an unconventional life and to pursue a series of literary vendettas; he revenged himself on Southey with his "Vision of Judgment" (1822). Became champion of oppressed nationalities, and joined the Greek struggle for independence as a volunteer. He died of malaria. Byron's poetry is one of the highlights of romanticism, and the adjective "byronic" is still in use. His reputation has always been higher in Europe than in England or the United States.

C

Caballero, Fernan

Spanish novelist (1796-1877).

Pen name of Cecilia Boehl de Faber. Born in Switzerland, died in Seville. Her father was a hispanophile German, who served in various consular posts in Spain, her mother a Spaniard. She became a protégée of Queen Isabella II and wrote a number of novels about her adopted country of which one, "The Seagull" (1849) is still important. It started the *costumbrista* school of novel writing which deals at length with the customs and traditions of various Spanish regions; it also contributed towards making Seville the popular image of Spain as foreigners imagined it to be.

Cabell, James Branch

American writer (1879-1958).

Born in Richmond, Va. Invented a medieval kingdom, Poictesme, of which he writes chronicles, in which fantasy mingles with reality. Also a novelist, with "Jurgen" (1919) and "Figures of Earth" (1921).

Caedmon

Anglo-Saxon poet (Seventh Century).

Flourished about 670-680. A Northumbrian herdsman who, according to Bede, received in a dream the divine call to "sing of the beginning of the created things." The "Hymn" which he thus wrote is preserved in Bede's Latin version and in an Anglo-Saxon retranslation. Accepted by the Abbess Hilda as an inmate of the monastery at Whitby. There he wrote the "Caedmon poems," Anglo-Saxon paraphrases of the biblical books of Genesis, Daniel, and Exodus, and original religious poems. Recent criticism holds that the poems were partly reworked by other hands.

Caesar, Julius

Roman politician and writer (100-44 B.C.).

Born and died in Rome, after becoming its sole ruler. His place in literature was assured by his "Commentaries" on the Gallic War (58-52), and the "Civil War" that followed it. The latter, completed by one of his lieutenants, Aulus Hirtius, is written in a less direct and more polished prose than the former. Historians have seriously endangered Caesar's reputation as straightforward reporter of facts; but their researches have not affected the clarity and vigor of his language, which has made the "Gallic War" the ideal introduction to Latin for school boys for two millennia.

Calderon de la Barca, Pedro

Spanish dramatist (1600-1681).

Born and died in Madrid. Educated by the Jesuits and at Salamanca University. For thirteen years fought in Philip IV's army, taking part in the Catalan campaign of 1640. Became Philip's court poet. Took holy orders and rose to become the superior of the Brotherhood of Saint Peter and honorary chaplain to the king. Composed some 120 worldly and 80 religious plays of all kinds, mostly dealing with ethical and religious problems. Calderon's death marked the end of the Spanish Golden Age. For well over a century he was almost forgotten, even in Spain. He was rescued from oblivion by the German romanticists— Goethe staged one of his plays at Weimar in 1811— and his place as one of Europe's major dramatists is now assured. His chief plays are: "The Mayor of Zalamea," "The Constant Prince," "The Physician of His Honor," "Life's a Dream," "The Spirit of the Air," "The Purgatory of Saint Patrick," "The Tetrarch of Jerusalem."

Caldwell, Erskine
American novelist (born 1903).

Born at White Oak, Georgia. Educated at Universities of Virginia and Pennsylvania. Worked as journalist, cotton picker, stagehand, professional football player, book reviewer, editor, and scriptwriter for Metro-Goldwyn-Mayer. His books, with their realistic descriptions of life and sex, advocate the ideas of the New Deal and include "The Bastard" (1930), "Poor Fool" (1930), "Tobacco Road" (1932) (which made him a best seller), "God's Little Acre" (1933), "Journeyman" (1935), "Trouble in July" (1940), "Tragic Ground" (1944), "House in the Uplands" (1946), "Opossum" (1952), "Estherville" (1952).

Caldwell, (Janet) Taylor
American novelist (born in 1900).

Born in Prestwich near Manchester, England; came to U.S. in 1907. Chief works: "The Dynasty of Death" (1938), "The Eagles Gather" (1940), "This Side of Innocence" (1946), and "Let Love Come Last" (1949).

Callimachus
Greek poet (about 305-about 240 B.C.).

Born in Cyrene, North Africa, died in Alexandria. Worked in the great library of Alexandria, was patronized by Ptolemy II and III and included favorable references to them in his poem "The Lock of Berenice." Callimachus was a typical "Alexandrian" poet, strong in style and taste, weak in feeling and staying power. He made the best of his limited powers, wrote hymns and epigrams, including: "A big book is a big ugliness" that might serve as his epitaph.

Camoes, Luis Vaz de
Portuguese poet (1524-1580).

Born and died at Lisbon. Educated at Coimbra, joined court of King John III, wrote lyrical poems and plays. Was banished from court because of a love affair with one of the Queen's ladies-in-waiting, Caterina de Ataide. Became a soldier, fought in Morocco, where he lost an eye (1550); India, where he was imprisoned for attacking the abuses of the government; and Macao in China. Meanwhile wrote the "Lusiads" (1556, published 1572), epic of the Portuguese discoveries. On one occasion, saved the manuscript by swimming with it from a wrecked ship. A collection of prose reflections and maxims was lost. In 1570, had to borrow money to return to Portugal, where after the death of King Sebastian, whose patronage he had gained, he lived in bitter poverty, tended by his faithful slave, Jao. His death coincided with the end of Portugal's greatness.

Campbell, Thomas
Scottish poet (1777-1844).

Born in Glasgow, died in Boulogne sur Mer (France). A lawyer, became a poet to express his feelings about the war against Revolutionary and Napoleonic France. His best-known poems in this vigorous vein are "Hohenlinden" and "The Battle of the Baltic."

Campe, Heinrich
German writer (1746-1818).

Born in Deensen near Braunschweig; died in Braunschweig. Tutor to the Humboldt family and educational reformer of the Duchy of Braunschweig. Best remembered for his "Dictionary of the German

Language" (1807-1811) and his novel "Robinson the Younger" (1779) based on Defoe.

Campo, Estanislao del

Argentine poet (1835-1888).

Born and died in Buenos Aires. One of the best representatives of the gaucho poetry. His "Faust" (1865) is the narrative of a gaucho who saw a performance of Gounod's opera in Buenos Aires and believed that it was real life.

Campoamor, Ramon de

Spanish poet (1817-1901).

Born in Navias in Asturias, died in Madrid. Gave up law for literature and used literature as a stepping stone to politics. Was immensely successful in his day because his facile and tearful romanticism satisfied the sentimental side of his middle class readers. Although Havelock Ellis called him the best poet of modern Spain in his "Soul of Spain," he is now mercifully forgotten in his native land. Only some of his epigrammatic "Small Poems" are still read for pleasure.

Camus, Albert

French dramatist, novelist, and essayist (1913-1960).

Born in Oran in Algeria of a French father and a Spanish mother. Died in an automobile crash on the road to Paris. After father's early death, had a hard childhood and youth; worked at a large variety of jobs. The drama was his first love and he became an actor and producer. Moved to France, where he was due to direct Sartre's "Flies," when the Gestapo postponed the performance by arresting the actress who was to play the female lead. In the meantime Camus wrote his first novel "The Stranger" (1941) which brought him instant fame as an interpreter of 20th-century man. He returned to the drama with "Caligula" (1944). Until the end of the war he was active in the

French Resistance and his concern for human values continued after hostilities ceased. In 1945 he published "Letter to a German Friend," and followed it up with a second novel, "The Plague, 1947" a political essay, "The Rebel," short stories, plays, etc. Was awarded the Nobel Prize in 1956, one of the youngest writers to be so distinguished. Is usually classed as an existentialist, though he does not accept this classification, and his relations with Sartre have been tempestuous.

Capek, Karel
Czech writer (1890-1938).

Born in Male Svatonovice, died in Prague. A doctor's son, he studied in Prague, Berlin and Paris. Became a journalist and later a novelist; was the most representative figure of Masaryk's republic and enjoyed an international reputation. His novels are of the fantastic "science fiction" variety e.g. "Krakatit" (1924) and "War with the Newts" (1936) but written on a much higher literary level. His plays include "R.U.R." (1920) which gave the world the word and concept of "robot"; "The Insect Play" (1920, written with his elder brother Joseph); "The White Sickness" (1937) and "The Mother" (1938), forecasting the coming of Nazism to his country and preaching resistance to it. Munich broke his heart and killed him—his brother Joseph, not so fortunate, died at Belsen.

Carducci, Giosue
Pen name of Enotrio Romano. Born at Val di Castello (Tuscany); died at Bologna, where he was professor of the history of literature. Nobel Prize winner for 1906. His verses are classical in style and apply classical metres to modern Italian. Defended classical paganism against Christianity and acted as Champion of Satan. Chief works: "Satan" (1879); "Barbarian Odes" (Three Series, 1887-89).

Carlyle, Thomas
Scottish writer (1795-1881).

Born at Ecclefechan (Dumfriesshire), died in London. Studied at Edinburgh, taught in Scotland and moved to London in 1824, where he soon became a leading literary figure. Came to be known as "The Sage of Chelsea." Did much to popularize German literature and thought in England. Among his first works was a biography of Schiller (1824) and a translation of Goethe's "Wilhelm Meister." Later (1851-1865) he wrote an extensive "History of Frederick the Great," for which he did research in Germany. His treatment of the king was sympathetic, unlike his treatment of the French Revolution, in a book of that name published in 1837. He became attracted by historical heroes, wrote "Heroes and Hero Worship" in 1840, and found his English hero in "Oliver Cromwell" (1845). His "Sartor Resartus" (1833-34) is partly autobiography, partly a discussion of philosophical creeds. Was an acute critic of Victorian England from a Tory point of view: "Past and Present" (1843); "Latterday Chartism," etc. His "Reminiscences" (written 1866, published 1881) reflect his growing personal bitterness and misanthropy.

Casanova, Jacopo Giovanni
Italian adventurer and writer (1725-1798).

Born in Venice, died in Dux (Bohemia). Son of a family of actors. Expelled from Seminary of Saint Cyprian, where he studied for the priesthood, 1741. Was soldier, preacher, alchemist, cabbalist, musician, gambler, etc., all over Europe as far as Turkey. Upon returning to Venice in 1755 was imprisoned in the Piombi jail but made a sensational escape after a year. The telling of the story became his stock in trade and he published an account of it, anonymously, in French, "The History of My Escape" (1788). In addition to innumerable love affairs, had dealings with Louis XV (for whom he headed the French lottery), Frederick the Great (for whom he refused to work), the Pope (who gave him the Papal order of the Golden Spur), Catherine the Great, Voltaire, Madame de Pompadour, Cagliostro, etc. He finally settled down at Dux as librarian for the Count of Waldstein (1782). It was there that he wrote his "Memoirs." The German firm which published them in 1826-1838 left out the most juicy bits. These are lost irretrievably through the bombing of Leipzig in World War II but Casanova's reputation as lover and adventurer has survived the loss.

Castelo Branco, Camilo
Portuguese novelist (1825-1888).

Born in Lisbon, died in Sao Miguel de Seide. Brought up in the remote province of Tras os Montes, his life was as ultra-romantic as any of his novels. When he was fifteen, two women fought a duel over him. He was imprisoned for eloping with a married woman, and tried in vain to defeat the calls of the flesh by entering a theological seminary. Then came recognition, the title of viscount and an article of twelve pages in the "Universal Encyclopedia" of Lisbon, which gave only two pages to Brazil. Finally disease, blindness and suicide. His novels are all but innumerable but one of them still lives: "The Love Which Leads to Perdition" (1862) in which all the protagonists die or get killed because of a romantic entanglement. The book ends because there are no characters left.

Castiglione, Balthazar Count
Italian humanist (1478-1529).

Born at Casatico Castle near Mantua; died in Toledo. Diplomat, attached to courts of Milan and Urbino. Sent by Clement VII as papal nuncio to

Spain. After sack of Rome by Spanish troops (1527) was accused of treachery and had to remain in Spain. Left the court of Charles V to become bishop of Avila. Famous for his "Courtier," a book translated into most European languages. The ideal courtier blends the accomplishments of the Ages of Chivalry and of the Renaissance.

Castro, Rosalia
Spanish poetess (1837-1888).

Born in Santiago de Compostela, died in Padron. Her whole life was overshadowed by her birth as the illegitimate daughter of a priest and a lady of quality. Married the historian Manuel Murguia who took her to live in Madrid, where she pined for her native Galicia. She suffered from poverty, ill-treatment by her husband (who did, however, foster her literary career) and bad health, largely caused by overwork in caring for five children. Wrote at first in Galician— "Galician Songs" (1862) and "New Leaves" (1884)— then in Castilian, the language of her last book, "On the Shores of the Sar." "Rosalia," as she was generally called, brought to Spanish poetry the melancholy of her native region and also the highly developed technique of its medieval poetry. She is one of the main formative influences on modern Spanish poetry.

Cather, Willa
American novelist (1876-1947).

Born in Winchester, Va., died in New York. Brought up in the Nebraska prairie country which she put on the literary scene with "O Pioneers" (1913), "The Song of the Lark" (1915) and "My Antonia" (1918). Travel broadened her literary horizons: "Death comes for the Archbishop" (1927) deals with the Spanish Southwest, and "Shadows on the Rock" (1931) with French Quebec. Her excellent style was formed under the influence of classical and English literature which she taught at one time.

Cato, Marcus Portius

Roman writer (234-149).

Born in Tusculum, died in Rome. Known as "Cato the Elder," to distinguish him from his great-grand-son, "Cato the Younger," the opponent of Caesar. Cato was a rabid exponent of the Republican virtues of Rome. He ended every speech in the Senate with the remark: "Besides, I think that Carthage should be destroyed." He died three years before its destruction. He attacked Greek influences and accused the Greeks of a plot to poison all Romans, but learned Greek shortly before he died. His treatise "On Agriculture" is preserved, but not his "Origins," a history of Rome in which he takes a dim view of the cult of personality. He wrote on the Punic Wars without mentioning the names of either Scipio or Hannibal; the only name mentioned is that of Hannibal's elephant.

Catullus, Gaius Valerius

Roman poet (about 87-54 B.C.).

Born in Verona. Belonged to "modernist" circle called "Neoteroi" which wanted to adapt to Latin the fine Greek style of the Alexandrine poets. Some 116 poems of Catullus are preserved, mostly lyrical and satirical. The love poems addressed to "Lesbia," generally identified with the notorious Clodia, and the satires against Caesar, are best remembered. Catullus' language is a strange but successful mixture of the exquisite and the coarse.

Cavalcanti, Guido

Italian poet (about 1255-1300).

Born and died in Florence. Member of a prominent Florentine family, took part in local politics, was exiled for a short time. A friend of Dante, who admired his work and with whom he quarrelled for reasons that still remain obscure. Some 50 poems can be safely ascribed to him, mostly dealing with love. They express the poignant feelings of a lonely and suffering lover in a lucid style.

Cech, Svatopluk
Czech poet (1846-1908).

Born in Osterdek in Bohemia; died in Prague. Romantic poet, influenced by Byron. Wrote the epic poem "The Adamites" (1873) about the extreme Hussites who went about naked, the historical novel "Dagmar" (1885), and "Songs of Slaves" (1894), poems.

Cela, Camilo Jose
Spanish novelist (born 1916).

Born in Iria Flavia, Galicia. Fought on Franco's side in the Civil War. Startled the literary world with his picaresque novel "The Family of Pascual Duarte" (1942), the first sign that Spanish literary life did—as was widely feared—entirely expire under Franco's heel. Cela was able to publish the book because he worked as a censor at the time. Since then he has written a series of novels, including the "existentialist" "Hive" (1952), and acted as the *enfant terrible* of Spanish letters. Of late, he has much sobered and acts as leader of the younger generation of Spaniards who wish to lift the country out of the regime's political and moral mire.

Celakovsky, Frantisek Ladislav
Czech poet (1799-1852).

Romantic poet. Published a collection of Slav folk songs (1822-27). His own chief work is "Centifolia" ("100 leaves," 1840).

Cellini, Benvenuto
Italian artist and writer (1500-1571).

Born and died in Florence. Goldsmith and sculptor who led an adventurous life in the service of the Pope, the king of France and the Grand Duke of Tuscany. His literary fame and somewhat scandalous reputation rests on his "Autobiography" (started 1558), mostly preserved in a version he dictated to a 14 year old secretary, which accounts for its racy colloquial style.

Celtes or Celtis, Konrad

German humanist (1459-1508).

Born in Wipfed in Franconia; died in Vienna. Studied at Heidelberg, wandered through Germany and Italy. Was crowned poet laureate by Emperor Frederick III in 1487. Taught at Ingolstadt and Vienna, where he directed plays for Emperor Maximilian I. Promoted classical studies and wrote in Latin "Odes," "Loves," and an "Art of Versification and Poetry."

Cervantes, Miguel de

Spanish writer (1547-1616).

Full name: Miguel de Cervantes Saavedra. Born at Alcala de Henares; died in Madrid. Born of an impoverished noble family, educated by an Erasmist tutor in his native town, by Jesuits in Seville, and at the University of Salamanca. Served in Spanish army in Italy, entered the service of Cardinal Giulio Aquaviva (1570). Fought for Spain at Lepanto (1571), where he lost use of left arm, at Tunis and at Corfu. On his way back to Spain, captured by pirates and spent five years as slave in Algiers until he was ransomed. Returned home in 1575, married, and occupied a number of minor official posts. Twice jailed for debt, often in extreme poverty, could not settle at any place or in any job. In 1613 joined the Third Order of Saint Francis at his birthplace. His last years were brightened by the patronage of the Duke of Lemos and the success of his masterpiece, "Don Quixote," which sold 30,000 copies in his lifetime. Works: "Don Quixote" (Part I, 1605; Part II, 1606), a landmark in the history of the novel and one of the great books of all times; "Galatea," a pastoral novel (1585); plays, including "Numancia," "Journey to the Parnassus" (1614); literary criticism in verse; "Exemplary Novel" (twelve tales, 1613); "Persiles and Segismunde" (a fantastic tale, 1616); many poems, especially sonnets.

Chaadayev, Pyotr Yakovlevich
Russian writer (1793-1856).

Born and died in Moscow. Flashed into prominence by the publication of his "Philosophical Letters." Originally written in French, a Russian translation of the first was published in "The Telescope" magazine. Chaadayev, writing under the influence of French Catholic philosophers like De Maistre and De Bonald, attacked the problem of Russia's relations with the West. His thesis was simple—Russia is backward—and so was his solution—Russia must be Westernized. This started off the dispute between Westernizers and Slavophiles that lasted for the best part of a century. As for Chaadayev, Tsar Nicholas I had him officially proclaimed mad and forbade him further publication.

Chamisso, Adalbert Von
German writer (1781-1838).

Born at Boncourt castle in the Champagne; died in Berlin. Came to Berlin when his family, French nobles, had to leave France in 1790. In Berlin, became page of the Queen of Prussia, and later was Prussian officer. When his family returned to France, he remained in Germany and fought against the French in 1805. Naturalist, went round the world with Russian scientific expedition, and became curator of Berlin botanical garden. Best known for his "Poems" (1831), including the nostalgic "Castle Boncourt," and his prose story "Peter Schlemihl," the story of the man who lost his shadow, symbolic of Chamisso's homelessness.

94

Char, René

French poet (born 1907).

Born in L'Isle-sur-la-Sorgue. Started as a surrealist and, even after he grew out of it, incorporated its achievements in his verse. Friend of Albert Camus (q.v.), took part with him in the Resistance movement. His poetry, which has been much read in Anglo-Saxon countries, includes: "Furor and Mystery" (1948) and "The Sun of the Waters" (1951).

Chartier, Alain

French poet (about 1385-about 1429).

Born in Bayeux in Normandy, held important offices under the Dauphin, later Charles VII. Wrote in both French and Latin. Was deeply concerned with the causes, both political and moral, of his country's misfortunes in the Hundred Years' War. He analyzed them in the "Invective Quadrilogue" (1422). His poems are expressions of his patriotic sentiments in a courtly and refined form.

Chateaubriand, François, René Vicomte de

French writer (1768-1848).

Born in Saint-Malo; died in Paris. Of old French nobility, passed his happiest days at the family castle of Combourg in Brittany. Served in French army. Became a lover of nature and of primitive peoples under the influence of Rousseau (q.v.). Went to the United States in 1791, spent a year in the woods living with Indians. Returned to Europe to fight against the French Revolution in the emigre army (1792). After the defeat of Thionville, spent eight years in English exile (1792-1800). Returned to France, joined diplomatic corps but resigned his post after Napoleon's execution of the Duc d'Enghien (1804). Thenceforth opposed Napoleon and supported the Bourbons. Travelled extensively in Mediterranean countries.

After return of Bourbons, rejoined diplomatic service, was ambassador to England (1822) and Minister of Foreign Affairs (1823-24). Became increasingly isolated and died a forgotten man. His writings, which are said to have inaugurated the Romantic movement in France, include "Atala" (1801), "The Genius of Christianity" (1802), "Rene" (1802), "The Martyrs" (1809), "The Natchez" (1826), "The Last of the Abencerages" (1829), "Memoirs From Beyond the Grave" (1849-50).

Chatterji, Bankim Chandra
Indian novelist (1838-1894).

Born in Calcutta, wrote in his native Bengali a number of historical novels under the influence of Sir Walter Scott. They deal with the struggles between Hindus and Muslims in an exalted and sentimental manner. The most popular of them was "Ananda Math" (The Abbey of Bliss, 1822) which contains the song "Bande Mataram" (Hail to Thee, Mother), now the national anthem of India. Chatterji is one of the founders of the Indian novel; he greatly influenced Tagore (q.v.) who, however, purged his excesses.

Chatterton, Thomas
English poet (1752-1770).

Born in Bristol, died in London. Forged a number of poems in what he conceived to be medieval English and pretended to have found them in the church of Saint Mary Redcliffe in Bristol. He palmed them off as the work of a 15th century author, Thomas Rowley. Chatterton had great poetic gifts and appealed to local pride and the prevailing interest in the middle ages. He was acclaimed in Bristol but failed to impress London. He committed suicide there and was buried in a pauper's grave.

Chaucer, Geoffrey
English poet (about 1340-1400).

Born and died in London. Son of a vintner, represented the rising middle class. Became page to the wife of the Duke of Clarence, son of Edward III. Fought in English army against France in 1359, taken prisoner and ransomed a year later. For ten years on diplomatic missions in Flanders, France, and Italy, where he met Boccaccio and perhaps Petrarch (q.v.). In 1374, appointed comptroller of London customs. Obtained pensions from Edward III, John of Gaunt, Richard II, and Henry IV, surviving changes of regime and dynasty, but undergoing periods of poverty and hardship. IIc is buried in the Poet's Corner at London's Westminister Abbey, fittingly, since modern English literature may well be said to have started with him. His writing, first reflecting French and later influences, assimilated these influences and did much to create the English literary language. French influences predominate in "The Book of the Lyon" and "The Book of the Duchess," contemporary with his translation of the "Roman de la Rose," Italianate tendencies are seen in the narrative poem "Troilus and Creseide," modelled on Boccaccio (whose "Teseide" Chaucer translated), "The House of Fame," and "The Parliament of Fools." Toward the end of his life Chaucer wrote his masterpiece the "Canterbury Tales," which marked the final triumph of English as his country's language over French and Latin.

Chekhov, Anton Pavlovich
Russian writer (1860-1904).

Born in Taganrog (South Russia); died in Baden-weiler (Germany). Studied medicine in Moscow; started writing literary sketches to amuse himself. He discovered literature as his vocation (although he insisted that "medicine is my wife and literature my mis-

97

tress") through a letter from D. V. Grigorovich, a writer then famous and now forgotten, imploring him not to waste his talent on trifles. His greatest achievements are in plays and short stories, in which humor, irony, pathos, and despair mingle inextricably. Chekhov was the last Russian writer of the "classical" Russian tradition. He is greatly appreciated in the West, but the Russians often object that the Western attitude toward Chekhov tends to be sentimental and to stress form at the expense of content. Westerners tend to consider him "quaint" when he is not gloomy, and to ignore his faith in progress and his consistent championing of the underdog, e.g., his exposure of the inhuman conditions on the island prison of Sakhalin, achieved at great cost to his health. Chekhov also was one of the great stylists of the Russian language—a quality not easily transmitted in translation. He died of tuberculosis. Chief works: "Colorful Tales" (1886); "Dusk" (1870); "Gloomy Men" (1890); "Sakhalin Island" (1894); "Novellas and Tales" (1894); "The Seagull" (1896); "Uncle Vanya" (1900); "Three Sisters" (1901); "The Cherry Orchard" (1904).

Chenier, Andre
French poet (1762-1794).

Born in Constantinople, died in Paris. His father was a French consul, his mother a Cypriot. Brought to Paris as a child and grew up there among the poets and painters who frequented his mother's *salon*. Entered the diplomatic service and was secretary to the French embassy in London (1787-1790). He welcomed the Revolution but soon condemned its excesses, was jailed and executed after a mockery of a trial. His poetry was transitional between classicism and romanticism. Only fragments of his work were published in his lifetime but the 1819 edition of his "Poems," including his masterpiece "The Captive Girl" was hailed by the young poets of the day.

Chernyshevsky, Nikolai Gavrilovich
Russian writer and critic (1828-1889).

Born and died in Saratov. Said of himself that "having found no man or woman worthy of my attachment, I decided to devote myself to the service of mankind." Wrote critical articles on both literary and social questions, suffered exile to Siberia (1862-69). Won great popularity with a political novel, "What Is to Be Done?", a title that Lenin later used for one of his pamphlets.

Chesterton, Gilbert Keith
English writer (1874-1936).

Born in London, died in Beaconsfield, Bucks. A convert to Roman Catholicism, acted as one of its most powerful apologists. Prominent as writer, critic and a formidable wit. His work includes novels, such as, "The Napoleon of Notting Hill" (1904); detective stories like "The Man Who Was Thursday" (1908); biographies, critical essays, short stories and straightforward apologetics. Paradox was his strongest literary —and religious—weapon.

Chikamatsu, Monzaemon
Japanese dramatist (1653-1725).

Pen name of Sugimori Nobumori. Born in Kyoto, died in Osaka. Wrote plays for both the Kabuki actors' theater and the puppet theater and has been called, with pardonable exaggeration, "the Shakespeare of Japan." Chikamatsu can well stand on his own feet; he excelled in characterization and dialogue. Among the best-known of his numerous plays are "The Battles of Coxinga" and "Double Suicide at Amijima."

Chocano, Jose Santos
Peruvian poet (1875-1934).

Born in Lima, died in Santiago de Chile. Leader of the "modernist" movement which revolutionized Spanish-American letters. His strong social conscience especially moved by the sufferings of the oppressed Indians, found its expression in verses of Parnassian clarity and purity, e.g. in the sonnets of "The Soul of America" (1906).

Choderlos de Laclos, Pierre
French novelist (1741-1803).

Born in Amiens, died in Taranto (Italy). Professional soldier, lost his commission in 1786 for criticizing the theories of Vauban, the military genius who died almost a century earlier. Resumed his army career in 1792 and died a general. Wrote "Dangerous Acquaintances" (1782), a novel that pioneered in the psychology of sexual relations and offended the contemporary readers by its cool and detached treatment of the subject. It is now recognized as a classical French novel.

Chrestien de Troyes
French poet (1140/50-before 1191).

Born at Troyes in the Champagne. Court poet of Henry I of France and Count Philip of Flanders. His verse versions of Arthurian romances are a landmark of European literature and were widely imitated. They include "Percival," "Erec and Enide," "Yvain," "Cliges," "William of England."

Christine de Pisan
French writer (1365-1430).

Born in Venice. Her father was an Italian astrologer and physician to Charles V of France. Widowed at 25 after a happy marriage, she took up writing to support her family. Her biography of Charles V (1404) has been much praised, and her poetry strikes a personal note. It is, however, marred by bluestocking pedantry. Her "City of Women" is a spirited defense of her sex against attack by contemporaries like Jean de Meung.

Chu Hsi

Chinese philosopher (1130-1200).

Born in Yu-chi, died in Kao-ting. Had a long and distinguished official career, culminating in the post of tutor to the Sung emperor Ning-tsung. Founder of neo-Confucian school which combined the teachings of Confucius with elements taken from Buddhism and Taoism and became the official philosophy until the end of the Chinese Empire in 1911. In addition to editing the Confucian classics, he wrote "The Book of Domestic Rites," "The Morality of Youth," etc.

Chu Yuan

Chinese poet (343-277).

Also spelled "Chou Yuan." His life is wrapped in legend and his very existence has been doubted. His surviving verse makes him China's first personal poet giving vent to his feelings. He had a strong social consciousness which has made him a favorite of the Communist regime in China and of Mao Tse-tung personally. Large Chinese editions and many foreign translations of his work have been officially sponsored.

Chuang Tsu

Chinese philosopher (4th century B.C.).

A disciple of Lao Tse and a prominent Taoist. Refused all government patronage and became the model of an independent Chinese intellectual. His "Book of Chuang Tsu" is full of much quoted personal anecdotes. The most famous tells of how he dreamed that he was a butterfly and wondered, after he awoke, whether he was Chuang Tsu who dreamed about being a butterfly or a butterfly who dreamed about being Chuang Tsu.

Churchill, Sir Winston

English politician, writer and orator (born 1874).

Born in Blenheim Palace, the family seat in Woodstock, Oxfordshire. While his writing was mostly done in interludes between terms of political office, his magnificent speeches were not the least of his contributions as Prime Minister in World War II. Received Nobel Prize for Literature in 1953. Writings include a single novel, of the Ruritanian variety, "Savrola" (1902); lives of his father (1906) and his ancestor Marlborough (1933-36), the autobiographical "My Early Life" (1930) and histories of the two world wars.

Cicero, Marcus Tullius

Roman orator and writer (106-43 B.C.).

Born in Arpinum; died near Cajeta. Studied law, oratory, Greek literature, and philosophy. Became lawyer, earning big fees. Went through full career of Roman official, becoming consul in 63 B.C. It was then that he foiled the conspiracy of Catiline. Banished from Rome for a short time (58-57); returned as partisan of Pompey, who rewarded him with the post of proconsul in Cilicia (Asia Minor). Became reconciled with Caesar after his victory, but after Caesar's assassination attacked Mark Antony, which led to his proscription and death at the hands of Mark Antony's hired assassins. Cicero, using Greek models, gave Latin for the first time a literary prose, capable of dealing with the great tasks awaiting it. Of his speeches, the most famous are those against Catiline, against Mark Antony (known as "Philippics," from the model of Demosthenes, [q.v.]), and against Verres, the rapacious Roman governor of Sicily. He also wrote treatises on

Rhetoric, on the Orator, on Friendship, on the State, on Laws, the Nature of Gods, etc.

Claudel, Paul

French dramatist and poet (1868-1955).

Born at Villeneuve sur Fere; died in Paris. In diplomatic service after 1892, served as minister and ambassador to Brazil, Denmark, Japan, and the United States. After a conversion from youthful atheism, he became one of the chief spokesmen of French Catholicism. It was in this capacity that he corresponded with Gide. He failed to achieve Gide's conversion, but their exchange of letters became part and parcel of French literature. His Catholicism tended to be mystical and aesthetic. It is expressed in poems written under the influence of symbolism and especially in his dramas. Poems: "Five Great Odes" (1922), "Two Summer Poems" (1914), "War Poems" (1915). Plays: "The Tidings Brought to Mary" (1912) and "The Satin Slipper" (1928).

Claudius, Matthias

German poet (1740-1815).

Born in Reinsfeld (Holstein); died in Hamburg. Studied at Jena, worked as secretary in Copenhagen, and moved to Hamburg, where he published (1771-1775) the magazine "Wandsbecker Bote." Lyrical poet, whose simple and moving language made many of his poems into folk songs.

Clement of Alexandria

Greek scholar (150-214).

After the death of Pantaenus, (*ca.* 200 A.D.) he became for a short time the director of the Catechetical School at Alexandria. He was not only familiar with Scripture and all Christian literature before his time, but possessed an amazingly wide knowledge of pagan Greek literature. He cites more than 360 pagan authors. His chief extant writings, forming a kind of trilogy, are the *Exhortation to the Greeks (Protreptikos)*, the *Pedagogue (Paidagogos)*, and the *Carpets (Stromateis* or *Stromata)*. The last work is a long miscellany dealing primarily with the relations of Christianity to secular culture and especially to Greek philosophy. His style at times reaches poetic heights. In stressing the importance of secular knowledge as a preparation for religious instruction and study, Clement was the first to establish a harmony between Christianity and pagan literature and thus to make the pagan Classics an essential part of Christian education.

Cobbett, William
English writer (1762-1835).

Born in Farnham, died in Guildford. A political journalist who wrote under the pen name of "Peter Porcupine" in "The Weekly Political Register." His views were a uniquely English blend of Toryism and radicalism, and his language was terse, plain and biting. His pen spared no one, and he edited the "Political Register" for two years from the jail to which he had been confined after attacking the practice of flogging in the British army.

Cocteau, Jean
French writer (born 1892).

Born at Maison-Lafitte near Paris. Flew a French plane in World War I. Influenced by futurism and surrealism. Excelled in many literary genres—poetry, plays, film direction, and the creation of ballets. For many years one of the chief fixtures of the Paris literary and artistic scene; enjoyed playing part of "enfant terrible" and shocking the bourgeois. Surprised his friends and his enemies by becoming member of the French Academy in 1955. Chief works: "The Great Distance" (1923), "Opera" (1925), "Oedipus King"

(1927), "Orpheus" (1927), "Antigone" (1928), "The Terrible Children" (1929), "The Terrible Parents" (1938), "The Eagle Has Two Heads" (1941).

Coleridge, Samuel Taylor

English writer (1772-1834).

Born at Ottery Saint Mary (Devonshire); died at Highgate (London). Studied at Cambridge where, under influence of the French Revolution, he adopted extreme views in politics and religion. He dropped his studies in 1793 to enlist in the Dragoons, was bought out by his brother soon afterwards. In 1794 wrote a drama "The Death of Robespierre." Went to America to help start a Utopian community on the banks of the Susquehanna under the influence of Southey (q.v.); returned to England after its failure. Preached in Unitarian chapels, started a weekly magazine that failed, and became an addict to laudanum in 1796. Joined forces with Wordsworth (q.v.) and Southey to form the school of Lake poets, a landmark of English romanticism. In 1798 started collaborating with Wordsworth on the "Lyrical Ballads" to which he contributed, among other things, "The Ancient Mariner." The firm of Wedgwood granted him an annuity on condition of his devoting himself to literature. Visited Germany in 1798-99, returned to introduce to England German idealistic philosophy and methods of literary criticism. His criticism revolutionized our appreciation of Shakespeare. Suffering from poverty and addiction to opium (after 1803), he kept on writing, while his views became more and more conservative. Chief works include a translation of Schiller's "Wallenstein" (1800), "Christabel" (1816), "Kublai Khan" (1816), "Aids to Reflection" (1825), "Table Talk" (1835).

Colette

French novelist (1873-1956).

Full name: Sidonie Gabrielle Colette. Born in Sauveur-en-Puysaye, died in Paris. Started writing about her Burgundian childhood under the pen name of her first husband "Willy." After their divorce, she earned her living as a dancer and mime. A second marriage brought her social as well as literary acclaim. Though her sex excluded her from the French Academy, she became member of the Royal Belgian Academy in 1935 and of the Goncourt Academy in 1945. In the last years of her life she was one of France's great literary celebrities, but this never went to her head. The world of her novels is that of children, animals and —above all—women. They include: "Claudine" (1900-03), "Mitsou" (1919), "Cheri" (1920) and "Gigi" (1945).

Collodi, Carlo

Italian writer for children (1826-1890).

Pen name of Carlo Lorenzini. Born and died in Florence. Author of "The Adventures of Pinocchio" (1880), still read by children the world over.

Concolorcorvo

Peruvian writer (18th century).

The mystery of the man writing under this pen name remains, but most critics favor his identification with Carlos Bustamante. Concolorcorvo's "Lazarillo de Ciegos Caminantes" (A Guide for Blind Wayfarers) was published in 1773 ostensibly in Gijon (Spain) but actually in Lima. In the form of an itinerary from Buenos Aires to Lima, it offers a vivid picture of colonial days and a remarkably ambivalent view of Spanish-Indian relations: Concolorcorvo sometimes defends and attacks Spanish racial arrogance on the same page.

Confucius

Chinese philosopher (551-479 B.C.).

Latinized form of Kung Fu-tsu. Born in Kufu or Chüfu in the state of Lu, now the province of Shantung, where his descendants in the 76th generation still live. Studied ancient writings at an early age and soon won a reputation for scholarship. Became prime minister of his native state of Lu, and proved to be a good administrator, but resigned (495 B.C.) when his ruler rejected his moral precepts and turned to debauchery. Spent the rest of his life wandering through China in the company of his disciples. His teachings did not achieve a quasi-monopoly on Chinese thought and life until almost three centuries after his death; they maintained that dominion with more or less strength until the end of the Chinese Empire (1911 A.D.), and even beyond, for Generalissimo Chiang Kai-shek started his abortive "New Life Movement" in the 1930's on Confucian lines. Confucius' main emphasis was on ethics of a very practical sort: he was more concerned with good behavior than with right belief. He also laid stress on the importance of social position. At one time the entire classical literature of China was attributed to him. This is no longer believed to be the case, but the "Analects" are ascribed to him, and he is believed to have had a hand in the editing and preserving of other writings.

Congreve, William
English playwright (1670-1729).

Born in Bardsey, Yorkshire, died in London. Educated at Trinity College, Dublin, turned to writing and became perhaps the best-known author of the "Restoration Comedy." But his best play, "The Way of the World" (1700) had but a lukewarm reception and he wrote little more.

Conrad, Joseph
English novelist (1857-1924).

Real name: Josef Konrad Karzeniowski. Born in Mohilow, Poland; died in Bishopsbourne, Kent. Worked as seaman in the French (1874-78) and British (1878-94) merchant marine; qualified as captain in

1886. Became a naturalized British subject and took the name of "Joseph Conrad." Left the merchant marine in 1894 to devote himself to writing. The subjects of his novels and short stories were mostly taken from his own experiences. They include "Almayer's Folly" (1895), "An Outcast of the Islands" (1896), "The Nigger of the Narcissus" (1897), "Lord Jim" (1900), "Typhoon" (1903), "Nostromo" (1904), "Under Western Eyes" (1911), etc.

Constant, Benjamin
French novelist (1767-1830).

Born in Lausanne (Switzerland) of a French Huguenot family, died in Paris. Took prominent part in French politics as a liberal. Wrote a psychological novel, "Adolphe" (1816) which analyzes—and over-analyzes—his liaison with Madame de Stael (q.v.).

Cooper, James Fenimore
American writer (1789-1863).

Born in Burlington, N. J.; died in Cooperstown, N. Y. Educated at Yale, spent three years in the U.S. Navy, settled down as a gentleman farmer. Gained fame as writer of "The Pilot" (1824), and of the "Leatherstocking Tales," inspired, it is said, by the career of Daniel Boone (1823-1841). These include "The Pioneers," "The Last of the Mohicans," "The Prairie," "The Pathfinder," and "The Deerslayer." Traveled widely in Europe between 1826 and 1833, returned to America critical of conditions he found there. His "Home as Found" was violently attacked. He won several libel suits but lost a good deal of his popularity. Wrote a "History of the Navy of the United States" (1839).

Corbiere, Tristan
French poet (1845-1875).

Real name: Edouard Joachim Corbiere. His poems,

including "Yellow Loves" (1873), deal with the grimmer aspects of his native Brittany and his personal life in a rugged language. They have had considerable influence on modern English and American poetry.

Corneille, Pierre
French dramatist (1606-1684).

Born in Rouen; died in Paris. Member of Norman bourgeois family, studied law and practiced it for a time, but gave it up to devote himself to writing. His play, "Cid" (1636), had a great success. It roused the jealousy of Scudery (q.v.) who made the French Academy proclaim the rule of the three unities of time, place, and action for plays. (The "Cid" did not observe these unities.) He also roused the ire of Cardinal Richelieu, who objected to Corneille's glorification of the duel—which the cardinal was trying to abolish—and of Spain, with whom France was at war at the time. Subsequently, Corneille adopted the three unities and the Cardinal, moved by his talents and steadfastness, relented and granted him a pension. His later years were clouded by lack of success—the public preferring the plays of Racine (q.v.)—and by dire poverty. His thirty plays, which inaugurated the French classical drama, included in addition to the "Cid": "Medee" (1635), "The Horace" (1640), "Cinna" (1640), "Polyeucte" (1642?), "The Death of Pompey" (1643), "Rodogune" (1643 or -44), "Oedipus" (1659), "Semiramis" (1662), "Sophonisbe" (1663), and "Othon" (1664), all tragedies; and "The Liar" (1643), his only comedy.

Courteline, Georges
French dramatist and novelist (1858-1929).

Pen name of Georges Moineaux. Born in Tours, died in Paris. His novels and plays present the life of French lawyers, officers and bureaucrats with biting satire and rollicking humor. Like so many great wits,

Courteline was a sad man, whose melancholy was all but suicidal. Wrote: "The Joys of the Barracks" (1866), "The Bureaucrats" (1893), "Boubouroche" (1893), "Article 330," etc.

Crabbe, George
English poet (1754-1832).

Born in Aldeburgh, Suffolk, died in Trowbridge. Came to London, where he was befriended by Dr. Johnson and Edmund Burke. He became a clergyman of the Church of England and died as rector of Trowbridge. His best poetry, especially "The Village" (1783), is inspired by his memories of Suffolk. But Crabbe did not idealize village life; he viewed it with a rather grim realism.

Crane, Harold Hart
American poet (1899-1932).

Generally called Hart Crane. Born in Garrettsville, Ohio, died by jumping off a ship in the Gulf of Mexico. His work, though fragmentary, is among the most influential among American poets today. He has, in many ways, become a symbolic figure: the poet, driven to suicide by the uncomprehending attitude of his environment and the overwhelming pressures of his family. Wrote: "White Buildings" (1926) and his masterpiece, the unfinished "The Bridge" (1930).

Crane, Stephen
American poet (1871-1900).

Born in Newark, New Jersey, died in Badenweiler, Germany. Spent his youth in New York, which was the setting of his "Maggie: A Girl of the Streets" (1892). It met with scant success, and it was only the Civil War story "The Red Badge of Courage" (1895) that gave him recognition as the master of the new realistic novel in America. He became a reporter, covered wars in Mexico, Cuba and Greece, and wrote short stories, including "The Open Boat and Other Tales of Adventure" (1898).

Croce, Benedetto

Italian philosopher, historian and critic (1866-1952).

Born in Pescasseroli, died in Naples. Studied in Rome, returned to Naples to found the monthly review "La Critica," one of the strongest influences in Italy's intellectual life. More than any other source it acquainted Italy with intellectual developments abroad. Croce was an active politician on the liberal side. He became senator in 1910, Minister of Education (1920-21) and an untiring opponent of Mussolini, who did not dare to touch him. His philosophical system is expounded in the four volumes of "The Philosophy of the Spirit" (1902-17). It rejects materialism in favor of an aestheticizing spiritualism. Croce's historical studies revolutionized our conceptions of Italy in the Baroque Age.

Cronin, Archibald Joseph ("A. J.")

British novelist (born 1896).

Born in Cardross, Scotland. Studied medicine at Glasgow and practiced it as a ship's doctor and as a general practitioner in London and South Wales. Overwork forced him to give up his practice, so he started writing. His novels include: "Hatter's Castle" (1931), "Three Loves" (1932), "The Grand Canary" (1933), "The Stars Look Down" (1935), "The Citadel" (1937)—a powerful exposé of the medical profession, "The Keys of the Kingdom" (1942), "The Green Years" (1944).

Cruz, San Juan de la

Spanish poet (1542-1591).

Was the classical mystic: poet, theologian, philosopher. Imprisoned for trying to reform the Carmelite Order, he found there the decisive symbolism of his mystic system, the dark night of despair that finally leads to the morning of Divine vision. He presents his doctrine through poems of his own, upon which he comments. His *Spiritual Canticle* (pub. 1627) is an adaptation of the *Song of Songs* to Spanish landscape and concepts. Its style is a refined synthesis of Andalusian, Italian, Biblical, Arabic, popular, and learned elements.

Cruz, Sor Juana Ines de la

Spanish writer in Mexico (1651-1695).

Real name: Juana Ines de Asbaje. Born and died in Mexico City. Became a nun after the death of the man she loved. Had difficulties with the convent authorities about her writing and scientific activities. Two years before her death she sold her library and scientific instruments and gave the money to the poor, having been forbidden to write. She wrote religious plays in the manner of Calderon and poetry, some of it in the Nahua language of the Aztecs. A strong feminist and a precursor of Mexican nationalism. Hailed as "The Tenth Muse" by contemporaries and later critics.

Cues, Nicholas of

German philosopher and theologian (1401-1464).

Born in Cues (Rhineland); died in Todi (Italy). Studied theology and jurisprudence, became priest in 1430. His "On the Catholic Concord" tried to mediate between the Pope and the Conciliar movement. His chief work, also written in Latin, is "Of Learned Ignorance" (1440). Cusanus, as he is known from the Latin form of his name, has been described as the first modern philosopher. Actually he is on the borderline between the middle ages and modernity. His humanism and his anticipations of the Copernican theories are modern; but his mysticism and his views of the Church are still rooted in the middle ages.

Cullen, Countee
American Negro poet (1903-1946).

Born in New York City, took a prominent part in the "Harlem Renaissance" of the twenties. His poetry, sensitive and proud, includes "Color" (1925), "The Ballad of the Brown Girl" (1928) and "The Black Christ" (1929).

Cunha, Euclides da
Brazilian novelist (1866-1909).

Born in Santa Rita do Rio Negro, killed by the jealous husband of his mistress. Wrote "Os Sertoes" (1902, translated as "Rebellion in the Backlands") an eyewitness account of the campaign against Antonio Conselheiro, a strange religious mystic who defied the Brazilian government and was defeated after a campaign in which both sides fought without scruples. Da Cunha turned journalism into both art and history, both of a very high order. His book is generally considered a masterpiece—if not the masterpiece—of Brazilian literature.

Cynewulf
Anglo-Saxon poet (eighth century).

Northumbrian, flourished about 750. Latin scholar. Accepted author of poems "Juliana," "Elene," "The Ascension," and "The Fates of the Apostles." Credited, but not universally, with authorship of "Christ," "St. Guthlac," "Andreas," and "The Dream of the Rood."

Cyrano de Bergerac, Savinien de
French writer (1620-1655).

Born at Bergerac (southwestern France); died in Paris. Fought three years in French army (1637-40), severely wounded. Survived to fight many duels over love affairs and sneers at his outsize nose. Wrote poems, plays, and novels. The "States and Empires" of the Sun and the Moon (1656, 1662) anticipated science fiction and inspired Swift (q.v.). Rostand's play, which revived his fame, has but a slender basis in the facts of his life.

D

Dach, Simon

German poet (1605-1659).

Born at Memel (East Germany, now Lithuania);
died at Koenigsberg (East Germany, now Russia).
Lyrical poet in the baroque manner, member of a
poetic circle called "The Musical Pumpkin Hut."
Best known for his poems and songs which became
genuinely popular.

Dahn, Felix

German novelist (1834-1912).

Born in Hamburg; died in Breslau. Was professor
of history of law at various German universities and
his novels belong to the genre known as "professorial
novels." They deal with German and Germanic history, which they helped to popularize. Chief work:
"A Struggle for Rome" (1876), an epic novel of the
Ostrogoths in four volumes.

Dana, Richard Henry

American writer (1815-1882).

Born in Cambridge, Mass., died in Rome, Italy. A
lawyer by profession, his fame rests on his autobiographical "Two Years Before the Mast" (1840), the
story of a trip to California round Cape Horn and
a precursor of Melville's "Moby Dick."

Dandin

(Sanskrit, *ca.* 7th century A.D.).

Colorful and picturesque Sanskrit author of a

picaresque novel, *Dasakumāracharita* (*The Adventures of the Ten Princes*). The play *Mricchakatika* is attributed to him by some.

D'Annunzio, Gabriele
Italian writer (1863-1938)

Born in Francavilla near Pescara; died in Gardone. Educated at Florence and Rome universities; started writing novels under pen name of "Duca Minimo." Wrote novels in "Byzantine" decadent style of great linguistic brilliance. Became famous as a Don Juan. Went to live at Arcachon (France) in 1902-15, when Italy became too hot to hold him. Engaged in the campaign to bring Italy into the war on the side of the Allies. When Italy joined the belligerents, fought in Italian army, navy, and air force. Gained fame for sensational exploits, including a flight over Vienna; lost an eye in aerial combat. After the war became involved in Italo-Yugoslav controversy over the port of Fiume. Published a violent pamphlet against Wilson, whom he judged insufficiently pro-Italian, and occupied Fiume in September 1919 at the head of a force composed of Italian soldiers and adventurers. He had acted without orders from the Italian government, and became head of the "Republic of the Quarnaro," governing it in a fashion that did much to inspire Mussolini's fascism. Forced out of Fiume in December 1920, and retired to his villa at Gardone on Lake Garda. Was created "Prince of Monte Nevoso" in 1924, after the scene of one of his wartime exploits, but lived in haughty retirement till his death. Chief works: poems, including "First Verses" (1879), "New Song" (1881), "Naval Odes" (1893); short stories, collected in the "Tales of Pescara" (1898); dramas, e.g. "La Gioconda" (1898), "Francesca da Rimini" (1902), "The Daughter of Jorio" (1904), his masterpiece, "The Ship" (1908); novels,

116

like "The Pleasure" (1889), "The Triumph of Death" (1894), and "Fire" (1904); and many political pamphlets, manifestos, and articles.

Dante Alighieri
Italian poet (1265-1321).

Born in Florence; died in Ravenna. Studied at Bologna, Padua, Paris, and possibly Oxford. Said to have met Beatrice Portinari, the great inspiration of his poetry—she is the "Beatrice" of the "Divine Comedy"—when he was eight or nine, and to have seen her briefly for a second time just before she died. Member of the intellectual elite of Florence; friend of writers Guido Cavalcanti and Brunetto Latini and of painter Giotto. Became active politically about the age of thirty on the side of the Guelphs, for whom he had fought at the battle of Campaldino (1289). After he had executed various diplomatic missions, he was elected Prior of Florence in 1300. His politics veered from Guelph to Ghibelline, and he was exiled from his native city two years later, never to return, by Charles of Valois, ally of Pope Boniface VIII. After brief stays in various Italian cities, settled in Ravenna about 1315 and stayed there till his death. Dante's poetry, influenced by French, Provençal, Sicilian, and (as was proved recently) Arabic forerunners, marked the birth of Italian as a full-fledged literary language. Since his day literary Italian has always had a Tuscan foundation. His "sweet new style" has never been surpassed. (T. S. Eliot calls him "the great master of the simple style.") But his masterpiece, the "Divine Comedy" (1307-1321) belongs to Europe, and indeed to the world, as well as to Italy. It consists of 100 cantos in tercets describing Dante's journey through Hell, Purgatory, and Paradise, accompanied through the first two by Vergil and through the last by Beatrice. Dante also wrote in Italian a collection of thirty-one love poems dedicated to Beatrice; the "New Life" (1292-95); and a number of prose works. In Latin he wrote, among other things, "On Vulgar Speech," about the position of Latin and the new European languages, and "On the Monarchy," the fullest expression of his Ghibelline views, where he came out in favor of a world-wide monarchy under the Holy Roman Emperor.

Dario, Ruben
Nicaraguan poet (1867-1916).

Real name: Felix Ruben Garcia Sarmiento. Born in Metapa; died in Leon (Nicaragua). After he gained fame as a poet, was named by his government to diplomatic posts in Brazil and Spain. Spent most of his later life in Europe—France and Spain—returning home to die. His work revolutionized the Spanish poetic language, largely under French influence (Dario was a friend of Verlaine and Mallarmé, q.v.). He inaugurated the era of "modernism" in Spanish literature. Chief works: "Azul" (i.e., "Blue"; the collection of verse and prose that made him famous, 1893); "The Strange Ones" (1893); "Profane Proses" (1896); "Songs of Life and Experience" (1906).

Daudet, Alphonse
French writer (1840-1897).

Born in Nimes; died in Paris. Settled in Paris in 1857 as a teacher, later as a writer. His verses "Les Amoureuses" (1858) won him the post of secretary to the Duke of Morny. His greatest successes were his stories and novels of his native Provence, especially "Letters From My Windmill" (1866) and "Tartarin of Tarascon" (1872). Also wrote plays, including "Sappho" (originally published as a novel, 1884).

David ap Gwylim
Welsh poet (about 1340-1370).

Member of a noble family of Pembrokeshire. His

love and nature poems, written with remarkable poetic invention, made him the greatest poet of medieval Wales.

De Coster, Karel
Belgian novelist (1827-1879).

Born in Munich (Germany); died in Ixelles near Brussels. His father was a Belgian official working for the papal nuncio to Bavaria, and he came to Belgium as a child. He spent many years in various occupations until he found his true vocation, literature. He wrote in French, but his books deal with Flanders, whose heroes they glorify. His masterpiece is "The Legend and Heroic, Joyous, and Glorious Adventures of Ulenspiegel and Lamme Godzak" (1867), in which he tells the story of the picaresque hero and his companion, nicknamed "The Stomach of Flanders." Also wrote "Flemish Legends," "Brabant Stories," and "The Honeymoon."

Defoe, Daniel
English writer (1659/60-1731).

Born and died in London. A man of strong Puritan views; suffered persecution by the Anglicans under Charles II and by the Catholics under James II. As a merchant he made wide journeys in Europe(1680-82), later became active as a journalist. Employed fitfully by various English governments after 1698. First became famous for his satire, "The True-Born Englishman" (1701). Fined, imprisoned, and pilloried for his "Short Way With Dissenters" (1702). Acted as English government secret agent in Scotland (1706-07) to prepare the union of the two countries. Wrote pamphlets in favor of Whigs, Tories, and Jacobites, according as political winds blew. Turned to fiction when nearly sixty and wrote his world-famous "Robinson Crusoe" (1719) on the basis of the experiences of Alexander Selkirk. Within the next two years published, among other works, "Moll Flanders" (1722) and "Journal of the Plague Year" (1722). Published a series of lives of famous English criminals, and much miscellaneous prose. Spent his last years in hiding under the name of "Andrew Moreton."

Dehmel, Richard

German poet and dramatist (1863-1920).

Born in Wendisch-Hermsdorf (East Germany); died in Blankenese near Hamburg. One of the leaders of the impressionist movement in German poetry, strongly influenced by the ideas of Nietzsche. Works include "Woman and the World" (1896) and "The Metamorphoses of Venus" (1907).

Deledda, Grazia

Italian novelist (1871-1936).

Born in Nuoro (Sardinia); died in Rome. Her novels and stories, for which she won the Nobel Prize in 1926, deal mostly with Sardinian life, and include "Sardinian Stories" (1893), "Ashes" (1903), "Elias Portolu" (1903), "Reeds in the Wind" (1913), and "Annalena Bilsini" (1928).

Democritus

Greek philosopher (about 460-about 371 B.C.).

Born in Abdera in Thracia. Known as the "laughing philosopher" because of his cheerful disposition. Was the first to develop an independent ethics, in which he postulated man's duty to be happy. Proclaimed the irrational origin of poetry. Best known for his atomic theory, which he extended to all material and psychical phenomena. Only fragments of his sixty treatises remain.

Demosthenes

Greek orator (about 385-322 B.C.).

Born in Athens; died in Kalaureia. Generally regarded as the greatest orator of Greece and of classical antiquity. Leader, after 352, of Athenian policy of resistance against Philip of Macedon. After Philip's victory was exiled from Athens. Recalled after the death of Philip's son Alexander the Great (322), he had to flee again when Athens was occupied by Alexander's lieutenants Antipater and Craterus in 322. Poisoned himself to avoid capture. His most famous speeches are the "Philippics," whose name became proverbial, the "Olynthides," "On the Peace," "On the Embassy," and "On the Crown" which commemorated the dead of the battle of Chaironea won by Philip in 338.

De Quincy, Thomas
English writer and critic (1785-1859).

Born in Manchester, died in Edinburgh. Son of prosperous merchant, ran away from school and roamed through England and Wales until he married and settled near Lake Grasmere as friend of Wordsworth and the Lake Poets, of whom he wrote "Recollections." Best-known for his essays and "The Confessions of an English Opium Eater" (1821).

Derzhavin, Gavril Romanovich
Russian poet (1743-1816).

Born in Kazan, died in Saint Petersburg. Son of a petty nobleman, became a civil servant and rose to high rank. His poetry is written in an exalted and rather high-faluting style, tempered by a sly humor. The former quality prevails in his ode on the death of Prince Meshchersky, the latter makes the servility of his "Ode to Felitsa" (i.e. Catherine the Great) a little bit more bearable. Derzhavin was the "official" poet of the Age of Catherine. He was eclipsed by the outburst of poetic genius inaugurated by Pushkin but the political and literary values for which he stood have once more come to the fore in the officially-sponsored "socialist realism."

Desbordes-Valmore, Marceline

French poetess (1786-1859).

Born in Douai, died in Paris. A singer and actress as well as a writer, she led an unhappy life, not overmuch brightened by a hopeless passion for Henri de Latouche. Her poems, e.g. "Elegies and Romances" (1819) and "Laments" (1833) were much admired by Lamartine, Victor Hugo and Verlaine. By influencing the work of the latter, she has a place in the story of the birth of modern poetry.

Descartes, René

French philosopher (1596-1650).

Born in La Haye in the Touraine; died in Stockholm. Educated at the Jesuit college of La Flèche; joined the French army. Took part in various Dutch and German campaigns of the Thirty Years' War. Left the army to go live in Holland, where he spent twenty years (1629-1649) working out his philosophy. Queen Christina of Sweden invited him to Stockholm to help found an Academy of Sciences on the French model, but he could not endure the climate and died within a year. Descartes' masterpiece is the "Discourse on Method" (1637) which established the Cartesian system, a landmark in the growth of modern philosophy—and in the development of modern French prose. Descartes' emphasis on logic and mathematics was opposed by Pascal (q.v.) in the name of intuition and metaphysics. The "Discourse" was supplemented by essays on Geometry, Meteors, and Dioptrics. Descartes also wrote "Principles of Philosophy" (1644), "Of Man" (1664), etc.

Dewey, John

American philosopher and educationist (1859-1952).

Born in Burlington, Vermont, died in New York.

Dewey's importance in the growth of American culture is twofold. As philosopher, he developed the pragmatism of William James (q.v.) into an all-embracing and all-applicable system. As educationist, he revolutionized American schools by his pedagogical theories which emphasized practical activities and persuasive rather than compulsive methods. Writings include: "The School and Society" (1899), "How We Think" (1910), "Freedom and Culture" (1939).

Diaz del Castillo, Bernal

Spanish chronicler (about 1498-after 1568).

Born in Medina del Campo, died in Mexico. Joined the expedition of Cortes against Mexico and took part in the Conquest. At Cortes' recommendation, Charles V granted him some land in Guatemala. After reading in 1552 Lopez de Gomara's history of the Conquest, he wrote his own "True History of the Conquest of New Spain" (first printed in 1632) as a protest against its injustices and inaccuracies. His plain and unvarnished account has become a classic of both history and the Spanish language.

Dickens, Charles

English novelist (1812-1870).

Born in Landport near Portsmouth; died in Gladshill Place, near Chatham. Had a very hard childhood; was forced to work at a blacking factory at the age of ten or eleven. His father was imprisoned for debt and the child's humiliation and resentment aroused his social conscience. Dickens had very little formal education, but managed nonetheless to become a reporter at the House of Commons for a number of newspapers. He published, in various periodicals, sketches under the pen name of "Boz" (1836 onwards), which represented his first steps on the ladder of success. The "Pickwick Papers" (1836-37) established his fame. Then came a stream of novels including "Oliver Twist"

(1837-39), "Nicholas Nickleby" (1838-39), "Old Curiosity Shop" (1840-41), "Barnaby Rudge" (1841), "Martin Chuzzlewit" (1843-44), "A Christmas Carol" (1843), "Dombey and Son" (1846-48), "David Copperfield" (1849-50), "Bleak House" (1852-53), "Hard Times" (1854), "Little Dorrit" (1855-57), "A Tale of Two Cities" (1859), "Great Expectations" (1860-61), "Our Mutual Friend" (1864-65), "Mystery of Edwin Drood" (1870, left incomplete). The dates of his novels indicate the manner in which they were written—as newspaper serials, often at top speed. Unlike Balzac, who wrote his novels in much the same way, Dickens does not rank high as a literary artist. But his books have been read, reread, and loved, for over a century because of the sentiments that animate them and the characters that Dickens created for them. Throughout his life Dickens fought for philanthropic and social causes; he was committed to the side of the common man. He traveled a good deal, including America, though his "American Notes" (1842) show neither America nor Dickens at their best. His popularity was world-wide and has remained so.

Dickinson, Emily

American poetess (1830-1886).

Born and died in Amherst, Mass. After attending college and leading the social life normal to a girl of her social condition, retired to her house at the age of 26 following a tragic love affair. She shunned all social contacts and wrote some 500 short poems of great intensity. Only 5 were published by the time she died —they were not submitted by her—and she ordered all her manuscripts destroyed after her death. Her wish was not carried out and the poems were gradually published. They attracted little attention at first, and it was only in the 1920's that she was recognized as one of the great lyric poets of America. She has been called "a New England mystic" and "a feminine Blake"—the trivial and the sublime mingle in her writings as they did in those of St. Theresa (q.v.).

Diderot, Denis
French philosopher (1713-1784).

Born in Langres; died in Paris. Educated by the Jesuits, studied literature and languages against his father's will. After the publication of his first important philosophical work, "Letter on the Blind" (1749), was thrown in prison. Conceived the plan of the "Great Encyclopedia" in 1750, and worked on it for over twenty years (1751-1772) with D'Alembert, Voltaire, Rousseau, Montesquieu, Buffon, Quesnay, etc. The theater was his other main interest; he wrote some acute dramatic criticism and two plays, "The Natural Son" (1758) and "The Family Father" (1759), which helped establish the French bourgeois comedy. Diderot traveled all over Europe and spent some time in Russia at the invitation of Catherine the Great, an admirer of his work.

Dionysius of Halicarnassus
Greek writer (late 1st c. B.C.)

Was a representative of the group of literary critics whose studies of the great prose writers of the classical period brought about a renaissance of Greek prose writing in the period of the early Roman Empire. Dionysius' critical works are largely concerned with technical matters of style, except for his appreciation of Demosthenes, and his disparagement of Thucydides as a historian—a judgment based on rhetorical grounds. Rhetoric and moralizing vitiated his own historical work, the *Roman Antiquities,* but his talents lay rather in the close analysis of style; his importance, in pointing the way to the writers of the New Sophistic movement.

Dodgson, Charles
English novelist (1832-1898).

Wrote under pen name "Lewis Carroll." Born in Daresbury, Cheshire, died in Guilford, Surrey. Educated at Rugby School and Oxford, taught mathematics at Christ Church, Oxford. His literary activities, indulged in strictest secrecy, include the two classical children's tales of fantasy "Alice's Adventures in Wonderland" (1865) and "Through the Looking Glass" (1871), written for Alice Liddell, daughter of the Dean of his college, and the nonsense poem "The Hunting of the Snark" (1869). They have enriched the English language by numerous stock phrases and have brightened the lives of many readers, ranging in age from infancy to senility.

Doeblin, Alfred
German novelist (1878-1957).

Born in Stettin, of Jewish origin. Physician, specializing in treatment of nervous diseases. Forced to leave Germany by Hitler's victory in 1933; returned there after 1945. The best of his novels give a realistic picture of the poor quarters of Berlin, e.g. "Berlin, Alexander Square" (1930), his masterpiece.

Donne, John
English writer (1572-1631).

Born and died in London. Much mystery still surrounds the facts of his early life. After studies at Oxford and Lincoln's Inn, London, he seems to have taken place in Elizabethan expeditions to Cadiz and the Azores and to have been a Member of Parliament. His worldly career was wrecked by his marriage: his father-in-law, Sir George More, had him dismissed and imprisoned. Donne went through some difficult years but found new patrons, especially James I who, after his conversion from Roman Catholicism to the Church of England, fostered his ecclesiastical career which culminated in the deanship of Saint Paul (1621). His poems, including a number of "Epithalamia" and his sermons mingle religious and erotic motives in the best baroque manner. They remained all but forgotten for almost three centuries until they were re-published by Sir Herbert Grierson (1912). They have become one of the main sources of modern English poetry, especially of Pound and Eliot; but only time will show whether he has not been as over-valued lately as he had been under-valued before.

Dos Passos, John

American novelist (born 1896).

Born in Chicago, of Portuguese parentage. Educated at Harvard. His first novel, "Three Soldiers" (1921), was based on his war experiences. But it was only with "Manhattan Transfer" (1925) that he inaugurated his best vein: novels that present a critical picture of the American society of his day, drawn with modern literary means and some effects taken from other arts, notably film and radio. His trilogy "U.S.A." (The 42nd Parallel; 1919; The Big Money, 1930-36) shows this technique at its best in an anatomical study of New York. Since then Dos Passos has tended to accept rather than criticize the facts of American life. His voluminous writings lack "bite" and are not on the level of his earlier works.

Dostoyevski, Fedor

Russian novelist (1821-1881).

Born in Moscow; died in Saint Petersburg. His father was a physician who owned a property near Moscow. He was killed by his rebellious peasants in an atrocious way that might have come straight from one of his son's novels. Dostoyevski served three years (1841-44) in the army; resigned to devote himself to writing. Published his first novel, "Poor Folk," in 1846.

Joined the "Brotherhood of Saint Cyril and Methodius," a mildly reformist organization, and was condemned to death as a dangerous revolutionary (1849). Was pardoned by the Tsar while standing on the gallows with a noose round his neck, and was sent to a prison camp in Siberia where he spent five years (1849-1854). He described his experiences in his "Notes From the House of the Dead" (1861). After his return to freedom, resumed literary work. A magazine he founded was suppressed by the government; another failed. Spent many years abroad (Germany, Switzerland) to escape financial troubles; returned to Russia in 1871 and founded in 1876 his third magazine. "An Author's Notebook," which found favor with the government, proved a popular success. Dostoyevski became the accepted spokesman of "official" Russia, and he made a famous speech at the tomb of Pushkin (q.v.) extolling Russia's genius and mission. But his worldwide reputation—never higher than at present—rests upon a series of novels in which he explored the depths of the Russian soul and of the human heart. They include "Crime and Punishment" (1866), "The Idiot" (1868), "The Demons" or "The Possessed" (1871-72), and his great masterpiece "The Brothers Karamazov" (1880). The 75th anniversary of his death (1956) was celebrated both in the West and in the Soviet Union, where he had been in eclipse.

Doughty, Charles
English travel writer (1843-1926).

Born in Theberton Hall, Suffolk, died in Sissinghurst, Kent. An Englishman who lived as an Elizabethan in the age of Victoria. His "Travels in Arabia Deserta" (1888) give an account of his daring journeys into the heart of Arabia. The book, written with more than a touch of poetry, has inspired many imitators including T. E. Lawrence (q.v.).

Doyle, Sir Arthur Conan
English writer (1859-1930).

Born in Edinburgh; died in London. Studied medicine at Edinburgh and practiced at South Sea near Portsmouth (1882-1890) until his fortune as a writer was assured. Creator of Sherlock Holmes and Dr. Watson, still the most famous heroes of detective fiction. They first appeared in "The Sign of Four" (1889), which was followed by "The Adventures of Sherlock Holmes" (1891), "The Hound of the Baskervilles" (1902), etc. Doyle also wrote historical romances, fantasy adventures, straight novels, and apologies for spiritualism.

Drachman, Holger
Danish writer (1846-1908).

Born in Copenhagen; died at Hornbeck in Zealand. Professional painter specializing in marines. Wrote romantic verse "Poems," (1872), "Muffled Melodies," (1875), novels, and plays.

Dreiser, Theodore
American novelist (1871-1945).

Real name Thedore Dresser. Born in Terre Haute, Indiana; died in Hollywood, California. Son of poor family of German origin; his elder brother Paul gained wealth and reputation as a song writer. Dreiser's own life was one of tough struggle which led him, toward the end of his life, to join the Communist Party. Wrote plays, essays, and short stories, but best known for his novels, in which he champions the underdog and depicts American society in a pioneering realistic and naturalistic manner. These novels shocked their contemporaries by their probings and descriptive powers. They include "Sister Carrie" (1900), "Jennie Gerhardt" (1911), "The Financier" (1912), "The Titan" (1914), "The Genius" (1915),

"An American Tragedy" (1925) probably his master-piece, the novelization of a real life event. Also wrote autobiographical "A Book About Myself" (1925).

Drinkwater, John

English writer (1882-1937).

Born and died in London. Was an insurance clerk. Became poet, dramatist and theatrical director. His plays include one on Abraham Lincoln (1918) which was a great success on both sides of the Atlantic.

Droste-Huelshoff, Annette Von

German novelist and poet (1797-1848).

Born in Castle Huelshoff in Westphalia; died in Meersburg on Lake Constance. Member of one of the oldest families of Westphalian Catholic nobility. Educated at home by her mother and a tutor. Influenced by romanticism and especially the Grimm brothers. Wrote lyrical and nature poetry, and novels of which "The Jew's Beech" (1842) is the best-known.

Dryden, John

English writer (1631-1700).

Born in Aldwinkle Northamptonshire; died in London. Educated at Cambridge; moved to London to live as a professional writer. Became clerk to his cousin, who was Cromwell's chamberlain, and wrote Cromwell's panegyric when he died, the "Heroic Stanzas" (1658). Three years later, he wrote a "Panegyric" on the Restoration. His religious sympathies were also floating between the Church of England and Roman Catholicism, until he embraced the latter. But in literature he remained faithful to classical and French models, which made him the great molder of English literary prose. Became court poet to Charles II, whom he had welcomed home in "Astraea Redux" (1660). Wrote a number of topical historical writings directed against the Spanish and the Dutch, England's chief rivals at the time. Also: "Annus Mirabilis" (The Wonderful Year, 1667), describing the Great Fire of London and other events of 1666; "All for Love" (1678), a tragedy about Antony and Cleopatra in blank verse which he said he wrote not for the stage or for the public, but for himself; "Absalom and Achitophel" (1681), a sharp satire against those, including Charles II who wanted to exclude the Duke of York from succession; etc. Lost his positions and pensions after the Revolution of 1688 when he refused to swear loyalty to the new government. In the last years of his life busied himself mostly with translations and adaptations.

Du Bellay, Joachim
French writer (1522-1560).

Born in Lire (Anjou), died in Paris. Friend and fellow-student of Ronsard (q.v.), launched with him the association of seven poets called "the Pleiad" through his manifesto "The Defense and Illustration of the French Language" (1549) in which he argued for the abandoning of the medieval literary traditions and their replacement by the classical tradition as restored by the Renaissance. In the same year he published a sequence of 115 sonnets, "The Olive." Served under his uncle, the cardinal Du Bellay in Rome from 1553 to 1557. He was unhappy and felt himself exiled; his Roman stay inspired "The Regrets" (1558) another sonnet sequence even more personal than the first. His poems, delicate in their irony and nostalgia, are second only to Ronsard's.

Dudintsev, Nikolai
Russian writer (born 1916).

Fought in World War II, created a sensation inside and outside Russia with his novel "Man Does not Live by Bread Alone" (1956) in which an individualistic inventor faces a solidly entrenched political and economic bureaucracy. Widely criticized as anti-regime, the author escaped serious punishment largely because Khrushchev himself recognized his good intentions. His "New Year Fable" (1959) has made him once more spokesman of the dissatisfied.

Duhamel, Georges
French novelist (born 1884).

Born in Paris. Son of a chemist, became a doctor and wrote while practicing medicine. Evolved with Jules Romains (q.v.) the doctrine of unanimism or the belief that groups have minds of their own. His experiences in World War I inspired "The Life of Martyrs" (1917) and "Civilization." Wrote two series of psychological novels, one in five volumes on "The Adventures of Salavin" (1920-32) and one in ten volumes, called "The Pasquier Chronicles" (1933-45). They give a somewhat acid picture of French society.

Dumas, Alexandre (father)
French novelist and playwright (1802-1870).

Born at Villiers-Cotterets (Picardy); died at Puys (Normandy). Son of a mulatto who became a general of the French Revolution and Napoleon. After some years of clerking and other occupations Dumas became a playwright. His "Henry III and his Court" (1829) and "Antony" (1831) became landmarks of the French historical and psychological drama respectively. But he became world-famous only by his historical novels, still read in cheap editions the world over. "The Three Musketeers" (1844) started an all but interminable flood of novels, which by their author's death numbered 254, many of them written by "negres" (ghostwriters) from Dumas' outlines. Among the more noteworthy are "Twenty Years After" (1845) and "The Vicomte de Bragelonne" (1848), two sequels to "The Three Musketeers"; "The Count of Monte Cristo" (1844); "Queen Margot" (1845); "The Lady of Monsoreau" (1846).

Dumas, Alexandre (son)
French writer (1824-1895).

Born in Paris; died in nearby Marly-le-Roi. Natural son of the novelist who called him "my best work," an opinion with which posterity, on the whole, has not agreed. Young Dumas worshipped and imitated his father. After a collection of verse appropriately called "Sins of Youth" (1847), gained a fame of his own with the novel "The Lady of the Camelias" (1848), which fathered in turn, many stage and screen versions. Later turned to writing plays, and the title of one of his plays, "The Half-World" (1855), passed into French and many other languages.

Dunash ibn Labrat
Jewish medieval poet (920-980).

Born in Baghdad, died in Fez. Came to Spain where he enjoyed the patronage of the powerful Jewish minister Hasdai ibn Shaput and inaugurated the Golden Age of Spanish-Jewish literature by importing Arab meters and the principles of Arab grammar into Hebrew. Wrote liturgical songs and odes for patrons.

Dunbar, Paul Lawrence
American Negro poet (1872-1906).

Born in Dayton, Ohio, son of an escaped slave. Worked as elevator boy until his poems, "Majors and Minors" (1895) received favorable notice from William Dean Howells (q.v.), who wrote an introduction to his second volume, "Lyrics of Lowly Life" (1896). These two volumes established him as the first American Negro poet of standing.

133

Dunn, Olav

Norwegian writer (1876-1939).

Born on the island Ja, off Namsos; died in Holmestrand. Elementary school teacher till 1927. His masterpiece; "Ragnhild" (1929-33); "God Smiles" (1935); "Man and Power" (1938).

E

Ebner Eschenbach, Marie Von
Austrian writer (1830-1916).

Born Marie Countess Dubsky, on the family property Zdislavic in Moravia; died in Vienna. Married Captain Von Ebner Eschenbach who rose to the rank of Lieutenant-Field Marshall. First wrote a drama, "Mary of Scotland" (1860), then realistic novels and stories about the life of the Austrian nobility and the conditions of the countryside, especially "Stories of Castle and Village" (1883) and "Lotti, The Watchmaker" (1881). Toward the end of her life became ardent and vocal pacifist.

Ebreo, Leone
Jewish philosopher and poet (about 1460-about 1535).

Born in Lisbon died in Naples. Real name: Judah Abrabanel. Son of Isaac Abrabanel, Bible commentator and treasurer of the kings of Portugal, Spain and Naples. Physician by profession, became a humanist and neo-platonist under the influence of Pico della Mirandola (q.v.). His "Dialogues of Love" (1535), known only in an Italian translation of the Spanish or Hebrew original, are a landmark in the development of European sensibility.

Eca de Queiroz, Jose Maria
Portuguese novelist (1845-1900).

Born in Pova de Varzim, died in Paris. Studied law at Coimbra; worked in the diplomatic service; looked at Portugal with an ironical eye. Was at first much under the cultural influence of France and described himself as "a Frenchman who happened to write in Portuguese"; but later changed his mind on this and other matters. His early novels, like "The Crime of Father Amaro" (1876) were often violently anticlerical. Social satire dominates others like "Cousin Basilio" (1878) and "The Maias" (1888). After his death, a number of books were published showing a more mature and balanced view, notably "The City and the Mountains" (1901). Eca de Queiroz' great merits as a novelist are only now becoming known abroad through translations into English, French etc.

Echegaray, José
Spanish dramatist (1832-1916).

Born and died in Madrid. An engineer, economist and financier, was several times a minister of the Spanish cabinet. Started a new career as dramatist at the age of 40 and was so successful at it that he won the Nobel Prize in 1905. But his plays, considered daring at the time, are now quite dated. They treat traditional subjects, like the conflict between love and honor, in a manner that is modernistic rather than modern, e.g. "Madness or Sainthood" (1877) and "The Great Gallion" (1881).

Echeverria, Esteban
Argentine writer (1805-1851).

Born in Buenos Aires, died in Montevideo. Lived in Paris (1826-30) and brought European romanticism to his native land when he returned. Was one of the first to oppose Spanish cultural influences and to replace them by the French. Of his poetry "The Captive Girl" (1837), a Byronic tale set in the pampa has survived best. His prose includes "The Socialist Dogma," a political essay, and "The Slaughterhouse," a description of the bloody tyranny of Rosas presented as a slaughterhouse.

Eckermann, Johann Peter
German writer (1792-1854).

Born at Winsen near Hanover; died in Weimar. From 1823 secretary of Goethe, to whom he played Boswell in his "Conversations With Goethe" (three volumes, 1836-48). After Goethe's death, published editions of his work.

Eckhart
German mystic (about 1260-1327).

Generally known as "Master Eckhart"; at least five alternative spellings of his name have been preserved. Born in Hochheim near Gotha; died in Cologne. Dominican monk, became master of theology in Paris (1302), was Dominican provincial in Saxony (1303-1311), and vicar-general in Bohemia (from 1307). Taught at various places, from 1314 at Cologne. Accused of heresy by the Franciscans in 1327; his teachings condemned by the Pope in the following year. Eckhart's system is pantheistic influenced by Neoplatonism and Arab and Jewish sources. But it has a native foundation, and he became father of German mysticism and—since he wrote in German—of the German philosophical language. Chief works: "Speeches of Difference"; "The Book of Divine Consolation"; "Of Noble Man."

Edwards, Jonathan
Colonial American logician (1703-1758)

Puritan logician, constructed a lofty system of Calvinism buttressed by current philosophy. In *Religious Affections* (1746) he defended his idea of the Great Awakening and worked out his basic psychological concept, that the passions (affections) are the root of all action. He then argued that *Freedom of the Will* (1754) is liberty of action, but *not* of willing, since the will's activity depends upon the understanding's invariable choice of the stronger motive. However, *The Nature of True Virtue* (1755) is "disinterested benevolence," and natural man—shorn of that virtue at the Fall (*The Doctrine of Original Sin,* 1758)—has only culpable self-interest unless divinely elected (*Decrees and Elections*) to receive a supernatural affection— "Efficacious Grace"—to make the choices by his Understanding constantly good.

Ehrenburg, Ilya Grigoryevich
Russian writer (born 1891).

Born in Kiev, of Jewish origin. Joined the Communist Party in 1906, arrested by Tsarist police two years later. Escaped to Paris in 1909, lived there until he settled in Russia following the Revolution (after a temporary return to Paris). His talents as political chameleon have enabled him to survive purge after purge and to be the semi-official spokesman for successive regimes. After his "Poems" (1921), wrote a series of novels that made him famous in the 1920's, including the fantastic "Julio Jurenito" and the realistic "Leizor Rotschwantz," about the life of Russian Jews. Relatively silent in the 1930's. In 1941 won Stalin Prize for his novel "The Fall of Paris." His wartime writing is likely to prove ephemeral but his novel "The Thaw," published after Stalin's death, is likely to survive as a landmark in Russian cultural history, if not literary.

Eichendorff, Joseph Baron Von
German writer (1788-1857).

Born at the family castle of Lubowitz in Upper Silesia; died in Neisse (Lower Silesia). One of the leading writers of German romanticism, friend of Novalis and the Schlegels (q.v.). A fervent Roman Catholic,

138

and for fourteen years Prussian government councilor on Catholic affairs. Best known for his poems and the novel "From the Life of a Ne'er-do-well" (1826).

Eike Von Repgow
German jurist (1180/90-after 1223).

Saxon nobleman who wrote, about 1220, the "Saxon Mirror," the first German law book. Considered by some author of "Saxon World Chronicle."

Eilhart Von Oberge
German poet (flourished 1187-1207).

Official at Oberge near Braunschweig. Wrote in 1180's the first German version of the "Tristan" story, from a French model.

Einhart
Frankish writer (about 770-840).

Born in the Main area; died in Seligenstadt. Architect and secretary to Charlemagne, whose Latin biography he wrote. "The Life of Charles the Great" is one of the best medieval biographies.

Eliot, George
English novelist (1819-1880).

Pen name of Mary Ann Evans. Born on Arbury Farm, Warwickshire; died in London. Born of simple family; educated herself. Learned German and Italian, studied music. Became a convinced atheist after reading D. F. Strauss' "Life of Jesus." Her views were also influenced by Comte and Spencer. They are reflected in the realism of her novels which she began to write only in her late thirties. For twenty-four years (1854-1878) lived with her publisher George Henry Lewes in a relationship that she, though not society, considered marriage. After Lewes' death married New York banker John W. Cross. Wrote "Scenes From Clerical Life" (1858), "Adam Bede" (1859), "The Mill on the Floss" (1860), "Silas Marner" (1861), "Romola" (1863), "Daniel Deronda" (1874-76), etc.

Eliot, Thomas Stearns

British poet, dramatist, critic (born 1888).

Born in Saint Louis, Missouri; resident in London after 1914; naturalized British subject who adopted Anglo-Catholic faith. Worked in bank; now partner in a publishing house. Started his poetical career with "Prufrock and Other Observations" (1917) and continued it with, among others, "The Wasteland" (1922), a name that became a judgment on our civilization, and "The Four Quartets" (a series of poems first published as a whole in 1944). Started dramatic career with blank verse play "Murder in the Cathedral" (1935), which he followed with "The Cocktail Party" (1949), "The Confidential Clerk" (1954), etc. His critical views, strongly conservative, are embodied in "Selected Essays" (1932), "The Idea of a Christian Society" (1939) etc. Eliot won the Nobel Prize for Literature in 1948.

Eluard, Paul

French poet (1895-1952).

Born in Saint-Denis, died in Charenton. Fought in World War I and was gassed. Started writing poetry under the influence of Rimbaud and Apollinaire. Joined Andre Breton's (q.v.) surrealist movement and signed the first surrealist manifestos. Defended the cause of the Spanish Republic and took part in the French Resistance movement. Became a Communist in 1942 but he never let Marxist dogmas interfere with his deep humanitarianism. Poems include "Dying of Not Dying" (1924); "Thorns of Thunder" (1936). His "Poetry and Truth," published secretly in 1942, did much to inspire resistance to the Nazis.

Emerson, Ralph Waldo
American writer and philosopher (1803-1882).

Born in Botosani, died in Bucharest. His first poems Graduated from Harvard in 1821, became Unitarian minister in Boston, resigned in 1832 because of doctrinal differences. Went to Europe, met Wordsworth, Coleridge and Carlyle. Was friend and correspondent of the latter for over forty years, in spite of very different opinions on almost everything. Settled in Concord in 1834. His friends there included Thoreau, Hawthorne, Bronson Alcott, and Margaret Fuller. Preached and gave public lectures. His first published work, "Nature" (1836), expounds his transcendentalist philosophy, in which outward phenomena are viewed as symbols of man's inner life. His address to the Phi Beta Kappa society of Harvard, "The American Scholar" (1837), applied his philosophy to intellectuals, stressing the need for freedom and self-reliance. Editor of "The Dial" (1842-44). His "Essays" (1841, 1844) give him international fame. Became abolitionist spokesman in the 1850's. Later works include "Representative Men" (1850), "English Traits" (1856), and "The Conduct of Life" (1860). His early work was collected in "Poems" (1847).

Eminescu, Michael
Romanian poet (1850-1889).

Born in Botosani, died in Bucharest. His first poems were published when he was still at school. At 16 he ran away with a company of strolling actors and was its prompter for three years. Studied at Vienna and Berlin universities but failed to get a degree at either. Returned to Romania in 1874, worked as librarian and newspaper editor, died insane. A romantic dreamer, whose best poem is "The Evening Star," he gained a European fame.

141

Empedocles
Greek philosopher (about 490-about 430 B.C.).

Born in Acragas (Sicily); died by throwing himself into the creater of Etna. Physician and natural philosopher credited with miraculous feats. Fragments of his treatise "On Nature" and of his "Song of Repentance" make it possible to reconstruct his philosophy, in which four elements (earth, air, fire, water) are moved by two principles (love and hate).

Engstroem, Albert
Swedish novelist (1869-1940).

Born in Loenneberga; died in Stockholm. Painter and writer. Wrote: "A Book"; "Ink and Salt Water"; "To Cross and to Land."

Ennius, Quintus
Roman poet (239-169 B.C.).

Born in Rudiae in Calabria, died in Rome. Served in the Roman army in Sardinia. Cato the Elder (q.v.) brought him to Rome, where he earned a living teaching Greek. His "Annales," an epic on Roman history written in hexameters, earned him the title of "father of Roman poetry." His versification is still rough but he created the quantitative hexameter, later used by Ovid and Vergil.

Epicurus
Greek philosopher (341-270 B.C.).

Born on the island of Samos, son of an Athenian colonist; died in Athens. Taught philosophy at the "Garden of Epicurus" in Athens. Only fragments of his many works survive, but his basic teachings are fairly well known. They only partly justify the adjective "epicurean." While he taught that pleasure is the only good and the foundation of morality, he emphasized that a genuine life of pleasure must be a life of prudence, honor and justice.

Erasmus, Desiderius

Dutch philosopher and humanist (1466-1536).

Real name: Gerhard Gerhards or Geert Geerts. Born in Rotterdam; died in Basel (Switzerland). His father died early, and his guardian destined him for an ecclesiastical career. Became Augustinian monk without feeling any great vocation. Studied theology in Paris, Rome, and Turin. Lived in England (1498-99 and 1510-14) where he befriended Saint Thomas More, Linacre, and Grocyn, and taught Greek at Cambridge. Later lived in Freiburg and (after 1521) Basel. Concerned with restoration of the West's classical heritage and with reform of the Catholic Church from within. Edited a Greek New Testament with a Latin translation in 1516. Opposed Luther in the name of church unity. Wrote, in Latin, "Collected Adages" (1500), "Handbook of a Christian Soldier" (1502), "In Praise of Folly" (1509, perhaps his masterpiece), "On Writing Letters" (1521). His name has lived on for his championship of tolerance and humanity.

Ercilla y Zuniga, Alonso de

Spanish poet (1533-1594).

Born and died in Madrid. Page of Philip II, accompanied the King to England and Flanders. Fought in Chile against the fierce Araucanians, an experience which inspired his "Araucana" (three parts, 1569-1589), the greatest Spanish Renaissance epic and the first great poem to be inspired by America.

Esenin or Yesenin, Sergei Alexandrovich

Russian poet (1895-1925).

Born in Konstantinovo, died in Leningrad. Son of a peasant, remained steeped all through his life in the peasant values of "wooden Russia." Had practically no formal education. His first book of poems, pub-

143

lished in 1916, was a hymn of love of the soil. Greeted the Revolution with a messianic enthusiasm, but was soon bitterly disappointed. Tried in vain to find consolation in drink and travel, as described in his "Confession of a Hooligan" and "Persian Motif." Nor did his marriage to Isadora Duncan turn out any happier. He still wrote about a vanished rural Arcadia, but in the end, even this vision could not sustain him and he committed suicide. Gorki called him, not without reason, Russia's greatest lyrical genius since Pushkin.

Espronceda, Jose de
Spanish poet (1808-1842).

Born in Almendralejo near Badajoz, died in Madrid. His life was as romantic as his verse. Involved in his first conspiracy while a schoolboy of 15, fled to Gibraltar three years later. Fought on the liberal side in Holland and on the Paris barricades of 1830. Attacked the Spanish despotism of Ferdinand VII—the king who made the classical complaint about "that disastrous mania of thinking—with both sword and pen." His two masterpieces are the "Song of Theresa," a poignant and disillusioned poem of love and freedom, and "The Student of Salamanca" (1839), one of the best exercises on the Don Juan theme.

Euripides
Greek dramatist (about 480-407 B.C.).

Born on the island of Salamis, in the year of the great naval battle that saved Greece; died at the court of King Archelaos of Macedon. Started writing fairly late in life, and his first play, performed in 455, was not successful. He did not reach the height of his powers until the Peloponnesian Wars, when he wrote "Medea." Although he won five prizes in Athenian dramatic contests, did not become really famous until after his death. He reaped his finest,

144

posthumous, triumph when the victorious Spartans decided not to carry out their plan to destroy Athens after witnessing a performance of one of his plays. Euripides shifted the dramatic emphasis from external fate to the workings of man's psyche; he was the first Greek dramatist to treat seriously the problems of women. Of his ninety-two plays, eighteen have survived: "Alcestis," "Medea," "Hippolytus," "Hecuba," "Andromache," "Ion," "The Supplicants," "Heracleidae," "Mad Hercules," "Iphigenia on Tauris," "The Trojan Women," "Helen," "The Phoenician Women," "Electra," "Orestes," "Iphigenia at Aulis," "Bacchae," "Cyclops."

Evelyn, John

English diarist (1620-1706).

Born and died in Wotton, Surrey. Studied in London and Oxford, fought with the Royalist army and went into exile after the King's defeat. Returned to England in 1653. His "Diary" (complete edition published only in 1654) is a written-up work of art rather than a daily notebook and is remarkable for its range of interest rather than for its style.

F

Fadeyev, Alexander Alexandrovich

Russian novelist (1901-1959).

Born in Tver province, of peasant origin. His writing was realistic, under the influence of Tolstoy, but was bogged up later in socialist realism. At his best in his novels of Civil War Siberia, "The Debacle" and "The Last of the Udeghs." His "Young Guard" (1945) about partisan resistance to the Germans followed the official line and made him one of the literary glories of the regime. Was often put in charge of foreign writers visiting the Soviet Union. But his real character came into bitter conflict with his official mask, which drove him to drink and finally suicide.

Fallada, Hans

German novelist (1893-1947).

Real name: Rudolf Ditzen. Born in Greifswald; died in Berlin. Started writing during the Great Depression, and his novels describe the fate of the "little man" caught in the toils of economic forces whose working he cannot comprehend, let alone control. Wrote: "Peasants, Bosses, Bombs" (1930), "Little Man, What Now?" (1932), "Who Once Ate From a Brass Dish" (1934), "Everybody Dies Alone" (1947), "The Drunkard" (1950).

Farid, Ibn-al-

Arab mystic (1181-1235)

An Egyptian of Syrian ancestry, was born in Cairo.

He surpassed all other mystics of Islam in the intense glow of his utterances. He combined grandeur of ideas, power of phrase, and vibrant music, in the blaze of a consuming ecstasy. After a 15-year sojourn in Mecca, he settled in Cairo where he came to be venerated as a saint. In his anthology of mystical odes, the longest piece is a hymn of divine love, permitting comparison with the Biblical *Song of Songs,* and giving rise to the accusation that he favored the doctrine of God's incarnation in human beings. His verse is thoroughly Arabic in form and content. His style, pregnant with verbal subtleties (betraying the influence of al-Mutanabbi) is still inspiring.

Farrell, James T.
American novelist (born 1904).

Born in Chicago. Brought up in bitter poverty, wrote a trilogy on the grim life of a young Chicago Irishman, "Studs Lonigan" (1932-34), that was largely autobiographical. It was much read at the time. Farrell has not been able to match its success since.

Faulkner, William
American novelist (1897-1962).

Born in New Albany, Mississippi. Educated at the University of Mississippi, fought in Britain's Royal Air Force in World War I. His novels written in a forthright manner show a profound understanding of the South, which he helped to put back on America's literary map. Faulkner's outlook is tragic, though not always hopeless. His novels which won him the Nobel Prize, include: "The Marble Faun" (1924), "Mosquitoes" (1927), "Sartoris" (1929), "As I Lay Dying" (1930), "Sanctuary" (1941), "Light in August" (1932), "Pylon" (1935), "Absalom, Absalom" (1936), "The Unvanquished" (1938), "Go Down Moses" (1942), and "A Fable."

Fedin, Konstantin Alexandrovich
Russian novelist (born 1892).

Born in the Saratov province. Writes in the psychological tradition of Chekhov and Turgeniev. His first novel, "Cities and Years" (1924), had a Civil War theme. His best is perhaps "No Ordinary Summer" (1950), a poignant evocation of provincial life before the Revolution.

Feffer, Itzik
Jewish writer (1900-about 1950).

Born in the Kiev district, of working class family. Published his first poems at 20. Supported the Communist regime, toured England and the United States in 1943 as its spokesman. Was killed at Stalin's orders during the purge of Yiddish writers. Wrote: "A Stone on a Stone" (1926); "The Red Army Man" (1942); "The Barricades of the Warsaw Ghetto" (1944).

Fenelon, François Salignac de la Mothe
French writer (1651-1715).

Born, of noble family, at Castle Fenelon near Perigord; died in Cambrai. A priest, who distinguished himself by his severity in the forcible conversion of the Huguenots. His pioneering "Treatise on the Education of Girls" drew the attention of Louis XIV, who appointed him tutor of his grandson, the Duc de Bourgogne (1689). He wrote, for his pupil, "Fables," "Dialogues of the Dead," "Abbreviated Lives of Ancient Philosophers," "Telemaque." Got into trouble with Louis XIV over his support of the hysterical mystic, Madame Guyon, whose "quietist" doctrines were condemned by the Pope; and also over his "Telemaque," which the king interpreted as a satire on princes, including himself. None the less, Fenelon was appointed Archbishop of Cambrai in 1695. Fenelon's writings are among the models of classical French prose. His views made them favorite readings of Quakers in Britain and America.

Fernandez de Lizardi, Jose Joaquin
Mexican writer (1776-1828).

Born and died in Mexico City. Founded a magazine called "The Mexican Thinker" (1812) and is often called by that name. Wrote a picaresque novel, "The Mangy Parrot" (1816), a wildly satirical account of the Mexico of his day.

Feuchtwanger, Lion
German novelist (1884-1958).

Born in Munich, died in California. Won worldwide success with novels which applied modern psychology to the traditional historical novel. His first works—"The Ugly Duchess" (1923); "Jew Suess" (1925) and a trilogy on the Jewish historian Josephus (1932-35)—had some power and originality, but he then settled down to writing according to formula.

Fichte, Johann Gottlieb
German philosopher (1762-1814).

Born at Rammenau (Lusatia, East Germany); died in Berlin. Pupil of Kant whose philosophy he developed further in the direction of transcendentalist idealism. Professor at Jena after 1794, where he published "A Treatise on Science" (1794) and a book "On the Development of the Concept of Religion" which involved him in a serious controversy. Accused of atheism, had to leave his job and moved in 1799 to Berlin, where he gave private lectures and wrote political, linguistic, and economic treatises. Fichte became increasingly the champion of German nationalism and of German resistance to Napoleon. It was in Berlin that he made (1807-08) his famous "Speeches to the German Nation." Fichte also exercised a considerable influence on the development of nationalism among the non German peoples of Central and Eastern Europe.

Fielding, Henry
English writer (1707-1754).

Born near Glastonbury, died in Lisbon. Educated at Eton, studied law and became a magistrate at Bow Street, London. Organized a police force to cope with lawlessness, but also made serious efforts to understand the social causes of crime and the personal motives of the criminal. He was as pioneering in literature as in criminology: his "Joseph Andrews" (1742); "History of Tom Jones, A Foundling" (1749) and "Amelia" (1752) made him the effective founder of the English novel which reached its classical expression with Dickens. He drew upon the French and Spanish traditions—especially Cervantes and the picaresque—but his humor and humanity were part of his English heritage as well as of his personal character. This is made clear by his post-humous "Journal of a Voyage to Lisbon" (1755).

Firbank, Ronald
English novelist (1886-1926).

His books, written with considerable dash, color and subtlety on themes that verged on the fantastic, had a considerable success among sophisticated readers on both sides of the Atlantic. They include: "The Princess Zoubraroff" (1920) and "Concerning the Eccentricities of Cardinal Pirelli" (1925).

Firdausi
Persian poet (932-1020).

Real name: Abual-Qasim Hasan. Born and died in Tus (Khorasan in Northeast Persia). Court poet of King Mahmud of Ghazni. Spent thirty-five years in writing his "Book of Kings," an epic of 60,000 rhyming couplets of legendary and historical kings of

Persia prior to the Arab conquest of the country. His book has remained to this day a truly national epic, whose verses are recited and enjoyed by rich and poor, educated and illiterate alike. Mahmud paid the amount he promised Firdausi in silver instead of gold coins. The poet revenged himself with a bitter satire and had to flee for his life to Baghdad where he wrote another poem, "Yusuf and Zuleika," based on the story of Joseph and Potiphar's wife, as retold in the Koran. Shortly before his death, there was a reconciliation with Mahmud, which enabled the poet to return home.

Fischart, Johann
German satirist (1547-1590).

Born in Strasbourg; died at Forbach in Lorraine. Humanist, travelled all over Western Europe, settled to practice law in Strasbourg, later at Speyer. Translated, or rather, adapted Rabelais' works into German. His own satires include "The Flea Hatz" (1576) and "The Fortunate Ship of Zurich" (1576).

Fitzgerald, Edward
English poet and translater (1809-1883).

Real name Edward Purcell; assumed his mother's maiden name of Fitzgerald. Born near Woodbridge, Suffolk. Remembered today only for his rhymed translation of Omar Khayyam's (q.v.) "Rubaiyyat" from the Persian. Also translated plays of Sophocles and Calderon, and wrote "Euphranor: A Dialogue on Youth" and "Polonius: A Collection of Wise Saws and Modern Instances."

Fitzgerald, Francis Scott Key
American novelist (1896-1940).

Born in Saint Paul, Minn., died in Hollywood. In the 1920's he played the part of a "young man from the provinces" who came to the great metropolis and became a success. He experienced some setbacks—he went to Princeton but couldn't make the football team, served in the armed forces but was never sent overseas—but his rise as a writer came quickly and effortlessly. His "This Side of Paradise" (1920); "The Beautiful and the Damned" (1922) and "Tales of the Jazz Age" (1922) were instant and overwhelming best-sellers. But success did not last. Fitzgerald could not handle it, and his emotional problems were deepened by a marriage to a brilliant but unstable woman. He saw through the shams of his day and presented his bitter conclusions in three novels, reflecting the three stages of his later life. "The Great Gatsby" (1925) punctured the myth of success; "Tender is the Night" (1934) tells a sad story of expatriate life of American intellectuals in France; "The Last Tycoon" (published posthumously in 1941, unfinished) settles his accounts with Hollywood, where he killed himself trying to earn a living as a scriptwriter. All but forgotten in the 1930's and 1940's, he experienced an astonishing post-humous revival in the 1950's. Time alone will tell whether it was caused by a general nostalgia for the "Jazz Age" or by the more solid qualities of his writing.

Flaubert, Gustave

French novelist (1821-1880).

Born in Rouen; died in Croisset near Rouen. A typical Norman in appearance and mental outlook. Studied medicine but dropped his studies to devote himself to writing. Published his first work, "The Memoirs of a Lunatic," at the age of 17. But he spent almost twenty years painstakingly polishing his next novel, "Madame Bovary" (1857), a masterpiece of the naturalistic school. Prosecuted for immorality in his painfully detailed descriptions of adultery, but was acquitted. Wrote also: "Salambo" (1862, an historical novel), "Sentimental Education" (1869),

"The Temptation of Saint Anthony" (1874), "Three Stories" (1877), and "Bouvard and Pecuchet," (1881) unpublished satire on French petty bourgeoisie and its intellectual pretensions.

Flecker, James Elroy
English writer (1884-1915).

Born in London, died in Switzerland. Studied at Oxford, became English consul at Beirut and fell in love with the East. Member of the "Georgian group" of poets, wrote "The Golden Journey to Samarkand" (1913) and the play "Hassan" (published posthumously in 1922). Died of tuberculosis.

Fleming, Paul
German poet (1609-1640).

Born in Hartenstein in the Ore Mountains; died in Hamburg. Studied medicine at Leipzig, and practiced toward the end of his life. Spent two years in Russia and Persia as companion of the Duke of Holstein. Best-known German poet of the early baroque; some of his religious and worldly poems have become folksongs.

Fletcher, John
English playwright (1579-1625).

Born in Rye, Kent, died in London. Son of a clergyman who became bishop of London. Chiefly known as collaborator of Francis Beaumont (q.v.) with whom his name is invariably coupled.

Fogazzaro, Antonio
Italian novelist (1842-1911).

Born and died in Vicenza. Wrote lyrical poetry but chiefly known for his psychological novels, mainly dealing with love and the reconciliation of science and religion from a liberal Catholic point of view. Chief works: "The Saint" (his masterpiece, 1905), "The

Little World of Yesterday" (1896), "The Little World of Today" (1901), "Leila" (1910).

Fontane, Theodor
German writer (1819-1898).

Born in Neuruppin near Berlin; died in Berlin. Born of a family which emigrated to Germany from France. Served as apprentice in a drug store but soon devoted himself to writing, beginning with journalism. Was editor of the ultra-conservative "Kreuzzeitung" (1860-70), which attacked Bismarck as a dangerous liberal. Later (1870-89) dramatic critic for the liberal "Vossische Zeitung." Wrote of critical reportages from England, and two books of ballads; but achieved his full literary stature as the great novelist of Berlin, Brandenburg, and Prussia generally. A realist and naturalist in style, but an idealist in his sentiments. Among his books are "Meanderings, Whirls" (1888), "Effie Briest" (1895), two novels of Berlin; "The Stechlin" (1896), a sympathetic novel of the Junkers; and "Wandering Through Brandenburg" (four volumes, 1862-89), an intimate travel book.

Ford, Ford Madox
English novelist (1874-1939).

Born in Merton, Surrey, died in Deauville, France. Brought up among pre-Raphaelite painters and writers, his own novels cooler and more self-possessed than the neo-romantic creations of his companions. None the less they exhibit some pre-Raphaelite qualities. They include: "The Good Soldier" (1915); "Some Do Not" (1925) and "A Man Could Stand Up" (1926).

Forster, Edward Morgan
English novelist (born 1879).

Born in London. Became the novelist of the English middle class in its decline. Less sardonic than H. G.

Wells and less pedantic than Galsworthy, his two fellow chroniclers, Forster has remained consistently attached to the liberal values that the English middle class created but he has never shut his eyes to its shortcomings. He is a good stylist and his characters are psychological portraits. Novels include "Where Angels Fear to Tread" (1905), "A Room with a View" (1908), "Howard's End" (1910) and "A Passage to India" (1924), his judgment on the English adventure in India in which he had participated in a modest way as secretary to an Indian princeling.

Foscolo, Ugo
Italian poet (1778-1827).

Born on the Ionian island of Zante, died in Turnham Green, London. His father was Italian, his mother Greek. Educated at Padua and Spalato. Supported the French Revolution and Napoleon, for whom he wrote an "Ode" (1797) but gradually became disillusioned with French rule in Italy though he served in Napoleon's army till 1806. His "Ode on the Sepulchres" (1806) was inspired by a Napoleonic decree on the burial of the dead and attacks bureaucratic interference with human remains that ought not to be disturbed. Foscolo's romanticism found its full expression in his novel "The Last Letters of Jacopo Ortis" (1802-14), modelled on Goethe's "Werther." He refused to accept Austrian rule in Italy and lived in England from 1814. After some initial success as writer and critic he died in poverty. His remains were transferred to Florence in 1871.

Fouqué, Friedrich Baron de La Motte
German poet (1777-1843).

Born in Brandenburg, of a family descended from French immigrants. Officer in Prussian army; glorified the spirit of Prussian nobility. Romantic poet, who roused public interest in German and Scandinavian folk-lore. Wrote: "The Hero of the North" (1810), "Undine" (1811), "The Magic Ring" (1813), "The Journeys of Thidolf the Icelander" (1815), etc.

Fox, George
English religious leader (1624-1691).

Born in Fenny Drayton Leicestershire; died in London. Founder of the Religious Society of Friends (Quakers). Fox wrote many tracts and "Epistles" which now are read only by Quakers; his wider reputation is based on his "Journal," the remarkable record of a remarkable man. Like its author, the "Journal" is highly idiosyncratic; it portrays Fox's unflagging vigor, his extraordinary spontaneity, his piercing moral vision, his pugnacity which produced the gentlest of faiths. It is written in a clear uneducated (but by no means illiterate), Biblically-derived prose, and is characterized by startling imagery. The "Journal" was written for propagandistic purposes and was "toned down" by its editors to suit an era when Quakers had become respectable; but the latest edition has been scrupulously unedited, and reveals that this highly original man was even more original than his admirers had hoped.

France, Anatole
French novelist (1844-1924).

Real name; Anatole Thibault. Born in Paris; died in La Bechellerin near Tours. Started as a poet, soon veered to novels, with occasional excursions into the drama. Satirist and humorist, attacked conventions in a language marked by charm, irony and an exquisite style. Perhaps the most distinguished successor of Voltaire. After a period of political quietism took a prominent part in the defense of Captain Dreyfus at the side of Zola (q.v.). Among his works, which earned him election to the French Academy in 1896 and the

Nobel Prize in 1921, are "The Crime of Sylvestre Bonnard" (1881), "Thais" (1890), "The Rotisserie of Queen Pedauque" (1893), "The Life of Joan of Arc" (1908), "Penguin Island" (1909), "The Gods Are Thirsty" (1912), "The Revolt of the Angels" (1914)—his artistic and political testament.

Francis of Assisi, Saint
Italian religious writer (1181-1226).

Real name: Giovanni Francesco Bernardone. Born and died in Assisi. After a youth of debauchery, consecrated himself to poverty and religion in 1206 and formed the order named after him, approved by Pope Innocent III in 1209. Retired as hermit to Monte Alverno, received stigmata there in 1224. Canonized two years after his death. In literature his place is assured by his lyrics, singing the beauties of faith and nature in Italian rather than in Latin, and by the "Little Flowers of Saint Francis," a crop of legends that gathered around his figure and which were published shortly after his death.

Francis of Sales, Saint
French religious writer (1567-1622).

Born at his family's castle of Sales near Thorens in Savoy; died in Lyons. Studied law at Padua, ordained priest in 1593. Sent on a mission of converting Calvinists in 1594; bishop of Geneva in 1602. Founded, with Saint Jeanne de Chantal, Visitationist order. Canonized in 1665, proclaimed patron saint of Catholic writers. Wrote two religious classics: "Introduction to the Life of Devotion" and "The Love of God."

Franck, Sebastian
German writer (1499-1542).

Born in Donauwoerth; died in Basel. Humanist and free thinker, who was in succession Catholic priest, Lutheran preacher, and agnostic. In constant trouble with the authorities; led a wandering life. Best known for his collection of German proverbs (1541).

Franklin, Benjamin

American politician, scientist and writer (1706-1790).

Born in Boston, died in Philadelphia. The landmarks of Franklin's literary career are: his "Poor Richard's Almanack," which he edited for 32 years (1732-64) and which is still read for its laconic wisdom; "The Way to Wealth" (1857), a collection of maxims; and the masterly "Autobiography" (first complete edition, 1818). His letters and numerous miscellaneous writings often throw a brilliant light on his political activities and scientific discoveries. Franklin was perhaps the first American writer in the full sense of the word: both his virtues and his faults can often be traced in later American literature.

Franko, Ivan

Ukrainian writer (1856-1916)

Was the best known writer of Western Ukraine. He spent most of his life in Lvivi as a journalist, man of letters, and leader of popular thought. He achieved success in almost every field of literature: poetry, prose writing, drama, criticism, political writing. A socialist, he preached a sincere and active democracy, but he realized that the conditions of the late 19th c. called for sober work rather than for grandiloquent gestures. His poems range from brief treatments of social themes to such philosophical poems as *The Withered Leaves,* and *Moses,* where he portrays the fate of a leader whose vision leads him too far ahead of his people. If it was the task of Shevchenko to rouse his people to a knowledge of their past, it was the task of Franko to teach them to live in the present and to be ready for the future, and he did his work well. The enormous welcome that he received on the occasion of the 40th anniversary of his literary career and his majestic funeral show he had won the regard of his people.

Frederick II, Holy Roman Emperor
German writer (1194-1250).

Born at Jesi; died in Palermo. Frederick was not only a great patron of arts and letters but also a writer. His poems in the Sicilian dialect are a landmark in the growth of Italian literature. His Latin "Of the Art of Hunting With Birds," a treatise on falconry, attacks Aristotle's authority on the basis of observations of nature. Widely credited with authorship of mythical treatise "On the Three Impostors," i.e., Moses, Jesus, and Mohammed.

Frederick II, King of Prussia
German political writer (1712-1786).

Born in Berlin; died in Potsdam. Frederick the Great has a place in Eighteenth Century literature as an influential political writer. He wrote in French, "The History of My Time," "Memoirs," "Political Testament," "On German Literature" (exceedingly critical of it). Best known for his youthful "Anti-Macchiavelli" (1740), which his political enemies have ever used to quote against him.

Freiligrath, Ferdinand
German poet (1810-1876).

Born in Detmold; died in Cannstadt. Worked as clerk in business offices at Amsterdam and Bremen, obtained a Prussian government pension in 1838 at the instance of Alexander of Humboldt, but gave it up because it did not accord with his liberal opinions. Welcomed German Revolution of 1848, arrested after its failure, became editor of "Neue Rheinische Zeitung." Best known for his political lyrics, e.g. "New Political and Social Poems" (1849-51).

Freneau, Philip
American poet (1752-1832).

Born in New York. A Jeffersonian newspaper editor and sea captain, he sang of liberty and the sea. Became "Poet of the Revolution" and wrote violent satires against the British, especially "The British Prison Ship" (1781).

Freud, Sigmund
Austrian psychologist and critic. (1856-1939).

Born in Freiberg, Moravia; died in London. Freud has a twofold claim to inclusion in a dictionary of literature. Contemporary literature and, in particular, the modern novel, simply cannot be described without reference to his theories of the unconscious, his interpretations of sex, life and death and his techniques of psychoanalysis. Proust, Kafka, Joyce and innumerable lesser men have written under their influence. Also, Freud's own writings, beginning with "Studies of Hysteria" (1895) and "The Interpretation of Dreams" (1900) are written in a language so excellent that the city of Frankfurt conferred on him its Goethe Prize for Literature.

Freytag, Gustav
German writer (1816-1895).

Born in Kreuzling (Silesia); died in Wiesbaden. Started as a journalist; editor of the Leipzig "Grenzboten" from 1848 to 1870. Used his experience in a popular comedy, "The Journalists" (1855). Champion of liberalism, the middle class, and German nationalism. Wrote novels of contemporary life—"Assets and Liabilities" (1856)—and of German history notably "The Ancestors" (six volumes, 1872-81).

Froeding, Gustav
Swedish poet (1860-1911).

Born in Alster (Vaermland province); died in Stockholm. Journalist, suffered nervous breakdown in 1888 and went temporarily insane. Wrote lyrical poems about his home province and on patriotic themes. Wrote "Guitar and Harmonica" (1890), "New Poems" (1894), "Old and New" (1897), "Convalescence" (1898).

Frost, Robert
American poet (born 1875).

Born in San Francisco. Is so associated in the American mind with New England—where he resides and about which he writes—that most Americans are surprised to hear that he is a Californian by birth. Actually, he left California at the age of 10. He studied at Dartmouth and Harvard, then earned his living as bobbin boy in a mill, school teacher, cobbler and farmer. Failed to get his poetry published in America, went to England for three years (1912-15) and published there "A Boy's Will" (1913) and "North of Boston" (1914). He returned home to become professor of English at Amherst (1916-38). His reputation gradually grew and today he is the "Grand Old Man" of American poetry. He uses creatively the colloquial speech of New England.

Fry, Christopher
English playwright (born 1907).

Born in Bristol. Quaker and pacifist, conscientious objector in World War II. His plays which revived the English poetic drama that had languished since Elizabethan days include "A Phoenix Too Frequent" (1946), "The Lady's Not For Burning" (1949), "Venus Observed" (1950).

Fucik, Julius
Czech writer (1903-1943).

Critic and journalist. Took part in the Czech resistance to the Nazis as a Communist. Arrested and executed by the Gestapo after tortures. His "Written under the Gallows" (1945) is a diary he secretly wrote in the Gestapo jail. It was smuggled out after his death. It is a tragic but heart-warming document of human courage under extreme pressures.

Furmanov, Dmitry Andreyevich

Russian writer (1891-1926).

Born in Kineshma, died in Moscow. His "Chapayev" (1923) is the story of the peasant guerilla leader of that name who fought for the Communists against Kolchak in the Ural region. It gives a vivid picture of the Civil War but tends to gloss over the frictions between Chapayev and the Commissars.

Futabatei Shimei

Japanese novelist (1864-1909).

Born in Tokyo, died at sea. Started by translating Russian novels of Turgeniev, Tolstoy, Gorki etc. In his own novels he applied the lessons of the great Russians, notably in "Mediocrity" (1907), an autobiographical story that tells of the general plight of the Japanese intellectuals.

Fuzuli or Faizuli

Turkish poet (1494-1555).

Born in Hilla, Iraq, died in Baghdad. Greatest Turkish poet of the classical school, wrote in the Azerbaijan dialect. When Suleiman the Great conquered Iraq in 1534, he wrote a panegyric to him but failed to get the patronage he hoped for. Wrote a Turkish version of the love story of Leyla and Mecnun and some intensely personal lyrics.

G

Gale, Zona
American novelist (1874-1938).

Born in Portage, Wisconsin died in Chicago. Her
first stories idealized American small town life; but
she gave a more realistic picture of it in "Birth"
(1918) and "Miss Lulu Bett" (1920). A dramatization
of the latter won a Pulitzer Prize.

Galib, Sheyh
(Turkish, 1759-99).

Was the last great poet of the old Turkey. His
fame depends almost entirely on the long allegorical
"mesnevi" poem, *Love and Beauty* (*Hüsnü Ashk*),
written when he was 21. He was for some time the
"sheyh" (shaikh), or grand master, of the Mevlevî
(whirling dervish) tekke in Pera, and his tomb may
still be seen there.

Gallegos, Romulo
Venezuelan writer (born 1884).

Born in Caracas. Took prominent part in the politics of his country, defending the liberal cause against
dictators; was president for a short time. His novels,
of which "Dona Barbara" (1929) is the best give an
unvarnished picture of Venezuelan conditions.

Galsworthy, John
English novelist and playwright (1867-1933).

Born in Coombe, Surrey; died in London. Studied
law and was called to the Bar, but never practiced.

His novels and plays, once highly praised for their portrayals of the English upper middle class are under a cloud now and are considered rather pedestrian. Galsworthy was awarded the Nobel Prize in 1932. His works include "The Island Pharisees" (1904), "The Forsyte Saga": this epic of the British bourgeoisie, includes "The Man of Property" (1921), "The White Monkey" (1924), "The Silver Spoon" (1926), "Swan Song" (1928).

Garcia Lorca, Federico
Spanish writer (1899-1936).

Born in Fuentavaqueros near Granada; died in Granada. Son of a well-to-do farmer. Studied law at Granada, became first known to local intellectual circles as a poet, musician and painter. Manuel de Falla befriended him. Then came acclaim from Madrid and fame in Spain. His poetry combines the inspiration of surrealism with that of the popular Spanish tradition. He also learned from older men like Antonio Machado (q.v.) who revived Spanish poetry at the turn of the century. Although Lorca travelled to the United States and Cuba, it was only the Civil War and his tragic death that gave him an international reputation. Lorca was murdered by a squad of fanatical Falangists and has been widely regarded as a martyr of the Franco regime. Although fundamentally non-political, he had accepted the Republic and worked for it, e.g. in the "cultural missions" that the government sent to the villages. He had also roused the wrath of the "solid citizens" by his unconventional opinions and morals. Recent attempts by the regime to disclaim responsibility for his death do not sound very convincing. Lorca's place in literature is, however, assured by solid achievements and needs no support from extraneous circumstances. As a poet, he was of the "Andalusian" school, as can be seen from his "Gypsy Romancero" (1928) and the "Lament for Ignacio Sanchez Mejia" (1935). He transcended local limitations in the posthumously published "Poet in New York". He also wrote plays that are increasingly produced the world over, e.g. "The Blood Wedding" (1933) and "The House of Bernarda Alba" (First published 1949). Lorca's fate, not an unusual one for a Spaniard, has been over-estimation abroad and underestimation at home. While he is certainly not, as his foreign admirers seem to think, Spain's great poet, he is a greater poet than the fanatic admirers of other Spanish poets believe him to be.

Garcilaso de la Vega

Spanish poet. (1503-1536).

Born in Toledo, died in Nice. Courtier and soldier of Charles V, was killed in the Emperor's war against Francis I of France. Much of his verse was inspired by his unhappy love for Isabel Freyre; it was all published posthumously by the widow of his friend Juan Boscan (q.v.) in 1543. His great technical achievement is the adaptation of Italian meters to Spanish poetry; but he is read and admired as "the Prince of Castilian Poets" also for the delicacy of his feelings, and their tender expression; his poetic and personal integrity, and his virile language. Considered one of Spain's greatest poets, his reputation has proved remarkably safe from the usual ups and downs.

Garland, Hamlin

American novelist (1860-1940).

Born in West Salem, Wisconsin, died in Los Angeles. His "Son of the Middle Border" (1917) tells the story, based on his own experiences, of a farm boy growing up in a prairie made drab and shoddy by man. None of his later work came up to its level of writing—or sincerity.

Garshin, Vsevolod

(Russian, 1855-1888).

Russian writer of novellas. Lived his short adult life in melancholy frustration, suffering from experiences in Serbian and Turkish wars. Committed suicide. Stories permeated with urgent sense of justice and compassion.

Gautier, Theophile

French writer (1811-1872).

Born in Tarbes, died in Neuilly near Paris. First studied painting, but gave it up for literature. Became an arch-romanticist who "shocked the bourgeois"—the phrase is his—by wearing a red waistcoat. He was the first to elaborate the theory of art for art's sake. Earned his living as a literary journalist, wrote novels, e.g. "Mademoiselle de Maupin" (1835) and "Captain Fracasse" (1863) and a number of travel books—he was one of the first to discover the exoticism of Spain.

Geibel, Emmanuel

German poet (1815-1884).

Born and died in Lubeck. Wrote political and lyrical poems, some of which, like "May Has Come," have become folksongs. The kings of Prussia and Bavaria acted as his patrons.

Gellert, Christian Fuerchtegott

German writer (1715-1769).

Born at Hainichen in the Ore Mountains; died in Leipzig. One of the forerunners of classical German literature; was active in many fields. Remembered today for his hymns, his comedies, his novel "The Life of the Swedish Countess" (1746), and above all, for his ever-popular "Fables" (1754).

George, Stefan

German poet (1868-1933).

Born at Budesheim on the Rhine; died in Locarno

(Switzerland). Studied philosophy and art history; leader of group of poets and critics who formed the "George Circle." His lyrical poetry, modeled to some extent on Baudelaire, Mallarmé, and the English pre-Raphaelites, is highly polished, very form conscious, and often obscure. At one time George had sympathies with the Nazis—he wrote "The New Reich" (1928)—though he treated their coming to power with aristocratic disdain. Chief works: "Hymns" (1890), "Maximin" (1906), "The Seventh Ring" (1907), "Three Songs" (1921).

Gerhardt, Paul
German poet (1607-1676).

Born in Graefenhainichen, Saxony; died in Luebben near Berlin. Writer of Protestant hymns, many of which are still sung in Protestant churches the world over, such as "Jesus, Thy Boundless Love to Me," and his version of "O Sacred Head Now Wounded."

Gibbon, Edward
English historian (1737-1794).

Born and died in London. Studied in Oxford, where he became converted to Roman Catholicism and served in the Hampshire militia which he found "not useless to the historian of the Roman Empire" that he became. The decision to write "The History of the Decline and Fall of the Roman Empire" (six volumes, 1776-88) was taken on a visit to Rome in 1764. He wrote it at Lausanne, where he settled for many years. His masterpiece contains some deep historical insights but it is a masterpiece of literature rather than of history. This explains why Gibbon is regarded as a great historian by the English-speaking peoples but is practically ignored on the continent of Europe.

Gibran, Khalil
Syrian-American writer (1883-1931).

Born in Bsherre, Lebanon, died in New York. His

167

Maronite parents took him to Boston in 1895. He returned home to study literature at Beirut University. Then he went to Paris to study art under Rodin. Came back to America in 1912. Wrote in both Arabic and English, painted and preached mysticism. Became known as the "William Blake of the Twentieth Century" and his English poem, "The Prophet" (1923), was a best-seller.

Gide, André
French writer (1869-1951).

Born and died in Paris, scion of a well-known French Protestant family. Son of a famous jurist, brother of Charles Gide, economist and economic historian. André Gide aimed at a synthesis of classicism and romanticism, and his works mirror the French scene of his long life. He won the Nobel Prize, but his works were placed on the Papal Index in 1892. He is still a controversial figure both in France and abroad, but his influence is undeniable. Chief works: "Terrestrial Nourishments" (1897), "The Immoralist" (1902), "The Return of the Prodigal Sons" (1907), "The Narrow Gate" (1909), "The Caves of the Vatican" (1914), "Pastoral Symphony" (1919), "If the Grain Does Not Die" (1924), "The Coiners" (1925), "Journals" (from 1929). Gide also wrote literary criticism, reportage (including a disillusioned "Return From the U.S.S.R." —1936—that made headlines in the 1930's), travelogues, plays, and translations, especially from English (Shakespeare, Whitman, Blake).

Gilbert, Sir William S.
English librettist and humorist (1836-1911).

Born in London; died in Harrow Weald, of heart failure, while rescuing a young woman from drowning. A prolific and successful author of plays, verse, and libretti, his reputation rests today on the series of musical comedies which he wrote in collaboration with Sir Arthur Sullivan, in which he showed himself a consummate master of satire. In "Trial By Jury" he poked fun at British courts; in "Pinafore" he mocked the British navy and Victorian class-consciousness; in "Patience" he jeered at the aestheticism of fin-de-siècle English letters—always with such sparkling wit and good humor that, though the occasion of his plays is now long past, Gilbert and Sullivan continue to be performed and loved all over the world. Queen Victoria was not amused at Gilbert's irreverence, and passed him by when she knighted Sullivan; Gilbert was not knighted until 1907, by King Edward VII. Gilbert was a cantankerous man with an acid wit and a taste for lawsuits, and most of his life was engaged in quarrels with somebody; his famous partnership with Sullivan finally broke up in an argument over the cost of a carpet for their theater. Gilbert revolutionized English stagecraft; and, with Sullivan, he made the native musical theater respectable in England. Chief works: "Bab Ballads" (two series, 1869 and 1873), and , with Sullivan, "Trial by Jury" (1875), "The Sorcerer" (1877), "H.M.S. Pinafore" (1878), "The Pirates of Penzance" (1879), "Patience" (1881), "Iolanthe" (1882), "Princess Ida" (1884), "The Mikado" (1885), "Ruddigore" (1887), "The Yeomen of the Guard" (1888), "The Gondoliers" (1889), "Utopia, Limited" (1893).

Giono, Jean

French novelist (born 1895).

Born at Manosque in the Provence, which is the scene of his best novels. Partly under the influence of Hamsun (q.v.), he defends rural values and people against the monster-city of Paris. Politically confused: tried Communism, pacifism, Petainism, and has now settled to a tired political agnosticism. Wrote: "The

Hill" (1928), "Harvest" (1930), "The Great Herd" (1932), "Moby Dick" a tribute to Melville, (1936-39), "The Hussar on the Roof" (1944).

Gippius, Zinaida Nikolayevna
Russian poetess (1869-1945).

Born in Belevo, died in Paris. Leading member of the symbolist school; her poetry tended towards the morbid and mystical. Her novels and short stories were pretty pale imitations of Dostoyevsky. Married Dmitry Merezhkovski (q.v.) and emigrated with him to Paris after the Revolution. Her best book is "Living Faces" (1925), sketches of her contemporaries.

Giraudoux, Jean
French writer (1882-1944).

Born in Bellac, near Limoges; died in Paris. Studied classical philology in Germany, and all through his life had ambivalent feelings about Germany, first expressed in his "Siegfried and the Limousin" (1922). Although a man of pacifist sympathies, acted as French propaganda chief in 1939-40. Giraudoux tried his hand at several literary genres: novel—"Bella" (1926); political essay—"Full Powers" (1939); and, most successfully, plays—"Amphitryon 38" (1929), "The Trojan War Will Not Take Place" (1935), and "The Madwoman of Chaillot" (1945).

Gissing, George
English novelist (1857-1903).

Born in Wakefield, Yorkshire, died in Saint-Jean-de-Luz, France. Lived a poor and frustrated life and wrote "The Nether World," a Victorian three-decker about life in the slums (1889) under the influence of Dickens. Gissing specialized in describing the more sordid aspects of Victorian life and did not suffer from lack of material.

Gjellerup, Karl

Danish writer (1857-1919).

Born at the parsonage of Roholte on the island of Seeland; died in Dresden. Studied theology, but turned against Christianity under the influence of naturalist novels and the Danish critic Georg Brandes. Later influenced by German and Greek classicism, and finally by Buddhism. Received Nobel Prize in 1917. Wrote: "The Pilgrim Kamanita" (1906), "The Friend of the Gods" (1916), "The Golden Bough" (1917).

Gladkov, Fedor Vasilyevich

Russian novelist (born 1883).

Born of peasant stock, started writing under the influence of Gorki. Had a great success with a documentary novel, "Cement" (1925), but failed to live up to it since.

Glasgow, Ellen

American novelist (1874-1945).

Born and died in Richmond, Va. Her novels are a history of modern Virginia. She viewed the Civil War as the "expiring gesture of irony" and held that "what the South needs is blood and irony." Wrote: "The Battle-Ground" (1902), "The Builders" (1919), "The Barren Ground" (1925), etc.

Glaspell, Susan

American dramatist (1882-1948).

Born in Davenport, Iowa, died in Provincetown, Mass. Started writing plays for the Provincetown Players, a group which she organized with her husband, George Cram Cook and which gave Eugene O'Neill (q.v.) his first chance. Wrote: "Trifles" (1917), "Inheritors" (1921), "Alison's House" (1930).

Gleim, Johann Wilhelm

Prussian poet (1719-1803).

Born in Ermsleben; died in Halberstadt. Classical

poet, whose odes are hymns to Prussia. Best known for his "Prussian War Songs" (1758).

Glickel Von Hameln
Yiddish writer (1645-1727).

Born in Hamburg, died in Hamelin. Her autobiography, in seven volumes, is the first great prose work in Yiddish. It gives a vivid and often delightful account of Jewish life in Germany, as observed by a remarkable woman.

Goethe, Johann Wolfgang Von
German writer (1749-1832).

Born at Frankfurt am Main; died at Weimar. Studied law at Leipzig (1765-8), where he attended Gellert's (q.v.) lectures and published his first works, "Annette" (1767) and "Leipzig Songbook" (1768). It was here that he met Kaethchen Schoenkopf, the first of the almost innumerable women in his life. Continued his studies at Strasbourg (1770-2) where he fell under the influence of Herder, who persuaded him to drop his plan to write in French; and where he enjoyed an idyll with Friederike Brion, daughter of a village parson. After return to Frankfurt, published his first play, "Goetz Von Berlichingen" (1773), a typical product of the "Storm and Stress" period. But his literary emotions cooled somewhat under the influence of the critic Merck. Meanwhile he went to Wetzlar, to practice law at the Imperial Tribunal, where he met Charlotte Buff, who inspired "The Sufferings of Young Werther" (1774), a sentimental masterpiece, which has been recently popular in such unlikely places as Peron's Argentina and Communist China. In 1774 Goethe first met Duke Karl August of Weimar, who was soon to become his lifelong patron. After a broken engagement with Lile Schoenemann, daughter of a Frankfurt banker (1774-5), he moved to Weimar in 1775. There he became the Duke's minister and leader of literary life, associating with Wieland, Herder, and later, Schiller. In 1776 met Charlotte Von Stein, who inspired some of his finest lyrics. His literary talents were further stimulated by two Italian journeys (1786-8 and 1790), which marked his discovery of classical antiquity and made him assume his "Olympian" prose. Wrote dramas: "Iphigenia on Tauris" (1787), "Egmont" (1788), and "Torquato Tasso" (1790). Meanwhile formed an attachment with Christiane Vulpius, who gave him a son in 1789 and whom he married in 1808. Pursued scientific study and made a number of discoveries in optics and biology. The French Revolution inspired an account of the campaign of Valmy, which he observed at first hand, and the epic poem "Hermann and Dorothea" (1797) on the plight of the refugees. After 1788, close friendship with Schiller, with whom he collaborated on various magazines and a collection of verse, the "Xenien." These years, until Schiller's death in 1805, marked the peak of his literary activity. It was then that he wrote his ballads, the animal epic "Reineke the Fox" (1794), the novel "The Years of Learning of Wilhelm Meister" (1795-6), and the first part of his masterpiece "Faust" (not published until 1806). After Schiller's death Goethe felt increasingly lonely, although he continued to fall in love with, among others, Bettina Von Arnim, Minna Herzlieb, Marianna Von Willemer, and Ulrike Von Levetzow. His later years were also marked by his discovery of the East, especially of Persian and Indian literature, which found expression in his "West-East Divan" (1814). He also wrote his autobiography, "Poetry and Truth" (1811-31), the novel "Selective Relationships" (1809), "The Years of Wandering of Wilhelm Meister" (1829), and the second part of "Faust" (1832). Eckermann (q.v.) was the Boswell of his last years. The celebration of the 200th anniversary of his birth (1949) indicated Goethe's continued stature as a giant of world literature.

Gogol, Nikolay Vasilyevich
Russian novelist and playwright (1809-1852).

Born in Sorochintsy in the Ukraine; died in Moscow. Member of Russified Ukrainian peasant family; spent childhood and youth in poverty. Wanted to become an actor but gave it up when his eight tales, published as "Evenings on a Farm near Dikanka," were hailed by the critics and won him the friendship of Pushkin. He followed them up with another collection of tales, "Mirgorod" (1835), which included "Taras Bulba," a story of the Ukrainian cossacks that is a classic of Russian and world literature. Gogol's early work was realistic, and together with Pushkin's created modern Russian literary prose. His comedy "The Inspector-General" (1836), a biting satire, is still played and has been adapted in many languages. Gogol went on a series of travels to Europe and the Holy Land, and spent most of the rest of his life in Rome. In 1842 he published "The Dead Souls," another bitter satire, which made him, for all of Pushkin's and Lermontov's pioneering work, the father of the "Russian novel," as that term is understood in the West. Gogol moved toward mysticism in religion and reaction in politics; his liberal friends were shocked by the "Selected Letters to Friends" which he published in 1848. His last years were clouded by mental troubles.

Goldfaden, Abraham
Yiddish poet (1840-1908).

"Father of the modern Yiddish Theatre," poet and composer. Born in a small town in the Ukraine, he graduated from the state rabbinical seminary in Zhitomir. He wrote popular and Maskillic songs,

depicting typical characters of his Jewish environment, then tender Zionist poems. Edited (with J. J.
Linietsky) the weekly *Yiskolik*. In 1876 he founded
the first modern Yiddish theatre, in Yassay, Rumania.
Later he directed a theatre in Russia till its closing
in 1883, by order of the Czarist regime. He wrote
the text and the music to a large number of op-
erettas, which were at first humorous and descriptive of the mode of life (e.g., *The Two Kuni-
Lemlehk; Shmendrik*) and later historical-national
and full of pathos (e.g., *Bar Kokhba; Shulamis*).

Goldoni, Carlo
Italian playwright (1707-1793).

Born in Venice, died in Paris. A lawyer who reformed the Venetian theater and wrote some 250
plays in Italian, French and the Venetian dialect.
They revived the old Italian "commedia dell'arte" by
injecting into it the technical lessons that Goldoni
learned from France, especially from Molière (q.v.).

Goldsmith, Oliver
Anglo-Irish writer (1728-1774).

Born in Pallasmore, Ireland; died in London.
Studied medicine at Edinburgh. After graduating,
roamed for a year all over Europe and settled in London where he tried, and failed, to practice as a physician. Started literary career by doing hackwork for
a living. A man of very attractive character and
"Irish" charm, he became a friend of many leading
writers of the day and a permanent member of Dr.
Johnson's circle. Goldsmith's literary talents were
varied and he excelled in a number of literary genres.
Chief works: "An Enquiry Into the Present State of
Polite Learning in Europe" (1759), "The Traveller"
(didactic poem, 1764), "The Vicar of Wakefield"
(novel with sentimental overtones, 1766), "The Deserted Village" (poem, defending rural and conserva-

tive values against the prevailing "Whig" liberalism, 1770), "She Stoops to Conquer" (light comic play, 1773).

Goncharov, Ivan Alexandrovich
Russian novelist (1812-1891).

Born in Simbirsk (now Ulanovsk); died in Saint Petersburg. Civil servant in Russian Ministry of Finance. The only exciting event in his life was a circumnavigation of the world (1862), in which he took part as secretary to Admiral Count Putyatin. He left a description of the Cruise, and wrote a novel "Oblomov" (1855) which became a Russian classic and was drawn from the rest of his life. Oblomov is inertia personified. He lives a "dressing-gown existence," is full of plans and schemes but is too lazy to do anything about them. Oblomov depicts one side of the Russian character and most of Goncharov's.

Goncourt brothers—Edmond de and Jules de
French novelists and critics.

Started as historians and art critics, turned to writing novels e.g. "Germinie Lacerteux" (1865) and "Manette Salomon" (1865). Their best-known work is, however, their "Journals" (9 volumes, 1887-1895), which is less a personal document than a picture of the artistic and literary life of their time. The Goncourt Academy, with a highly valued annual literary prize, was founded with money for this purpose by Edmond's will.

Gongora y Argote, Luis de
Spanish poet (1561-1627).

Real name: Luis de Argote y Gongora, but he reversed his names and took his mother's name as his own. Born and died in Cordoba. Wrote at first in simple, popular style, later veered to a highly complex and artificial language, ultimately based on Roman rhetoric as started by Spanish-born Romans like Seneca and Quintilian, but developed through the centuries and enriched by his own contributions. His language is full of baroque "conceits," extremely personal and obscure. Hence the changes in Gongora's literary fame. Popular in his own day, his influence spread to various European countries in the Seventeenth Century. Then, for almost three centuries, he was reviled and all but forgotten. At the beginning of this century came a revival in Spain and a second blossoming of universal fame. Chief works: "Fable of Polyphemus and Galatea" (1613), and his masterpiece, the unfinished "Solitudes" in two parts (1611).

Gonzalez Martinez, Enrique

Mexican poet (1871-1954).

Born in Guadalajara. Practised medicine and wrote only occasionally until he was forty. Then he took the lead among the younger elements of the modernist school, founded the review "Mexico Moderno," and led the reaction against the exoticism and exaggerated symbolism of Ruben Dario (q.v.). His most famous poem asked his fellow poets "to wring the swan's neck." Occupied a number of diplomatic posts, including that of minister to Madrid, in his later years.

Gonzalez Prada, Manuel

Peruvian writer and critic (1848-1918).

Born and died in Lima. Descendant of one of the aristocratic families of Lima, he rebelled against his heritage, became a virulent atheist and a critic of the small group of families that governed Peru since the Conquest—and, in a way, still does. He inspired the movement for the uplift of the Indian that assumed political shape in the APRA party. His prose has been gathered in "Free Pages" and "Hours of Struggle"; his poetry, that can be as tender as his prose can be acid, in "Minuscules" (1901); "Presbyterians" (1909); "Exotics" (1911).

Gorbunov, Ivan Fyodorovich

Russian actor and writer (1831-1895).

Famous for his monologues which he delivered as "General Dityatin" (from *ditya,* the Russian word for "child"), a retired warrior who boasted that he had his brains removed in an operation and delivered himself of appropriate comments on the events of the day.

Gordon, Judah Loeb

Hebrew poet (1830-1892).

Writer of the Haskalah, was born in Vilna, Lithuania, of a well-to-do cultured family. He received a thorough Hebrew and secular education, and became an ardent advocate of the Enlightenment. A facile and capable writer, his poems are distinguished for their flowing and easy style, rich and colorful metaphor, rather than depth of emotion or lofty thought. He devoted his pen, both in prose and in poetry, toward the spread of enlightenment and education. He satirized the old-fashioned orthodox rabbis, their manners, their customs. He combatted ignorance, advocated secular learning and the way of life of the Gentile world. For this, he was denounced to Russian authorities as a revolutionary and spent some time in prison. However, the younger generation devoured his poems and his satirical essays. He was of inestimable service to the spread of enlightenment and reform among the Jews in Russia. The pogroms and persecutions of the 1880's disillusioned him of his ideas of assimilation. He wrote a few poems in a new vein, in the spirit of the new nationalistic movement; but he could not adjust himself entirely to the new trend of ideas, and died a broken-hearted man.

Gorki, Maxim

Russian novelist and playwright (1868-1936).

Real name: Alexei Peshkov. Born at Nizhni Novgorod, renamed "Gorki" in his honor at the order of Stalin in 1932; died in Moscow. Orphaned at an early age, he had a desperately poor, adventurous, and wandering childhood and youth. Had little formal education and worked at various trades from the ages of 10 to 22. Became journalist, used the pen name "Gorki" (The Bitter One) for the first time in submitting sketches to a Tiflis newspaper (1892). Became famous in the 1890's by his realistic stories and plays describing the life of the lowest strata of society. After the premiere of "The Lower Depths" (1903) his fame became world-wide. None the less, he was ignominiously deported when visiting the United States, because the immigration authorities took umbrage at his "moral turpitude," i.e., his living with a woman not his wife. Until World War I he was prominent in Russia as champion of advanced causes and of oppressed peasants, workers, and Jews. He proclaimed the virtues of humanitarianism and pacifism, but enlisted in the Russian army at the outbreak of World War I and fought bravely on the Galician front until incapacitated by wounds. By then he was a Communist sympathizer. The Revolution made him an active Communist; he was chief of the Soviet propaganda bureau (1918) and member of the Petrograd Soviet (1919). None the less, he spent eleven years (1921-32) in Italy for reasons of both health and, it is said, politics. Stalin hailed his return to Russia as a personal triumph. The ensuing Communist apotheosis of Gorki is said to have gone to his head though there is some contrary evidence to the effect that he did not endorse Stalin's methods and their results wholeheartedly. When he died, Stalin accused his enemies of having poisoned him and the accusations played a prominent part in the Great Purge trials. After his death, Gorki's hesitations were forgotten and he became enshrined as the founder of socialist realism, creator of the "positive hero," and Number One glory of Soviet literature. The Gorki Publishing House is still the chief publisher of translations from world literature. Gorki's chief works are: short stories; novels, including "Forma Gordeyev" (1900), "Mother" (1907), "The Affair of the Artamonous" (1925); plays, especially "The Lower Depths" (1903) ["The Night Shelter" (1907)], autobiographical works, e.g. "Reminiscences of My Youth" (1924), biographies of Andreyev, Lenin, and Tolstoy; diaries (published 1924).

Gosse, Sir Edmund
English writer (1849-1928).

Born and died in London. Biographer, critic and essayist, but is best-known for his "Father and Son" (1907), a portrait of his father, who lived up to all the stereotypes of Victorian fatherhood.

Gottfried of Strasbourg
German poet (about 1200).

Born in Strasbourg of bourgeois origin, one of the first of his class to achieve prominence in medieval letters. Wrote a verse version of "Tristan," which was completed after his death by Ulrich Von Tuerheim and Heinrich Von Freiburg, and furnished Wagner the theme for his opera.

Gotthelf, Jeremias
Swiss writer (1797-1854).

Real name: Albert Bitzius. Born in Murten; died at Luetzelfluh in the Emmenthal. Studied theology, history, and physics, became pastor of Luetzelfluh in 1831. His novels, written in the Swiss dialect, pioneered in their realistic descriptions of peasant life. He took his pen name from the hero of his first novel, "Peasant's Mirror" (1837). Also wrote: "How Uli the Laborer Became Happy" (1841), "Kathi, the Grandmother" (1847), "Uli the Farmer" (1849).

Gottsched, Johann Christoph
German writer (1700-1766).

Born in Juditten (East Prussia); died in Leipzig. Professor of poetry at Leipzig after 1730. Gottsched is less important for his own writings than for his work in clearing the German language and literature of the remnants of decadent baroque formlessness and emotionalism. He thus cleared the way for the coming of German classical literature. Gottsched acted under the influence of French classicism but his main motive power was perhaps his own typically "Prussian" character. The title of one of the many literary magazines he edited, "The Reasonable Critics," is typical of the man. He wrote a number of critical works and a tragedy "The Dying Cato" (1732).

Gower, John
English poet (about 1330-1408).

Place of birth unknown, died in Southwark, London. Chief rival of Chaucer, wrote in French, English and Latin. Works include: "A Voice Clamoring in the Desert" (a political satire); "In Praise of Peace" (a ballad); "The Lover's Confession" (dialogues on love).

Gozzi, Carlo Count
Italian playwright (1720-1806).

Born and died in Venice. Spent three years in Dalmatia as cavalry officer, then returned to Venice to take part in literary activities and battles. Opposed Goldoni's (q.v.) reform of the Italian comedy on French lines in the name of the pure Italian tradition of the "Commedia dell'arte." Wrote ten "fiabe" i.e. dramatizations of popular Italian and Oriental tales

181

(1761-65), including "Turandot" which was to enjoy a long dramatic and operatic career.

Grabbe, Christian

German dramatist (1801-1836).

Born and died in Detmold. Worked as lawyer and theatre director but succumbed to drunkenness. Wrote historical dramas which, during the triumph of romanticism, prepared the coming of realism; e.g., "Napoleon and the Hundred Days" (1831), "Hannibal" (1835), "The Battle of the Teutoburg Forest" (1836).

Graca Aranha, Jose

Brazilian novelist (1868-1931).

Famous for his single novel, "Canaan" (1902), which shows the impact of European immigrants, especially Germans, on a Brazil still living in the traditional way.

Gracian, Baltasar

Spanish writer (1601-1658).

Born in Calatayud (Aragon), died in Taragona. A Jesuit who acted as army chaplain during the French invasion of Catalonia. Wrote treatises on the hero (1637); the politician (1640, a eulogy of Ferdinand the Catholic); and the discreet man (1646). The publication of his chief work, "El Criticon," (1651) an allegory on human life showing the necessity of experience and prudence, made him fall in disgrace with his superiors and he died in close confinement. Gracian deliberately wrote a difficult and baroque Spanish in order to make his lessons stick in the minds of his readers through the efforts needed to acquire them. Was much read in France, England and Germany, where Schopenhauer was his great admirer.

Grahame, Kenneth

English writer of children's books (1859-1932).

Born in Edinburgh, died in Pangbourne. Spent

many years working for the Bank of England, was its secretary 1898-1908. The other side of his nature found its expression in very popular children's books, especially "The Wind in the Willows" (1908), which was dramatized as "Toad of Toad's Hall" in 1930.

Granada, Luis de
Spanish writer (1504-1588).

Typical Renaissance ascetic writer and preacher. His moral themes, especially in his *Guide For Sinners* (1567), are so steeped in his ponderings over the beauty of nature that the amazing descriptions sometimes overpower the ascetic concern. His Ciceronian style, in close imitation of the Latin rhetoric, developed the most redundant yet balanced prose of classical Spain.

Graves, Robert
English writer (born 1895).

Born in London son of Sir Alfred Percival Graves, Welsh collector of Irish folklore. Fought in World War I; took a long time to recover from its impact. His autobiography, published in 1929, was significantly titled "Goodbye to All That." He followed it with an eccentric historical novel, "I, Claudius" (1934) and an even more eccentric biography of Christ, "King Jesus." His "Collected Poems" (1948) were much admired. Lives in Mallorca.

Gray, Thomas
English poet (1716-1771).

Born in London; died in Cambridge. Studied at Cambridge, came back to London, accompanied Horace Walpole on his continental Grand Tour in 1739-41, described it in his "Letters and Journal of a Tour in Italy." Returned to Cambridge as professor of modern history. His poetry is classical, perfectionist in its language, and cool in its emotions. None the less it inspired strong and contradictory emotions: Dr. Johnson accused Gray of having invented a new kind of monotony, while James Wolfe exclaimed that he would rather have written Gray's masterpiece, his "Elegy Written in a Country Churchyard" (1751), than have taken Quebec.

Green, Henry
English novelist (born 1905).

Went to Oxford, lived for some time as manual worker and described his experience in "Living" (1929). Since then has been a prosperous Yorkshire manufacturer who publishes a novel now and then, including "Party Going" (1939), "Caught" (1943), "Loving" (1945) and "Nothing" (1950). Highly esteemed as a craftsman.

Green, Julien
French novelist (born 1900).

Born in Paris, of American parents. Much influenced by Anglo-Saxon literature, especially Blake, Dickens and Hawthorne. His novels tend to be exceedingly metaphysical, fantastic and pessimistic. Their heroes are "dead in life." Wrote: "English Suite" (1927), "The Keys of Death" (1928), "The Visionary" (1934) etc.

Greene, Graham
English novelist (born 1904).

Born in Berkhamsted, Hertfordshire. Studied at Oxford, where he joined the Communist Party for one day, leaving it in disgust. His conversion to Roman Catholicism proved more permanent. Worked as journalist for London "Times" and "Spectator." Travelled widely in Europe, Mexico, the United States, Africa, and Asia; and his travelling experiences supplied him with backgrounds for his writings. Greene's view of man and life is an almost unredeemed pessimism, with overtones of disgust, as is so prominent among the intellectuals of our time. Chief works: "The Man Within" (1929), "England Made Me" (1935), "Brighton Rock" (1938), "The Power and the Glory" (1940), "The Heart of the Matter" (1948), "The End of the Affair" (1951).

Gregory, Lady Augusta
Irish dramatist (1852-1932).

Born in Roxborough, County Galway, died in Galway. After the death of her husband, Sir William Gregory, in 1892 became interested in Irish folk lore and history. Became patroness of the Irish Literary movement and "godmother of the Abbey Theatre." Her own plays, mostly historical dramas or contemporary comedies, were written in racy Irish speech and were successful on the stage.

Grey, Zane
American novelist (1875-1939).

Born in Zanesville, Ohio, died in Altadena, California. Was unsuccessful as dentist but a great success as writer of Western stories, which he turned into a literary genre—if not, necessarily, literature. His "Riders of the Purple Sage" (1912) set a pattern that has been widely imitated.

Griboyedov, Alexander Sergeyevich
Russian dramatist (1795-1829).

Served in Russian diplomatic service, was killed by a Persian mob which stormed the Russian legation in Teheran. Wrote poems and plays but his fame rests entirely upon a single comedy, "The Misfortune of Being Clever" (1823-24) about an intellectual in love with a girl who was anything but an intellectual. In addition to offering a satirical picture of Moscow "society" it is so well written that almost all its verses have become popular quotations.

Grillparzer, Franz

Austrian dramatist (1791-1872).

Born and died in Vienna. Studied law. After early death of his father, was a tutor for four years (1809-13), then became a civil servant. Dogged by family misfortunes, his mother committed suicide. Won a great success with his first play, "The Ancestress" (1817), a "tragedy of fate." His theatrical public proved fickle, but his fame as one of the greatest dramatists of the German language has remained. Plays include: "Sappho" (1817), "The Golden Fleece" (a trilogy, 1820), "A True Servant of His Master" (1870), "The Waves of Sea and Love" (1840), "Woe to Him That Lies" (1837), "Libussa" (1872), "The Jewess of Toledo" (1873). Grillparzer also wrote lyrical poems and short stories, and essays. He was a penetrating critic of his time and a prophet of things to come, as witnessed by his celebrated epigram, "The course of mankind's new education is from humanity through nationality to bestiality."

Grimm, Jacob

German writer and philologist (1778-1863).

Born in Hanau near Frankfurt; died in Berlin. Studied law, became librarian in 1808 and in 1829 professor of German antiquities at Goettingen. Was one of the "Goettingen Seven," the seven professors who lost their jobs by protesting against the King of Hanover's abolition of the constitution. Moved to Berlin. Grimm has two titles to fame: he founded modern philological study of the German language, and he collected the German "Maerchen" (1812), the tales that have become the delight of children the world over.

Grimm, Wilhelm

German writer (1786-1859).

Born in Hanau; died in Berlin, brother of Jacob

(q.v.), acted as his assistant and collected most of the "Maerchen."

Grimmelshausen, Christoffel Von
German writer (about 1625-1676).

Born in Gelnhausen; died in Renchen (Southwest Germany), where he administered a farm and became village elder. Took part in Thirty Years' War as soldier and regimental secretary, and his experiences prompted him to write a picaresque novel, "The Adventurous Simplicius Simplicissimus" (1660), a masterpiece of the genre and an imperishable testimony to the horrors and deeds of inhumanity of that war.

Grin, Alexander
Russian novelist (1880-1932).

Pen name of Alexander Stepanovich Grinevitsky. Born in Vyatka. Wrote fantastic novels of the "science fiction" variety, published mostly in the 1920's. They have been extremely popular with the Soviet reading public which reads into his fantasies allusions to Soviet realities. His best-known books are "The Golden Chain" and "The Road to Nowhere."

Grundtvig, N. F. S.
Danish poet (1783-1872).

The greatest influence in Danish literature, culture, and folk life, moulding it into self-conscious form, and giving it national expression. His historical and mythological works are invaluable; his poetry inspirational. Among his poetic contributions are his hymns, which are incomparably majestic.

Gryphius, Andreas
German poet (1616-1664).

Real name: Grief. Born and died at Glogau in Silesia. The greatest lyrical and dramatic poet of the

German baroque. Wrote sonnets and plays, including "A Spook in Love" (1660) and "Horribilicribrifax" (1663).

Guarini, Battista

Italian poet (1538-1612).

Born in Ferrara, died in Venice. Succeeded Tasso (q.v.) as the court poet of the Estes of Ferrara. Went on diplomatic missions to Poland, Spain and the Pope. His "Faithful Shepherd" (final text fixed by Guarini in the twentieth edition, dated 1602) is a pastoral drama with strong lyrical overtones which greatly influenced European writing in the 17th century.

Guillaume de Lorris

French poet (first half of the 13th century).

Born in Lorris in Central France. Started the allegorical love poem, the "Roman de la Rose" which was finished in the next century by Jean de Meung (q.v.). The first important secular allegory of European literature, it deals with love in a courtly spirit and style.

Guillen, Jorge

Spanish poet (born 1893).

Born in Valladolid. Taught at the Sorbonne, at Murcia, Seville and Oxford. Moved to the United States in 1938 and has occupied various teaching posts there. His poetry is contained in a single book "Canticle" which has grown in successive editions, beginning in 1928. It is more cerebral than the average run of Spanish poetry and excels in the rendering of visual experiences.

Guiraldes, Ricardo

Argentine novelist (1886-1927).

Born in Buenos Aires, died in Paris. Brought the Argentine gaucho literature to its culmination with his "Don Segundo Sombra" (1926), a novel in which gaucho traditions are enshrined with the aid of techniques that he learned from Spanish modernist poetry and modern French prose.

Gumiliev, Nikolai Stepanovich

Russian poet (1886-1921).

Born in Kronstadt. Started as a symbolist, rebelled against the symbolist vagueness and pseudomysticism and organized in 1912 the "acmeist" group which demanded clear ideas and strong language. His own poetry is excellent in its craftsmanship, e.g. in "Pillar of Fire" (1921). A strong opponent of the Revolution, he was shot by the Bolsheviks.

Gunnarson, Gunnar

Icelandic writer (born 1889).

Born in Valthjoefsstadur. Poet and novelist, writes mostly in Danish, but also in Icelandic. First Icelandic writer to become known in the outside world. Wrote "Seven Days' Darkness," "The Night and the Dream," "Ships in the Sky, " "The Good Shepherd" (1940).

Gutzkow, Karl

German dramatist (1811-1878).

Born in Berlin; died in Sachsenhausen. Leading writer of the "Young German" school. Man of advanced political views; was jailed and his works banned in 1835 by the Parliament of the German Confederation. Suffered from persecution mania in later years, tried to commit suicide. Best known for his dramas, including "Pigtail and Sword" (1844), "Uriel Acosta" (1847), "The King's Lieutenant" (1852).

Guzman, Martin Luis

Mexican novelist (born 1887).

Born in Chihuahua. Took part in the Mexican Revolution until his exile in 1914. Spent many years in New York and Madrid, did not return until the 1930's. It was in exile that he wrote "The Eagle and the Serpent" (1928). This is generally considered as one of the best "novels of the Revolution"; but it is actually not a novel but an only slightly dramatized version of Guzman's revolutionary experiences, with some acute and often acid commentaries. At present edits the news magazine "Tiempo."

H

Hafiz
Persian poet (about 1320-1389).

Real name: Shams-ud-Din Mohammed. Became
known as "Hafiz" i.e. the preserver, meaning a man
who knows the entire Koran by heart and thus helps
to preserve it. Born and died at Shiraz. Studied the
mystical philosophy of sufism under a chief of an order
of dervishes; later joined the order. Became professor
of Koranic exegesis at a religious college that a Persian vizier founded specially for him. His poems were
gathered after his death in a "Divan" (collection) and
published by Mohammed Gallandam. They are lyrical poems, singing the joys of religion, nature love,
and wine. Among Hafiz' Western admirers was Goethe,
who imitated him in his "West-East Divan."

Hakim, Tewfik El
Egyptian novelist and playwright (born 1902).

Born in Alexandria. Takes his material from Arab
and Greek history and the Bible—he translated the
Song of Songs in 1940. But at his best he deals with
Egyptian realities, as in his novel of Egyptian village
life, "The Maze of Justice" (1937), available in English translation.

Halide Adib Adivar
Turkish writer (born 1883).

Born in Istanbul. Daughter of a civil servant, she
was educated by tutors and later attended Robert

College. Became a writer and journalist, made her name under the Young Turk regime. Did relief and medical work in Syria during World War I, aiding her second husband, Dr. Adnan Adivar. Became a corporal in the Nationalist army during the Turkish War of Independence, took part in battles and organized the Anatolian News Agency. Her relations with the victorious Ataturk and his successor Izmet were stormy on occasions. She writes in English and Turkish, and is at her best in her novels "The New Turan" (1912) and "The Clown and His Daughter" (1935) and her two-part autobiography, "Memoirs" (1926) and "The Turkish Ordeal" (1928).

Haller, Albrecht Von

Swiss writer (1708-1777).

Born and died in Berne. Naturalist and physician by training, professor at Goettingen (1736-1753). His writings, especially "The Alps" (1729), pioneered in the love and understanding of Europe's wild nature. Haller was, in this respect, a predecessor of his countryman Rousseau (q.v.).

Hallstroem, Per

Swedish writer (born 1866).

Born in Stockholm. Chemist, who exercised his profession in Sweden and in the United States. Became a writer, member of the Swedish Academy in 1908, its permanent secretary since 1931. Overcame a youthful pessimism and became a believer in manly virtues of courage and determination. Wrote "Lost Birds" (1894), "Thanatos" (1900), "The Four Elements" (1906).

Hamann, Johann Georg

German writer and critic (1730-1788).

Born in Koenigsberg (now Kaliningrad) in East Prussia; died at Muenster in Westphalia. After a youth of debauchery became a sincere and pietistic Christian. His writings, obscure and disorderly, are a defense of the irrational aspects of human nature in the Age of Enlightenment, and exercised a considerable influence on the romantic reaction to that age. His discovery of Vico's philosophy paved the way to Hegel and through Hegel to Marx. He was known as "The Magus of the North." Works include "Socratic Memorabilia" (1759), "Crusades of a Philologist" (1762).

Hamsun, Knut

Norwegian novelist (1859-1952).

Real name: Knut Petersen. Born at Lom in Gudbrandsdal; died on the island of Hammeroeg. Born of a peasant family; left his ancestral home and worked as farmer, teacher, laborer, leading a wandering life and often suffering from hunger. Went to America and tried his luck as streetcar conductor in Chicago, but returned to Norway in 1884 after a serious illness. His first novel, "Hunger" (1890), patently autobiographical, was an instant success. His later novels, influenced by Bjoernson, Nietzsche, Dostoyevski, and Strindberg, veered from a defense of rural against industrial values to outright Fascism. Hamsun became one of the few prominent Norwegians to support the Nazis and the Quisling government they set up. The Nazi propaganda made good use of his prestige, backed by the Nobel Prize he had won in 1920. After the liberation of Norway he was tried for collaborationism. His old age—he was by then in his late eighties—made him escape punishment; but his irate countrymen expressed their feelings by mailing all his books in their possession to his home. Hamsun died unrepentant. His novels include: "Pan" (1894), "Victoria" (1898), "The Blessing of the Earth" (1917), "The Last Chapter" (1923), "The Tramp" (1927), "August" (1930).

Han Fei-tsu

Chinese philosopher (died 233 B.C.).

Died in Hsien-yang. Pupil of the philosopher Hsuntsu (q.v.). Founded the "legalist" school, whose fundamental belief was that the empire can best be governed not by rites, as Confucius believed, but by a fixed code of laws. Strangely enough, his philosophy became the foundation of imperial despotism, and—even more strangely—Han Fei-tsu derived the metaphysical basis of his teaching from Lao Tse's Taoism.

Han Yu

Chinese essayist and poet (768-824).

Died in Ch'ang An. Teacher in imperial school and censor, was punished by exile on two occasions for opposing the emperor's will. On the second of these occasions, in 819, he wrote his famous memorial of protest against the worship of an alleged bone of the Buddha's foot, brought to China at great expense. He advocated a return to pure Confucianism and to the simple style of the Confucian classics.

Hardy, Thomas

English novelist (1840-1928).

Born in Bockhampton, Dorset; died in Dorchester. Studied architecture, but soon devoted himself to writing. His chief theme is the invasion of his native Dorset heath by the industrial civilization of the Nineteenth Century and the disastrous results. Hardy's feelings are pessimistic, his style realistic and naturalistic. He lived as a recluse. Obtained Order of Merit (1911). Novels include "Under the Greenwood Tree" (1872), "Far From the Madding Crowd" (1874), "The Return of the Native" (1878), "The Mayor of Casterbridge" (1886), "Tess of the D'Urbervilles" (1892), "Jude the Obscure" (1896). Hardy also wrote a poetic drama on Napoleon in three parts, "The Dynasts" (1903-08).

Hariri

Arab writer (1054-1122).

Born near Basra (Iraq), died in Baghdad. Wrote 50 *maqamas* (short stories in rhymed prose) about an adventurous hero, Abu Zeid, which influenced literature in the West as well as in the East.

Harris, Joel Chandler

American writer (1848-1908).

Born in Eatonton, Georgia, died in Atlanta. Worked on the Atlanta "Constitution," where he published the first of his "Uncle Remus" and "Brer Rabbit" stories, derived from Negro folklore but fashioned by his masterly hand.

Harte, (Francis) Bret

American writer (1836-1902).

Was a pioneer in local color fiction, with popular tales and poems of California. Born in Albany, N. Y. he lived from 1854 to 1871 as an itinerant journalist and teacher in the midst of the gold-rush, and then spent the rest of his life in the East or abroad unsuccessfully striving to match his early successes in *The Luck of Roaring Camp* (1868), *The Outcasts of Poker Flat* (1869), *Tennessee's Partner* (1869) and *Plain Language from Truthful James* (1870). Although the matter of these was realistic, the manner (influenced by Irving, Dickens, and Poe) was consciously artistic, theatrical, rather fastidious, and basically sentimental in its combined appeal to pathos and humor. His *Condensed Novels* (1867) contains amusing parodies of popular novelists of the day.

Hartmann Von Aue

German poet (about 1170-1215).

A Swabian who served an unidentified lord "Von Aue." In addition to lyrics wrote a number of epic poems: the Arthurian "Erec" and "Yvain"; "Gregorius" on the legend of Pope Gregory the Great; and "Poor Heinrich," the story of a knight stricken with leprosy. He began the great flowering of German literature under the Hohenstaufen dynasty; was much admired by later German writers like Gottfried Von Strasburg and—in our own time—by Gerhart Hauptmann and Thomas Mann, who re-wrote his epics as novels.

Hasek, Jaroslav
Czech writer (1883-1923).

Born in Prague; died in Lipnice na Svetle. Journalist, editor of "The World of Animals." Soldier in World War I, taken prisoner by the Russians. Converted to Communism; was Bolshevik official in Eastern Siberia. Returned home disillusioned, torn between love of Communist ideals and attractions of the bourgeois existence that he satirized in his writings, but craved in his life. Died of dipsomania, his conflicts unresolved. Left a novel based on his wartime experiences, "Adventures of the Brave Soldier Schweik" (1921 ss., four volumes by Hasek, last two completed by his friend Karel Vanek), a bitter and riotously funny satire that is one of the most important documents of our time. Schweik, playing the fool and surviving a hostile world by his feigned stupidity, has become both a Czech and universally human symbol.

Hauptmann, Gerhart
German writer (1862-1946).

Born at Obersalzbrunn in the Giant Mountains; died in Agnetendorf, Silesia. Studied at Breslau and Jena Universities. At first influenced by naturalism, was a spokesman of strong social protest in his plays and novels. Later moved toward neoromanticism, aestheticism, classicism, and an "Olympian" prose a la Goethe. Won Nobel Prize in 1912. Chief works: "Before Sunrise" (1899), "The Weavers" (1892), "The Beaver Fur" (1893), "Hannele's Journey to Heaven" (1894), "Florian Geyer" (1896), "The Sunken Bell" (1896), "Carter Henschel" (1899), "And Pippa Dances" (1906), "The Fool in Christ Emanuel Quint" (1910), "The Island of the Great Mother" (1924), and an autobiography (three volumes, 1929-37).

Hawthorne, Nathaniel

American writer (1804-1864).

Born in Salem, Massachusetts; died in Plymouth, New Hampshire. Studied at Bowdoin with Longfellow; graduated in 1825. Worked as customs official in Boston (1849-41) but left job to become a professional writer. Lived at Brook Farm for a year, then at Concord (1842-45). Moved to Salem, where was surveyor of port (1845-49). In U.S. diplomatic service, consul at Liverpool (1853-58); spent next two years in England and Italy, finally returned to Salem. Hawthorne's writing is largely determined by his Puritan descent and his ambivalent attitude toward the Puritan outlook. More than most of his contemporaries, he probed beneath the surface. Chief works: "Twice-Told Tales" (1832), "The Scarlet Letter" (1850), "The House of the Seven Gables" (1851), "The Blithedale Romance" (1852), "Tanglewood Tales for Girls and Boys" (1853), "The Marble Faun" (1860).

Hazaz, Chaim

Israeli novelist (born 1898).

Born in the Ukraine. After the Revolution went to Istanbul and Paris, emigrated to Palestine in 1931. There he became interested in the Yemenite Jewish community. He has lived among them and has practically become one of them. His novels and short stories present the Yemenites to their fellow-Jews in Israel.

Hazlitt, William

English critic and essayist (1778-1830).

Born in Maidstone, Kent, died in London. Son of a Unitarian minister, became first a painter, then a journalist. His critical essays are spiced with wit.

Hearn, Lafcadio

American writer (1850-1904).

Born on the Greek island of Leucas, died in Tokyo. A journalist who settled in Japan, married a Japanese woman and became a Japanese citizen. Best known for a number of books he wrote on his adopted country, e.g. "Kokoro." They reflect an enchantment that slowly turned to disappointment.

Hebbel, Christian Friedrich

German dramatist and poet (1813-1863).

Born in Wesselburen; died in Vienna. Born of poor family; studied at home, later at University of Heidelberg and Munich. From 1839 to 1846 lived in Hamburg, where his mistress and mother of his children, Elise Lensing, helped him to educate himself and to travel in Europe. From 1846 lived in Vienna, where he was employed in theater. Hebbel wrote poems, important dramatic criticism, and plays, including "Judith" (1841), "Genoveva" (1843), "Mary Magdalen" (1844), "Herodes and Mariamne" (1850), "Agnes Bernauer" (1855), "Gyges and His Ring" (1856), "The Nibelungs" (a trilogy, 1862).

Hebel, Johann Peter

German poet (1760-1826).

Born at Basel; died at Schwetzingen near Heidelberg. Professor at Karlsruhe, he inaugurated poetry in the Alemannic dialect with his "Alemannic Poems" (1803) highly praised by Goethe (q.v.).

Hegel, Georg Wilhelm Friedrich

German philosopher (1770-1831).

Born in Stuttgart; died in Berlin. Educated at Tübingen University; became a friend of Hoelderlin and Schelling. Tutor at Berne and Frankfurt am Main (1793-1800). Taught at Jena (1801-7), rector at Nuremberg Gymnasium (1808-16), professor at Heidelberg (1816-8) and Berlin (1818-31). His philosophical system is a philosophy of the Absolute, but its most striking feature is the dialects, a dynamic interpretation of all phenomena. Hegel dominated the Western philosophical scene for some fifty years after his death. His philosophy has served to defend all kinds of political systems, mostly extreme, from Prussian absolutism to Communism. Marx developed his dialectics from Hegel, substituting his materialism for Hegel's idealism. Hegel also profoundly affected the development of science, both natural sciences and the humanities. His general revivifying force must be balanced against the more pernicious aspects of his absolutism. Anti-Hegelians are more vocal than Hegelians today, but this is because Hegelianism has been so universally absorbed. Chief works: "Phenomenology of the Spirit" (1807), "The Science of Logic" (1812-6), "Outline Encyclopedia of Philosophical Sciences" (1817), "The Philosophy of Law" (1821).

Heidenstam, Verner Von

Swedish poet (1859-1940).

Born at Olshammer on Lake Vaetter; died in Oevralid. Scion of old aristocratic family of German origin. Had to give up schooling in Stockholm because of illness; moved to Italy, where he became a painter. Returned to Sweden in 1883, became friend of Strindberg (q.v.). He became the chief representative of Swedish neoromanticism, revived interest in the country's great past. Tried his hand at many literary genres;

obtained Nobel Prize in 1916. Wrote "Poems" (1892), "King Charles XII and His Warriors" (1897-98), "Saint George and the Dragon" (1900), "Saint Brigitta's Pilgrimage" (1901), "The Folkungs" (1905-07), "New Poems" (1915).

Heine, Heinrich

German poet (1797-1856).

Born at Duesseldorf of Jewish merchant family; died at Paris. Became a Christian in 1825, but this does not seem to have affected his Jewish feelings and attachments. As an adolescent, he fell desperately in love with his cousin Amalia, and wrote for her love lyrics which revealed his poetic talents. He became the leader of the Young Germany school, characterized by political liberalism and romantic irony. Studied at Bonn, Göttingen and Berlin, then traveled in England and France. He settled in Paris in 1831 and lived there until he died, confined for the last 11 years of his life to his mattress dungeon by an incurable disease of the spine. His writings were forbidden in Germany by a decision of the Federal Parliament. His feelings towards Germany were as ambivalent as his feelings toward Judaism. He was a master of the German language in both poetry and prose and excelled in tender lyricism, satire and irony. Works: "Poems" (1822); "Travel Pictures" (1826-1831); "The Book of Songs" (1827), which contains his two most popular poems, "The Lorelei" and "You Are Like a Flower," which became German folksongs; "History of the New German Literature" (1833); "The Romantic School" (1836); "Germany: A Winter's Tale" (1844); "New Poems" (1844); "The Romanzero" (1851); "Journey in the Harz" (1853).

Heliodorus

Greek novelist (3rd century A.D.).

Born in Emessa, Syria, later to have been bishop of

Tricca in Thessaly. His romantic novel, "Aethiopica" was much read in Byzance and translated into several European languages in the Renaissance, influencing the birth of the modern novel.

Hemingway, Ernest

American novelist (1898-1961).

Born at Oak Park, Illinois. The strongest impressions of his childhood and youth came from the prairies and woods of the Middle West that had not yet been reached by industrialization. This became his "paradise lost" and, as a writer, he has constantly measured civilized man against primitive man, and has always found the former wanting. Served in World War I with an American ambulance unit at the French and Italian fronts. Went to Greece as a war correspondent. After the war, was European correspondent of the Toronto "Star," later Paris correspondent for Hearst's Syndicated News Service. Started literary career with "Three Stories and Ten Poems" (1923). His verse was distinguished more for its pornographic than its literary qualities, but his true literary vocation was prose—as a short story writer and novelist. Hemingway became the spokesman of America's "Lost Generation" of literary exiles who settled in Paris. He revolutionized the literary language by writing as if man were a creature of emotions barely, if at all, checked by reason. His clipped style has had an influence that by now is world-wide and not confined to the English language. With Faulkner (q.v.), he has been the chief banner-bearer of America's new literary hegemony. Chief works: "The Sun Also Rises" (1926), "Men Without Women" (1927), "A Farewell to Arms" (1929), "Death in the Afternoon," (1932), "Green Hills of Africa" (1935), "To Have and to Have Not" (1937), "For Whom the Bell Tolls" (1940), "The Old Man and the Sea" (1952), that won him the Pulitzer Prize.

Hemon, Louis

French novelist (1880-1913).

Born in Brest, died in Chapleau, Ontario, Canada. Wrote a novel of French Canada, "Maria Chapdelaine" (first published posthumously in the Paris newspaper "Le Temps," 1914), remarkable for its descriptions and psychological penetrations. Although Hemon spent only 18 months in Canada, his novel has been generally accepted as "the national novel" by French Canadians.

Henry, O.

(William Sydney Porter, American, 1862-1910).

Imaginative, ironic storyteller, famous for surprise endings. At one time America's most widely read story writer. Author of some 600 tales. Characters drawn from everyday life, with sympathy for the underdog. Titles of collections: *Cabbages and Kings, The Four Million, Heart of the West.*

Herculano, Alexander

Portuguese historian and novelist (1810-1877).

Born in Lisbon, died in Val de Lobos. He richly merited his self-composed epitaph: "Here lies a man who conquered for History, mistress of the future, some important truths." Single-handed he rewrote Portuguese history from authentic sources which he gathered and published. Was much attacked for proving the falsity of many patriotic legends. His historical novels, "Enrico the Presbyter" (1844) and "The Cistercian Monk" (1848) were similarly attacked for tackling the ticklish theme of clerical chastity. They remain, nonetheless, among the best novels inspired by Walter Scott.

Herder, Johann Gottfried

German poet (1744-1803).

Born at Mohrungen (East Prussia); died at Weimar.

His parents were poor, but he managed to study at Koenigsberg University under Kant and Hamann (q.v.). Teacher and preacher at Riga (1764-1769) and from 1776 till his death at Weimar, where the Grand Duke had called him upon the recommendation of the young Goethe, whom he had befriended at Strasbourg. Herder rose to the position of court preacher and general superintendent of the Weimar church district. Herder is one of the most important figures of classical German literature, but his influence is not confined to Germany. In his reaction against the Enlightenment, he pioneered in many directions and inaugurated a number of new trends. He became a spokesman for the primitive man and his values in language, art and history, but he also was a prominent advocate of humanitarianism. His world wide collection of folk-songs, his defense of Shakespeare, his philosophy of history, his defense of human emotions made him a leader in Germany's intellectual life and one of the chief influences in the re-birth of the "Forgotten peoples" of Central and Eastern Europe. Chief works: "On Modern German Literature" (1767-68), "Critical Forests" (1769), "On German Character and Art" (1773), "The Oldest Document of the Human Race" (1774-1776). Also "A Philosophy of History for the Education of Mankind" (1775), "The Causes of Lowered Tastes Among Various Peoples" (1775), "Voices of Peoples in Songs" (1778-79), "Ideas on the Philosophy of History of Mankind" (1784-87), "Letters on Fostering Humanity" (1793-97).

Heredia, Jose Maria de

French poet (1842-1905).

Born in Cuba, died in Bourdonne (France). His father was Spanish, his mother French. Spanish was his mother tongue, but he became one of the masters of French verse of the coldly perfect Parnassian school.

Wrote: "The Trophies" (1893), a sequence of 118 sonnets and a few longer poems.

Hergesheimer, Joseph

American novelist (1880-1954).

Born in Philadelphia. Wrote historical novels in a better style than is usual today in that genre. His "Three Black Pennies" (1917) deals with Pennsylvania iron masters, "Java Head" (1919), with Salem and its China trade.

Hernandez, Joseph

Argentine poet (1834-1894).

Born in Pueyrredon, died near Buenos Aires. Wrote the epic of the gaucho in two parts: "Martin Fierro" (1872) and "The Return of Martin Fierro" (1879). Hernandez wrote about a kind of life he knew from personal experience and whose passing he regretted. But his writing is anything but primitive and embodies the Spanish epic tradition as developed from the Cid onwards.

Hernandez, Miguel

Spanish poet (1910-1942).

Born in Orihuela, died in Alicante. Started life as a goatherd, educated himself and became one of Spain's leading poets. Was a Communist, fought in the Republican army and died in a Franco jail of ill-treatment aggravated by semi-starvation. His poems, e.g. "Wind from the Village" (1937) were written in a strong and passionate language of remarkable craftsmanship. The verses he wrote in jail are poignant documents. He is today one of the leading influences among Spanish poets, and his works are published in Spain, though in truncated form.

Herodotus

Greek historian (c. 480-424 B.C.).

Born at Halicarnassus, a Dorian colony in Southeast

Asia Minor; died in Thurii in southern Italy, where he settled as a colonist. Traveled widely in Greece and the then known parts of Asia and Africa, lived on Samos and, under Pericles, in Athens. Known as the "Father of History," his "Historiae" (Inquiries), later divided into nine books named after the nine Muses, is generally recognized as the first work of history. It deals with the history of the Greco-Persian Wars until 479 B.C., but includes also considerable geographical and ethnological material, gathered on his travels. Herodotus' style is anecdotal and his history is not yet scientific. But recent research tends to confirm a good deal of his facts. Herodotus was a pupil of Herataeus, who absorbed the Egyptian and Babylonian historical traditions. But this does not affect his position as the man who inaugurated the writing of history in the western world.

Herrick, Robert
English poet (1591-1674).

Born in London, died in Dean Prior. Apprenticed to a goldsmith, he ran away to study at Cambridge, became a clergyman of the Church of England. Vicar of Dean Prior with an interruption during Cromwell's regime. Excellent epigrammatist and lyricist whose verse is a useful reminder to the modern reader that the 17th century was devoted to physical as well as metaphysical pursuits.

Hersey, John
American novelist (born 1914).

Born in Tientsin, China. A journalist and war reporter, gained fame with his first report on Hiroshima, to which the "New Yorker Magazine" devoted an entire issue in 1946. His best novels, "A Bell for Adano." (1944) and "The Wall" (1950), on the struggle of the Warsaw Ghetto, have war themes.

Herzen, Alexander Ivanovich

Russian writer (1812-1870).

Born in Moscow, died in Paris. Moved in the "advanced" circles of Moscow and Saint Petersburg, and knew the realities of the Russian countryside from first-hand experience as exile and, later, as official. In 1847 he left Russia to wage his campaigns against serfdom and Tsarist autocracy. His newspaper "The Bell" and his magazine "The Polar Star" were smuggled into Russia and were widely read there. Herzen moved among the leaders of European radicalism but Russia remained his chief concern. His essays, collected in "From the Other Shore" (1851) are still worth reading. Herzen veered from Westernism to an agrarian socialism that helped to create the Populist and Social Revolutionary movements in Russia.

Hesiod

Greek poet (eighth century B.C.).

Born in Boethia, where he lived and worked as a peasant. His poetry is as homely as Homer's is heroic. Wrote "Works and Days" about life on the land, and "Theogony" on the origin of the world and of the gods.

Hesse, Hermann

German novelist and poet (born 1877).

Born at Calw in Wuerttemberg. Went to live in Switzerland as mechanic, bookseller, and finally writer. His lyrical poetry and his novels reflect his inner conflicts, his skepticism, and his cultural pessimism. Indian religion has exercised an increasing influence on him. Works include "Poems" (1912), "Peter Camenzind" (1904), "From India" (1913), "Siddharta" (1922), "The Steppe Wolf" (1927), "Narziss and Goldmund" (1930), "The Glass Pearl Game" (1943). He won the Nobel Prize for 1946.

Heyse, Paul Von
German writer (1830-1914).

Born in Berlin; died in Munich. Moved to Munich in 1854 at the invitation of King Maximilian I of Bavaria, became head of the "Munich Poets' Circle" and was ennobled in 1910. His writings are realistic, with aesthetic and psychological overtones. He opposed the neo-romantic currents at the turn of the century in the name of bourgeois classicism. The neo-romantics replied with bitter attacks, but Heyse became in 1910 the first German writer to win the Nobel Prize. Works include "Treasury of German Stories" (1870), "Children of the World" (1872), "In Paradise" (1876), "Stories of Lake Garda" (1902).

Hino, Ashihei
Japanese novelist (born 1907).

Pen name of Tamai Katsunori. Educated at Waseda University, Tokyo, specializing in English. Was reporter in Sino-Japanese War, wrote a remarkably dispassionate account of it in his autobiographical "War and the Soldier" (1937-38).

Hitomaro Kakinomoto
(Japanese, *ca.* 655-710).

Greatest of the Japanese Manyō poets. Nothing known of his life. Surviving work collected in the *Manyōshū*—scores of long poems and several hundred *tanka*, vigorous epics and delicate lyrics.

Hoelderlin, Friedrich
German poet (1770-1843).

Born at Lauffen in Swabia; died in Tübingen. Studied theology at Maulbronn and Tübingen, where he met Hegel. Became a tutor, fell in love with Suzette Gontard, daughter of a Frankfurt banker, whom he immortalized as "Diotima." After wandering all over Europe, went insane in 1807 and was confined to an asylum. Hoelderlin's work combines the highest ideals of German romanticism and Greek classicism in a language of great depth and inspiration. Works: "Hyperion" (a novel in letters, 1797-99), "The Death of Empedocles" (tragedy, 1798-9), "Night Songs" (1805)

Hoelty, Ludwig

German poet (1748-1776).

Born in Mariensee near Hanover, died in Hanover. Lyrical poet, member of the "Göttingen Grove" circle. His tender lyrics are overshadowed by presentiments of an early death from tuberculosis, but they include some exuberantly gay poems in the Anacreontic mood. His poem "Be Always Honest and Loyal" became a German folk song.

Hoffmann, Ernst Theodor Amedeus

German writer and composer (1776-1822).

Born in Koenigsberg; died in Berlin. Studied law and was a Prussian civil servant. Became leader of a group of German writers of the late romantic school, which emphasized the demonic and the grotesque. His influence has been felt throughout Europe. His "Undine" (1816) inspired Offenbach's opera "Tales of Hoffmann" and contemporary ballet and plays. His short stories on the "Serapion Brotherhood" (1819-21) gave that name to a group of Soviet writers in the 1920's.

Hoffmann Von Fallersleben, August

German poet (1798-1874).

Born at Fallersleben near Hanover; died at Corvey Castle. Became professor of German literature at Breslau University, later librarian of Corvey Castle. Romantic poet, with strong patriotic overtones; author of "Deutschland, Deutschland Über Alles" (1841). Also philologist and historian of German literature.

Hoffman von Hoffmannswaldau, Christian
German poet (1617-1679).

Born and died in Breslau. Traveled widely in Europe, then settled at Breslau as Imperial Councilor. Leader of the "Second Silesian School of Poets." His poetry is baroque, his language artificial and full of "conceits." But he also wrote a few simple poems in the popular vein. Chief work: "A Hundred Epitaphs in Long and Short Rhymes" (1663).

Hofmannsthal, Hugo Von
Austrian writer (1874-1929).

Born in Vienna; died at Rodaun near Vienna. Studied philology at Vienna University, then settled at Rodaun. Edited review "Tomorrow," became leading figure of the Vienna cultural scene, a friend of Rilke, Stefan George, and the composer Richard Strauss. His lyrical poems are symbolist and complex in their language; his plays, poetic, revived the Greek tragedy and the Christian mystery play. Works: "Yesterday" (1891), "The Death of Titian" (1892), "The Fool and Death" (1893), "Electra" (1903), "Rosenkavalier" (1911), "Ariadne on Naxos" (1912), which inspired operas, and "Everyman, A Play on the Death of a Rich Man," a mystery play first staged at the Salzburg Festival. Hofmannsthal is one of the last great figures of Austrian culture and of the Europe that went down in World War I.

Holberg, Ludwig
Norwegian-Danish writer (1684-1754).

Born in Bergen (Norway); died in Copenhagen. Orphaned at an early age. Tutor in Holland, Germany, England, France, and Italy; professor at Copenhagen from 1718. When the first Danish theater opened at Copenhagen four years later, Holberg wrote some thirty comedies for it, popular in subject matter,

French in style, and voicing the ideas of the Enlightenment. Most popular was "Jeppe on the Mountain." Holberg also wrote moral and historical treatises, a heroic poem "Peder Paars" (1719), and a novel.

Holmes, Oliver Wendell
American writer (1809-1894).

Born in Cambridge, Mass., died in Boston. Professor of medicine at Harvard. Started writing career with "The Autocrat of the Breakfast Table" (1858) and continued it with occasional pieces, essays and poems including "The One Horse Shay," a perennial favorite.

Holz, Arno
German writer (1863-1929).

Born in Rastenburg, East Prussia; died in Berlin. Naturalist poet and literary critic; had strong influence on young Gerhart Hauptmann (q.v.). Wrote: "Papa Hamlet" (1889), "The Selicke Family" (1890), "Revolution in Lyric Poetry" (1899).

Homer
Greek poet (about ninth century B.C.).

Various dates have been suggested for his birth, ranging from 1250 B.C. to 800 B.C. Herodotus suggested 850 B.C. and Homer was certainly older than Hesiod (q.v.), who knew his works. Traditionally, Homer's birth was ascribed to seven different Greek cities. The island of Chios has perhaps the best claim to him. Tradition also made him a blind singer and ascribed him the authorship of the "Iliad," epic of the Trojan War, and of the "Odyssey," epic of the wanderings of Ulysses, as well as the so-called "Homeric Hymns." The "Homeric Question" was started in 1794 by the German critic Friedrich August Wolf, who in his "Prolegomena to Homer" denied the Homeric authorship of the epics and claimed that they were written by several authors. The controversy still rages among critics but the more extreme Wolfian views, which went so far as to deny Homer's existence altogether, are hardly upheld today. Homer is generally acknowledged as the author of the two poems that are a cornerstone of Greek and hence of Western civilization. The authorship of the "Hymns" is still a matter of dispute.

Hood, Thomas

English poet (1799-1845).

Born and died in London. Wrote verse that is humorous and sentimental; but his "Song of the Shirt" stirred his contemporaries and still stirs modern readers as a voice of social protest.

Hopkins, Gerard Manley

English poet (1844-1889).

Studied at Oxford, where he was converted to Roman Catholicism under the influence of Cardinal Newman. He became a Jesuit and destroyed all the poems he had written so as to devote all his poetry —on orders of his superiors—to the glory of God. His poems, published posthumously, include "The Wreck of the Deutschland," "The Windhover," and "Vision of the Mermaids." They are religious and philosophic, strongly influenced by Celtic models, and pioneering in their literary techniques which include sprung rhythms and outrides.

Horace

Roman poet and critic (65-8 B.C.).

Full name: Quintus Horatius Flaccus. Born at Venusia in Lucania (Southern Italy); died in Rome. Son of a freed slave, received good education in Athens and Rome. Supported the murderers of Caesar, and fought on the side of Brutus at the battle of Philippi (42 B.C.). Following the defeat of Brutus, his property was handed over to soldiers of the victorious army. Horace had to go to Rome and earn his living as a writer. His friendship with Vergil led to a meeting with Maecenas, who became his patron. He became reconciled to Augustus, Caesar's heir, and wrote poems in his praise. He spent his last years on a small property near Mount Soracte in Tuscany where he enjoyed a life of ease and leisure. In his poetical career, he was at first under the influence of the native Roman tradition, but his later work gave increasing evidence that "captured Greece overcame her savage captor" (i.e., Rome), as one of his verses put it. Horace's poetry is marked by chaste language and restrained feelings. His work of criticism, "The Art of Poetry," based on Aristotle, was highly influential in medieval and Renaissance Europe. His poetic work consists of satires, odes, epodes, epistles, and the "Secular Poem" in praise of Augustus.

Housman, Alfred Edward

English poet (1859-1936).

Is known to the world as author of *A Shropshire Lad* (1898), a volume of ballads about the everyday life of the Shropshire people. Like Fitzgerald he voiced a philosophy of pessimism and defeat. Even his gayest poems reveal an inner sadness. Housman's verse is condensed and stripped of all superfluity of ornament, having as its outstanding virtue an extraordinary simplicity of tone. His poems are fastidious, small, limited in range, and restricted in outlook, but considered by many as nearly perfect as lyrics can hope to be.

Howells, William Dean

American writer and critic (1837-1920).

Born in Martin's Ferry, Ohio, died in New York. Brought up on the Ohio frontier, educated himself in his father's printing office. Wrote a campaign biography of Lincoln that earned him a consulship in Venice. He reached the acme of literary respectability as editor of the "Atlantic Monthly" (1871-1881) and tried, at least with outward success, to make his friend Mark Twain equally respectable. Howells is not easy to classify. On the one hand, he asserted that "the more smiling aspects of life are the more American." On the other hand, he pioneered in portraying the less smiling aspects of American life in novels like "The Rise of Silas Lapham" (1885).

Hrotsvitha Von Gandersheim

German writer (about 935-1002).

Nun at the Benedictine convent at Gandersheim near Brunswick. First German poetess. Wrote verse, chronicles of Emperor Otto I, legends, dialogues, and six plays which were modeled on Terence but permeated with Christian morality.

Hsu Chih-mo

Chinese poet (1896-1931).

Born in Hai-ning, died in Tsinan. Studied at Peking National University, Columbia and Cambridge. The most powerful influence on him was English, exercised as it was through personal contacts with, among others, E. M. Forster and Katherine Mansfield (q.v.). Returned to China in 1922, taught at various universities. Under the influence of Hu Shih (q.v.) started writing poetry in the Chinese vernacular, experimenting with English metres. Founded, with Hu Shih and others, the "Crescent Moon Society" to spread their ideals. His influence has been much felt.

Hsun-tsu

Chinese philosopher (3rd century B.C.).

Was magistrate at Lan-ling in the state of Ch'u (Central China). He was a systematizer rather than an original thinker, but it was he who was primarily responsible for the victory of Confucianism over its rivals around 200 B.C.

Hu Shih

Chinese scholar and critic (born 1891).

Born in Chi-ch'i. Studied in the United States, took English literature, philosophy and political science courses at Cornell, took his doctor's degree at Columbia (1916). Returned to China to revolutionize its cultural life by his successful advocacy of the use of the Chinese vernacular (pai-hua) in "respectable" literature. Taught at Peking National University, was ambassador to Washington in World War II. Although Ch'en Tu-hsiu, who did much to ensure the literary success of pai-hua, turned Communist (and was shot as a Trotskyist), Hu Shih has remained a staunch adherent of Generalissimo Chiang and now lives in Formosa.

Huch, Ricarda

German writer (1864-1947).

Born in Braunschweig; died in Schoenberg. Leading German neo-romanticist, concerned with religious and patriotic themes. Wrote "Memories of Ludwig Ursleu the Younger" (1892), "Life is a Short Dream" (1903), "The Struggle for Rome" (1907), "Luther's Creed" (1916), "The Jewish Grave" (1916), "The Era of the Religious Split" (1937).

Hudson, William Henry

English naturalist and writer (1841-1922).

Born in Quilmes, Argentina, of English parents; died in London. Spent most of his life in dingy London rooming houses, but never forgot the "purple land" of his childhood and youth. He described it in "The Purple Land" (1885); made it the scene of his novel "Green Mansions" (1904) and went back to it nostalgically in his autobiography, "Far Away and Long Ago" (1918).

Hughes, Langston
American Negro writer (born 1902).

Born in Joplin, Missouri. Has lived mostly in New York, but has traveled a good deal. His poetry is remarkable for its use of blues rhythms, e.g. in his "Weary Blues" (1926). His "Ways of White Folks" (1934) are sardonic stories of Negro life. Of late he has created a Negro character called "Simple" as effective spokesman of his views.

Hugo, Victor
French writer (1802-1885).

Born in Besançon; died in Paris. Son of Count Joseph Hugo, one of Napoleon's best generals and writer on military subjects. Spent childhood in his father's company in Italy and Spain. Moved with him to Paris in 1812. At 17 won three prizes for poetry at the Floral Games (poetic contests) at Toulouse. Three years later (1822), he published "Odes and Various Poems" which won him recognition in Paris and a pension from King Louis XVIII. During the 1820's, established his leadership of the Romantic movement through his verse and dramas. The Paris premiere of his "Hernani" (1830) was accompanied by riots and was followed by a battle royal between classicists and romanticists. Hugo accepted the bourgeois morality of Louis Philippe and received various honors from it—including membership in the French Academy (1841) and peerage (1845). But his views became increasingly liberal and when the monarchy fell through the February Revolution of 1848, he became a member of the Constituent Assembly. He opposed Louis Napoleon's ambitions and had to leave France in 1850. During his twenty years' exile, spent mostly on the Channel Islands of Guernsey and Jersey, he wrote several attacks against Napoleon III, whom he called "Napoleon the Little." His political views veered still further to the left and culminated in a vague and humanitarian socialism. Returned to France in 1870, became member of the National Assembly after the overthrow of Napoleon III, resigned his post after the outbreak of the Commune. For the rest of his life he was honored as the Grand Old Man of French literature both in France and abroad, even though Flaubert (q.v.) demurred and called him "the best poet of France—alas." Hugo's rhetorical romanticism was widely imitated, especially in Latin countries, but his reputation today is much lower than in his own time. Chief works: "Han d'Islande" (romantic novel, 1823), "Cromwell" (a drama, with important "Preface," 1827), "Hernani" (1830), "The Hunchback of Notre Dame" (1831, novel), "Marion Delorme" (1831), "The King Enjoys Himself" (1832), "Ruy Blas" (1838), "The Burgraves" (1843)—all plays; "Autumn Leaves" (1831), "Chastisements" (1853), "The Legend of the Centuries" (1859-83)—poems; "Les Miserables" (1862, ten volumes), "The Man Who Laughs" (1869), "Ninety-three" (1874)—novels.

Humboldt, Alexander
German naturalist and traveler (1769-1859).

Born and died in Berlin; brother of Wilhelm (q.v.). Educated at several German universities and the Freiburg Mining Academy. Became superintendent of mines in Franconia in 1792. Traveled with French naturalist Aimé Bonpland over most of Latin America (1799-1804), settled in Paris after his return. From 1827, lived in Berlin, traveled on diplomatic missions for the Prussian government and in Russian Asia (1829) for the Tsar. His travel descriptions are important literary as well as scientific documents, but his magnum opus was "Kosmos" (1845-62), an epoch-making attempt to describe and analyze the whole of nature. Humboldt was a humanitarian idealist.

Humboldt, Wilhelm, Baron
German writer (1767-1835).

Born in Spandau; died on the family property of Tegel near Potsdam. Linguist, philosopher, and educationalist. Founded Berlin University in 1810. Wrote literary criticism on works of Schiller and Goethe, and helped develop comparative philology by his posthumous "On the Difference in the Construction of Language and its Influence Upon the Intellectual Development of the Human Race."

Hume, David
Scottish philosopher and historian (1711-1776).

Born and died in Edinburgh. Studied in France (1734-37), returned to Edinburgh, where he was Keeper of the Advocates' Library and occupied a number of secretarial posts. His philosophy is based on sensualism and scepticism which made him refute the experimental and formal proofs of causality in his "Treatise on Human Nature" (1739-40) and "Essays Concerning Human Understanding" (1748). Hume exercised a revolutionary influence on the minds of his century. His historical works, including a "History of England" (1754-61) are quite dated, unlike his philosophy.

Hus, John
Czech religious reformer (1369-1415).

Born in Husinec, burned on the stake at Constance (Germany). Studied at Prague University, became its rector in 1402. Attracted attention by his sermons which spread the reforming ideas of the Englishman John Wyclif and added some of his own. Attacked the sale of indulgences and had to leave Prague. Condemned as heretic at the Council of Constance and burned in spite of the safe conduct granted by the emperor Sigismund. Hus was a voluminous writer in

Czech and Latin: his theological writings, letters and hymns made him one of the great figures of Czech literary as well as European religious history.

Hutten, Ulrich Von
German humanist (1488-1523).

Born of noble family at Steckelberg Castle in Hesse; died on the island of Ufenau in Lake Zurich. His parents wanted him to become a priest, but he ran away from the monastery school to which they sent him. Studied at Cologne and Erfurt University, became acquainted with leading German humanists. Wrote mostly in Latin. The second volume of the humanist attack on the obscurantist clergy, "Epistles of Obscure Men," is now attributed to him. Strong supporter of Luther, for whom he wrote "Complaint and Warning Against the Power of the Pope" (1521). His best known German poem starts with the line, "I have dared." Emperor Maximilian I made him a knight and crowned him as a poet at a ceremony in 1518.

Huxley, Aldous
English novelist (born 1894).

Born in Godalming. Grandson of the Darwinian scientist Thomas Huxley, brother of the biologist Julian. His satirical novels like "Crome Yellow" (1921) and "Point Counter Point" (1928) were popular with the sophisticated readers of the twenties. Later he turned to more serious subjects, sometimes successfully as in his bitter utopia "Brave New World" (1932), at others producing, under the influence of Yoga, "a blend of sublime mysticism and nonsense." Lives in Southern California.

Huysmans, Joris-Karel
French novelist (1848-1907).

Born and died in Paris. His father was Dutch and

Huysmans described himself, not without reason, as "a Dutchman putrefied by Parisianism." Moved from a decadent naturalism to a not much less decadent defense of spiritual values. Chief Works: "Against the Grain" (1884) and "Down There" (1891).

I

Ibara, Saikaku

Japanese novelist (1642-1693).

Born and died in Osaka. Born of a merchant family, he had an excellent knowledge of the prosperous middleclass of his native city. After trying himself out as a poet of haiku verse he found his true vocation as the chronicler of the demi-monde in some two dozen novels that are as penetrating as they are licentious. They include "The Life of a Voluptuous Woman" and "The Story of a Young Man About Town."

Ibarbourou, Juana de

Uruguayan poetess (born 1895).

Born in Melo. Was active for only a short time (1918-30) but her love lyrics won wide acclaim. A vote organized in Latin America in 1929 proclaimed her "Juana of the Americas." Verse includes "Diamond Tongues" (1918) and "The Rose of Winds" (1930).

Ibn al Arabi, Muhiddin

Arab poet and theologian (1165-1240).

Born in Murcia, Spain, died in Damascus, Syria. His poems and theological treatises, written in a subtle and paradoxical style, are a fountainhead of European mysticism, Christian and Jewish as well as Muslim.

Ibn Ezra, Abraham

Jewish poet and critic (1092-1167).

Born in Tudea (Navarre), died in Calahorra (Aragon). Spent many years travelling in Italy, the Provence and England. His verse is light and humorous on secular topics and deep and philosophical on the religious side. A grammarian, he wrote at least six textbooks of Hebrew grammar. A scientist, he translated many scientific treatises from Arabic into Hebrew and wrote a commentary on the Bible that is a pioneering work of Biblical criticism.

Ibn Ezra, Moses
Jewish poet and critic (1060-1139).

Born in Granada, died in Northern Spain. High official at the court of Granada, was patron of Judah ha-Levi (q.v.). Wrote both secular and liturgical poems, marked by a deep pessimism and—in Arabic—a study of Hebrew poetry in Spain that is a prime source for its "Golden Age."

Ibn Gabirol, Solomon
Jewish poet and philosopher (about 1020-about 1057).

Born in Malaga, died in Valencia or Saragossa. Protege of Samuel ha Nagid. Started writing at 16, composed at 19 a Hebrew grammar in verse. His secular verse is mainly concerned with his own cruel fate and descriptions of nature. His liturgical songs are still sung in synagogues. He expressed his philosophy in a Hebrew poem, "The Royal Crown" and in an Arabic treatise, "The Crown of Life" which was translated into Latin and influenced Duns Scotus, Spinoza and Schopenhauer. For eight centuries the authorship of "The Source of Life" was attributed to a mythical Arab philosopher "Avicebron," it was only in 1859 that Solomon Munk proved that Gabirol wrote it.

Ibn Guzman
Arab poet (died 1160).

Local ruler of Seville, wrote poetry in the popular vein. His subjects are taken from the city's low life and his language is the local vernacular. Influenced the development of both Arab and Christian poetry of Spain.

Ibn Hazm

Arab writer (993-1064).

Born and died in Cordoba, Spain. A man of wide learning and independent mind, defended traditional Islam in theological works. Wrote the first history of comparative religion, the "Fisal," and "The Collar of the Dove," a book on love that presents an analysis unequalled until Stendhal (q.v.).

Ibn Khaldun

Arab historian (1332-1406).

Born in Tunis, died in Cairo. Member of a distinguished family which had emigrated from Spain. Served as adviser to rulers of Tunis, Morocco, Granada, Biskra and Tlemcen until 1382 when he became lecturer at the Al Azhar University of Cairo and subsequently Chief Justice of Egypt. In 1401 he met the great conqueror Tamerlane, who treated him with respect. He wrote his masterpiece, a history of the Muslim World, in a four years' retreat in the Sahara desert. Its most famous part, the "Prolegomena," is a pioneering work that earned him the title of precursor—if not father—of both philosophy of history and sociology.

Ibn Rushd

Arab philosopher (1126-1198).

Commonly known as Averroes. Born in Cordoba, died in Marrakesh (Morocco). Chief judge in Seville and Cordoba, wrote commentaries on Aristotle which were translated into Latin and Hebrew and helped to create Western scholasticism. A staunch rationalist he attacked in his "Incoherence of Incoherence" the anti-rationalism and mysticism of Al Ghazali.

222

Ibn Sina

Arab philosopher (980-1037).

Born near Bokhara, died in Hamadan (Persia). A prominent physician, he wrote the "Canon of Medicine," that ruled medical science until the Renaissance. His books on philosophy, written both in Arabic and Persian (his native tongue), include: "The Recovery of the Soul from Error" and "The Salvation of the Soul from Error." Ibn Sina is an Aristotelian but with strong neo-Platonic and Islamic mystical elements. His books tend to be encyclopedias of the then existing knowledge.

Ibn Tufail

Arab writer (1105-1185).

Born in Cordoba, Spain, died in Marrakesh, Morrocco. Wrote a philosophical novel on the adventures of a man who spent the first 50 years of his life on a desert island and educated himself into a superior kind of human being. Translated into Latin for Pico della Mirandola (q.v.) it had a considerable influence on Renaissance and Enlightenment minds.

Ibsen, Henrik

Norwegian playwright (1828-1906).

Born in Skien; died in Oslo. Studied medicine and worked as chemist's assistant at Grimstad (1844-50). Edited a weekly (1850-1), became stage director and dramatist of the National Theatre, then director (1851-62). His career as dramatist was started by an unsuccessful "Catiline" (1850), published under the pen name of "Brynjolf Bjarme." Received a government travelling scholarship (1863) and pension (1866), but disapproved of Norwegian politics and lived abroad, mostly in Italy and Germany, from 1863 to 1891, when he returned to Oslo. Ibsen's plays deal mostly with Norwegian history, legends, and social problems, but his stagecraft made them epochal in the history of European drama. If his influence is under an eclipse right now, it is largely because it has been so thoroughly assimilated. Ibsen advocated causes, like women's emancipation, was full of indignation at the "lies of society," and attacked corruption in business and politics. But his search for truth was made with a cold, calculating mind rather than with warm emotions. Chief works: "The Warriors of Helgeland" (1858), "The Pretenders" (1864), "Brand" (1866), "Peer Gynt" (1867), "The Pillars of Society" (1877), "A Doll's House" (1879), "Ghosts" (1881), "An Enemy of the People" (1890), "The Master Builder" (1892), "Little Eyolf" (1894), "When We Dead Awaken" (1899).

Ilf, Ilya Arnoldovich and Petrov, Evegenii Petrovich

Russian writing team (1897-1939) and (1903-1942).

Petrov, whose real name was Evegeny Katayev, was killed in the siege of Sebastopol. Together with Ilf he wrote humorous stories, of which the best are "The Twelve Chairs" (1928) and "The Little Golden Calf" (1931). Their hero is the picaresque Ostap Bender whose epitaph speaks for itself: "He loved and suffered. He loved money and suffered from lack of it." Ilf and Petrov were, understandably, under a cloud in the Stalin-Zhdanov era.

Imru'al Qays

Arab poet (6th century A.D.).

Son of a Bedouin prince of Nejd in Central Arabia who was banished by his father on account of his love affairs and led a wandering life. Stories about the "Wandering Prince," as he was called, include one that he went to Constantinople and was named by the Byzantine Emperor governor of the Syrian border tribes. He was the greatest of the pre-Islamic Arab poets who is said to have "invented" many of the

characteristic features of Bedouin poetry which have
marked Arab poetry ever since.

Iqbal, Sir Muhammad

Muslim Indian writer and philosoper (1873-1938).

Born in Sialkot, Punjab, died in Lahore. Educated
at Government College, Lahore, under Sir Thomas
Arnold, Cambridge and Munich. Wanted at first
to become a lawyer, but gave up law for literature. Started writing poetry in Urdu, with "The
Sound of the Caravan Bell" (1924), a symbolic title
showing his desire to stir his torpid co-religionists.
Then he switched to Persian, a language he found
more suitable for expressing philosophical ideas. It
was in Persian that he wrote his best poems, gathered
in "The Secrets of Self." It was in English that he
wrote "The Reconstruction of Religious Thought in
Islam" (1934), a seminal book. Iqbal advocated Muslim nationalism and is acknowledged as the spiritual
father of Pakistan.

Irving, Washington

American writer (1783-1859).

Born in New York; died at his home, "Sunnyside,"
near Tarrytown, N.Y. Son of a wealthy merchant.
Leader of literary group that published "Salmagundi"
(1807-8), social and critical essays on the lines of Addison (q.v.). It was in these essays that the name "Got-
ham" was first applied to New York. Irving followed
this with his gently satirical "History of New York by
Diedrich Knickerbocker" (1809), which made him
famous. Lived in England (1815-18) as representative
of the family firm; turned to writing for a living when
firm failed. Wrote under a number of pen names including "Geoffrey Crayon" and "Fray Antonio Aga-
pida." Travelled widely in Europe, and worked for
U.S. diplomatic service—he served as minister to Spain
from 1842 to 1846. His initiative helped save the

Alhambra from wreckers who wanted to pull it down for building materials. Later works include "History of . . . Columbus" (1828), "Spanish Sketchbook" (1829), "Alhambra" (1832), lives of Mahomet and Washington, and short stories, of which the most popular were "The Legend of Sleepy Hollow," introducing Ichabod Crane, and "Rip Van Winkle." Irving, the first American writer to earn European fame, was perhaps the last great American writer to feel really at home in his culture, even though he turned from America's materialistic present (he coined the phrase "Almighty Dollar") to her legendary past for inspiration.

Isaacs, Jorge
Colombian novelist (1837-1895).

Born in Cali, died in Ibague. Of Jewish origin. His "Maria" (1867), a tragic love story set in the Cauca valley, is a Latin American classic.

Isocrates
Greek educator (436-338 B.C.)

Born and died in Athens. One of the great prose writers and educators of 4th c. Greece. He established a school of rhetoric in Athens and, through his students and pamphlets, had considerable influence on Greek letters and political thought. In his writings the periodic style of Greek prose is brought to a smooth perfection and, by his political pamphlets, Isocrates had some effect in preparing the way for the unity of culture that characterised the Hellenistic age. His educational methods were criticised by his contemporaries, and they had the unfortunate effect of giving a rhetorical turn to Greek historiography through the work of his pupils. Yet his dignified, easy type of prose was carried on by his school and played a part in the molding of Cicero's style, which had the greatest influence on European prose.

Istrati, Panait

Roumanian writer (1884-1935).

Born in Braila, died in Bucharest. His father was a Greek smuggler, his mother a Roumanian washerwoman. Left home at 12 and led for 20 years a roaming life of great hardships. In 1921 he tried to commit suicide in Nice but failed. He wrote to Romain Rolland (q.v.) a forty page letter and got a reply that persuaded him to become a writer. His first book, "Kyra Kyralina" (1925) brought him instant fame as "the Balkan Gorki." He wrote this, and subsequent books, in French. Became a Communist and went to Russia in 1927, but came back disillusioned in 1929. His last years were darkened by bitter poverty, tuberculosis and loneliness.

Ivanov, Vyacheslav

Russian writer (1866-1950).

Born in Moscow; died in Rome. Studied at Moscow and Berlin Universities, at the latter under Mommsen. Became professor of history at Baku University, emigrated to Italy in 1924. Leading member of Russian symbolist movement, helped to remodel the Russian literary language by his literary writings and by his philosophical studies. Wrote "Guiding Stars" (1903, poems), "Tantalus" (play), "Tender Secrets" (1912), etc.

J

Jacob, Max
French poet (1876-1944).

Born in Quimper, Brittany, died in Drancy. Of Jewish origin, attended the School of Colonial Administration in Paris. Became a painter and then a writer. His verse, first published in "A Cornet of Dice" (1915), is surrealist, fantastic and mystical (he became a Catholic in 1915). Became a prominent figure in the Paris artistic and literary scene, friend of men like Picasso and Apollinaire, universally respected and liked for his eccentricities. During the Nazi occupation, had some hair-raising escapes, but was finally caught when working as doorkeeper of the church of Saint-Benoit-sur-Loire. The Nazis put him in a concentration camp, where he died.

Jacobsen, Jens Peter
Danish writer (1847-1885).

Born and died in Tisted. A botanist by profession, was one of the first adherents of Darwin in Denmark. Turned to literature under the influence of Georg Brandes (q.v.). Became one of the pioneers of naturalism, though his minute descriptions of life are overshadowed by a weary pessimism. Wrote "A Cactus Springs Up" (1869-70), "Mrs. Marie Grubbe" (1876), "Niels Lyhne" (1880), "From My Sketchbook" (1881).

Jacobus de Voragine
Italian writer (about 1230-1298).

Born in Varazzo, died in Genoa. A Dominican

preacher who became archbishop of Genoa in 1292. Wrote "The Golden Legend" (1255-66), a collection of saints' lives that was one of the most popular books of the later middle ages. Caxton published two English translations in 1483 and 1488.

Jacopone da Todi
Italian poet (about 1225-1306).

Born in Todi, Umbria, died in Collazone, Umbria. A lawyer who suffered a religious crisis after the sudden death of his wife and became a Franciscan (1268). His zeal for church reform made him an enemy of Pope Boniface VIII who had him excommunicated and jailed. Wrote hymns in Latin and Italian, of which the best known is the "Stabat Mater" on the sufferings of Our Lady.

James, Henry
American novelist (1843-1916).

Born in New York, died in London. Younger brother of the philosopher William James (q.v.). Was largely educated in Europe where he spent a good deal of his time and finally settled. Became a naturalized British subject in 1915. His novels, written under the influence of Flaubert and Turgenev, often tackle the contrasts and complex relations between America and Europe. They include: "The American" (1877), "The Bostonians" (1886), "The Princess Casamassima" (1886), "The Wings of the Dove" (1902) and "The Ambassadors" (1903). James is what the critics call a "major" novelist, but he is destined to be read by the few rather than the many. An excellent stylist and craftsman, his complexity and preciosity put off the general reader.

James, William
American philosopher (1842-1910).

Born in New York City. Educated at Harvard,

taught there, from 1872, anatomy, physiology and hygiene. One of the founders, with Dewey, of the typically American philosophy of pragmatism, which he crystallized in a book under that title (1907). His other title to fame is his "Varieties of Religious Experience" (1902), in many ways a pioneering book.

Jami

(Mullā Nūr al-Dīn 'Abd al-Rahmān; Iranian, 1414-92).

Was one of the most remarkable poets of Iran. The six greatest poets of Iran are considered to be: *Firdausi,* for epic poetry, *Nizāmī* for romance, *Rūmī* for mystical poetry, *Sa'dī* for his verses on ethical subjects, *Hāfiz* for lyrics, and *Jāmī* for general excellence in all these forms. He is regarded as the last of the classical poets of Iran. He wrote numerous works. His poetry, not including minor productions, consists of 3 *Dīvāns* of lyrical poetry, and 7 romantic masnavīs which are collectively known as the *Sab'a (Septet)* or *Haft Awrang (Seven Thrones).* The fifth of the *Seven Thrones,* the *Romance of Yūsuf and Zulaykhā,* is by far the most popular and accessible, both in the original and in translation.

Jammes, Francis

French poet (1868-1938).

Born in Tournay, died in Hasparren. Became a symbolist, then a Catholic poet, singing the praises of his Pyrenean region in "Franciscan" verse, strongly influenced by Verlaine. Wrote: "The Christian Georgics" (1911-12).

Jean de Meung

French poet (died about 1305).

Real name: Jean Chopinel or Clopinel. Born in Meung, died in Paris. Completed the "Roman de la

Rose" of Guillaume de Lorris (q.v.) in a far coarser and more bourgeois spirit.

Jeffers, Robinson

American poet (born 1887).

Born in Pittsburgh. Settled in Carmel, on the wild California coast. His style is largely derived from Whitman, but he is as determinedly pessimistic as Whitman was optimistic. Wrote: "Flagons and Apples" (1912), "Roan Stallion, Tamar and Other Poems" (1925), "Apology for Bad Dreams" (1930).

Jensen, Johannes

Danish writer (1873-1950).

Born at Farsoe in Vesthimmerland. Lyrical poet and novelist, leader of neoromantic school which opposed Brandes (q.v.). Inspired by the legends of his native land and the exploits of the Vikings, his chief work, "The Long Journey" (six volumes, 1909-22), aims at creating "The Myth of the New Man," deals with history from the Vikings to the rise of the technological age.

Jerome, Saint

Latin writer (about 348-420).

Born in Dalmatia, died in Palestine. Born a pagan, was baptized in Rome where he went for education. Wrote the standard Latin translation of the Bible, known as "Vulgate," and a history of the world.

Jewett, Sarah Orne

American writer (1849-1909).

Born in South Berwick, Maine novelist and short story writer, influenced by Harriet Beecher Stowe. Best known for "The Country of Pointed Firs" (1896), stories about her native state.

Jimenez, Juan Ramon

Spanish poet (1881-1958).

Born in Moguer, died in San Juan, Puerto Rico.

Educated at a Jesuit school and at Seville University. Lived mainly in Madrid until the Civil War drove him into exile, first in the United States and finally in Puerto Rico. Was awarded the Nobel Prize in 1957. As a poet, he carried forward the "modernist" revolution inaugurated by Ruben Dario (q.v.). His "Spring Ballads" (1910, "Diary of a Recently Married Poet" (1917), "Stone and Sky" (1919) show him as a sensitive and rather cerebral poet. His "Platero and I" (1917), based on his reminiscences of Moguer, is the story of a donkey and a man that seems destined to survive as one of the best children's books.

Jodelle, Etienne

French poet and playwright. (1532-1573).

Born and died in Paris. A member of the "Pleiad" literary group. Wrote the first French tragedies in the classical style, "Captive Cleopatra" (1552) and "Self-sacrificing Dido" (1555).

John Chrysostom, Saint

Byzantine theologian (about 354-407).

Born in Antioch, died in Byzantium. John surnamed 'Chrysostom the Golden-mouthed' disputes with Bossuet the distinction of being the greatest orator ever to be heard from a Christian pulpit. He was educated in rhetoric and the classics by the famous pagan teacher Libanius; and Diodorus of Tarsus, in theology and biblical exegesis. Becoming a monk after his baptism in 372, he soon won fame as a writer of apologetic and other works, notable among the latter the moving dialogue on the nobility and responsibilities of "The Priesthood," still required reading in every Catholic seminary, and the interesting treatise on "Vainglory and the Education of the Child."

John of Salisbury
English historian and educator (1115-1180).

Born and died in Salisbury. The best educated man of the Middle Ages, a pupil of Abailard. His knowledge of the Classics was incomparable, his (Latin) style rivals that of Cicero. He was an intimate of Thomas a Becket, Bernard of Clairvaux, Nicholas Breakspear (Adrian IV, the only English Pope), and his admired master, Abailard. A vigorous defender of humanistic education against the proponents of a "modern, scientific curriculum" in his "Metalogicon." His "Policraticus" is a mine of information about his times; it contains his political theory, the organic nature of the State and a Mirror of the Prince. His account of the teaching method of Bernard of Chartres is our most detailed source for the educational method of the 12th century.

John of the Cross, Saint
Spanish religious poet (1542-1591).

Full name: Juan de Yepes. Born in Fontiveros near Avila, died in Ubeda. A Carmelite who suffered exile and imprisonment for his attempts to reform the order. Canonized in 1726. His three mystical poems are perhaps the best of their kind. They combine the highest flights of religion with a poetic technique learned from the best models of Spain and Italy.

Johnson, Samuel
English writer, critic and lexicographer (1709-1784).

Born in Lichfield, Staffordshire; died in London. Son of a bookdealer; educated at Oxford (1728-9). Opened a school near Lichfield, in which the actor David Garrick was one of the first pupils. Went with Garrick to London in 1737, became a contributor to the "Gentleman's Magazine." Pubished a satirical poem, "London" (1738), in imitation of Juvenal. In

1747 started on his dictionary of the English language, on which he worked for eight years, and which brought him fame and made him leader of a circle of writers and painters that gathered around him and met in taverns, later at a club. When Lord Chesterfield made a belated offer of patronage for the Dictionary, Johnson rejected it in a famous letter. Received various honors, including honorary degrees from Oxford and Trinity College, Dublin, and a government pension. Edited various magazines, including "The Rambler" (1750-2) and "The Idler" (1758-60). Published an important critical edition of Shakespeare (1765) and wrote "Lives of the Poets" (1779-81). His novel "Rasselas, Prince of Abyssinia" (1759), a variation on the "noble savage" theme was hugely successful and is still reprinted and translated. Met his future biographer James Boswell (q.v.) in 1763, travelled with him to Scotland and published "Journey to the Western Isles of Scotland" in 1775. Johnson was recognized as the leading literary figure of his time and was buried in Westminster Abbey. He lives on as the compiler of the "Dictionary," the first modern dictionary of the English language, as literary critic, and as conversationalist, whose wit and wisdom were transmitted to us by Boswell.

Jokai, Mauris

Hungarian novelist (1825-1904).

Born in Komarom, died in Budapest. The most popular of Hungarian novelists, widely read abroad in translations. Today his novels are quite dated. They include: "Midst the Wild Carpathians" (1852) and "A Hungarian Nabob" (1853-54). Jokai wrote all kinds of novels with equal facility and equal shallowness.

Jonson, Ben

English poet and playwright (about 1573-1637).

Born and died in London. Studied at Westminster

School and perhaps at Cambridge. Served with the English army in Flanders (1592), returned to London to become an actor and playwright. Generally regarded as the first Poet Laureate, although William Davenant was the first official recipient of the title, a year after Jonson's death. Friend of Shakespeare, for whom he wrote "To the Memory of My Beloved Master William Shakespeare" (1623). Jonson's plays, which realistically attack the abuses of his time, were often satirical and made him many enemies, who undermined his position at court. They are influenced by the Greek tragedy. Plays include "Every Man in His Humour" (1598), "Every Man Out of His Humour" (1509), "Cynthia's Revels" (1600), "The Poetaster" (1601), "Volponc" (1605), and a number of court masques. His poems, published in 1616, include the famous "Drink to Me Only With Thine Eyes."

Josephus, Flavius
Jewish historian (37/8-about 100 A.D.).

Born in Jerusalem, died in Rome. Visited Rome in 64. Prominent leader of the Jewish Rising against the Romans, he went over to the enemy in 67 and gained the favor of Vespasian and Titus. Lived in Rome for the rest of his life and wrote, in Greek, "The History of the Jewish War," "Jewish Antiquities" "Autobiography" and "Against Apion" (an anti-Jewish rabble rouser from Alexandria). His deeply split personality has ever caused controversy among both Jews and Gentiles.

Joyce, James
Irish novelist (1882-1941).

Born in Rathgar, Dublin, died in Zurich. Educated at Jesuit schools and at the Catholic University, Dublin, where he studied modern languages and graduated in 1902. He was a gifted musician, competed at music festivals and published an attack on Yeats and the

Irish Literary Theatre, "The Day of the Rabblement" (1901) for not staging European masterpieces as an incentive for young Irish dramatists. In 1904 he left Ireland, determined to express himself in "silence, exile and cunning," a vow that he was destined to carry out in the face of most unpromising circumstances. Dogged by poverty and ill health, earning a precarious living by language teaching in Trieste, Paris and Zurich, he stuck to his literary guns, aided by occasional generous patrons. He remained undaunted through family misfortunes and the onset of blindness. His first works, the autobiographical "Portrait of the Artist as a Young Man" (1916), the short stories "Dubliners" (1914) and the Ibsenian drama "Exiles" (1918) were merely preludes to his magnum opus, "Ulysses" (1922) which has been called the greatest modern novel, worthless pornographic trash, and anything in between. Completed and published in the face of what seemed insuperable odds with the aid of a few who believed in his genius, "Ulysses" seems destined for immortality, whatever the final judgment of posterity on its merits. Certainly no one can understand 20th century fiction without reference to it. In "Finnegan's Wake" (1939), Joyce tried to take language beyond the limits of accepted meaning—and succeeded.

Juan Manuel, Infante

Spanish writer (1282-1349).

Born in Escalona near Toledo. Nephew of Alfonso X of Castile. Wrote several collections of tales including "Count Lucanor" and "Book of Estates" which incorporate a good deal of Oriental material.

Judah, Ha-Levi

Jewish poet (1080-after 1145).

Born in Tudela (Navarre), died in Palestine. A physician by profession, he lived in Granada, Toledo and

Cordoba. Wrote in Arabic "Al Kuzari," a dialogue on Jewish religion and history. His poetry, in Hebrew, was gay and brilliant at first but grew more serious and culminated in "The Songs of Zion," a heartrending expression of his nostalgia for the Holy Land. He went there in 1141 and reached it after a stay in Egypt; but there is no further news of him. Generally considered the greatest medieval Jewish poet.

Juenger, Ernst
German writer (born 1895).

Born in Heidelberg. Officer in World War I; his first works are based on that experience: "In a Tempest of Steel" (1920), "The Wood Number 125" (1925), "War as an Inner Experience" (1922). Settled in Berlin, became a leading spirit of the nationalist opposition to the Weimar Republic, developed an ambivalent attitude toward the Nazis, and wrote two books which analyzed the society of his time: "Total Mobilization" (1931) and "The Worker" (1932). In the first years of the Nazi regime, remained in a vague "inner opposition" which crystallized in the symbolic novel "On Marble Cliffs" (1939), published in Germany just before the war. In active service in World War II in French and Russian campaigns; wrote a series of diaries which he continued after the war. Toward the end of the war, became associated with the anti-Hitler movement of officers and aristocrats, circulated a manuscript treatise "On Peace" advocating unity of Europe, but managed to escape the consequences of the plot on Hitler's life. After World War II, was for a long time in disfavor with occupation authorities because of his persistent German nationalism. Wrote several novels and two books on the problems of postwar man: "Going to Woods" (1951), an appeal for individual opposition to the modern state, and "The Glass Bees," an attack on technological man.

Jung-Stilling, Johann Heinrich

German writer (1740-1817).

Real name: Johann Heinrich Jung; used pen name "Heinrich Stilling." Born at Grund in Hesse; died in Karlsruhe. Studied medicine at Strasbourg, where he met Herder and Goethe; became professor of economics and privy councilor to the Grand Duke of Baden. His writings are animated by a spirit of mysticism which he acquired through a Pietist upbringing. Most important of them is his autobiography in five volumes (1777-1804), partly edited by Goethe.

Junichiro Tanizaki

(Japanese, 1886-   ).

One of Japan's most distinguished modern novelists. Started his career under Western influence of Baudelaire, Wilde and Poe. After earthquake of 1923, turned to classical Japanese literature and wrote most important novels, including *Some Prefer Nettles*. Recently engaged in new translation of *The Tale of Genji*.

Junqueiro, Guerra

Portuguese poet (1850-1923).

Born at Freixo, leader of Republican party and a founder of the Republic in 1910. His lyric poems and satires are highly symbolic in their language and metaphors.

Juvenal

Roman poet (about 60—about 140).

Full name: Decimus Julius Juvenalis. Born at Aquinum; died in Rome. His five books of satires, containing sixteen poems, castigate the corruption of Rome, especially under the emperor Domitian. Among his targets are the rich, women, and oriental immigrants to Rome. His satires are very sharp and full of moral indignation, which has earned him the nickname of "Ethical." Little is known of his life and doubts have been cast as to his motives, but his critics have found no proofs so far. There is no reason to doubt that Juvenal was in dead earnest when he wrote, "It is difficult *not* to write a satire."

K

Kaestner, Erich

German writer (born 1899).

Born in Dresden. During the Weimar Republic he was a bitter satirist, e.g. in his novel "Fabian" (1930) and in poems, in which he mocked German militarism, e.g. "Do You Know the Land the Cannon Blossoms?" But his gentler side came to the fore in his children's books, especially the classic "Emil and the Detectives" (1928). He still writes in both veins.

Kafka, Franz

German writer (1883-1924).

Born in Prague, of Jewish origin; died at Kierling near Vienna. Had difficult relations with his authoritarian father. Earned his living as an insurance clerk, while writing in the expressionist manner. Member of a circle of writers which included Max Brod and Franz Werfel. While he published a good deal in his life—including "Observations" (1913), "The Sentence" (1916), "In the Penal Colony" (1919), "A Country Doctor" (1920)—he was known only to a small circle of Prague intellectuals. His fame and reputation as one of the great novelists of the Twentieth Century was entirely posthumous. It is based on four novels lovingly edited and published by his literary executor Max Brod against Kafka's own wishes (his will asked Brod to burn his manuscripts): "The Trial" (1925), "The Castle" (1927), "Amerika" (1927), and "The Chinese Wall" (1931). Kafka's characters move in a magical dream world of their own; they are lonely and alienated from the world of reality, with which they are unable to establish contact, although it condemns them. Kafka was the first to give literary expression to the existentialist predicament of modern man, caught in the terrifying coils of a world which is beyond his understanding. His hero, "Joseph K.," has become a universal symbol, and Kafka has found disciples wherever man feels alone and betrayed.

Kaiser, Georg
German playwright (1878-1945).

Born in Magdeborg; died in Ascona (Switzerland). Expressionist, became a leading dramatist of the Berlin stage during the Weimar Republic. His plays, suppressed and burned under Hitler, include "The Jewish Widow" (1911), "Gas" (two parts, 1918 and 1922), "Colportage" (1924).

Kagawa Kageki
(Japanese, 1768-1843).

Leading *tanka* poet of his day. A prodigy who composed verse as a child. Earned living as instructor of poetry. Famous collection of verse: *Keien Isshi*. Also prepared important editions of early Japanese texts.

Kalidasa
Indian writer (about 450-500).

Lived under the Gupta dynasty but very little is known of his life. One of the classical writers of Hindu literature, especially in drama, which earned him the reputation of "the Shakespeare of India." His masterpiece "Sakuntala," is now part of the repertoire of theaters throughout the civilized world. Also wrote the court drama "Malavika and Agnimitra," the epic "Story of the Raghu Family," lyrical poems, etc.

Kan Kikuchi

(Japanese, 1888-1948).

Contemporary Japanese short story writer, novelist and playwright. Precise, clear-cut stylist. Influenced by West, helped introduce realism into Japanese theater. Plays translated: *The Miracle, Love and Four Other Plays, The Father Returns, The Madman on the Roof, Better Than Revenge.*

Kant, Immanuel

German philosopher (1724-1804).

Born and died in Koenigsberg, a city that he hardly ever left. Educated as a Pietist, studied at Koenigsberg University and under private tutors. Became professor of philosophy, anthropology, and physical geography at Koenigsberg. He sympathized with the French and American Revolutions, developed liberal religious views, and advocated universal peace, all of which was not to the liking of the Prussian government, with which he came into conflict in 1790-2. Kant overcame his early admiration for the views of Leibnitz and Hume and created a critical and transcendentalist philosophy which tried to determine the limitations of man's knowledge and to avoid the pitfalls of both dogmatism and scepticism. Kant's chief works, which are landmarks of the growth of philosophy, are the three "critiques": "Critique of Pure Reason" (1781-7), "Critique of Practical Reason" (1788), and "Critique of Judgment" (1790). He wrote, in addition, works on cosmogony, morals, history, etc.

Karadzic, Vuk Stefanovic

Serb writer and lexicographer (1787-1864).

Born at Trsic on the Drina; died in Vienna. Founded Serbo-Croat literary language, collected "Serb National Songs" (nine volumes, 1822-33), and "Serb National Tales" (1853); wrote a Serb grammar and dictionary. Was in friendly contact with Goethe and the Grimm brothers (q.v.), and put Serbia on European literary map.

Karamzin, Nikolai Mikhailovich
Russian writer (1766-1826).

Born at Mikhaiovka near Orenburg, of a Tartar family; died in Saint Petersburg. Edited a number of magazines from 1785 to 1789. Travelled in Western Europe (1789-90) and described his experiences in "Notes of a Russian Traveller" (1790-2). Published two novels of the sentimental variety, "Poor Liza" (1792) and "Natalia, the Boyar's Daughter" (1792); two anthologies of literary masterpieces; and a "History of Russia" (twelve volumes, unfinished, 1819-26). Pushkin sneered at its reactionary views: "In his history beauty and necessity prove without bias the necessity of the autocracy and the charm of the knut" —but Karamzin wrote the first modern history of Russia of any literary standing. Karamzin's chief importance lies in his reform of the Russian literary language, whose modern prose form he virtually created. This he did by permeating Russian with French idioms and syntax.

Karlfeldt, Erik
Swedish poet (1864-1931).

Born at Folkaerna in Dalarna; died in Stockholm. Lyrical poet, member of the Swedish Academy and its permanent secretary after 1912. Wrote "Fridolin's Songs" (1898) and "Horn of Autumn" (1927).

Karo, Joseph
Jewish religious writer (1488-1575).

Born in Toledo, Spain, died in Safed, Palestine. Taken out of Spain in 1492, went to Constantinople and reached Safed in 1525. His writings reveal a split religious personality. There is, on the one hand,

"The Covered Table," a dry and ritualistic treatise on religious customs that was used extensively by Eastern European Jewry; on the other, the verse that he wrote in Safed, which is in the most exalted vein of mysticism.

Kasprowicz, Jan
Polish poet (1860-1926).

Born in Szymborze; died in Poronin near Zakopane in the Tatra Mountains. Lyrical poet of the symbolist school; wrote of man's relationship to God and nature. Chief works: "Christ" (1894) "To a Dying World" (1910). Translated into Polish many masterpieces of world literature.

Katayev, Valentin
Russian writer (born 1897).

Born in Odessa. Started as a picaresque critic of Soviet realities in the novel "The Embezzlers" (1926) and the play "Squaring the Circle" (1937), developed into a singer of hymns to the Soviet things that be.

Kavafis, Konstantinos
Greek poet (1863-1933).

Born and died in Alexandria, Egypt. Revived the Hellenistic spirit of the city founded by Alexander of Macedon in poems like "The Town" and "Waiting for the Barbarians" (1912). His language is archaic, but his spirit modern.

Kaverin, Venyamin
Russian novelist (born 1902).

Pen name of Venyamin Alexandrovich Zillberg. Born in Odessa. His novels are of the psychological variety, with fantastic overtones. Influenced by Poe and Hoffman, he was a leading member of the "Serapion Brothers" in the twenties. It was then that he did his best work, in "Masters and Apprentices" (1923) and "Nine Tenths of Fate" (1926). His "Artist Unknown" (1931) is a timely plea for ethical values in writing. "The Larger View" (1934-35) shows a falling-off of his talents.

Keats, John

English poet (1795-1821).

Born in London; died in Rome. Son of a hostler, studied medicine but never practiced it. Published his first sonnet in 1816, followed it by another "On First Looking Into Chapman's Homer," in the same year. A small inheritance enabled him to publish his "Poems" (1817). Later published "Endymion" (1817), "The Eve of Saint Agnes" (1819), "La Belle Dame Sans Merci" (1819), "Lamia and Other Poems" (1820). He was befriended by Shelley and Leigh Hunt, but his last years were darkened by a hopeless love for Fanny Brawne, poverty, lack of recognition, and tuberculosis. He went to Italy for his health, but in vain. His tomb in Rome is still the object of literary pilgrimages. His friend Shelley's tender epitaph, "Adonais," helped to establish his literary stature as one of the great poets of English romanticism.

Keller, Gottfried

Swiss novelist (1819-1890).

Born and died in Zurich. Son of a poor craftsman, educated fitfully; tried at first to be a painter. A government grant enabled him to study at Heidelberg University at the age of 31. After his return to Zurich he became a secretary in the municipal government (1861-75). Keller is the master of the Swiss realistic novel, but his realism is shot through with poetry. Chief works: "Poems" (1846), "The People of Seldwyla" (1856), "Romeo and Juliet in a Village," (1870), "Zurich Stories" (1878).

Kerouac, Jack

American writer (born 1933?).

Born in Lowell, Mass., educated at Columbia. Moved to California, has since returned to New York. His "On the Road," a novel as disjointed as it is ecstatic, made him the leading writer of the so-called "beat generation." Its success has made the incoherent expression of assorted forms of joy and misery—mostly the latter—flavored with a dash of what is believed to be Zen Buddhism, the most lucrative literary endeavor in the world today.

Ki no Tsurayuki

Japanese writer (862-940).

Court official at Kyoto. Charged by the emperor with compiling the "Kokinshu" anthology of poetry, which includes over 100 poems of his own. He preceded it by a famous "Introduction" which discusses Chinese and Japanese poetry (date given variously as 905 and 922). His "Tosa Diary" is a charming piece of writing in simple and unaffected language.

Kierkegaard, Soren

Danish philosopher and theologian (1813-1855).

Born and died in Copenhagen. Led a lonely and melancholy life. After giving up his fiancee in 1843—a step which he justified in his book "Either/or"—he devoted himself entirely to philosophical and theological studies. Attacked Hegelianism and the Danish (Lutheran) State Church for its worldliness. Went through a religious crisis in 1848 in which he posed the dilemma of the incompatibility of religion and church and demanded an unconditional Christianity. He held that while man's relation to God was an individual matter, this relation inevitably involved sufferings. Published a number of books, from which Twentieth Century existentialism largely derived its philosophical basis. They include: "On the Concept of Irony" (1841), "Fear and Trembling" (1845), "The Concept of Fear" (1844), "Sickness Unto Death" (1849), "Training in Christianity" (1850), "Stages on Life's Way" (1845). Had practically no influence on his own time. Interest in him was first revived by his countryman Georg Brandes (q.v.). The Spanish philosopher Unamuno learned Danish in the 1890's to read him in the original. But Kierkegaard's rediscovery was not really complete until Martin Heidegger in the 1920's. Sartre took over many Kierkegaardian views from Heidegger. His existentialism started a world conquest with the discovery of Sartre by the outside world after the Liberation of France.

Kingsley, Charles
English writer (1819-1875).

Born in Hone, Devonshire; died in Eversley, Hampshire, where he was rector. Studied at King's College, London, and at Cambridge. Clergyman of the Church of England, rose to be chaplain to Queen Victoria. Professor of modern history at Cambridge. Man of broad social sympathies, one of the founders and leading exponents of the Christian Socialist movement. Two early novels, "Alton Locke" (1849) and "Yeast" (1849), showed some sympathy with the social and political ferment of Chartism. Wrote a number of historical novels, including "Westward Ho!" (1855, about the Elizabethan mariners) and "Hereward the Wake" (1866), as well as two very popular books for children, "Greek Fairy Tales" (1856) and "The Water Babies" (1863).

Kipling, Rudyard
English writer (1865-1936).

Born in Bombay (India); died in Burwash, Sussex. Son of Engish artist who was head of the Art School and Museum at Lahore (now Pakistan). Started as a reporter on the "Civil and Military Gazette" of Amritsar, but moved to England (1889) after his first literary successes. Became famous as spokesman for England and her imperial mission, descriptions of India, and children's books. Was also one of the first to offer literary treatment of the Industrial Revolution —engineers are among his favorite heros. Chief works: "Plain Tales From the Hills" (1886), "Soldiers Three" and other poems (1888-9), "The Light That Failed" (1891), "Barrack Room Ballads" (1892), "The Jungle Book" (1894), "Second Jungle Book" (1895), "Captains Courageous" (1897), "Stalky and Co." (1899), "Kim" (1901), "Just So Stories" (1902), "Puck of Pook's Hill" (1906), "Something of Myself" (autobiography, published 1937).

Kisfaludy, Alexander

Hungarian poet (1772-1844).

Born and died in Suemeg. Professional soldier, turned to literature after coming across the poems of Petrarch (q.v.). Under his influence wrote the very popular "Himfy" lyrics. Also wrote romantic epics about his native region round Lake Balaton.

Kisfaludy, Karoly

Hungarian poet (1788-1830).

Younger brother of Alexander (q.v.). Born in Tet; died in Budapest. Poet who started the Hungarian romantic school, and whose plays started the Hungarian drama. Also wrote short stories including "Tihamer" (1825). As important as his creative work was his publication of the literary journal "Aurora" (from 1822), around which the young Hungarian writers gathered.

Kivi, Alexis

Finnish writer (1834-1872).

Real name: Alexis Stenvall. Born in Nurmijaervi;

died in Tuusola. Born in very poor circumstances, had a very hard childhood and youth. Disapproval of the prudish bourgeoisie of his time drove him into alcoholism and mental disease; he died after two years of insanity. Wrote "Kullervo" (1859), a drama based on an episode from the Finnish national epic, Kalevala; "The Shoemakers of the Heath" (1864); "Seven Brothers" (1870) the novel that made him Finland's national novelist, a book of epic stature that tells of the clearing of one of Europe's last forests.

Kleist, Heinrich Von

German dramatist, poet, and novelist (1777-1811).

Born in Frankfurt on the Oder; died by suicide in Berlin. Son of a Prussian officer of a Junker family which originated in Pomerania. Served as officer in guards regiment 1792-9, left service to study. Underwent a spiritual crisis after reading Kant's "Critique of Pure Reason": traveled in Europe with his sister Ulrike. Returned to Prussia in 1802, became civil servant. Was granted a pension by Queen Louise. After Prussia's defeat by Napoleon in 1806, briefly imprisoned by the French, and developed a pathological hatred of them. Spent two years in Dresden (1807-9), during which did most of his best writing. Committed suicide with Henriette Vogel, whom he loved. Most of his work was published only posthumously. The Prussian vigor and simplicity of his language and his penetrating insights into human nature made him soon a classic of German literature. But he was not appreciated abroad until World War II, when his dramas were rediscovered and staged in Paris. Chief works: "The Schroffenstein Family" (1803), "Amphitrion" (1808), "Penthesilea" (1808), "Kaethchen Von Heilbronn" (1810), "Stories" (1810-11), "The Broken Jar" (1811), "The Battle of Arminius" (1821), "The Prince of Homburg" (1821).

Klinger, Maximilian Von
German dramatist (1752-1831).

Born in Frankfurt am Main; died in Dorpat (Estonia). Had a turbulent youth, was a friend of young Goethe, then settled down to a military and diplomatic career in Russia. Is still remembered for his youthful play "Storm and Stress" that gave its name to an era.

Klopstock, Friedrich Gottlieb
German writer (1724-1803).

Born in Quedlinburg; died in Hamburg. First great figure in German classical literature; represents the transition between baroque and classicism. Brought up as a Pietist, educated at Pforta school, studied at Jena and Leipzig. Lived many years in Copenhagen under the patronage of King Frederick V, then moved to Hamburg. Became Germany's Milton with his epic "The Messiah" (1748-73), which successfully used the hexameter and combined baroque pathos with classical dignity. Also wrote "Odes" (1771), and a number of works on the battle of the Teutoburg Forest, in which Arminius defeated the Romans. His interest in the ancient Teutons made him an important forerunner of German romanticism and of the Scandinavian literary revival.

Kluyev, Nikolai Alexeyevich
Russian poet (1887-1937).

Born in the Lake Onega district, of peasant stock belonging to the heretical "Old Believers." Welcomed the Revolution, but was consumed, like his fellow peasant poet Esenin (q.v.) by a nostalgia for the "wooden Russia." His poem to Lenin (1924) was written in a religious vein. He became labelled as the poet of the kulaks, the rich peasants, was arrested in the great purges and is supposed to have died in a concentration camp.

Knigge, Adolf Baron Von
German writer (1752-1796).

Born in Bredenbeck near Hanover. Wrote "On Dealings With Men" (1788), a classic of polite Eighteenth Century etiquette.

Knox, John
Scottish religious reformer (1513-1572).

Born in Haddington, died in Edinburgh. Became Calvinist in 1547, spent the next two years a prisoner on French galleys. From then on he devoted his life to the cause of the Reformation in England, Geneva and Scotland. His "First Blast of The Trumpet against the Monstrous Regiment of Women" (1558) is primarily directed against Mary Queen of Scots. His "History of the Reformation . . . in Scotland" (1586) is a valuable though, of course, not unbiased document.

Kochanowski, Jan
Polish poet (1530-1584).

Born in Sycyn, died in Czarnolas. Educated at Cracow and Padua, traveled widely in Europe and was a courtier and favorite of King Sigismund II until he retired in 1575 to his farm in Czarnolas. Kochanowski lifted the Polish language from an uncouth state into an instrument capable of expressing the finest feelings of a Renaissance man. His tragedy "The Dismissal of the Greek Envoys," on a Homeric theme, is the first Polish drama worthy of the name. But he excelled as a lyric poet, be it the gay "Trifles" or the sublimely tragic "Laments" (1580) for his favorite daughter Urszula.

Koerner, Theodor
German poet and dramatist (1791-1813).

Born in Dresden; died in battle at Gadebusch in Mecklenburg. His poem, "Lyre and Sword," and his dramatic works, were both published posthumously in 1814. They are written in a spirit of romantic nationalism, which made him join the fight against Napoleon.

Koestler, Arthur

Hungarian-Jewish novelist (born 1905).

Born in Budapest, studied at Vienna University. Went to Berlin, became a noted journalist. Hitler and other circumstances drove him to Communism, and he spent a couple of years in Russia in the thirties. Then moved to England, covered the Spanish Civil War for an English newspaper, was caught by Franco forces, condemned to death but later released. His novels, written in English, mirror our "age of anxiety," a phrase Koestler coined. The most powerful of them is "Darkness at Noon" (1940), a fictional version of the Moscow purges.

Kolbenheyer, Erwin Guido

German writer (born 1878).

Born in Budapest. Lyric poet, dramatist, and story teller, won many literary prizes and was one of the few major German writers to take a positive attitude to the Nazi regime. His chief work is a novel in three volumes, "Paracelsus" (1917-25), on the life of the mystical scientist of the Renaissance.

Kollar, Jan

Slovak poet (1793-1852).

Born in Mosovce, died in Vienna. A Protestant who studied theology in Bratislava and Jena (1817-19) where he was much influenced by Herder and a German girl whom he idealized as "Mina" and married in 1835. He became a Protestant minister in Budapest and in 1849 professor of archeology at Vienna. His poem "The Daughter of Slava" (various editions starting in 1824) though inspired by the German "Mina" became one of the main inspirations of Panslavism.

Komenski, Jan Amos
Czech philosopher and educator (1592-1670).

Born in Uhersky Brod, died in Amsterdam. Born of a family of Moravian Brethren, he became a minister in 1615 after theological studies in Germany. The Protestant defeat of 1620 sent him into exile during which he lived in many European countries including England. His religious writings include "The Labyrinth of the World" (1631) and "The Testament of the Dying Mother Unity of the Brethren" (1648). His pedagogical treatises, especially "The Gate of Languages" (1631) make him one of the great forerunners of modern education.

Korolenko, Vladimir Galaktionovich
Russian novelist (1853-1921).

Born in Zhitomir, died in Poltava. Of Polish-Ukrainian origin, his writing was influenced by Turgenev and Chekhov. Its main feature is a belief in humanity that left him undaunted even through years of exile in Northern Russia and Siberia. His sympathy goes out to the poor and the oppressed and he was populist in his outlook. But he also had the saving grace of a strong and gentle sense of humor. Attacked the Tsarist government for its misdeeds but rejected the Revolution because of its terrorism. Wrote: "Makar's Dream" (1883), "The Blind Musician" (1887) and "The Story of My Contemporary" (1907-10). Was widely read in the West of his day.

Koskenniemi, Veikko Antero
Finnish writer (born 1885).

Real name: Forsnaes. Born in Oulu. Professor at Abo University and chairman of the Finnish PEN Club. His poetry reflects his preoccupation with classical antiquity and Finnish nationalism. Wrote "Collected Poems" (1930), "Young Goethe" (1932), "New Poems" (1932).

Kotzebue, August Von
German dramatist (1761-1819).

Born in Weimar, died in Mannheim. Had an adventurous life in the Russian civil service, which included a spell in Siberia (1800-1); was killed by a German nationalist student who resented his pro-Russian attitude and his attacks on German students. Kotzebue was a hard-hitting critic, who fought against romanticism and did not hesitate to attack Goethe. Of his two hundred plays, the most popular are his comedies, which are still played on German stages. They include: "The Female Jacobin Club" (1791), "The Widow and the Horse" (1796), "The German Petty Bourgeois" (1803).

Krasinski, Count Zygmunt
Polish writer (1812-1859).

Born and died in Paris. Of noble Polish family. Studied at Warsaw University (1829-31), emigrated to Switzerland after the Polish Rising of 1830-31, returned to Poland in 1832. His Polish patriotism made him clash with his pro-Russian father, and his aristocratic views conflicted with those of the more democratic Polish patriots. Became one of the "Big Three" of Polish romanticism, with Mickiewicz and Slowacki (q.v.). An ardent Roman Catholic, his "Un-Divine Comedy" (1835) resolves the conflict between aristocracy and democracy by the victory of religion. His views on the social conflicts of the day anticipated those of Pope Leo XIII. Another play, "Irydion" (1836), celebrated the triumphs of Christianity over pagan Rome. His "Psalms of the Future" (1845) represent a turn to mysticism.

Kraszewski, Josef Ignacy
Polish writer (1812-1887).

Born in Warsaw. Best known for his historical novels, in a belated imitation of Walter Scott, including "Kordecki" (1852), about the heroic defense of Czesto-chowa monastery against the Swedes in the Seven-teenth Century, and "An Old Tale," about prehistoric Poland. Also wrote verse plays, and novels about con-temporary social problems.

Kraus, Karl
Austrian writer (1874-1936).

Born in Cziczin (Bohemia, now Czechoslovakia); died in Vienna. Lived most of his life in Vienna, where he became known as a biting satirist and editor of the magazine "Die Fackel" (The Torch) which spared no authority and no pretense. One of the most brilliant representatives of Austrian culture. He trans-lated Shakespeare's sonnets into German (1933). His deep pessimism found expression in his expressionist drama "The Last Days of Mankind" (1922). His last days were darkened by the rise of Hitler, which he dis-missed with the bitter epigram, "I can't think of any-thing funny about him."

Kreutzwald, Friedrich
Estonian poet and scholar (1803-1882).

Born in Joepere manor, died in Tartu. Teacher and physician, compiled the popular epic "Son of Kalevi" (1857-61) from folk songs under the influence of German romanticism and the Finnish literary re-vival.

Krige, Uys
South African writer (born 1910).

Born in Bonteboksvlei in the Cape Province, of Afrikaner stock. Writes poetry and dramas in Afri-kaans which are strongly lyrical and "modern." Served as war correspondent in Italy, was imprisoned by the Italians and escaped. Told the story of his escape in

"The Way Out" (1946). His work does not gloss over South African realities.

Krylov, Ivan Andreyevich
Russian poet (1768-1844).

Born in Moscow; died in Saint Petersburg. Worked as civil servant, journalist, and tutor, and from 1816 as librarian at the Imperial Public Library (till 1841). Made Imperial Councilor in 1830. Wrote his first comedy, "The Coffee House Hostess," at 16; followed it with a number of others. They were realistic and attacked various abuses, but they found no success with the public and earned him the enmity of influential people. Krylov found his true vein through translating La Fontaine's fables, which led him to writing fables of his own (various collections published 1809-43). Krylov's fables are practically unknown outside Russia, but they are classics of Russian literature. Moreover, they give clues to Russian national character that are so acute that they can usefully be applied to any analysis of Russian policy today.

Kuo Mo-jo
Chinese writer and politician (born 1893).

Born in Lo-shan, Sze-chuan province. Studied medicine in Japan, wrote poetry while there and founded the "Creation" literary society after he returned to China. Strongly involved in politics from his youth, he accompanied Chiang Kai-shek on his victorious advance, which he described in his "A Poet with the Northern Expedition." But he broke with Chiang and went to Japan, where he stayed until the Sino-Japanese War and published books on Chinese prehistory and archaeology. Embraced communism and is a much publicized figure in China today. Became Minister of Culture and Education in 1951, and has been in charge of cultural activities, especially of contacts with foreign countries. Important translator.

Kuprin, Alexander
Russian novelist (1870-1938).

Born at Narouchat; died in Leningrad. Emigrated after the Revolution, lived in exile (mostly Paris) until 1937, when he returned to Russia. A realist and naturalist, his novels and short stories deal with barracks, factories, and brothels. A moralist in his youth, he later became a pessimistic skeptic. Wrote: "The Duel" (1904), "The Pit" (1910), "The Wheel of Time" (1930), "Jeannette, Princess of Four States" (1933), "Stories" (twelve volumes, 1906-16).

Kurbski, Prince Andrei
Russian poet (1528-1583).

A favorite of Ivan the Terrible, deserted to Poland after a defeat in Livonia. From the security of his exile he exchanged letters with Ivan that contain some of the most serious arguments on the methods and necessity of Russian despotism.

Kuzmin, Mikhail
Russian poet (1875-1936).

Born at Yaroslav. A melancholy and aestheticizing decadent, whose poems are written in a symbolistic style. Wrote "Alexandrian Songs" (1900), "The Adventures of Aimé Leboeuf" (1908), "The Journeys of Sir John Fairfax Through Turkey and Other Notable Lands" (1910).

Kyd, Thomas
English dramatist (1558-1594).

Born and died in London. A friend of Marlowe and suspected of sympathy with his atheism. Said to have written a play on which Shakespeare based his "Hamlet," but which is lost. His fame rests on "The Spanish Tragedy" (1587), one of the bloodiest and most poetic of Elizabethan plays.

L

La Bruyere, Jean de

French writer (1645-1696).

Born in Paris; died in Versailles. Studied in Paris together with Racine, Bossuet, and Boileau. Lawyer by training; became, through Bossuet's patronage, tutor to Louis de Bourbon, grandson of the military leader Condé, and a prominent figure at the French court. In 1687 La Bruyere published his masterpiece, "The Characters," or, to give it its full title, "The Characters of Theophrastus, Translated From the Greek, Together With Characters and Habits of This Century." Later editions contained additional material. La Bruyere's work, written in a simple and impeccable French prose, was an immediate success. He takes a pessimistic view of human nature and of his fellow man.

La Fayette, Madame de

French novelist (1634-1693).

Born and died in Paris. Maiden name: Marie Madeleine Pioche de la Vergne; married François Mothier, Count of La Fayette, in 1655. Their home became a prominent salon, frequented by the literary lights of her time. Wrote a number of novels, including "The Princess of Montpensier" (1662), "Zayde" (1670), and "The Princess of Cleves" (1678)—her masterpiece, written under the influence of the "Portuguese Letters" of Mariana Alcoforado (q.v.), and generally considered a pioneering psychological novel.

La Fontaine, Jean de

French poet (1621-1695).

Born at Chateau-Thierry in the Champagne; died in Paris. His father was a forester, and La Fontaine exercised this profession for a brief time. But he soon deserted his post and his family and moved to Paris, where he became a friend of Racine, Moliere, and Boileau. Member of the French Academy after 1684. Best known for his "Fables" in twelve books. The first six were published in 1668 and dedicated to the Dauphin; the next five, published 1678-9, were prefaced with a eulogy to Madame de Montespan; the last, which came out in 1694, was dedicated to the Duke of Burgundy. The exquisite "Fables" are his chief title to glory as one of the great men of "The Age of Louis XIV." His sources were mainly Aesop and Phaedrus. But La Fontaine became, in turn, an influence on writers of fable the world over. Less known are his spicy "Contes" (Tales, 1664-74), his poems, and his opera libretti.

Laforet, Carmen

Spanish novelist (born 1920).

Born in Barcelona. Was taken to the Canary Islands at the age of 2, did not return to her native city until after the Civil War, to study at the University. Created a sensation with her first novel, "Nada" (1945) which won the Nadal Prize. It was a remarkably mature study of the disintegration of a family with some pungent descriptions of its Barcelona milieu. A second novel, "The Island and the Devil" is a sensitive study of adolescence in the Canary Islands.

Laforgue, Jules

French poet (1860-1887).

Born in Montevideo, Uruguay, died in Paris. Was for five years reader to the Empress Augusta of Germany, where he wrote most of his work including

"Complaints" (1885) and "The Fairy Council" (1886). But most influential were his free verse "Last Poems" (published 1890) from which English poets learned a good deal.

Lagerloef, Selma
Swedish writer (1858-1940).

Born and died in Marbacka in the province of Vaermland. Taught at a girl's school in Landskrona, 1885-95; then earned her living by writing. Won Nobel Prize in 1909; became in 1916 first woman member of the Swedish Academy. Novels include "Goesta Berling" (1891), "Tale of a Manor" (1899), "Jerusalem" (1901-2), "The Wonderful Journey of Nils Holgersson" (1907), "Anna Svaerd" (1928). Her novels are mostly evocations of Swedish history and of Sweden's countryside, written in the neoromantic mood.

Lagerquist, Per
Swedish novelist (born 1891).

Born in Vaexjoe of a peasant family. Wrote lyrical poems, romances, and essays; but best known for his novels. Expressionist in style. His outlook is determined by his sudden leap from the pious and conservative atmosphere of a small Swedish country town into cosmopolitan Stockholm, and by a crisis of cosmic dread induced by the coming of World War I. However, he moved from prostrating fear to a fighting and critical humanism. Won Nobel Prize for 1951. Wrote "Dread" (1916), "Chaos," (1919), "The Dwarf" (1944), "The Philosopher's Stone" (1947), and "Barabbas" his masterpiece (1950).

Lamartine, Alphonse de
French poet (1790-1869)

Born in Macon, of noble family; died in Paris. Officer of guards under Louis XVIII; quit service for reasons of health and devoted himself to writing. He became a leader of French romanticism with his "Poetic Meditations" of 1820. His strength lay in his fine language and descriptions of landscape, his love of God and nature. His chief weaknesses are sentimentality and superficiality. Published "New Poetic Meditations" (1823), "Political and Religious Harmonies" (1830). Disapproved of the July Revolution and of the regime of Louis Philippe; went on a journey to the Orient, about which he published a book in 1835. This was followed by two poems, "Jocelyn" (1836) and "The Revolt of an Angel" (1838). He greeted the February Revolution (1848) with enthusiasm and became Minister of Foreign Affairs in the Provisional Government. His humanistic exaltation reached its peak with "The Marseillaise of Peace," which he wrote at that time. Disillusioned with the coming to power of Louis-Napoleon, Bonaparte Lamartine withdrew to private life. He spent the last twenty years of his life in semi-retirement; published histories of the French Revolution and of the Girondin Party, and a book of memoirs.

Lamb, Charles

English essayist and critic (1775-1834).

Born and died in London. Educated at Christ's Hospital; worked as a clerk in India House (1792-1825). Lived in straitened circumstances, devoting himself to the care of his sister Mary Ann, who killed their invalid mother in a fit of insanity. Lamb himself was confined in an asylum for several months (1795-6). Friend of Coleridge, Leigh Hunt, and Godwin. Chief works: "Tales From Shakespeare" (1807-8), written with Mary Ann for Godwin's Juvenile Library, and the twenty-five "Essays of Elia" (two series, printed in 1823 and 1833). A man of gentle character, he has remained one of England's best-loved writers.

Landor, Walter Savage

English writer (1775-1864).

Born in Warwick, died in Florence. His poem "Gebir" (1798) won him the friendship of Southey; his lyrics were much praised by Wordsworth. Modern criticism has not always endorsed their enthusiasm. This also applies to his "Imaginary Conversations" (1824-29) written in a prose that is as ornate as the language of his poems is simple.

Langland, William

English poet (about 1332-about 1400).

Little is known of his life. Said to have been born in the West Midlands and lived in London. His "Vision of Piers Plowman" (variously dated from 1370 to 1398) is an allegorical and satirical poem with strong overtones of mysticism.

Lanier, Sidney

American poet and musician (1842-1881).

Born in Macon, Georgia, died in Lynn, N. C. Spent four years in the Confederate Army in the Civil War, died of tuberculosis he contracted at the time. Wrote "Poems" (1877); "Tiger Lily" (1877), a novel about the Civil War on the lines of Walter Scott; "The Science of English Verse" (1880) about the relation of poetry and music. His own verse, intensely musical, is the best literary production of the American South until its present literary renascence.

Lao She

Chinese writer (born 1896).

Pen name of Shu Ch'ing-Ch'un. Born in Peking. Leading satirist, turned patriotic in the Sino-Japanese War. Became president of the Writers League of China and wrote a successful novel about life in Japanese-occupied Peking. Best-known for his poignant "Rikshaw Boy" (1937).

Lao Tze

Chinese philosopher (about 634-531 B.C.).

Said to have been born in Honan province in North China and to have led a wandering life; but his very existence is doubted by many Chinese scholars. Reputed author of "Tao Te King" (The Book of the Way) and of Taoism, which started as an anarchist philosophy and developed into a popular religion. Taoism came close to becoming an established church; it exercised a strong influence on the more aesthetic aspects of Chinese culture, especially poetry and painting. According to the researches of Joseph Needham, it is also at the root of the Chinese scientific tradition. Throughout Chinese history, Lao Tze—or the book ascribed to him—acted as counterpoise to the authoritarianism of Confucius and his followers.

Lardner, Ring

American writer (1885-1933).

Born in Niles, Michigan, died in East Hampton, Long Island. Worked as reporter, specializing in baseball, whose slang he raised to literary status. He was also an acute critic of the shallower aspects of the "Jazz Age" in his stories collected in "How to Write Short Stories" (1924) and "The Love Nest" (1926).

La Rochefoucauld, Duke Francois de

French writer (1613-1680).

Member of one of France's most distinguished families. Intrigued against Cardinal Richelieu and joined the rising of the Fronde against his successor, Cardinal Mazarin. Treated the French monarchy, even that of Louis XIV, with an aristocratic disdain. Frequented literary circles in Paris, but was not a favorite at court. Best known for his collection of brilliant and cynical epigrams, "Reflections," which he published anonymously in 1665. Also wrote "Memoirs on the Regency of Anne of Austria" (1665).

Larra, Mariano Jose de

Spanish writer and journalist (1809-1837).

Born and died in Madrid. Educated in France, came back to Spain and became a brilliant journalist under the pen name of "Figaro." In the best romantic style, committed suicide by shooting himself in front of a mirror following an unhappy love affair. Wrote a novel and play on Macias the Lover, a medieval Galician troubadour. But Larra transcends romanticism as penetrating and relentless analyst of Spanish reality. To his bitter question "Where is Spain?", he answered even more bitterly: "Here lies half of Spain. Killed by the other half." With Larra begins the modern self-analysis of Spain.

Larreta, Enrique Rodriguez

Argentine novelist (born 1875).

Born in Buenos Aires. A cosmopolitan figure, fully at home in the great capitals of Europe. His "Glory of Don Ramiro" (1908) is a remarkable tour de force, a re-creation of Spanish life in the days of Philip II, written in an archaizing language that renders the flavor of the period. The patrician author characteristically revealed that he learned his Spanish from the Spanish servant girls employed in his parents' home. His second novel, "Zogoibi" (1926), an exercise on the gaucho theme, is much weaker.

Lasker-Schueler, Else

German Jewish poetess (1876-1945).

Born in Elberfeld, died in Jerusalem. Took leading part in the expressionist movement at the turn of the century. Her verse is a blend of stark realism and oriental fantasy. She expressed strong Hebraist convictions in ecstatic language. Spent her last years in Palestine. Wrote: "Hebraic Ballads" (1913); "My Blue Piano" (1943) etc.

Laube, Heinrich
German dramatist (1806-1884).

Born at Sprotten in Silesia; died in Vienna. Acted from 1850 to 1867 as manager of the Vienna Burgtheater, later managed other theatres in Vienna and Leipzig. Wrote novels, short stories, and dramas, mostly historical; e.g., "Struensee" (1847), "The Pupils of the Charles Academy" (1847, his best-known play, about Schiller's schooldays); "Essex" (1856). Wrote an important biography of Grillparzer (q.v.).

Lautreamont, Count
French poet (1847-1870).

Pen name of Isidor Ducasse, born in Montevideo, died in Paris. His prose epic "The Song of Maldoror" (published in 1890) is "diabolic," Byronic and obscene and makes him a precursor of surrealism.

Lavater, Johann Kaspar
Swiss writer (1741-1801).

Born and died in Zurich; Protestant pastor there after 1775. Religious mystic, opponent of the Enlightenment, wrote poems—"Swiss Songs" (1767)—and hymns. Friend of Herder and Goethe, whom he influenced. At one time had European fame as father of the so-called science of physiognomy, which explained a man's character by physiological signs, especially head bumps. Lavater expounded it in his "Physiognomical Fragments to Foster the Love and Knowledge of Mankind" (1775-84, four volumes).

Lawrence, David Herbert
English novelist (1885-1930).

Born in Eastwood, Nottinghamshire, died in Vence, Southern France. Son of a miner, remained conscious all through his life of his working-class and "lowly" origin. His mother encouraged him to study and he

265

became teacher at an elementary school. His short stories were published and he was encouraged by some established writers like Ford Madox Ford (q.v.) and Edward Garnett. His "Sons and Lovers" (1913) based on his family and emotional tangles established him as a novelist; but he never established a satisfactory relationship with his countrymen, and tended to behave like a working-class Byron. During World War I he was expelled from Cornwall because of his unorthodox views; two of his novels were banned in England as "indecent" and he spent most of his last years abroad, mostly in Italy and New Mexico. Lawrence has two reputations: one, a very wide one, as writer of pornographic stories, and another, confined to a narrower but more discerning number of readers, as the Western novelist who discovered the primitive. The first is based, almost exclusively on "Lady Chatterley's Lover" and its censorship troubles. The second, more solid for all of Lawrence's slapdash writing, on books like "Kangaroo" (1923) and "The Plumed Serpent" (1926) that introduced many people to Australia and Mexico respectively—not always, it must be added, with happy results.

Lawrence, Thomas Edward

English writer and soldier (1885-1935).

Born in Tremadoc, Wales, died in Bovington Camp Hospital following a motorcycle accident. Studied at Oxford, and became intoxicated, like so many of his countrymen, with the Arab world during a journey to gather material for his thesis on Crusaders' castles in Syria. During World War I, as British intelligence officer, organized the "Arab Revolt" and became "Lawrence of Arabia." His experiences—and subsequent disappointments about Arab developments—deeply upset him and he sought a new and anonymous existence as "Aircraftsman T. E. Shaw of the Royal Air Force." His "Seven Pillars of Wisdom" (1935) tells of his war-time exploits in a powerful, strange and sensitive—perhaps over-sensitive—manner.

Lawson, Henry
Australian writer (1867-1922).

Born near Grenfell, New South Wales, died in Sydney. His short stories introduced life in the Australian "bush," i.e. back country, to literature, with emphasis on its harsher aspects. His later life was made unhappy by drink, though he never quite lost his perspective—"beer makes you feel as you should feel without beer," he said. He was turned into Australia's national writer and was given posthumous homage by many people who would have turned up their noses at him when he was alive.

Laxness, Halldor
Icelandic novelist (born 1902).

Born in Reykjavik. Moved from religious enthusiasm to a socialism bordering on Communism. Received Nobel Prize in 1955 both for the considerable literary merits of his work, and as an expression of the Geneva spirit of coexistence. A great traveller, but he was the first modern writer to present the realities of Icelandic life in his novels. They are written in a rhapsodic style, and include "A Child of Nature" (1919), "The Russian Adventure" (1930), "Salka Valke" (1935), "An Independent People" (1934-5).

Lear, Edward
English poet (1812-1888).

Born in London, died in San Remo, Italy. A painter and illustrator who spent most of his life travelling. Founder of English nonsense verse with "The Book of Nonsense" (1846); "Nonsense Songs" (1871) and "More Nonsense" (1871). Lear was also responsible for another English institution—the limerick, which he popularized though he did not invent.

Leconte de Lisle, Charles

French writer (1818-1894).

Born on the island of Reunion, son of a French sugar planter, died in Louveciennes. His poetry is Parnassian, cool and classical; but his tales of horror occasionally surpass those of Poe as inducers of shudders, e.g. "The Torture of Hope."

Lee Hou-Chu

(Chinese, 937-978).

King of the South T'ang Kingdom in the time of the Ten Kingdoms, and greatest poet of his time. His administration, more devoted to arts than wars, fell easily to Sung Emperor. Great lover of music, women and Buddhism. Master of the *tzu,* a song set to a definite tune.

Le Fort, Gertrud Von

German writer (born 1876).

Born at Minden in Westphalia of a family descended from French Huguenot emigrants. One of Germany's leading Catholic writers. Her themes are religious, historical, and feminine, her tendencies mystical and neoromantic. Excels in both prose and verse. Chief works: "Hymns to the Church" (1924), "Hymns to Germany" (1932), "The Pope From the Ghetto" (1930), "The Eternal Woman" (1934), "Our Road Through the Night" (1949).

Leibniz, Baron Gottfried Wilhelm Von

German philosopher (1646-1716).

Born in Leipzig; died in Hanover. Educated at Leipzig, Jena, and Altdorf. Worked for the Archbishop of Mainz from 1667 to 1676, and for the Duke of Brunswick as librarian and privy councilor from 1676 to his death. Spent four years in Paris (1672-6) and visited London (1673); maintained a lifelong correspondence with many European savants; suggested to Elector Frederick III the foundation of the Prussian Academy in Berlin (1700). Leibniz was a universal genius who excelled in mathematics, natural science, philosophy, theology, history, law, politics, etc. His philosophy was based on his hypotheses of monads (independent spiritual entities) and of preestablished harmony. His optimism, which made him proclaim that everything was for the best in the best of all possible worlds, was ridiculed by Voltaire in Candide. His theological views, embodied in "Theodicee" (1705) and "Theological System" (not published until 1819), aimed at reconciling Catholicism and Protestantism. He also championed a united Europe and its expansion overseas. He favored a "Universal language" for all humanity. His outstanding scientific achievement was his codiscovery, with Newton, of the calculus. Leibniz published his results first, and the question of priority led to long controversy. Leibniz' influence was at its peak during the Enlightenment, but it is only now that some of his achievements are fully appreciated, e.g. his substitution of a "logic of relations" for Aristotle's "logic of chance."

Lenau, Nikolaus

German writer (1802-1850).

Real name: Nikolaus Niembsch von Strehlenau. Born in Csanad (Hungary); died in Vienna. Studied at Vienna, Bratislava, and Heidelberg; became friendly with leading German and Austrian writers of his day. Melancholy and unrest made him emigrate to the United States in 1832 but he soon returned to Europe, a deeply disappointed man. A hopeless love deepened his melancholy and he went insane in

1844. His lyrical and epic poetry express his deeply-torn character. Wrote "Poems" (1832), "Faust" (1836), "Savonarola" (1838), "New Poems" (1838), "The Albigensians" (1843), "Poems" (1844).

Leon, Luis de
Spanish religious writer (1527-1591).

Born in Belmonte, died in Madrigal. An Augustinian monk who studied and taught at Salamanca. Got into trouble with the authorities on suspicion of Judaism and was jailed for several years. He started the first lecture after his return with the classical remark: "As we were saying yesterday . . ." Wrote commentaries on various Old Testament books and poetical translations of the Psalms, the book of Job and The Song of Songs.

Leonov, Leonid Maximovich
Russian novelist (born 1899).

Born in Polukhino. Became member of the "Serapion Brotherhood" in 1922. Started writing under influence of Dostoyevski. Later developed an elaborate style which reveals reality by half-concealing it. His "Badgers" (1925) and "Thief" (1926) still deserve to be read, but he never reached this level again.

Leopardi, Count Giacomo
Italian poet (1798-1837).

Born in Recanati in Central Italy; died in Naples. Led a profoundly unhappy life, suffered from physical deformities and chronic ailment, had very unhappy relationship with his father and an even unhappier love affair. Classical scholar, wrote on classical philology. His enthusiasm for a free and united Italy inspired his first work, the patriotic poem "To Italy" (1819). The most marked feature both of his character and his work is a deep and brooding melancholy. Also wrote "On Dante's Monument" (1818), "Poems" (1824), "Songs" (1836).

Lermontov, Mikhail

Russian writer (1814-1841).

Born in Moscow; died at Pyatigorsk in the Caucasus. Studied at the Military Academy; after graduation became officer in a guards cavalry regiment. Published "The Masquerade" in 1834-5, became one of the literary circle around Pushkin, whom he greatly admired. After Pushkin's death in a duel (1837), published an ode which blamed the rottenness of the Tsarist regime for driving Pushkin to his death. Tsar Nicholas I judged the ode subversive. Lermontov was court-martialled, expelled from the guards and assigned to a line regiment in the Caucasus. This proved a blessing in disguise, for he was able to discover the beauties of the Caucasus, which later attracted other Russian writers, including Tolstoy. Lermontov used the Caucasian setting in his romantic poem "The Demon" and "Mtsyri" (1840). He also wrote "A Hero of Our Time" (1839), chronologically the first "Russian novel," published three years before Gogol's "Dead Souls." Its hero is the "problematic man" that was to dominate the Russian novel till Gorki. But, unlike Gogol and like Pushkin, Lermontov had practically no influence outside Russia—possibly because he was too Russian to be assimilated. Like his hero, Pushkin, he died in a duel.

Lesage, Alain Rene

French writer (1688-1747).

Born at Sarzeau in Brittany; died in Boulogne. A lawyer, practicing in Paris, who left the law for literature. Modelled his writing on Spanish models, especially on picaresque novels. Chief Works: "The Limping Devil" (1707), "Turcaret" (1709), "Gil Blas" (1715-35).

Leskov, Nikolai Semyonovich

Russian writer (1831-1895).

Born at Gorokhov in Orel Province; died in Saint Petersburg. Began as feuilletonist and short story writer; developed into a novelist. Practically unknown in the West, Leskov created some of the best descriptions of life in Old Russia, especially among the Orthodox clergy, in his novel "The Cathedral Clergy" (1872). His stories are realistic and his outlook traditionalist. One of the best stylists of the Russian language. Also wrote: "The Bewitched Pilgrim" (1873); "Pavlin" (1875); "At the End of the World" (1875); "Self-Love" (1887); "Old Christian Legends."

Lessing, Gotthold Ephraim

German writer and critic (1729-1781).

Born at Kamenz in Saxony; died in Brunswick. Studied at Leipzig University, moved to Berlin in 1758, where he became a journalist. Published, with Nikolai and Moses Mendelssohn (q.v.), the "Letters Concerning the Latest Literature" (1759-1765), a landmark of the Enlightenment. Lessing had already expressed his rationalist and progressive views in "The Young Scientist" (1747) and "The Freethinker" (1749). He wrote a plea for Jewish emancipation in the best Eighteenth Century spirit in "The Jews" (1749). His growing interest in the theater led him to accept the post of artistic manager of the Hamburg Theatre (1767-70). He had already written the first German bourgeois tragedy, on the English model, "Miss Sarah Sampson" (1755), and the classic German comedy, "Minna Von Barnhelm" (1767), one of the first literary expressions of the Prussian Spirit, based on his experiences as secretary to General Tauentzien (1760-5). His term at Hamburg revolutionized the German theater, because he favored the English drama against the prevailing French. He was one of the first Europeans to reach a full appreciation of the greatness of Shakespeare, in his dramatic criticism, published as the "Hamburg Dramaturgy" (1767-9). He also wrote a dramatic fragment on the Faust legend (1759); "Emilia Galotti" (1772), another "Bourgeois tragedy": and "Nathan the Wise" (1779), a noble plea for religious toleration. Toward the end of his life, Lessing became more and more interested in questions of aesthetics, and his "Laocoon or the Borders of Painting and Poetry" (1767), a repudiation of Winckelmann's classicism and a plea for a more expressive art, transcended the aesthetic limits of the Enlightenment. Lessing died as librarian to the Duke of Brunswick-Wolffenbuettel, a post hc oc cupied from 1770.

Levi, Carlo

Italian painter and writer (born 1902).

Born in Turin. Exiled to a remote part of Southern Italy for anti-Fascist activities, he wrote "Christ Stopped at Eboli" (1946), a book that discovered the Italian South for the foreign reader—and for many Italian readers. His "Watch" (1950) is a novel of postwar Italy, concerned with tracing the disappearance of the hopes and achievements of the war-time resistance movement.

Lewis, Cecil Day

English poet (born 1904).

Born in Ballintogher, Ireland. Was associated with W. H. Auden and Stephen Spender as one of a trio that tried to "modernize" English poetry and adapt it to the spirit of the time. Wrote "A Time to Dance" (1935) and "Overtures to Death" (1938). Successful writer of detective stories under pseudonym of "Nicholas Blake."

Lewis, Sinclair

American novelist (1885-1951).

Born in Sauk Center, Minnesota, son of a country doctor; died in Rome. Studied at Yale, then moved to New York, where he worked as journalist, editor, and publishing executive, with a short spell at the Utopian colony of Helicon Hall, organized by Upton Sinclair (q.v.) across the Hudson in New Jersey. Wrote many potboiler stories for magazines, and four novels of mediocrity tempered with promise, and finally got into stride with "Main Street" (1920), a novel which marked a new era in American letters. To his contemporaries, it was primarily an attack on "the village virus," but the novel had more dimensions: It embodied a critical view of the whole American civilization as it manifested itself in the Midwestern village —and the heroine who tried to reform it. Lewis followed "Main Street" with five books in the same vein, dealing with different aspects of American reality: "Babbitt" (1922), the story of a businessman whose name became a symbol; "Arrowsmith" (1925), the novel of a doctor, but also a critique of the relations between science and society; "Elmer Gantry" (1927), a bitter attack on the sordid side of religion; "The Man Who Knew Coolidge" (1928), a literary tour de force written as a long salesman's monologue; "Dodsworth," (1929), an evaluation of the relations between Europe and America. After "Dodsworth" there was a sharp break in Lewis' literary inspiration, parallel to a serious crisis in his personal life. After several years' silence, he wrote a number of books which reveal a decline, but have occasional flashes of greatness; e.g., "Ann Vickers" (1933), a study of the American emancipated woman; "It Can't Happen Here" (1935), a deep and often bitter analysis of American society. He then got a literary second wind, and wrote some books which, while nowhere near the level of the series inaugurated by "Main Street," showed a renewed satirical bite; "Gideon Planish" (1943), on organized philanthropy; "Cass Timberlane" (1945), an analysis of the American marriage; "Kingsblood Royal" (1945), a savage attack on race prejudice; "The Godseeker," a return to his Minnesotan roots. His last novel, "World So Wide," once more sets America against Europe. Lewis excelled as a social critic and satirist, and as an analyzer of American society and social realities. He continued the work of Mark Twain in turning America's common speech into a literary language; but his main deficiencies were aesthetic. He became, in the 1930's, the first American writer to win the Nobel Prize. Today, he is perhaps more appreciated abroad than in his native land, where he is overshadowed by the Faulkner-Hemingway school.

Lichtenberg, Georg Christoph

German writer and critic (1742-1799).

Born at Ober-Ramstadt in Hesse; died in Sachtingen, where he was professor of physics. Best known for his "Aphorisms," published posthumously in four volumes (1802-8), which offer some penetrating insights into the human mind.

Liliencron, Detlau Von

German poet (1844-1909).

Born at Kiel; died at Alt-Rahlstaedt near Hamburg. Officer in German army; took part in campaigns of 1866 and 1870-1; emigrated to the United States, then returned to Germany. Lived in great poverty, was rescued from it by literary pension granted by Kaiser Wilhelm II on his 60th birthday. His poetry hovers between naturalism and impressionism. Wrote: "Rides of a Military Aide" (1884); "Poems" (1889); "Life and Lies" (1908); "Last Harvest" (1909).

Lillo, George
English playwright (1693-1739).

Born and died in London. Wrote ballads, opera librettos and "The Merchant of London" (1731), the first "bourgeois tragedy," much imitated in England and on the Continent.

Lindsay, Vachel
American poet (1879-1931).

Born and died in Springfield, Illinois. Studied art, then went on long vagabond tours through the southern and eastern United States, distributing his pamphlet "Rhymes to Be Traded for Bread." Gained national fame with his "General William Booth Enters Heaven" (1913). Lindsay is one of the populist poets who became the nostalgic bards of the rural and small-town Middle West. They saw its passing— and regretted it.

Lin Ho-ching
(Chinese, 967-1028).

A rustic word painter of the Sung Period. Received classical Chinese education. Due to delicate health, retired to home in the country. Also a skillful painter, fond of plum trees. Poetry simple, serene, refined.

Lin Yu-T'ang
Chinese writer (born 1895).

Born in Ch'ang-chou, Fukien province. Became a Christian and studied at Saint John's University, Shanghai. After teaching English at Tsinghua University, studied philology at Harvard and Leipzig. Returned to teach at Peking National University (1923-26). Became editor of various magazines which often criticized conditions in China. In the thirties started writing in English, and wrote three books which have done much to explain his country to the world: "My Country and My People" (1935) a general introduction; "The Importance of Living" (1937), an exposition of Chinese philosophy and outlook on life; "Moment in Peking" (1939), a novel.

Li Po
Chinese poet (701-762).

Born, according to most sources, at Sujab in Sinkiang (or, according to some, in Szechuen province); died in Tang-tu near Nanking, by drowning in a drunken effort to embrace the moon in the Yellow River. Generally considered the greatest of all Chinese poets. Led a wandering and dissipated life, sponged on his relatives, and spent many years at the court of the Tang emperor Ming Huang. Friend of many distinguished contemporaries, and member of a group of talented and bibulous intellectuals who called themselves "The Eight Immortals of the Wine Cup." Known for long in Europe as "Li Tai Po," and called "The Chinese Anacreon." His lyrical poems are noted for the exquisite simplicity of their language, the wealth of their imagery, and the lightness of their cadences. They contain descriptions of natural scenery, reports of official and religious ceremonies, evocations of pleasure parties, personal tributes to friends, especially absent ones, and so on. Like most Chinese poets of his time, Li Po's inspiration was Taoist rather than Confucian.

List, Jacob
American writer and educator (born 1895).

Born in New York, educated at Syracuse University. Chief works, "Education for Living" (1961) "Living One Day at a Time" (1962), containing a philosophy for living based on his forty years' experience as an educator and guidance counselor.

Liu Chi

(Chinese, 1311-1375).

Most celebrated poet of the Mongol Period. Court adviser of first Ming Emperor. Prolific poet and author of philosophic dialogues. Poems distinguished by charm and feeling for beauty rather than by depth.

Livy

Roman historian (about 59 B.C.-17 A.D.).

Full name: Titus Livius. Born and died in Padua. Did not engage in active politics, but became a partisan of Augustus and his reforms. It was under this inspiration and on the model of the great Greek historians that he wrote his "Annals of the Roman People," a history of Rome in 142 volumes from the foundation of the city to the death of Drusus (9 B.C.). Of these, books 1 through 10 and 21 through 45 are extant, as well as fragments and epitomes of all but two of the others.

Locke, John

English philosopher (1632-1704).

Born at Wrington, Somerset; died at Oates. Lecturer in Greek, rhetoric, and philosophy. Was at first under the influence of Aristotle and the Scholastics, but soon turned to the philosophy of Bacon and Descartes and became the true founder of modern Anglo-Saxon empiricism, which swept the Western world in the Eighteenth Century. Locke was a tolerant deist and expressed his views in two essays, "An Essay on Toleration" (1667) and "The Reasonableness of Christianity" (1695). Took an active part in English politics of the Restoration as advisor and tutor to Anthony Ashley Cooper, later Lord Shaftesbury. Among the work he did for Cooper was drafting the constitution of the Colony of Carolina. Accused of complicity in Shaftesbury's plot, Locke had to flee to Holland in 1684. Returned to England after the Glorious Revolution of 1688; became its official spokesman and ideologist for the victorious Whigs. Became Commissioner of Appeal and adviser on coinage to the government. It was then that he wrote his most influential works: "An Essay Concerning Human Understanding" (1690), an analysis of morality and the limitations of human understanding of it, and "Two Treatises of Government" (1690), an apology for parliamentary monarchy on the Whig pattern. Locke's views were even more popular in America than in his native country and in Europe: the American Constitution is fundamentally Lockean, and philosophical observers like professor F. S. C. Northrop still analyze the American character in Lockean terms.

Loennrot, Elias
Finnish poet and scholar (1802-1884).

Born and died in Sammati. A physician by profession. Founded Finnish Literary Society in 1831 and crowned his life's work as collector of folklore by compiling the folk epic Kalevala (1835-49). This not only inspired Finnish writers and artists but also had a considerable echo abroad, including Longfellow's "Hiawatha."

Logau, Friedrich Von
German writer (1604-1655).

Born at Brockrut in Silesia; died at Liegnitz. Baroque poet, in the service of the Duke of Brieg. A deeply religious man and a moralist, best known for his rhymed epigrams, published in 1638 and 1654 under the pen name of "Salomon Von Golaw."

Lohenstein, Daniel Kaspar Von
German poet and dramatist (1635-1683).

Born at Nimptsch in Silesia; died in Breslau. The

German baroque reached the peak of its excesses in his poems and plays, mostly on Oriental subjects; e.g. "Ibrahim" (1653), "Cleopatra" (1661).

Lomonosov, Mikhail Vasilievich

Russian scientist and writer (1711-1765).

Born in Denisovka near Archangelsk, died in Saint Petersburg. A fisherman's son, went to Moscow to study at 19, lived there in great poverty. In 1736 was at the University of Marburg. Was forcibly enrolled in a Prussian regiment but escaped to Russia in 1741. A few years later he became professor of chemistry and member of the Academy of Sciences. He was a universal genius and excelled in many sciences. Was instrumental in founding Russia's first university in Moscow (1755). It was not without reason that the critic Belinsky called him the father of Russian literature: in addition to an epic on Peter the Great and 24 odes, he reformed Russian prosody, set up three styles—grand, middle and low—and practically founded modern Russian prose.

London, Jack

American novelist (1876-1916).

Real name: John Griffith. Born in San Francisco, died on his farm in Glen Ellen, California. Worked as sailor, lived for several years as hobo and waterfront loafer (1891-4). Became a Socialist, was arrested after a soapbox speech. Decided to educate himself and to become a writer. Spent a year at high school and some months at the University of California. Went to Klondike during the Gold Rush (1897-8), made good literary use of his experiences there. Began by writing stories for magazines, had no success at first and lived through grim months of hunger and cold. Persevered and became the most popular and best-paid magazine writer in America (1898-1900). In the next sixteen years, London produced 43 books and much miscellaneous work, necessarily of uneven value. Among the best are the books inspired by his life on the sea and in the Klondike, written in a lively "red-blooded" style and including "The Call of the Wild" (1903), "The Sea Wolf" (1904), and "White Fang" (1907). Two of his books stand apart: "The Iron Heel," a forecast of a Fascist regime, and "Martin Eden" (1909), a thinly disguised autobiography. London's Darwinian and Nietzschean views and his combination of Socialism and Anglo-Saxon racism were very popular in America at one time; today he is hardly read in his native land, except in school anthologies. He is still amazingly popular in Europe, especially east of the Iron Curtain: "The Iron Heel" is a best-seller in the Soviet Union, and a poll of Polish students in 1956 revealed Martin Eden as their most popular foreign hero.

Longfellow, Henry Wadsworth
American poet (1807-1882).

Born in Portland, Maine; died in Cambridge, Massachusetts. Studied at Bowdoin College, graduated in 1825, went on a study trip to Europe (Spain, France, Holland, Germany) and returned to America to become professor of modern languages at the age of 20. Taught at Bowdoin (1829-35) and Harvard (1835-54). From 1854 devoted himself entirely to his writing. His literary reputation was established by his "Ballads and Other Poems" and "Poems on Slavery," both published in 1841. Later he wrote narrative and dramatic verse. Chief works: "Evangeline" (1847), "Song of Hiawatha" (1857), "Tales of a Wayside Inn" (1865-73), and masterly translations of Goethe and Dante. Longfellow was the favorite poet of the rising American bourgeoisie, which greatly enjoyed the simplicity, optimism, and sentimentality of his verse. For the same reasons he also enjoyed a wide popularity in Europe. Today his poetic fame is at an exceedingly low ebb, especially in his native land, but this may merely be the prelude to a revival. Some of his poems, like "The Midnight Ride of Paul Revere," are still the perennial favorites of children.

Lope de Vega

Spanish dramatist and poet (1562-1635).

Full name: Felix Lope de Vega Carpio. Born and died in Madrid. Had a gay and dissipated youth; was banished from Castile in 1588 as the result of a duel. Served in the Spanish Armada and became secretary to the Duke of Alba. Became exceedingly pious in his old age; was ordained priest in 1614 and became doctor of theology in 1627. A man of prodigious productivity, he founded the Spanish national drama by writing some 1800 plays (other estimates go as high as 3000), of which 481 are extant (another count is 468). Was known, already in his lifetime, as "The Phoenix of Spain." Chief plays: "Fuenteovejuna," "The Mayor of Zalamea," "Trust Unto Death," "The Best Mayor Is the King." Also wrote a pastoral novel "Dorotea," an epic after the manner of Tasso, sonnets, prose romances, etc. The quality of Lope's output is necessarily uneven; its quantity makes a certain degree of superficiality inevitable. But Lope at his best is both good and deep, and his "Fuenteovejuna," for example, is not only still played today the world over, but is also one of the best expressions of the Spanish national character. Lope was also an excellent technician of the drama: He introduced the comic character "gracioso" and was a master of dialogue. Today his fame is as firmly established as ever and his petty squabbles with his contemporaries, including Cervantes, are mercifully forgotten.

Lorenzo the Magnificent

Italian poet (1449-1492).

Full name: Lorenzo de' Medici. Born and died in Florence, a city which he ruled after the death of his father Piero. Great patron of arts and artists, including Michelangelo. Fostered Italian letters by acting as patron of the Platonic Academy and of the Florentine Library. He thus helped to establish the Tuscan dialect as the literary language of Italy. His own prose and poetry mingled classical and popular inspirations. In his own time, his carnival songs were best remembered; today he chiefly lives as the author of a small poetic gem, a quatrain on the passing of youth.

Loti, Pierre

French novelist (1850-1923).

Pen name of Louis Viaud. Born in Rochefort, died in Hendaye. Naval officer, retired in 1910 with rank of captain, returned to service in World War I. His novels, based on his traveling experiences, made him one of the founders of modern exoticism: not only French, but many European readers learned about faraway countries from his books. Thus, he discovered Turkey for them in "Aziyade" (1879), Polynesia in "The Marriage of Loti" (1886) and Japan in "Madame Chrysanthemum" (1887). Closer at home, he did the same thing for Brittany in "The Iceland Fisherman" (1886) and the Basque country in "Ramuntcho" (1897).

Lowell, Amy

American poetess (1874-1925).

Born and died in Brookline, Mass. Born of a wealthy and cultured Boston Brahmin family, she was educated by private tutors and traveled a good deal abroad. In England she met Ezra Pound and started the imagist movement on the basis of her theories.

Her verses, which include "A Dome of Many-Colored Glass" (1912) and "Sword Blades and Poppy Seed" (1914) were as formidable as her appearance.

Lowell, James Russell
American writer (1819-1891).

Born and died in Cambridge, Mass. Of a Boston Brahmin family, was educated at Harvard where he taught modern languages for over 30 years. Was first editor of the "Atlantic Monthly" and U.S. Minister to Spain. Wrote poetry and "The Biglow Papers" (1848) which has been called "the high point of Yankee humor."

Loyola, Inigo or Ignatius de
Spanish religious writer (1491-1556).

Born at the family castle of Loyola in the Basque country, of which the tower is incorporated in the basilica built in his honor; died in Rome. Page in service of Ferdinand the Catholic; became soldier under the Duke of Najera. Severely wounded in the siege of Pamplona (1521), had a deep religious experience on his sickbed, and decided to dedicate himself thenceforth to the service of God. Spent some months as an ascetic in the wilderness, made a barefoot pilgrimage to Jerusalem (1523-4), and started his education at a grammar school at the age of 33. Studied at the Universities of Salamanca and Paris. It was in Paris (1534) that he decided to found the Society (or Company) of Jesus, dedicated to the conversion of infidels and the defense of Roman Catholicism against the onslaughts of the Reformation. After some initial difficulties, obtained approval of his order by the Pope (1540), and became its first general. Canonized in 1622. Wrote two classics of religious literature, the "Constitution" of the Jesuit Order and the "Spiritual Exercises" (1521-2), the latter remarkable for its psychological insights.

Lucan

Roman poet (39-65).

Full name: Marcus Annaeus Lucanus. Born in Cordoba, Spain; died in Rome. A poet who, in spite of his Republican views, enjoyed at one time the favor of Nero. But as his literary reputation grew, Nero became jealous of him and finally forbade public recitals of his poems. Joined the conspiracy of Piso against Nero, was betrayed and condemned to death. Escaped execution by suicide. His sole surviving work is the epic poem in ten books, "Pharsalia," celebrating not the victory of Caesar at Pharsalus, but the defeat of his Republican opponents. This view was expressed in his most famous line: "The victorious cause pleased the gods, but the defeated cause pleased Cato" (the Younger, who committed suicide after Caesar's victory). Lucan's poem is celebrated for the classical vigor and conciseness of his Latin, written in the old Roman tradition, as opposed to Hellenizing tendencies.

Lucian

Greek writer (about 125-about 180).

Born at Samosata in Syria; died in Athens. Wandered all over the Graeco-Roman world as a teacher of philosophy, finally settled in Athens. His writings, characterized by a very personal style, are remarkable for their comical and satirical touches. Chief works: "Dialogues of the Gods," "Dialogues of the Dead," "Banquet of Philosophers," "Auction of Philosophers."

Lucilius, Gaius

Roman poet (about 180-102 B.C.).

Born at Sessa Aurunca in the Campagna; died in Naples. Member of the intellectual circle around Scipio the Younger. Said to have invented the satire, the only literary genre of classical literature attributed to the Romans. His satires, social and political, were published in thirty books, of which only fragments survive.

Lucretius, Titus Carus
Roman poet (about 97-55 B.C.).

Died by suicide, according to tradition, in a fit of madness produced by a love philter administered to him by his wife. A disciple of the Greek philosopher Epicurus. Wrote a didactic poem in six volumes, "On the Nature of Things," based on Epicureanism, "to free men from the fear of the gods and from fear of death." The poem includes a forecast of the theory of evolution.

Ludwig, Emil
German biographer (1881-1948).

Pen name of Emil Ludwig Cohn. Born in Breslau, now Wroclaw in Poland, died in Ascona, Switzerland. During the 1920's, he created an immensely successful genre of biography, based on a pinch of history, more than a pinch of psychology and a good deal of knowledge of what his public wanted. He thus popularized the lives of Goethe, Napoleon, William II, Bismarck, Lincoln, etc.

Lu Hsin
Chinese writer (1881-1936).

Pen name of Chou Shu-jen. Born in Shao-hsinh, died in Shanghai. Sent to Japan to study medicine on a government scholarship. He did not complete his studies but turned to literature. Returned home in 1909, became a school teacher, and taught literature at Peking National University (1913-1926). Left Peking in 1926 when the government started persecuting radical intellectuals, and moved to Shanghai in the following year. Lu Hsin excelled as an essayist and a writer of short stories. His main concern was the condition of China and his "Story of Ah Q" has remained a classic picture of Chinese weakness. The sad role played by Chinese intellectuals drew his withering scorn. The Communists have made him their literary patron saint, but his humanitarianism might have well made him scorn them.

Lull, Ramon
Catalan writer (1235-1315).

Born in Palma de Mallorca, died according to tradition, of stoning in Tunis. One of the encyclopedic minds of the middle ages. Knew Hebrew and Arabic and urged Christians to learn Oriental languages if they wished to convert their speakers. Founded a school for missionaries on these lines in Mallorca and traveled on missionary journeys all over the Mediterranean world. His Latin "Great Art" was a treatise on thinking and persuasion, with liberal use of visual aids. His Catalan books include "The Book of Beasts," a collection of fables; "Blanguerna," a novel, and "The Book of the Lover and the Beloved," an early exposition of mysticism.

Luria, Isaac
Jewish mystic (1534-1572).

Born in Jerusalem, died in Safed. Composed Commentaries on the Book of Zohar of Moses de Leon (q.v.) which were widely read by Jews and did much to produce the Hassidic movement of the 18th century.

Luther, Martin
German religious reformer and writer (1483-1546).

Born and died at Eisleben in Central Germany. Son of a miner, studied at Erfurt University. Became an Augustinian monk and was ordained priest in 1507. Became professor at Wittenberg in the next year. On a mission to Rome (1510-11) was most unfavorably impressed by the artistic glories and moral corruption of the Eternal City and the Papacy which governed it.

287

Began to attack church abuses, especially the sale of indulgences, and to preach the doctrine of salvation by faith rather than by works. On October 31, 1517, Luther nailed 95 theses against indulgences to the door of Wittenberg church, an action generally regarded as the beginning of the Reformation. Debated his position with Cardinal Cajetan and Dr. Eck and refused to budge from it. Was excommunicated by Pope Leo X in 1520; publicly burned excommunication bill. Appeared before the Emperor Charles V at the Diet of Worms (1521) and finally took his stand with the famous words, "Here I stand, I can do no other, God Help me." The diet passed the Edict of Worms putting Luther under the ban of the Empire. He was saved by the protection of the Elector Frederick of Saxony, who kept him concealed at Wartburg Castle until the danger was over (1521-2). The remainder of his life was devoted to the organization of his church and to the family which he founded with a former nun, Katharina Von Bora. Luther's commanding place in German literature is that of the founder of the modern German literary language by his translation of the Bible at Wartburg. In it he combined the official or "chancery" language with popular and humanistic elements. His language was at its sharpest and crudest in the pamphlets he wrote against Leo X (1520), to the German nobility (1520), against the rebellious peasants (1525), etc.; it was at its simplest and gentlest in his "Table Talks." He is also the author of many hymns, still sung in Protestant churches of various denominations. The most famous of them is doubtless "A Mighty Fortress Is Our God."

Luzzatto, Samuel David

Jewish writer (1800-1865).

Born in Trieste, died in Padua. Professor at the Rabbinical College of Padua from 1829. His Hebrew poems (published in two volumes, 1825-79) mark the start of modern Hebrew literature. His "Moral Discourses" and "Historical and Religious Discourses" addressed in Italian to Jewish students viewed the Bible and Jewish religion in the light of nationalist and romantic emotion.

Lyly, John

English novelist (1554-1606).

Studied at both Oxford and Cambridge, became deputy master of choir boys at Saint Paul's, London, and Member of Parliament. His novel "Euphues" (two volumes, 1578-80) gives an aristocratic view of English life and was written in a highly polished and inflated style that created the adjective "euphuistic."

M

Macaulay, Thomas Babington

English historian and writer (1800-1859).

Born in Rothley Temple, Leicestershire, died in London. Won reputation as essayist with an essay on Milton published in the "Edinburgh Review" and maintained it steadily. His poetry is still part of Anglo-American school books, especially the "Lays of Ancient Rome" (1842). His reputation as historian rests on his "History of England" (5 volumes, 1849-61), a work whose literary qualities transcend its patent Whig bias.

Macha, Karel Hynek

Czech poet (1810-1836).

Born in Prague, died in Litomerice. Greatest of Czech poets, lived a typically romantic life. His poem "May" (1836) is a masterpiece of Slav literature, less important for its Byronic tale of a robber than for its lyrical interludes, its exquisite language and musical qualities.

Machado, Antonio

Spanish poet (1875-1939).

Born in Seville, died in Colliure, France. His father, a Galician, was a leading collector of folklore; his brother Manuel (1874-1947) was also a poet. He was educated in Madrid at the Free Institution of Learning and he was deeply influenced by its emphasis on active and social ethics. Taught French at a number of provincial secondary schools, including Soria, Baeza and Segovia. Started writing under the influence of Becquer and Ruben Dario, but soon developed a style of his own and became one of the greatest, if not the greatest, of modern Spanish poets. His early work, in "Solitudes" (1903), is soberly lyrical; but it was only in the "Fields of Castile" (1912) that he reached full mastery under the emotional impact of the overpowering Castilian landscape. In a language marked by "imperial brevity" he interpreted Spain, questioned her past, lamented her present, and maintained an unshaken faith in her future. He accepted the Republic and died as refugee during its last days. But his message for Spain transcends partisan lines, and he has now found a new generation of readers in his country, to whom he gives hope. Although the Nobel Prize Committee that gave the prize to Juan Ramon Jimenez, couples his name with those of Jimenez and Lorca, he is still very little translated. This omission should be soon remedied, for Machado represents the best that Spain can offer to the world.

Machado de Assis, Joaquim Maria
Brazilian novelist (1839-1908).

Born and died in Rio de Janeiro. Started as a poet of the Parnassian variety but developed into an ironic novelist who expressed bitter but shrewd opinions on the human race under the mask of a Dickensian humor. Chief works: "The Posthumous Memoirs of Braz Cubas" (1881) and "Dom Casmurro" (1900).

Machiavelli, Niccolo
Italian writer (1459-1527).

Born and died in Florence. Was secretary to the Council of Ten of the Florentine Republic (1498-1512), for which he carried out diplomatic missions in Germany, France, and Italy. Was deprived of his office by the returning Medicis, who imprisoned him for a time. He then retired to his estate at San Casciano, to devote himself to his literary work. Machiavelli is one of the glories of the Italian Renaissance; but he has always been fiercely criticized for his political morality or rather the lack of it, even by people whose moral standards were certainly no better than his, e.g. Frederick the Great of Prussia (q.v.). His masterpiece is "The Prince," a treatise on government inspired by the rule of Ferdinand the Catholic in Spain and of Cesare Borgia in Italy, and also by Machiavelli's own fierce desire for the union of Italy under a "Prince." Also wrote a "History of Florence" and "Discourses on the First Ten Books of Livy," a book that was greatly admired by Benito Mussolini. His two comedies "Clizia" and "Mandragola" are landmarks in the growth of the Renaissance drama, and had a European influence, especially the latter. Machiavelli's writings also include a treatise on the art of war, short stories, a satire on women, etc.

Mackay, Claude

American Negro poet and novelist (born 1890).

Born in Jamaica, British West Indies. Became poet, novelist and student of life in Harlem in his "Harlem Shadows" (poems, 1922); "Home to Harlem" (novel, 1927) and "Harlem: Negro Metropolis" (a social study, 1940). His message is one of self-reliance and "Fighting Back," the title of one of his best poems.

MacLeish, Archibald

American poet (born 1892).

Born in Glencoe, Illinois. Served in World War I, studied law at Harvard and practiced law. Went to Paris in the twenties, fell under the spell of Eliot and Pound, like so many of his fellow expatriates. In the thirties, developed a social consciousness and became a poet of the New Deal, e.g. in "Public Speech" (1936). Served as Librarian of Congress. Successful dramatist, lately with his "J.B.", based on the story of Job.

MacNeice, Louis
Anglo-Irish poet (born 1907).

Born in Belfast, Northern Ireland. Educated at Oxford, lectured at Birmingham, Cornell and London Universities. As poet, he belongs to the "school" of Auden and Spender. Had great success with radio plays. Wrote: "Agamemnon" (1936), "The Earth Compels" (1938), etc.

Macpherson, James
Scottish poet (1736-1796).

Born in Ruthven, Inverness; died in Belleville. Published in 1760 "Fragments of Ancient Poetry Collected in the Highlands of Scotland" which were one of the literary sensations of the age. On the strength of its success he obtained funds to collect, translate from the Gaelic, and publish "Fingal" (1762) and "Temora" (1766), two epic poems which he attributed to Ossian, a bard of Gaelic Scotland said to have lived sometime around the third century A.D. The poems created a furious controversy. Dr. Samuel Johnson accused Macpherson of concocting the epics himself from fragments of poems and stories; Macpherson defended himself but did not publish the alleged originals needed to rebut the charge of forgery. Among Macpherson's admirers and defenders were the Germans Klopstock, Herder, and Goethe; and among the most faithful readers of the Ossianic epics was Napoleon. Today, it is recognized that Macpherson edited the epics from existing materials; but his editorial procedures do not affect the poetic value of the epics nor their position as one of the great books of the pre-romantic movement of the eighteenth century.

Madariaga, Salvador de
Spanish essayist (born 1886).

Born in Corunna. Trained in Paris as an engineer,

subsequently embarked on a brilliant and diversified career that has included the Chair of Spanish Literature at Oxford University, an ambassadorship, and the directorship of a section of the League of Nations. Left Spain when Franco came to power. One of the chief interpreters of Spanish culture to other nations. Writes in Spanish, French and English, and in all three languages demonstrates exceptional clarity and brilliance of thought combined with elegance of style. Chief works: "Englishmen, Frenchmen, Spaniards" (1923), "Don Quixote, an introductory essay" (1935), "The Rise and Fall of the Spanish Empire" (1947). Novels: "The Sacred Giraffe" (1925), "The Heart of Jade" (1944). Poetry includes "La Fuente Serena" (1928).

Maeterlinck, Maurice

Belgian writer (1862-1949).

Born at Ghent; died at Nice. Though he was from Flanders and though his native tongue was Flemish, he wrote in French. Flanders inspired, however, some of his best work. He settled in Paris in 1896, where he came under the influence of the French symbolists. His own verse is symbolist and expressionistic, full of vague fears and yearnings, as befitted a neoromantic. His poems, prose, and dramas were very successful at the turn of the century; today most of his work seems antiquated. Maeterlinck won the Nobel Prize in 1911, was ennobled and became president of the International PEN Club. Had his last period of prominence during World War I when he did relief work and vigorously protested against the misdeeds of the Germans in his occupied country. During the last thirty years of his life, he was all but forgotten. Chief works: "Princess Maleine" (1889), "Pelleas and Melisande" (1892, later set to music by Debussy and given new life in a famous ballet), "The Treasure of the Poor" (1896), "The Life of the Bees" (1901), and "The

Blue Bird" (1908)—still popular, the first with adults and the second with children—"Death" (1913), "The Intelligence of Flowers" (1927), "The Life of the Ant" (1930).

Magnusson, Gudmundur

("Jón Trausti"; Icelandic, 1873-1918).

Who shares honors with Einar H. Kvaran as the leading novelist of the period, has achieved even greater success with his short stories. He interpreted rural life effectively in such novels as *Halla* (1906) and the series *Heidarbýlid* (*The Heath-Farm,* 1908-11), town life equally ably in *Borgir* (1909). His historical novels are also noteworthy. He has written excellent short stories of the life of the fishermen, splendid in characterization, and breathing the atmosphere of the sea. His narrative art is always vivid and fluent, and he succeeds in creating a number of strong, unforgettable characters. His novels on contemporary themes are a significant contribution to the cultural history of Iceland.

Mailer, Norman

American novelist (born 1923).

Born in Long Branch, New Jersey. Studied at Harvard, fought in the South Pacific in World War II and wrote "The Naked and the Dead" (1948) the most-praised novel of the war of some literary quality. His "Deer Park" took an equally dim view of Hollywood. Mailer has now found a new hero in the "hipster" and acts as a kind of literary father—or grandfather—of the "Beat Generation."

Maimonides, Moses

Jewish philosopher (1135-1204).

Westernized form of his name Moses ben Maimon. Born in Cordoba, died in Cairo. Had to escape from Spain because of persecution of Jews and settled in

Cairo after stays in Morocco and Palestine. Was physician to the Sultan of Egypt and rabbi to the Jewish community. Wrote in both Hebrew and Arabic. Composed commentaries on the Bible and the Talmud, wrote treatises on logic and grammar. Chief work is "The Guide to the Perplexed," a presentation of the Jewish religion which had a wide influence on Christians as well as Jews and caused deep controversies because of its Aristotelianism. It was banned to all under 25. Maimonides was the greatest mind of the Jewish middle ages.

Malaparte, Curzio
Italian writer and journalist (1899-1958).

Real name Kurt Suckert. Born at Prato in Tuscany of a German father; died in Rome. An early adherent of Fascism, later quarreled with Mussolini when he disclosed some of the Duce's secrets in his "Technique of the Coup d'Etat" (1931), his first taste of fame. Had a larger share of it with "Kaputt" a brilliant, nihilistic and journalistic account of the horrors perpetrated in Europe by the Nazis and their allies. Malaparte settled his accounts with his father by adopting a ferociously anti-Teutonic attitude. In "The Skin" (1953) he expressed the "Neapolitan" outlook, in which the preservation of one's own skin came before any other consideration. He made a journey to Communist China of which he wrote a reportage, paid a literary tribute to his native Tuscany, and became reconciled to Catholicism on his deathbed.

Malherbe, François de
French writer and critic (1555-1628).

Born at Caen in Normandy; died in Paris. Became court poet of Henry IV and Louis XIII. Wrote odes, sonnets, and occasional lyrics, the most famous of which is an ode he wrote in 1599 to console a friend, Du Perier, on the death of his daughter. He embodied his criticism in commentaries on the poems of a contemporary, Desportes. The clarity and simplicity of Malherbe's language became proverbial. He did much to make Parisian French the ideal instrument of French classical prose. His work as literary pioneer of "The Age of Louis XIV" inspired the line of Boileau (q.v.) which is Malherbe's best epitaph: "And finally Malherbe came."

Mallarmé, Stephane
French poet (1842-1898).

Born in Paris; died at Valvins-sur-Seine. One of the leaders of the Parnassian school, originally inspired by Baudelaire (q.v.). Chiefly concerned with use of words for expressing the most subtle thoughts and emotions. His style is abstract and allusive; the content of his poems is indicative of a flight from reality and often dwells in a borderline between dream and waking. Mallarmé greatly developed the use of symbols. He had great influence not only in France but throughout the West, in particular on the revival of English poetry through the work of two American poets, T. S. Eliot and Ezra Pound (q.v.). Mallarmé was a schoolmaster by profession; he taught English in a Paris girls' school. Chief works: "The Afternoon of a Faun" (1876, which inspired music and a ballet), "Poems" (1881), "Album of Verse and Prose" (1887-8), "Music and Letters" (1894), "Divagations" (1897), "A Throw of Dice Will Not Abolish Risk" (1897), and the posthumous "Circumstantial Verse" (1920) and "Igitur or the Folly of Elbehohn" (1925).

Malory, Sir Thomas
English writer (died 1471).

Has been tentatively identified with a Warwickshire knight of that name who spent 20 years of his life in jail. Wrote eight Arthurian romances in prose published by Caxton as "Le Morte Darthur" (The Death

of Arthur, 1485) which popularized the Arthurian
legend and provided a model for Tennyson (q.v.).

Malraux, André

French novelist (born 1901).

Born in Paris. Throughout his career, has led a life
of both letters and action. His experience in Indo-
china, where he worked as archeologist, produced
"The Royal Road" (1930) and "The Human Condition" (1933). A visit to Hitler's Germany led to "Days
of Contempt" (1935). Fighting for the Spanish Republic as aviator found its literary expression in "Days
of Hope" (1937). During the War, he was active in the
Resistance and established in 1944 a personal contact
with General De Gaulle. The German problem made
him write "The Walnut Trees of Altenburg." His
association with the general made him the organizer
of Gaullist propaganda and, in time, minister of the
Fifth Republic. He still found time to write his monu-
mental "Essays in the Psychology of Art." Malraux is
the 20th century intellectual as tortured man of action.

Mann, Heinrich

German novelist (1871-1950).

Born in Lubeck, elder brother of Thomas Mann
(q.v.); died in Santa Monica, California. A sharp critic
of the Germany of his time and of the bourgeoisie into which he was born, his irony tends to be more biting than that of his brother and fellow-critic, Thomas.
His strong anti-Nazi views made him emigrate to
France in 1933. Was surprised there by the defeat of
the French army in 1940 and spent some time in internment, but managed to escape to the United States.
During and after the war, his political views veered
more strongly to the left; and the German Communists claim that he died on the eve of returning to
East Germany. Chief works: "The Goddesses" (1902-4);
"Professor Unrat" (1906, the novel that became the

film "Blue Angel"); "The Small Town" (1909); "Short Stories" (1909-10); "The Road to Power" (1918); "The Head" (1925); "The Youth of King Henry IV" (1935); "An Era Is Viewed" (1945).

Mann, Thomas

German novelist and critic (1875-1955.)

Born in Lubeck; died in Zurich. His father was a Lubeck merchant, his mother a Brazilian lady, and the relations between the Nordic and Latin peoples were his lifelong concern. The family fortunes declined and he soon had to earn his own living. After a short spell at an insurance company and work for the humorous magazine "Simplicissimus," he settled at Munich as a writer. His first novel, "The Buddenbrooks" (1901), a story of the decline of a Lubeck family and of the bourgeoisie generally, made him famous. It it written in a poetical, post-naturalist style, of which the keynote is a subtle but not gentle irony. Until World War I, he was mostly concerned with aesthetic problems. The coming of the war proved that Mann, though critical of the German Bourgeoisie, was by no means condemning Germany herself—at that time. He wrote two wartime books that could be, and were, interpreted as support of the cause of the Central Powers: "Frederick and the Great Coalition" and "Considerations of an Un-Political Man." But he had a change of heart in 1918. He fully accepted democracy and the Weimar Republic, and became their official spokesman at home and abroad. His fame as a writer reached its peak with "The Magic Mountain" (1925), a landmark in the history of the European novel. It was consolidated by the Nobel Prize he won in 1929. The coming to power of the Nazis disturbed him profoundly for both political and personal reasons—his wife, Kathy Pringsheim, was Jewish and his children half-Jewish. He finally left Germany in 1934, moved to Switzerland

and, in 1938, to the United States. He settled his accounts with the Nazis by publishing a trilogy, "Joseph and His Brethren" (1933-40), a modern interpretation of the Old Testament story; and, during World War II, by his broadcasts to Germany, sponsored by the U.S. Office of War Information. His settling of accounts with Germany was embodied in the novel "Doctor Faustus" (1947). He also wrote: "Little Mr. Friedemann" (1898), "Tristan" (1903), "Royal Highness" (1909), "Death in Venice" (1913), "Confessions of the Confidence Man Felix Krull" (1923, second version 1955), "Goethe as Representative of the Bourgeois Age" (1932), "Lotte in Weimar" (1939), "An Essay on Schiller" (1955).

Manrique, Jorge
Spanish poet (1440-1479).

Born in Paredes de la Nava, died in Calatrava. A nobleman who took part in the innumerable civil wars of the time and died in battle. His "Verses on the Death of his father, Don Rodrigo" are four-line coplas which enshrine his ever popular meditations on life, death and the vanity of human existence.

Mansfield, Katherine
English writer (1889-1923).

Real name: Kathleen Beauchamp. Born in Wellington, New Zealand; died in Fontainebleau near Paris. Afflicted with tuberculosis, spent her last years in German, Swiss, Italian, and French sanatoria. Her short stories, modelled partly on Chekhov and the techniques of the impressionists, are concerned with the trivial and the commonplace and uncover their real nature. Wrote: "In a German Boarding House" (1911); "Bliss," her "Letters" and "Journal," which caused considerable stir in literary circles, were published posthumously by her second husband, the English writer John Middleton Murry.

Manzoni, Alessandro Count

Italian novelist (1785-1873).

Born and died in Milan. Had a romantic and sceptical youth, influenced by romanticism during his stay in Paris (1805-7). But he soon moved from romanticism to classicism and from scepticism to a deep, though quiet, Catholicism. Became a national celebrity through his historical novel "The Engaged Couple" (1825-6, three volumes) on an episode during the Spanish rule in Milan in the Seventeenth Century. It is still considered the greatest modern Italian novel and is read by the people as well as by intellectuals. Manzoni took part in the politics of the Risorgimento: He participated in the Milanese revolt of 1848 and was made senator (1860) by the new Kingdom of Italy. But his chief contributions to the rebirth of Italy were literary and linguistic—by his philological studies of the Italian literary language and of the Tuscan and Milanese dialects. Also wrote poetry, both sacred and profane; tragedies; historical studies.

Mao Tse-tung

Chinese politician and poet (born 1893).

Born in Hunan province. The present ruler of China has written numerous books, mostly of pamphlet size, on his interpretation of Communism and on various political and military problems. He is also a good poet in the Chinese classical tradition, and has been at his best in "Snow," verses he wrote while flying to Moscow on his first journey out of China. However he does not live up to the classical tradition in that his handwriting is execrable.

Mao Tun

Chinese novelist (born 1896).

Pen name of Shen Yen-ping. Born in Tung-hsiang, Chekiang province. Prominent in Chinese literary life since the twenties, when he edited the "Short

Story Monthly" and founded with Lu Hsin's brother Chou Tso-jen the Literary Research Society. His trilogy of novels on life in Shanghai, "Shih" (1931-33) established his fame. Helped to found "League of Left-wing Writers" in 1930, leading Communist and one of the most favored writers of the present regime.

March, Auzias

Catalan poet (1397-1458).

Born and died in Gandia near Valencia. His love poems to a lady called Teresa made him the greatest of Catalan poets. They are very modern in their psychological bias and their continuous self-torturings.

Marinetti, Filippo

Italian writer (1876-1944).

Born in Alexandria, Egypt, died in Bellagio. Founder of "futurism" which proclaimed the beauties of the machine age, the death of the past and the glories of the future—under Fascism. Proclaimed "war is the sole hygiene" and wrote poems like "Zang Tumb Tumb" which sound exactly like their title.

Marini, Marino

Italian poet (1569-1625).

Born and died in Naples. Had to seek the protection of Louis XIII of France and his Italian wife, Mary of Medici, following a literary quarrel with Gaspare Murtola which he fought first with sonnets, then with invective and finally with pistols. His long, pastoral and sensuous poem "Adonis" was much admired and imitated throughout the 17th century.

Maritain, Jacques

French philosopher (born 1882).

Born in Paris. A Catholic convert from Protestantism, he became the leading exponent of neo-Thomism, an adaptation of the teachings of Saint Thomas Aquinas to the needs of our day. A leading Christian

democrat, served as French ambassador to the Holy
See (1945-48). Wrote: "Of Christian Philosophy"
(1933); "Integral Humanism" (1936) etc.

Marivaux, Pierre Carlet de

French dramatist (1688-1763).

Born and died in Paris. Son of a rich banker,
started writing for fun and continued it for a living
when the family fortune disappeared in the economic
crisis of 1722 caused by the swindling schemes of
John Law. Became member of the French Academy in
1743. His comedies, of which "The Game of Love
and Hazard" (1730) is best, are psychological and ex-
plore human sentiments. Also wrote racy novels.

Marlowe, Christopher

English dramatist (1564-1593).

Born in Canterbury; died in Deptford, Kent (now a
part of London). Son of a shoemaker, studied at Cambridge, became M.A. in 1587. Became member of
"The Admiral's Men," the theatrical troupe of the
Earl of Northampton that produced most of his plays.
He was the most important of the predecessors of
Shakespeare. He discovered the vigor and variety of
English blank verse in "Tamburlaine the Great"
(1587). Also wrote "The Tragedy of Doctor Faustus"
(1588), the most important treatment of the German
legend until Goethe's "Faust"; "The Jew of Malta"
(1588); and "Edward II" (1593). He has been credited,
on internal evidence, with part-authorship of some of
Shakespeare's plays, notably "Titus Andronicus" and
"Henry VI." Translated Ovid and wrote lyrical verse.
Marlowe was denounced for atheism and immorality,
was condemned to death, but was killed in a tavern
brawl before the sentence could be executed.

Marot, Clement

French poet (1496-1544).

Born in Cahors, died in Turin. His verses represent

a transition between the middle ages and the Renaissance. In addition to epigrams and epistles, wrote the earliest French sonnets and a metrical version of the Psalms that were adopted by the Calvinists of Geneva. Had to flee from France on suspicion of heresy.

Marquand, John Phillips
American novelist (born 1893).

Born in Wilmington, Delaware. Studied at Harvard. Has written a series of novels, beginning with "The Late George Apley" (1937) that have made the "proper Bostonians," for the first time, popular figures.

Martial
Roman writer (about 40-about 104).

Full name: Marcus Valerius Martialis. Born and died in Bilbilis, Spain (now in Aragon). Came to Rome in 64 A.D. to practise law but soon turned to literature. Although he enjoyed the patronage of Emperors Titus and Domitian, he lived in poverty. When he decided to return to his native Spain in 98 A.D., he could not go until the Younger Pliny gave him money for the journey. Martial wrote panegyrics and other verse; but he is remembered today for his epigrams, witty and sharply moralizing. Some 1200 of them are preserved in fourteen books.

Martin Du Gard, Roger
French novelist (1881-1958).

Born at Neuilly near Paris. Started writing under influence of naturalism but overcame it under the influence of Gide (q.v.). He is a conservative, deeply concerned with the decline of moral standards in our time. Awarded the Nobel Prize in 1937. Chief work is a family chronicle in eight volumes, "The Thibaults" (1922-40). Also has written "Jean Barois" (1913), "The Testament of Pere Leleu" (1914), "Old France" (1933).

Marvell, Andrew
English poet (1621-1678).

Born in Winestead, died in London. Educated at Cambridge, served Cromwell and Charles II as civil servant. Represented Hull in Parliament from 1659 to his death. His "Miscellaneous Poems" are in the best baroque vein.

Masefield, John
English writer (born 1875).

Born in Ledbury, Herefordshire. Ran away to sea at 13. Spent a wandering youth, lived for two years in the United States, came back to England and settled near London (1897) to devote himself to writing. But the touch of the sea still marks most of his writing. Became England's Poet Laureate in 1930, was awarded the Order of Merit five years later. Chief works: "Salt Water Ballads" (1902), "Captain Margaret" (1908), "The Tragedy of Nan" (1909), "The Everlasting Mercy" (1911), "Gallipoli" (1916).

Massinger, Philip
English dramatist (1583-1640).

Born in Salisbury, died in London. Studied at Oxford but left without obtaining a degree and moved to London. Wrote plays for a number of actors' companies. They are in blank verse, well-written and rather superficial except for "A New Way to Pay Old Debts" (1631) with its full-blooded hero Sir Giles Overreach.

Masters, Edgar Lee
American poet (1869-1954).

Born in Garnett, Kansas. Grew up in rural Illinois which he immortalized in the "Spoon River Anthology" (1915), a group of some 200 epitaphs in verse, mostly sardonic. Masters is torn between nostalgia for the past glories of mid-western rural life and contempt for its present corruptions. Wrote biographies of Lincoln, Whitman, Twain and Vachel Lindsay (q.v.).

Mather, Cotton

American religious writer (1663-1728).

Born and died in Boston. A Puritan divine of the extreme variety who mortified his body and took part in the Salem witch hunts. His "Diary" is revealing: his "Magnalia Christi Americana or Ecclesiastical History of New England" (1702) hailed America as "the glorious renovator of the world."

Maugham, William Somerset

English writer (born 1874).

Born in Paris of English parents. Educated at Heidelberg University and Saint Thomas Hospital, London, where he graduated in medicine, though he never practiced it. Maugham gained his first great popular success with a series of plays that conquered the London stage and included "A Man of Honour" (1903) and "Lady Frederick" (1907). But in later years, his main success lay with novels and short stories; e.g., "Of Human Bondage" (1915, based on his own youth), "The Moon and Sixpence" (1919, based on the life of Gauguin), "On a Chinese Screen" (1922), "Cakes and Ale" (1930), "Rain" (1932), "The Razor's Edge" (1944). Maugham is a popular rather than a great writer. He excels in style, plot, character, and settings (especially Eastern and Pacific), but he has little to say and does not rise much beyond a maudlin sentimentality with "religious" overtones.

Maupassant, Guy de

French writer (1850-1893).

Born in Tourville-sur-Argues; died in Passy (now Paris). Descendant of old Lorraine nobility who worked at the Ministry of the Navy in Paris. Began writing as a protege of Flaubert (q.v.) and under his literary inspiration. But he soon moved toward a more ruthless and personal realism, which depicted human beings with a complete absence of sentimentality and idealization. Although he wrote six novels and four volumes of travel notes, his greatness as a writer rests almost entirely on his three hundred short stories, which established him as a master of the genre. The first of these was "Boule de Suif" (1880); it was followed by "The Tellier House" (1881), "Mademoiselle Fifi" (1883), and several collections. Among his novels are "Bel Ami" (1885), "Mont Oriol" (1887), and "Strong as Death" (1889).

Mauriac, François

French novelist (born 1885).

Born in Bordeaux, of bourgeois family. Started as a poet with "The Joined Hands" (1909) and "Farewell to the Adolescent Girl" (1911), but soon evolved into a novelist. His main preoccupations are moral and religious. His ardent Catholicism is obsessed with a sense of sin and reflects the gloomy outlook that is common in Southwest France and which previously expressed itself in Albigensianism and Jansenism. Mauriac is especially concerned with the decline of the Christian family under the pressures of modern individualism and materialism. He is an excellent literary craftsman; of late his political preoccupations have made him a star columnist of the Paris "Figaro," in which he attempts to act as the conscience of France and often voices unpopular opinions, e.g. on Algeria. Chief works: "The Child Loaded With Chains" (1913), "The Kiss of the Leper" (1922), "Genitrix" (1923), "The Desert of Love" (1927), "Therese Desqueyroux" (1927), "Destinies" (1928), "The Nest of Vipers" (1932), "The End of Night" (1935), "The Life of Jesus" (1936), "The Black Angels" (1936), "Asmodeus" (1938), "The Black Copybook" (1943), Mauriac was awarded the Nobel Prize for 1952.

Maurois, André
French writer (born 1885).

Real name: Emile Herzog. Born in Elboeuf, son of a prosperous manufacturer. Worked as a journalist in Paris. In World War I served as a liaison officer with the British forces, and his experiences inspired his first books,—"The Silences of Colonel Bramble" (1918) and "The Discourses of Doctor O'Grady" (1922)—and a lifelong preoccupation with things Anglo-Saxon. During World War II, Maurois left France after the defeat and lived in the United States. He defended the Free French cause and acted as its semi-official spokesman. Maurois is a very prolific writer, a good stylist, but with a tendency toward shallowness. Among his best works are "The Climates" (1928), a psychological novel on the changing moods of love; biographies, e.g. "Ariel, or the Life of Shelley" (1923) and "The Life of Disraeli" (1927); popular histories, as "The History of France" (1947), and "The History of England" (1937); essays, as "The Art of Living" (1935).

Maximilian I
German emperor and writer (1459-1519).

Born in Wiener Neustadt; died in Wels (Austria). Son of Habsburg Emperor Frederick III, whom he succeeded in 1490. Important patron of literature: In addition to promoting living writers, was responsible for gathering of medieval German writings in a manuscript preserved at Castle Ambras. Two narrative poems "Theuerdank" and "Weisskunig" are ascribed to him, but literary historians still dispute his actual share in the writing, though they agree that he invented the themes.

Mayakovski, Vladimir
Russian poet (1894-1930).

Born in Bagdady, died in Moscow. Became a futurist under the influence of Marinetti (q.v.) and his Russian follower Khlebnikov; but chose Communism instead of Fascism. His "Cloud in Trousers" (1916) is intensely egotistic, but he wrote ecstatic praises of the Revolution in "War and Peace" (1916) and "Mystery-Bouffe" (1917-18). He put his talents unreservedly in the service of Communism, writing anything for it from recruiting songs to advertisement. His panegyric on Lenin (1924) was deeply felt. But disillusionment came: the two plays "The Bedbug" (1928) and "The Bath" (1930) show it under cover of a grotesque and hyperbolic language. He finally committed suicide, as forecast by his line "the ship of poetry broken against the rock of state." Officially enshrined as "The poet of Communism."

McCullers, Carson

American writer (born 1917).

Maiden name: Smith. Born in Columbus, Georgia, married Reeves McCullers. Came to New York to study music, lost her tuition money in the subway on her second day in the city, and took odd jobs. Her first novel, "The Heart is a Lonely Hunter" (1940), takes a pessimistic view of attempts to overcome loneliness. Her "The Member of the Wedding" (1946), the story of a lonely adolescent girl in the South, was a great success, first as a novel and then as a play.

Melanchthon, Philip

German humanist and religious writer (1497-1560).

Real name Philip Schwarzerd, which he translated into the Greek "Melanchthon" in humanist fashion. Born at Bretten in Southwest Germany; died in Wittenberg. Nephew of John Reuchlin (q.v.) and pupil of Erasmus. Supported from the start Luther and his Reformation, but rejected Luther's negative view of classical antiquity. He was also more conciliatory than the irascible Reformer. Melanchthon tried to moderate Luther's outbursts and worked for reconciliation with the Catholics. But once he realized this was not possible at the time, he became the first great Protestant theologian. He became professor at Wittenberg, first of Greek (1518), then of theology (1526). Wrote, in Latin, "The Common-Places of Theological Things," a Protestant theology largely based on an Aristotelian framework that Luther rejected. Drafted the Augsburg Confession of 1530, the first definition of Lutheran Protestantism and still its authoritative creed. To the end of his life, Melanchthon was concerned with ethical questions and hopes of religious peace.

Melville, Herman

American novelist (1819-1891).

Born and died in New York. His father was of Scottish descent, his mother came from a Dutch patron family, and young Herman was brought up in an atmosphere heavy with Presbyterianism from both sides of the family. Ran away to sea at 18. Worked as sailor on the whaling ship "Acushnet" (1841-2), but deserted his ship at the Marquesas Islands and found a temporary refuge among their cannibal inhabitants. Escaped on the Australian whaler "Lucy Ann" but left her at Tahiti (1843). Served for a year on the American frigate "United States" (1843-4). Spent rest of his life at home; worked as U.S. customs inspector in the port of New York. His writing deals mainly with his sailing experiences in the Pacific. In addition to three volumes of poetry, Melville wrote several novels including his masterpiece "Moby Dick" (1851), the story of the chase of the white whale by Captain Ahab, which grows into a Homeric epic of man's destiny, civilization, willpower, and greed. Melville attracted little attention in his lifetime; it was not until the 1920's that he was taken seriously. Today,

"Moby Dick" rivals "Huckleberry Finn" as *the* American novel and has been the subject of innumerable critical studies. Melville's critique of civilized man when measured by the ethical standards of primitive man was made topical by the events of the last few decades. Melville also wrote "Typee" (1846), "Omoo" (1847), "Mardi" (1849), "Pierre, or the Ambiguities" (1852), several short stories (of which "Billy Budd" is the best known), etc.

Menander
Greek playwright (342-290 B.C.).

Born in Athens; died when bathing in the sea off Piraeus. Pupil of Theophrastus (q.v.) and friend of Epicurus. Chief figure of the Athenian "New Comedy" which, unlike the "Old Comedy" of Aristophanes, was not concerned with politics but with the study of character and with everyday life. His one hundred comedies, distinguished by wit and ingenuity, were great favorites in the Hellenistic and Roman eras, especially "The Court of Arbitration," "The Punished Kiss," and "The Peasant." Until 1905, only small fragments of the comedies survived, though the Roman comedies of Plautus and Terence were largely adapted from them. Since then, four considerable fragments have been located, and, more recently, a fairly complete play.

Mencius
Chinese philosopher (4th century B.C.).

Westernized form of the Chinese Meng-tsu who is said to have been born in the state of Tsou about 370 B.C. and to have received Confucius' teachings from the latter's grandson. Acted as adviser to various Chinese rulers, being more successful in this respect than his master. This is not surprising since his own teachings not only systematized those of Confucius but also smoothed off the rough edges of Confucianism and

311

turned it into a commonsensical "middle way." It is, however, to Mencius' credit that his own bias was a humanitarian one.

Mendele Moicher Sforim
Jewish writer (1835-1917).

Pen name of Sholem Jacob Abramovich. Born near Minsk, died in Odessa. Called "the grandfather of the Yiddish novel," created almost single-handed the Yiddish prose language, richly flavored with folk expressions. Wrote novels, e.g. "Fishke the Lame" (1869) and "The Mare" (1873).

Mendelssohn, Moses
Jewish writer (1729-1786).

Born in Dessau, died in Berlin. A principal figure of Jewish Emancipation. A friend of Lessing and other German writers of his day, he was a much respected figure in Berlin. He wrote German instead of Yiddish and encouraged other German Jews to do likewise. Wrote: "Phaidon or the Immortality of the Soul" (1767) and other philosophical treatises; literary criticism and "Jerusalem" (1783), a fervent plea for the emancipation of the Jews.

Mendes, Catulle
French writer (1841-1909).

Born in Bordeaux, died in Saint Germain en Laye. A very prolific writer and literary critic. Founded the "Revue Fantaisiste" in 1859 and was a leading Parnassian poet in "Philomela" (1864); "Poems" (1876) and "New Poems" (1893).

Meng Hao-Jan
(Chinese, 689-740).

Political satirist and lyricist. Spent early days studying in the mountains. When he failed to pass official examination, decided to devote remaining life to literature. Satirical poems incurred Emperor's wrath. Friend and disciple of famous Buddhist poet, Wang Wei.

Merck, Johann Heinrich
German critic (1741-1791).

Born and died in Darmstadt. Occupied an important post in the government; befriended young writers. Printed Goethe's "Goetz Von Berlichingen" at his own expense, but told him to burn his drama "Clavigo" because "others can write this kind of stuff, too." Goethe, who benefitted a good deal from Merck's criticism, revenged himself by making him the model of his Mephistopheles.

Meredith, George
English novelist (1828-1909).

Born in Portsmouth, died in Box Hill, Surrey. Tried his hand at poetry—notably in "Modern Love" (1862) —and journalism before he discovered his true vocation as a novelist. His novels are social and psychological, not easy to read but worth reading for their subtleties and poetic touches. Best known are "Beauchamp's Career" (1876) and "The Egoist" (1879), both in the Victorian three-decker tradition.

Merezhkovski, Dmitry Sergeyevich
Russian novelist (1865-1941).

Born in Saint Petersburg, died in Paris. Became a leading symbolist, with strong religious emphasis. Much concerned with relations between Russia and the West. Best-known for his trilogy: "Julian the Apostate" (1894): "The Revived Gods" (1896) and "Peter and Alexis" (1898). Emigrated in 1920 after relentless opposition to Communism. Kept up his anti-Communism in emigration, went as far as to hail, shortly before his death, Hitler's invasion of Russia.

Mérimée, Prosper
French writer (1803-1870).

Born in Paris; died in Cannes. Worked as a civil servant in various ministries, became inspector-general of historical monuments in 1834, and senator in 1853. Mérimée's writings do not rank very high by purely literary criteria, but he changed the literary geography of Europe by discovering its more exotic parts—Dalmatia, Corsica, Spain, and Russia. As a young man, he wanted to go to Dalmatia but had no money. He wrote and published "Guzla," purporting to be translations from Illyrian popular poetry. The book was an instant success, was hailed as an expression of the Slav literary genius by experts of the caliber of Pushkin and Mickiewicz, and permitted Mérimée, who had invented "Slav" poems, to visit Dalmatia on his royalties. Next came Corsica, with "Colomba" (1840), which described a dramatic vendetta. "Carmen" (1845) did for Spain what "Colomba" did for Corsica, and more. Besides all this, Mérimée was instrumental in introducing Eugenia de Montijo, an old family friend, to Napoleon III, whom she married. Finally, he translated many Russian literary classics and introduced them to France and so to Europe. He also wrote many historical novels on themes from French, Spanish, and Russian history. Successful in his time, they are forgotten today.

Metastasio, Pietro
Italian poet (1698-1782).

Born in Rome, died in Vienna. Left Rome at the age of twenty-one to become poet laureate of the imperial court at Vienna. His "Five Canzonets" (1719-49) express the essence of the Arcadian lyricism prevalent in his time. Wrote many operatic libretti in the lyrical genre. Drew largely on classical antiquity for the subjects of his dramas, which have been compared with French classical theatre. However, the conflicts which Corneille and Racine left tragically unresolved invariably find a pleasing and tender solution in the works of Metastasio.

Meyer, Conrad Ferdinand

Swiss writer (1825-1898).

Born in Zurich; died in Kilchberg. Member of a Zurich patrician family. His childhood and youth were overshadowed by the early death of his father and the melancholy of his mother. He became excessively shy and suffered a nervous breakdown in 1852. After the death of his mother, travelled in France and Italy (1856-58), started writing after his return. For ten years he wrote mostly poetry (1860-70); later he switched to prose. Married Luise Ziegler in 1875 and called himself, in gratitude, Meyer-Ziegler. Meyer excelled in both poetry and prose; his best points are literary portraiture of character and a Latin sense of form that is rare in German letters. Chief works: "Twenty Ballads of a Swiss" (1864), "The Last Days of Ulrich Von Hutten" (1871), "The Amulet" (1873), "Juerg Jenatsch" (1876), "The Saint" (1880), "The Wedding of the Monk" (1884), "The Temptation of Pescara" (1887).

Michelet, Jules

French historian (1798-1874).

Born and died in Paris. Self-educated son of a poor printer, attained the highest honors. His "History of France" (27 volumes, 1833-76) aimed at a "complete resurrection of the past." It is a magnificent piece of writing for all of its emotional romanticism and patriotic prejudice. It molded the image of French history throughout the world.

Mickiewicz, Adam

Polish poet (1798-1855).

Born at Zaosie in Byelorussia; died in Constantinople. Educated at Vilna University, taught school at Kovno. Inaugurated Polish romantic movement with his "Ballads and Romances," Arrested in 1824 for revolutionary activities and exiled to the interior of Russia. Spent five years in Saint Petersburg, Moscow, Odessa, and the Crimea; met Pushkin who befriended him and published a number of works, including the "Crimean Sonnets" (1824) and the historical poems "Konrad Wallenrod" and "Grazyna" (1827). Received permission to travel abroad; lived mostly in France. Taught Slav literature at Lausanne and at the College de France in Paris (1840-4); was dismissed from the latter post because his views alarmed the French government. His work moved into a national and religious mysticism in "The Ancestors" (especially Part III, 1832) and "Books of the Polish People and Pilgrimage" (1832); but in the deeply nostalgic "Pan Tadeusz" (1834) he achieved a classical simplicity in what is the last great epic poem of European literature. His last years were more and more occupied in political work for Polish independence, and he died of cholera while organizing a Polish legion that was to fight against Russia in the Crimean War. Mickiewicz is the greatest figure of Polish literature and a man of European stature.

Mikszath, Kalman

Hungarian novelist (1849-1910).

Born in Szklabonya; died in Budapest. Studied law and became a deputy to the Hungarian parliament. His realistic stories and novels, richly spiced with humor, include "The Miracle-Working Umbrella," "The Deaf Blacksmith," "The Young Noszty." He also wrote children's books, which have been translated into many languages.

Milarepa

Tibetan writer (1038-1122).

A wandering Buddhist monk, who begged for his living while spreading the gospel of Buddha. Wrote "Gurbun," the "Book of One Hundred Thousand Songs," a classic of Tibetan literature, still widely read today.

Millay, Edna Saint Vincent

American poetess (1892-1956).

Born in Rockland, Maine, died in Austerlitz, New York. Came to New York following the success of her first major poem, "Renascence" (1917). Became the leading poetic spirit of Greenwich Village with her "A Few Figs from Thistles" (1920), which contains her most famous poem, "My Candle Burns at Both Ends." Retired to Austerlitz following her marriage to Eugen Boissevain.

Mill, John Stuart

English philosopher (1806-1873).

Born in London, died in Avignon. Son of philosopher James Mill who educated his son at home in strict accordance with the principles of Bentham. Mill rebelled against these, acknowledging aspects of life that cannot be measured empirically. In the field of political economy he adhered to Ricardo in general, but took into consideration the possibility of a redistribution of wealth. Chief works: "Bentham" (1838), "System of Logic" (1843), "Principles of Political Economy" (1848), "On Liberty" (1859), "Thoughts on Parliamentary Reform" (1859), and "Three Essays on Religion" (1874).

Miller, Arthur

American playwright (born 1916).

Born in New York. Sharply critical of conditions in

America. His "Death of a Salesman" (1949) exposed the myth of success; "The Crucible" dealt with the Salem witchcraft trials with some obvious modern parallels; "A View From the Bridge" tackles the assimilation of immigrants.

Milton, John

English poet (1608-1674).

Born and died in London. His father was a minor writer and composer, who was disinherited when he was converted to Protestantism while a student at Oxford. Milton himself, an unwavering Protestant, went to Cambridge. He wrote his first poem in 1626 on the death of his sister's first child; wrote English and Latin verse while at Cambridge including a sonnet to Shakespeare. Thought of becoming a clergyman, but gave it up and studied classics at his father's home (1632-8). It was there that he wrote "L'Allegro" and "Il Penseroso" (1632), the masque "Comus" (1634) and the elegy "Lycidas" (1637). After traveling to France and Italy (1638-9), settled in London as a tutor, but soon became involved in politics. He became a staunch defender of the Puritan cause. His own Puritanism may have had something to do with the failure of his three marriages. He published several pamphlets on divorce; "Reformation of Church Discipline in England" (1641), a violent attack on episcopacy; "Areopagitica" (1644), a famous and classical defense of the freedom of the press. He defended the execution of Charles I and was appointed in 1649 Latin (i.e., Foreign) Secretary to the Council of State. Went blind in 1652 and was assisted in his duties by his fellow-poet Andrew Marvell. As secretary of state he pursued a policy of unity of Europe's Protestant powers. He also paid poetic tribute to that policy, notably in his sonnet on the massacre of the Waldensians in the Piedmont. He wrote poems in English,

Latin, and Greek in praise of the Commonwealth and its leaders, notably Cromwell and Fairfax. The Restoration cost him the greater part of his fortune, but he was included in the amnesty through the intercession of Marvell and perhaps Davenant and was not molested by the restored monarchy. None the less, Milton was bitterly disappointed by the inglorious end of the Puritan experiment in English politics, and he vented some of this disappointment in the lyrical drama "Samson Agonistes" (1671), a lament on his old age and the nation's apostasy, and also in his greatest work, "Paradise Lost" (1667-74, twelve books), the epic of the fall of man. Many commentators have felt that, for all his defeat by God, Satan really got the best of it in Milton's poem. "Paradise Regained" (1671) does not match "Paradise Lost." Milton lived through a bitter old age, despised by most of his countrymen as a regicide and out of touch with his age. The grammatical and logical works of his last years are of little value, and the theological "Treatise of Christian Doctrines," in which he shows himself an Arian, is only a curiosity. All this does not affect Milton's poetic greatness, which made him second only to Shakespeare, in the considered opinion of his countrymen, even though outside the Anglo-Saxon world he is overshadowed by lesser figures. He is perhaps most appreciated in Germany, where Klopstock (q.v.) modelled his "Messiah" on "Paradise Lost." Where Milton's influence has proved beneficial as well as universal is in his role as defender of freedom, as witnessed by the worldwide celebration of the 300th anniversary of "Areopagitica."

Miranda, Francisco de Sa de

(Portuguese, d. 1558).

Spent the years 1521-26 in Italy, and introduced the spirit and forms of the Renaissance in the literature of his country. Essentially an innovator, without great creative powers, he exercised a wide-spread influence on his contemporaries. The sonnet, which reached noble heights with Camões and Quental, was first cultivated by him. He also experimented with the tragic drama and wrote excellent verse in the traditional manner. Later in life he showed some bitterness at the changes that had overcome Portuguese society; in the field of literature he was largely responsible for the metamorphosis. An attractive personality of a certain patriarchal grandeur, he is one of the important figures of the productive Portuguese 16th c.

Mistral, Frederic

French poet in the Provençal language (1830-1914).

Born and died at Maillane in the Provence. Became early interested in a literary revival of the Provençal language, which had once sparked the birth of medieval European poetry through the Troubadours, but which had sunk, by his time, to the role of a peasant patois. Helped to found the "Felibrige," a movement of Provençal writers devoted to this revival. Published his first poems in 1852, followed it in 1854 with "Mireyo," a novel in verse, singing of the love of a poor laborer for the daughter of a rich peasant. It was crowned by the French Academy and, fifty years after its first appearance, Mistral was awarded the Nobel Prize for it. His other works include "The Treasury of the Felibrige" (1879-86), a Provencal-French dictionary in two volumes, "The Golden Age" (1875), "Nerto" (1884), "Queen Joan" (1890), "The Poem of the Rose" (1897). Mistral was the first major French writer in two or three centuries to live and flourish outside Paris; his regionalist credo has since found adherents in Provence and other parts of France.

Mistral, Gabriela
Chilean poet (1889-1958).

Pen name of Lucila Godoy de Alcayaga. Born in Vicuna; died in her home in suburban Long Island, New York. A schoolteacher in a lonely Andean valley, she leaped to fame with two brief collections of poems, called "Desolation" and "Tala." Her poems, in a starkly beautiful language, deal with her desperate solitude after a love; and with nature and children. She entered the Chilean diplomatic service in 1933, became Chilean consul in Madrid, Lisbon, Genoa, Los Angeles, etc. Was awarded the Nobel Prize in 1945, the first Latin American to be so honored.

Mitchell, Margaret
American novelist (1900-1949).

Born and died in Atlanta, Georgia. Worked as a journalist, married newspaper owner John R. Marsh, whose office served as a gathering place of Civil War veterans. Margaret Mitchell used their stories for "Gone With the Wind" (1936), the longest and most successful of all Civil War novels.

Moerike, Eduard
German writer (1804-1875).

Born in Ludwigsburg; died in Stuttgart. Was Protestant minister for ten years at Cleversulzbach, then taught literature at Stuttgart. One of the leaders of the Swabian romantic school. Wrote poetry, the novel "Painter Nolten" (two volumes, 1836), and short stories, including "Mozart on His Journey to Prague" (1856), generally considered one of the gems of German literature.

Moeser, Justus
German writer (1720-1794).

Born and died at Osnabrueck. Worked as government official. Strongly attached to Westphalian and

German traditions, he opposed the cosmopolitanism of the Enlightenment and the French Revolution. He was one of the pathbreakers of romanticism. Wrote "Essay of a Picture of the Morals of Our Time" (1747), "Arminius" (1749), "Patriotic Phantasies" (1774-8), "On German Language and Literature" (1787).

Mofolo, Thomas
South African Novelist (1875-1948).

Born in Khojane, died in Teyateyaneng. A Basuto, he wrote in his language "Chaka" (1925), a novel about the great Zulu conqueror and the first novel by a South African of African origin. It condemns Chaka on moral grounds and has been translated into English.

Molière, Jean Baptiste
French playwright (1622-1673).

Real name: Jean Baptiste Poquelin. Born and died in Paris. Studied law but gave it up because visits to the theater made him turn actor under the name of "Molière." Founded in 1643 the "Illustre Theatre" with which he performed in Paris and toured the provinces. Obtained royal patronage in 1658 and was given, two years later, the theatre of the Palais Royal. This became the nucleus of the "Comedie Française" which is still his "house" in Paris, where his plays are piously performed with the benefit of three centuries of loving experience. In his own lifetime, he was constantly under attack from the targets of his comedies. The bitterest attacks of all came from the clergy, which resented his exposure of religious hypocrisy. He was saved only by the personal intervention of the King, and when the hatred of the hypocrites pursued him even beyond death, it was Louis XIV who secured for him burial in consecrated ground. As with so many comic geniuses, his private life was extremely sad. His tragic marital experiences are mirrored in the attacks on women in which his comedies abound. But all this is merely incidental to Molière's genius. Starting from the French medieval tradition of farce, the Italian mime and the Spanish Comedy, his genius molded them into a uniquely personal form of comic drama of character. This is why Molière's comedies are the most universally appreciated of all the literary masterpieces of the "Age of Louis XIV." Not even the royal patronage could open to him, in his lifetime, the doors of the French Academy; but, not long after his death, the Academy placed his bust in a position of honor and adorned it with an epigram expressing its regrets. Of the many comedies that Molière wrote for his theatre, only thirty-two are left. They include "Les Precieuses Ridicules" (1659, his first great success), "The School of Husbands" (1661), "The School of Wives" (1662), "Don Juan" (1665), "The Misanthrope" (1666), "The Miser" (1668), "The Doctor in Spite of Himself" (1667), "Amphitryon" (1668), "Tartuffe (1669), "The Bourgeois Gentleman" (1670), "The Learned Women" (1672), "Le Malade Imaginaire" (1673), "The Man Who Thought He Was Ill," the play in which Moliere was playing when he was struck dead on the stage—a final piece of tragic irony.

Molina, Tirso de

Spanish dramatist (1571-1648).

Pen name of the Mercedarian friar Gabriel Tellez, born in Madrid, died in Soria. Wrote, some time before 1630, "The Mocker of Seville and the Stone Guest," the first play on the Don Juan theme and, in the opinion of some wise critics, still the best.

Molnar, Ferenc

(Hungarian, b. 1878).

Dramatist and novelist, pictures in his short stories woman who, by sex-appeal, selfishness, and unscrupulousness, turns man into her ever perturbed slave. *The Paul Street Boys* (*Pál uccai fiuk;* B'pest, 1907, trans. N. Y., 1927) is a moving story about children, their code of honor, their cruelties and sympathies. Outside Hungary, he is far better known as a dramatist. His masterpiece is *Liliom* (B'pest, 1909, trans. N. Y., 1929; adapted as the musical comedy *Carousel,* 1945). An idyl of the metropolis, it owes its great success to a combination of naturalism and romanticism, sophistication and sentimentality. The true-to-life characters of the big city 'tough' and his gentle mate, their inarticulate yet eloquent love, the harmless and hilarious satire on Heaven, the novel background, the transparent symbolism with its pathos and humor, are truly poetical. *Liliom* has local color, yet it is profoundly and universally human. Molnár's success is due partly to his sophistication, which is permeated with sentimentality, and partly to his skill in finding dramatic elements in any situation. This latter ability is, however, a source of weakness at the same time, for his themes are at times too flimsy to be of more than passing interest. Still, in moments of inspiration, Molnár is not only a craftsman but a poet. His apparent cynicism and sarcasm never hide completely his pity and compassion for suffering humanity.

Montaigne, Michel
French writer (1533-1592).

Full name: Michel Eyquem, Sieur de Montaigne. Born and died in Château de Montaigne, in Dordogne. Was courtier at the court of King Charles IX (1561-3) and was present with the king at the siege of Rouen. Withdrew from public life after the death of his father; travelled in Germany, Italy, and Switzerland; finally settled in the ancestral castle of Montaigne. Was mayor of Bordeaux for four years (1581-5) but generally kept out of the agitated politics of his time and devoted himself to his studies. Published a "Journal of a Journey to Italy, Switzerland, and Germany," but his fame rests exclusively on his "Essays" (three volumes, 1571, 1581, 1585), which created the literary genre of that name. Montaigne's outlook is a gentle and sceptical humanism, which reflects his own character and the experiences of his life and times. He was horrified by the religious strife of his day and kept neutral in the conflict between Catholics and Protestants, possibly because he had a Jewish mother. Another powerful influence on him was that of classical literature, especially Plutarch. Moreover, Montaigne was one of the first great writers of Europe to be affected by the Great Discoveries; he was the first to formulate the myth of the noble savage, later popularized by Rousseau. Montaigne's literary influence has been felt throughout the world; his essays are one of the classics of French literary style.

Montemayor, Jorge de
Portuguese writer in Spanish (about 1520-1559).

Born in Montemor O Velho, died in the Piedmont. Fought in the Spanish army in Flanders, was killed in a duel. His pastoral novel "Diana" (1559) was the first of its kind; it went through 39 editions in Spain alone and was much imitated all over Europe in the 16th and 17th centuries.

Montesquieu, Charles de
French philosopher (1689-1755).

Full name: Charles de Secondat, Baron de la Brède et de Montesquieu. Born at La Brède Castle near Bordeaux; died in Paris. Of good bourgeois family, trained as a lawyer, became counselor of the Bordeaux "parliament" (tribunal) in 1714, its president in 1716, was ennobled in the latter year. Withdrew from public life and settled at his castle of La Brède to study and to write. Travelled widely in the more accessible parts of Europe. His first book, published anonymously, "Persian Letters" (1721), won him instant fame. He became a member of the French Academy at the early age of 38. The "Persian Letters" uses a literary device common at the time: A critique of Western society is embodied in letters written by two fictitious Persians travelling in Europe. His next book, "Considerations on the Causes of the Greatness and the Decadence of the Romans" (1734), started the controversy on the causes of the fall of Rome that is still a topic of prime interest to historians. But Montesquieu's most important work is his "Spirit of the Laws," a classic of political philosophy. Montesquieu tried in it to codify the political experiences of his time, especially of the Whig monarchy in England, the generally admired model. In doing this, he had of necessity to do violence to the spirit of the English constitution which is unwritten in fact and almost by definition. But even Montesquieu's mistakes and oversimplifications proved fruitful: The doctrine of separation of powers which he distilled from the British political experience (though not from British political practice) was put into effect in the United States and was given the sanctity of a political dogma by the American Constitution. Montesquieu's influence was thus twofold: He was a pioneer of philosophical enlightenment and of political liberalism.

Montherlant, Henry de
French writer (born in 1896).

Born in Neuilly, of an aristocratic and strongly Catholic family. Gained fame as novelist in the thirties with bitter and sardonic novels like "Pity for Women" (1936).

Monti, Vincenzo
Italian writer (1754-1828).

Born in Alfonsine near Ravenna; died in Milan.

Born of poor parents, his literary talents were early noticed and won him the post of secretary to Cardinal Borghese in Rome. Monti's political allegiance was constantly shifting but he steadfastly maintained all through his life a great interest in classical antiquity. His "Essays in Poetry" (1779) were written in a classical style which he never abandoned. He attacked the French Revolution in the ode "Bassvilliana" (1793), but he made his peace with the invading French and Became secretary of the Cisalpine Republic, and later historiographer of the Kingdom of Italy and court poet of Napoleon. He then wrote "Gaius Gracchus" (1802) and "The Bard of the Black Forest" (1806). After the defeat of the French (1814) he kept his post as professor of rhetoric and adapted himself without much difficulty to the new regime. Monti also left some treatises on rhetoric and a translation of the Iliad.

Moore, George

Anglo-Irish novelist (1852-1933).

Born in Moore Hall, County Mayo, died in London. Gained fame with a naturalistic novel, "Esther Waters" (1894). Spent much time in Paris and London, but returned to Dublin to play a leading part in the Irish Literary Movement. His autobiographical trilogy, "Ave" (1911), "Salve" (1912), and "Vale" (1914) is a prime source for the story of that movement.

Moore, Thomas

Irish poet (1779-1852) .

Born in Dublin; died at Sloperton Cottage, Wiltshire, England. Educated at Trinity College, Dublin, and Middle Temple, London. Became Admiralty registrar in Bermuda in 1803. Published a translation of Anacreon and followed it with "Irish Melodies" (1807-34) , which established him as Ireland's national poet, a position which he still holds among nostalgic and sentimental Irishmen the world over. Published in 1817 an "oriental" poem, "Lalla Rookh," that earned him a European reputation. In the following year he was held responsible for an embezzlement of 6,000 pounds by his Bermuda deputy, had to go abroad to escape arrest. In Italy met Byron, who befriended him and entrusted him with his Memoirs. Moore destroyed the latter after Byron's death, and published in 1830 a bowdlerized version of the "Letters and Journal of Lord Byron" prefaced by a "Life" that drew Hazlitt's withering comment, "Poor Byron. But at least one thing was spared to him: He died before Moore published his life of him." Moore spent his last years in financial ease and at the height of his reputation. Today he is forgotten outside Ireland.

Moratin, Leandro Fernandez de

Spanish dramatist (1760-1828).

Born in Madrid, died in Paris. His father, Nicolas, was a poet, dramatist and critic who won great renown by his "Ode to Pedro Romero," the first of the great bullfighters. Leandro started as a goldsmith's apprentice but his literary talents soon became obvious and he was able to travel abroad under the patronage of Godoy, the ruling favorite, and Jovellanos, the leader of the political reformers. Moratin collaborated with the French invaders of Spain and went into exile after Napoleon's defeat, to escape from the Inquisition. He wrote in the French manner, but his spirit is unmistakably Spanish. His two best plays are "The New Comedy" (1792), in which he takes potshots at his fellow writers, and "The 'Yes' of the Girls" (1805), an unsentimental comment on marriage by parental choice.

Moravia, Alberto

Italian novelist (born 1907).

Born in Rome. Published at 22 a remarkable novel,

"The Indifferents," in which the people whose emotional life is dead, so typical of the twentieth century, are for the first time portrayed. It went through several editions before the Fascists caught on that they were Moravia's target, and they banned it. Since the war, Moravia has had an international public for novels like "Agostino" (1944) and "The Woman of Rome" (1947).

More, Saint and Sir Thomas

English humanist (1478-1535).

Born and died in London. Educated at Oxford. Became a leading figure among the English humanists and a friend of Erasmus. A successful lawyer, he deliberately subjected himself for four years (1499-1503) to the discipline of a Carthusian monk. Was elected to Parliament in 1504. Adviser to Kings Henry VII and Henry VIII, served them in a number of diplomatic missions. It was while he was in Flanders on such a mission (1516) that he wrote, in Latin, "Of the best state and of the new island Utopia," that introduced the word, though not the concept of "utopia." More's chief model was Plato, and his imitators were legion. The most successful was the Spanish Vasco de Quiroga, who organized the Tarascan Indians of Mexico on More's utopian principles, with beneficent results that have lasted to this day. More became, in 1529, England's first Lord Chancellor. He soon came into conflict with Henry VIII over the latter's assumption of authority over the English church. More, an earnest and fervent Catholic, refused to swear allegiance to Henry as head of the church. Was decapitated at Henry's order and his head fixed on London Bridge. Was canonized in 1935 by the Pope.

Morgenstern, Christian

German writer (1871-1914).

Born in Munich; died at Merano, now in the Italian

Tyrol. His earnest philosophical and theological treatises, e.g. on Oriental religions, were both read in his day, and are forgotten now. He lives by virtue of his satirical and parodistic nonsense poems, which he dashed off at odd moments and to which he attached no importance whatsoever, e.g. "Gallows Songs" (1905), "Palmstroem" (1910), etc.

Mori Ogai
(Japanese, 1860-1922).

Classical stylist, noted as both original writer and translator. As an army doctor, went to Germany to study army hygiene. Later translated many German classics into Japanese. Also author of over 60 novels and short stories. Major influence in modern Japanese literature.

Morris, William
English writer and craftsman (1834-1896).

Born and died in London. Educated at Oxford, was much influenced by Ruskin's aesthetic views and his friendship with the Preraphaelites. Advocated a return to the medieval traditions of solid craftsmanship as a corrective to the shoddiness encouraged by modern industrialism. Became a designer and printer, founded the Kelmscott Press to produce fine books. As writer, chiefly known for his translations from Anglo-Saxon and Old Norse and his Socialist utopia "News From Nowhere" (1891).

Morungen, Heinrich Von
German poet (about 1200).

Born at Sangershausen in Thuringia. One of the best of the "Minnesingers," the troubadours of medieval Germany. His verse sings the beauties of woman and nature.

Moscherosch, Johann Michael
German writer (1601-1669).

Born at Willstaedt in Alsace; died on a journey to

Worms. Baroque satirist; wrote, under the influence of Quevedo, "The Marvelous and Truthful Visions of Philander Von Sittenwald."

Moses de Leon

Jewish religious writer (about 1250-1305).

Born in Leon, died in Arevalo. A mystic who wrote the book "Zohar" in an artificial Aramaic and claimed that he merely published a manuscript written about 100 A.D. The "Zohar" is the fountainhead of all Cabbalistic lore.

Muenchhausen, Karl Friedrich Baron Von

German adventurer (1720-1797).

Born and died at Bodenwerder Castle near Hanover. Famous hunter and professional soldier who served with distinction as a Russian officer in war against Turkey. Told exaggerated and funny anecdotes about his real and imaginary exploits, with imagination growing ever more important than reality. His name is now proverbial for absurdly exaggerated stories. His exploits were put in book form by G. A. Buerger and R. E. Raspe (q.v.).

Multatuli

Dutch novelist (1820-1873).

Pen name of Edward Douwes Dekker. Born in Amsterdam, died in Niederingelheim, Germany. Spent many years in the Dutch East Indies as colonial official, was dismissed and wrote "Max Havelaar" (1860) a novel of social protest and humanitarian enthusiasm that caused a political storm by its condemnation of the colonial system. Multatuli was a prolific writer but nothing he wrote could approach the lyrical fervor and biting satire of his masterpiece.

Munk, Kai

Danish writer (1898-1944).

Born in Maribo, died in Hoerbylunde. A Lutheran parson on the West coast of Jutland. A leading Danish playwright, his plays dealt with the big problems of mankind—"the Word" (1932) with the reality of Christ's miracles; "The Melting Pot" (1938) with the persecution of the Jews; "For Cannae" (1943) with the question of power versus humanism. At first sympathized with the Fascists, but soon became a fearless spokesman of Danish resistance to Nazi occupation. The Nazis, after banning his books and trying vainly to silence him, finally dragged him out of his vicarage and murdered him in a nearby ditch.

Munthe, Axel
Swedish writer (1857-1949).

Born in Oskarshan; died in Stockholm. A physician by profession; caused a medical tempest in a teacup during World War I by his violently anti-German "Red Cross and Iron Cross," which he withdrew following a protest by German doctors. He settled on the island of Capri and won worldwide fame with the autobiographical and sentimental "Story of San Michele" (1930), a vivid and brilliant expression of the Northman's eternal nostalgia for the lands of the sun.

Murasaki, Shikibu
Japanese writer (about 978-about 1031).

Member of the powerful Fujiwara family. After a short-lived but very happy marriage, entered the service of Empress Akiko. Wrote "The Tale of Genji," a novel that is a classic of Japanese and world literature and has become available to Western readers through Arthur Waley's masterly translation. It is, essentially the story of a Japanese Don Juan, but viewed by a brilliant and critical woman who never loses her sense of proportion. Her "Diary" shows her as a shrewd observer of the Kyoto court, the scene of her great novel.

Murger, Henry
French novelist (1822-1861).

Born and died in Paris. Had a first-hand experience of the poverty-stricken life of intellectuals in the Latin Quarter of Paris which he described in "Scenes from the Life of Bohemia" (1847-49) that coined the word "Bohemian." Puccini's music was a great help to his words.

Musaeus
Greek writer (sixth century A.D.)

A grammarian by profession, wrote "Hero and Leander," one of the few love stories of classical antiquity.

Musaeus, Johann Karl August
German writer (1735-1787).

Ironist and satirist; wrote "Grandison the Second" (three volumes, 1760-2), a parody on Richardson, then at the peak of his popularity. Also wrote "Popular Tales of the Germans" (five volumes, 1782-6).

Musil, Robert
Austrian writer (1880-1942).

Born at Klagenfurt in Carinthia; died in Geneva. Wanted to become an officer in the Austrian army but became engineer and, later, a professional writer in Berlin, Vienna, and—following his emigration after the Anschluss—Geneva. He started as an expressionist but developed a metaphysical realism on the lines of Kafka. Wrote "Three Women" (1924), "On Stupidity" (1937), "The Man Without Qualities" (1930-42, three volumes; his chief work, left incomplete at his death).

Musset, Alfred de
French writer (1810-1857).

Born and died in Paris. Started writing at an early

age, published "Tales of Spain and Italy" at 19. Victor Hugo introduced him to the best writers of his day, and Musset soon became one of the banner-bearers of French romanticism. In 1833 started a passionate liaison with George Sand (q.v.), whom he accompanied to Italy. The affair continued for two years and was broken off amidst mutual recriminations and general scandalmongering which continued long after Musset's death. It was Musset who started the ball rolling with an autobiographical novel, "Confessions of a Child of the Century" (1836). George Sand, whose tongue could be as sharp as Musset's, waited until after his death to publish her side of the story, "She and He." But she reckoned without the poet's surviving brother Paul, who had the last word with "He and She," which revealed George Sand's infidelity. Alfred Musset's writings after the break with his mistress proved the truth of his saying, "Nothing makes us so great as a great pain." It was his love sorrow that inspired his tender lyrics gathered in "The Nights" (1835-7). After the pain subsided he wrote a good deal, but nothing nearly as good. However, some of the plays he wrote in his later years are still played on French stages. Musset became a member of the French Academy in 1852. At his best, he represents the tender, passionate, and melancholy moods of French romanticism.

Mu'tamid

(Arabic, 1040-1095).

A member of the Abbasid Dynasty, who became King of Seville when Moslem Spain was broken into petty states. Later lost his kingdom and was exiled to Morocco. Of some importance as a poet.

N

Nabokov, Vladimir Vladimirovich
Russian novelist (born 1899).

Born in Saint Petersburg, emigrated after the Revolution. Had a modest successs as emigré writer in Russia. Started writing in English in the 1940's with a biography of Gogol and a novel, "The Real Life of Sebastian Knight" (1945). Had a resounding success with "Lolita," first published in Paris, which catered, with a vengeance, to the current worship of erotic adolescence.

Naevius, Gnaeus
Roman writer (264-201 B.C.).

Born in Rome; died in Utica. First writer produced by the city of Rome after five centuries of historical existence. As is only to be expected, Naevius was a rough and clumsy writer in a language still unused to literary exercise. Naturally enough he turned to Greece for models, especially for his tragedies ("Danae," "Lycurgus") and his comedies. He was at his best and his most original in his epic poem "The Punic War." Naevius was a man of strong views and civic courage. He attacked in his poems the powerful Metelli clan and was imprisoned and exiled by their influence. He died in exile.

Natsume Soseki
(Japanese, 1867-1916).

Writer of bizarre and fantastic tales. Essayist, critic

and poet. Studied in England and taught English in Japan. First enormously successful novel: *I Am a Cat*. Later works: *Young Master, Kusamakura*. His style, marked by wit and urbanity, influenced the contemporary Japanese novel.

Nazim Hikmet

Turkish poet (born 1902).

Born in Salonica, son of a doctor from an upper class family. Educated at the Istanbul Naval College and Moscow University. First attracted attention with patriotic poems but his stay in Russia turned him into a Communist. He abandoned the old poetic traditions and introduced free verse and social themes into Turkish poetry, of which he is the greatest modern practitioner. Jailed for many years, was released by amnesty in 1951 and went to live in Russia.

Nedim, Ahmet

(Turkish, d. ca. 1730).

Is the last of the four most famous poets of the classic period. He lived in the famous "Tulip Period" (*Lale Devri*) and his poems reflect, as do those of few other poets, the spirit of his times, "the love of pleasure, the passion for beautiful things, and the all-pervading love of magnificence."

Nefi or Erzrum

(Turkish, d. ca. 1635).

The greatest poet of the reign of Murad IV, 1623-40. He gained fame as a writer of the *kasida,* an Arabic poetic form, usually a poem in praise of some great personage. He showed grandeur of imagination and brilliance of fancy, with imagery clothed in well nigh flawless language; yet his vocabulary and literary idiom and even his grammatical constructions were so Persian that he became known as the "founder of the artificial school." In his satires he sought revenge on many an enemy, and it is said that he was beheaded because of a violent satire on the Vezir Bayram Pasha.

Neidhart Von Reuenthal
German poet (about 1180-about 1250).

A knight of noble origin, he nonetheless created the "village poetry," i.e., poetry on peasant themes in the language of the courts. He was the first to make these lowly themes the theme of literature, and the people rewarded him by making him a popular figure of folklore as "Neidhart the Fox."

Nekrassov, Nikolai Alexeevich
Russian writer (1821-1878).

Born at Vinnitsa in the Ukraine; died in Saint Petersburg. His father was Russian, his mother Polish. Gave up university studies to become a journalist, and soon was made famous by his poems, moved by a strong sense of social indignation. Lenin was much moved by Nekrassov's poems, and some of them, like "Red-Nosed Frost" and "Fatherland," are still a regular part of Russian primers. He attacked serfdom in "Peasant Children," glorified the wives of the Dekabrist conspirators against Tsarist despotism in "The Russian Woman," and was one of the first to collect Russian popular tales and folklore. Intended to write a satirical epic "Who Is Happy in Russia?" but only its prologue appeared in 1866. The title became part of the Russian language. Nekrassov's fame owes more to his generous sentiments than to his literary skills.

Nemcova, Bozena
Czech writer (1820-1862).

Born Barbara Frankl in Vienna; died in Prague. One of the creators of modern Czech literature. Collected and published the popular tales of Bohemia (1845-7) and Slovakia (1857-8) under the influence of the prevailing romanticism, but she soon began to write in a pioneering realistic manner. She was one of the first fighters for women's emancipation. Best known for an autobiographical novel "The Grandmother," (1856). This gives a realistic picture of life in a Czech village and has been translated into many languages. Also wrote: "Poor People" (1857), "A Good Man" (1858), and "The Teacher" (1860).

Nepos, Cornelius
Roman historian (about 100 B.C.-after 32 B.C.).

Born in Rome of a distinguished family. Friend of Cicero, Atticus, Catullus, and member of their literary circle. Most of his works are lost, including "Chronicle," a history of Rome, and "Examples," stories to illustrate the severity of old Roman manners and morals. Of his "Lives of Illustrious Men," twenty-three biographies survive. Nepos is more esteemed as biographer than as historian. His style is of a classical ease and simplicity and has introduced to Latin many a schoolboy for whom Caesar's "Gallic War" was too advanced.

Neruda, Jan
Czech writer (1834-1891).

Born and died in Prague. Wrote prose and poetry in the spirit of realism; a well-known journalist who introduced the feuilleton to Prague. Chief works: "A Book of Verse" (1864), "Comic Songs" (1878), "Ballads and Romances" (1853), "Stories of Mala Strana" (1864), "I Am Not It" (1863), "Paris Pictures" (1864), "Poetic Entertainments" (1883-90).

Neruda, Pablo
Chilean poet (born 1904).

Pen name of Neftali Ricardo Reyes. Born in Parral. Influenced by Whitman, surrealism and—until recently —by strong Communist convictions. Best-known for his "Canto General," he is considered the great living poet of Latin America.

Nerval, Gerard de

French Poet (1808-1855).

Real name: Gerard de Labrunie. Born and died (by suicide) in Paris. The most representative poet of late romanticism. A melancholy dreamer and eccentric, much inspired by Germany, which he often visited. He made the best French translation of Goethe's "Faust" (he also translated other German works of the eighteenth and nineteenth centuries); was the first to recognize the literary talents of Jean Paul, and the musical genius of Wagner. Of his own writings the best known are the dreamy and often nightmarish "Chimeras" (1854) and "Sylvia" (1854), an idyll overcast by a dark fate. Nerval's later years were clouded by insanity.

Nestroy, Johann

Austrian humorist (1801-1862).

Born in Graz; died in Vienna. Professional actor on the popular stages of Vienna; starred in farces and comedies. He then started to write plays for himself, which he spiced with wit and satire without losing his typically Viennese melancholy. Nestroy is a typical product of Vienna and he is a regional Austrian, rather than a national German writer. But his wit and humor have a universal element, as was proved when one of his plays was adapted to the American scene and was played with considerable success on Broadway as "The Merchant of Yonkers." Nestroy wrote over sixty plays of which the following show him at his best: "Lumpazi Vagabundus" (1833), "The Mystery of the Gray House" (1838), and "Freedom at Kraehwinkel" (1848), a political satire on the Revolution of 1848.

Newman, John Henry

English religious writer (1801-1890).

Born in London, died in Edgbaston. Became a prominent member of the "Oxford Movement" for the renovation of the Church of England. Wrote for it religious tracts and hymns, including "Lead, Kindly Light" (1836). Became Roman Catholic in 1841, founded the Oratory at Edgbaston in 1847, created Cardinal in 1879. His two best-known writings of his Catholic days are "The Idea of a University" and the "Apologia pro Vita Sua" (1864) written in reply to Charles Kingsley (q.v.).

Nietzsche, Friedrich

German philosopher and writer (1844-1900).

Full name: Friedrich Wilhelm Nietzsche. Born in Roecken (East Germany); died in Weimar. Studied at Pforta School and the Universities of Bonn and Leipzig, where he met Wagner and came under the influence of Schopenhauer's philosophy. Took part in Wars of 1866 and 1870-1 as a hospital assistant in Austria and France. Specialized at first in classical studies and was professor of classical philology at the University of Basel, where he enjoyed the patronage of the Swiss historian Jacob Burckhardt. Suffered from serious nervous disorders from 1876; tried to obtain a cure on the Riviera and in the Engadin Valley. Became totally insane in 1889 and spent the last years of his life in Weimar under the care of his sister Elizabeth Foerster Nietzsche who survived him by many years. Nietzsche's view, achievements, and importance were controversial in his own day and are still seriously disputed. His controversy with Wagner, whom he admired at first and abhorred later, is now a matter of history. Nietzsche presented his side of it in "The Wagner Case" (1888). Nor is there much dispute about Nietzsche's great contribution to classical studies. His

"Birth of Tragedy From the Spirit of Music" (1870-1), which introduced the concepts of "Dionysian" and "Apollonian," revolutionized our ideas of classical Greece. But his philosophy, a "tooth and claw" version of Darwinism, culminated in the concepts of "the Superman" and "the blonde beast" and was embodied in works like "Human, All Too Human" (1878-9), "Thus Spake Zarathustra" (1883-5), "Beyond Good and Evil" (1886), and "The Will to Power" (1884-8); it is still very hotly disputed. Nietzsche's opponents pounce on his condemnation of Christian morality and his exaltation of the "Superman," and claim that Nietzsche's philosophy was one of the main influences that produced Hitler and Nazism. His defenders argue that Nietzsche was opposed to racism, praised the Jews and damned the Germans in extravagantly strong language (he even claimed with apparent seriousness that he was of Polish and not of German origin), and came out in favor of a united Europe. It is also claimed that Nietzsche's sister, a rabid German nationalist and a great admirer of Hitler, tampered with his work. This was recently proved for "The Will to Power," which was conclusively shown to be concocted by Frau Foerster from fragments of her brother's writings.

Niger, Samuel

(Yiddish, b. 1883).

Most prominent Yiddish literary critic. Born in White Russia, at an early age he joined the Jewish nationalist revolutionaries and became one of the leaders of the S. S. (Zionist-Socialist) party. Since 1907 he has devoted himself to literary criticism. Gained recognition through the *Literarische Monatshrift (Literary Monthly)*, which he edited in Vilna, (1908). After a period of study in Berlin and Berne, he edited (1913) the *Pinkes* (*Record*), a miscellany

341

devoted to philology and the history of literature, and (1913-15) a popular monthly *Di Yiddishe Velt* (*The Jewish World*). In 1919 he settled in New York and joined the staff of the monthly *Di Tsukunft* (*The Future*), and the daily *Tag* (*Day*). Since 1941, editor of the *Tsukunft*. He is considered the head of the Yiddishist movement, which maintains that the literature and the culture of the Jewish people are bilingual: Hebrew and Yiddish.

Nizami

(Abū Muhammad Ilyās Nizām al-Dīn; Iranian, 1140-1203).

Is acknowledged master of romantic masnavī (narrative couplets); his influence and popularity have remained unsurpassed in Iran and Turkey. He is considered second only to Firdausi in the romantic epic style. Of his *Khamsa* (*Five Treasures*), which took some 30 years to compose, the best poem is *Khosraw and Shīrīn* (ca. 7,000 couplets), a tale of the Sasanian king Khosraw Parvīz II (ruled 590-628). It was this work that established his claim to renown at the age of 40. The *Makhzan al-Asrār* (*Storehouse of Mysteries*), his first poetic production, is a work of religious didacticism rather than of romance, and contains the Sufi tinge of mystic speculation. *The Book of Alexander* is a combination of romantic fiction and philosophy written in epic form. Nizāmī's style is generally adorned with colorful figures and varied turns of rhythm. He has also composed theological and ethical poems and a *Dīvān*.

Nodier, Charles
French poet (1780-1844).

Born in Besancon, died in Paris. Librarian and journalist, took prominent part in politics. Did much to spread romanticism in France through his contacts with Germany and the "cenacles" or meetings of writers which he organized. His own writing, though voluminous, was less important. He is at his best in short stories.

Norris, Frank
American novelist (1870-1902).

Born in Chicago; died in San Francisco. Chief representative of the American naturalist novel, a disciple of Zola. However, he was not entirely proof against idealistic tendencies, especially in his last year. Norris pioneered in the description of American economic realities, especially the growth of big business, at which he looked with a discerning though disapproving eye. Worked as war correspondent in South Africa for the San Francisco "Chronicle" (1895-6), and in Cuba for "McClure's Magazine" (1898-9). Wrote "McTeague" (1899), "A Man's Woman" (1900), and a trilogy on wheat of which he lived to write only the first two volumes—"The Octopus" (1901) and "The Pit" (1902), dealing with the growing and marketing of wheat, respectively.

Notker the Stammerer
Medieval Latin writer (about 840-912).

Born in Heiligen, Switzerland; died in Sankt Gallen, Switzerland. Member of a noble family; became at an early age a monk at the Benedictine monastery at Sankt Gallen, where he taught and wrote. His writings are one of the high marks of medieval Latinity, especially the "Sequences," a series of poems, and "The Deeds of Charlemagne." Notker also translated a number of Latin classics into the nascent German language, which he thus helped to fix.

Novalis
German poet (1772-1801).

Pen name of Baron Friedrich Von Hardenberg.

343

Born at Oberwiederstedt in Thuringia; died at Weissenfels in Thuringia. Studied philosophy under Fichte; probably the most original creative writer of the German Romantic school. Novalis's most significant work is his unfinished novel, *Heinrich von Ofterdingen* (1799-1800), in which the hero goes through various symbolic stages of inner spiritual evolution in the attainment of his goal, the 'blue flower' of his romantic poetic ideal. After learning successively about nature, history, and poetry, Heinrich, through the death of his sweetheart—a motif that reflects Novalis's strongest personal experience, the untimely death of his betrothed, Sofie von Kühn—becomes capable of appreciating the ideal as well as the real world. Novalis's theory of magic idealism is derived from Fichte's philosophy. It seeks, by developing our will power, imagination, and faith to the highest level, to bring about the triumph of the inner over the outer world, and aims finally at a synthesis between nature and reason. As a lyric poet, Novalis made an important contribution by his religious songs with their heartfelt piety and sincerity, but his greatest lyrical achievement is the free-verse poem, *Hymns to the Night*. In it Novalis makes use of a motif frequently employed by romanticism, the celebration of, and longing for, night or death as a means of reunion with his betrothed in the world beyond.

O

Obstfelder, Sigbjoern
Norwegian writer (1866-1900).

Born in Stavanger, Norway; died in Copenhagen. Went to the United States to study engineering (1890-91). Returned to Europe and wrote neo-romantic verse and prose, with mystical and religious overtones. His style is polished, and influenced by symbolism. Chief works: "Poems" (1893), "Two Stories" (1895), "The Cross" (1896), "The Diary of a Priest" (1900).

O'Casey, Sean
Irish playwright (born 1884).

Born in Dublin, of working-class origin. Mostly self-educated, took part in the Irish labor and revolutionary movements, which he introduced on the Irish stage in "Juno and the Paycock" (1925), "The Shadow of a Gunman" (1925), and "The Plough and the Stars" (1926). The reception of his "Silver Tassie" (1928) was such that he preferred to emigrate to England. He lives in Devon, has written experimental plays and an autobiography.

Odets, Clifford
American playwright (born 1906).

Born in Philadelphia. Had bitter experience during the Depression, had to live at one time on ten cents a day. His "Awake and Sing" (1935), "Waiting for Lefty" (1935), and "Golden Boy" (1937) mirror the atmosphere of the more hectic days of the New Deal.

Since then, Odets has grown more prosperous—and tamer.

Oehlenschlaeger, Adam
Danish writer (1779-1850).

Born and died in Copenhagen. Started as an actor; became a writer. Wrote in German at first, soon switched to Danish, but maintained a lifelong interest in German literature and did much to popularize it in his native land. Traveled widely in Europe (1805-10) and made the acquaintance of famous people like Goethe and Madame de Staël; discovered romanticism and became its leading Danish exponent. Engaged in literary feuds with Danish classicists like Heiberg and Baggesen, but won through in the end. On his 50th birthday was crowned "King of Scandinavian poets" by the Swede Esaias Tegner (q.v.) at Lund. On his 70th birthday was publicly acclaimed as the national poet of Denmark. Oehlenschlaeger's output is varied and, on the whole, of high standard. He preached and practiced the romantic virtues of sentiment and imagination, but was by no means blind to classical restraint and concern with form. Chief works: "Poems" (1802), "Golden Horn" (1803), "Aladdin" (1820), "Hakon Jarl" (1848), "Baldur" (1808), "The Northern Gods" (1819), "Prometheus" (1832), "Socrates" (1836).

Oesterling, Anders Johan
Swedish poet (born 1884).

Born in Haelsingborg. Translated into Swedish many foreign classics including Goethe and Shelley. In his own work, began as a symbolist but became a realist under the influence of World War I. One of his perennial themes is the beauty of the Swedish landscape. Wrote "Preludes" (1904), "War Songs" (1917), "Sea Tones" (1933), etc.

Ognyov, Nikolai
Russian novelist (1888-1938).

Pen name of Mikhail Grigoryevich Rozanov. Wrote two novels, "The Diary of a Communist Schoolboy, Kostya Ryabtsev" (1927) and its continuation, "The Diary of a Communist Undergraduate" (1928) that are valuable pictures of the educational system—or rather, educational anarchy—of Russia in the twenties.

O'Hara, John
American novelist (born 1905).

Born in Pottsville, Pa. Came to New York and became associated with the "New Yorker" magazine and its slick type of fiction. Wrote: "Appointment in Samarra" (1934), "Butterfield 8" (1935), "A Rage to Live" (1949), etc.

Olyesha, Yuri Karlovich
Russian novelist (born 1899).

Born in Elizavetgrad. Member of the "Serapion Brotherhood." His "Envy" (1926), a tale of a "father and sons" conflict set in the Soviet era showing the author's clear-cut aversion to the coming mechanized era, created a good deal of controversy. Olyesha was silent in the later part of the Stalin era, has recently started publishing again.

Omar Khayyam
Persian poet (about 1050-about 1130).

Born and died in Nishapur. His name means "Omar the Tentmaker." Professional astronomer and mathematician, one of eight scholars appointed by the Sultan Jalal-al-Din Malik Shah to reform the Moslem religious calendar in 1079. Wrote a treatise on algebra and astronomical tables, "Ziji Malikshahi," which constitute his chief, if not his sole, claim to fame in his native land. More than seven centuries after his death he acquired a second kind of fame confined to the Western, if not the Anglo-Saxon, world, a fame that still causes astonishment among the Persians what they first hear of it. It stems from his collection of quatrains, "Rubaiyyat," translated—or better, adapted—into English in 1859 by Edward Fitzgerald (q.v.). Omar Khayyam became one of the favorite poets of Victorian England. The mixture of religion and skepticism, of sentimentality and mysticism, of austerity and alcoholism, was a ready-made recipe for satisfying the yearnings of the Victorian. Moreover, Fitzgerald, though a minor poet, was a poet. Today the Western and Eastern fames of Omar Khayyam are at last meeting.

O'Neill, Eugene

American playwright (1888-1958).

Full name: Eugene Gladstone O'Neill. Born and died in New York City. Had an adventurous youth as sailor, college student at Princeton and Harvard, actor, and theatrical manager. Settled down to become the true founder of the American drama. He was the first American whose plays influenced Europe and the whole civilized world; this was evidenced by the Nobel Prize for Literature, which he was awarded in 1936. O'Neill mingles reality and dream in a mixture that is often terrifying, though sometimes tender. His plays are mainly psychological, applying the lessons that O'Neill learned from Freud and Jung to an American environment that he knew, felt, and understood thoroughly. Through the presentation of his plays at the Provincetown Playhouse, he helped to reform American acting. A number of his posthumous plays continued to be produced in the late fifties, but the peak of O'Neill's influence was in the twenties and early thirties; since then, other and younger men have taken the lead. But O'Neill's place as the classic writer of

American drama seems secure, for all his bitter exaggerations and alcoholic meanderings. Chief plays: "Before Breakfast" (1916), "Moon of the Caribbees" (1919), "Beyond the Horizon" (1919), "Emperor Jones" (1921), "Anna Christie" (1922), "The Hairy Ape" (1923), "Desire Under the Elms" (1924), "The Great God Brown" (1925), "Lazarus Laughed" (1926), "Strange Interlude" (1927), "Mourning Becomes Electra" (a trilogy, 1931), "Ah, Wilderness" (1932), "Days Without End" (1934), "The Iceman Cometh" (1946), and "The Long Day's Journey Into Night."

Opitz, Martin

German poet and critic (1597-1639).

Full name: Martin Opitz Von Boberfeld. Born in Bunzlau in Silesia; died of the plague in Danzig (now Gdansk, in Poland). Led an unstable and dissipated life, which did not prevent him from becoming the champion of the classical virtues of steadiness and moderation. Was appointed historiographer to King Wladyslaw IV of Poland in 1635 or 1636. Wrote "Aristarchus" (1637), in which he championed the purity of the German language—writing in Latin. Wrote several didactic and idyllic poems in the baroque manner which earned him the title of founder of the first Silesian poetic school: "The Booklet of German Poetry" (1624, in German), which was to be to German literature what Horace's "Art of Poetry" was to Latin; "Daphne," which, set to music by Heinrich Schuetz in 1627, became the libretto of the first German opera.

Origen

Greek theologian (about 184-254).

Born in Alexandria, Egypt; died in Tyre, Syria. One of the Greek Fathers of the Church, surnamed "Adamanthius." Trained in classical Greek philosophy, he applied its methods to the Christian faith and became the founder of Christian theology. Was head of the catechetical school in Alexandria (about 211-232), later founded another school at Caesarea in Palestine. He defended Christianity against attacks, e.g. by the philosopher Celsus. His own interpretation of Christianity, which was too allegorical for some tastes, was by no means universally accepted among Christians. In fact, his teachings were condemned as neoplatonist and heretical at the Synod of Alexandria in 399. The condemnation has not, however, affected his position as a Father of the Church. Origen wrote textual exegeses of the Bible, a treatise on prayer, an exhortation to martyrdom, the treatise "Against Celsus," etc. His chief work, "The Main Teaching," survives only in a Latin version by Rufinus.

Ortega y Gasset, José
Spanish philosopher (1883-1956).

Born and died in Madrid. Educated at a Jesuit College and at the University of Madrid, and at several German universities, especially at Marburg where he came under the influence of the neo-Kantian Hermann Cohen. Returned to Spain; occupied after 1911 the chair of metaphysics at Madrid University. Founded a number of literary and cultural magazines, especially the "Revista de Occidente" (Review of the West), a landmark of Spanish cultural history, the main channel through which modern intellectual currents of the Western world were introduced to Spain. Was one of the men who prepared the coming of the Second Spanish Republic, under which he was a deputy at the Constituent Cortes and civil governor of Madrid. But Ortega soon tired of his brainchild, saying "The Republic is sad." Still, after Franco's victory he lived for many years in Lisbon because "the climate is better there." When he finally returned to Madrid, he was beset by troubles with the censorship and did not really feel at home under the dictatorship.

His funeral became a demonstration by Madrid students clamoring for intellectual freedom, and the press of the regime gave him the minimum of posthumous publicity required by his international stature. Ortega was a very prolific writer who wrote like Pico della Mirandola (q.v.) "on everything that can be written about and a few others." Apart from a mass of critical and expository writing, two books of his stand out: "Invertebrate Spain" (1922), an analysis of his country from the point of an unrepentant Castilian, and "The Revolt of the Masses" (1930), a landmark in European and, indeed, Western cultural history. Written under the influence of Plato, Nietzsche, and Bergson, it condemns the rise of the European proletariat in the name of aristocratic cultural values. Ortega's reputation has always stood higher abroad than at home, where his shallow and eclectic philosophy was called "the philosophy of the American bar." He cannot compete with the philosophical depths of his countryman Unamuno (q.v.). But Ortega stood out as a great "maestro," the teacher who acquainted Spain with the intellectual heritage of Europe.

Orwell, George

English novelist (1903-1950).

Pen name of Eric Blair. Born in India, of Scottish parents, died in London. Went to school and college in England, then became police officer in Burma. Returned to Europe and had the experiences described in his "Down and Out in Paris and London" (1932). His "Road to Wigan Pier" (1937) was a devastating documentary on a mining area plagued with unemployment. Fought in Spain on the Republican side, was severely wounded and wrote "Homage to Catalonia." During the war wrote mostly critical articles and essays. It was his two last books that at last gave him the fame he so long deserved: "Animal Farm"

(1945), a devastating satire on the ups and downs of Communism, and "1984," a grim forecast whose title became a stock phrase.

Ostrovskii, Alexander Nikolayevich

Russian dramatist (1823-1886).

Born in Moscow; died at Shchelykovo in Kostroma province. Showed his dramatic talents early, but had difficulties in getting his plays staged. His first play, "We Will Come to an Agreement" (1850), was banned by the Tsarist censorship; it was only three years later that the next one, "Cobbler, Stick to Your Last" (1853) was actually staged in Moscow. This was followed by a number of other plays, mostly comedies, including "Poverty Is No Disgrace" (1854), "A Well-Paying Post" (1856), "The Storm" (1860), "The Forest" (1872), "Crazy Money" (1870), "Talents and Admirers" (1882), "Innocenty Guilty" (1884), "Wolves and Sheep" (1875), "Snowwhite" (1873). Ostrovskii's plays are mostly staged in one social milieu, the old-fashioned patriarchal Russian merchant class, which Ostrovskii preferred to the smarter and more Westernized businessmen who were beginning to replace it in Russia. His tussles with the censorship show that his views on social conflicts were by no means conventional. After Gogol's pioneering, Ostrovskii consolidated the Russian theater; his plays are still a standard part of the Russian repertoire, e.g., at the Moscow Art Theatre. Following the artistic triumphs in Russia, they acquired a solid though modest following in Europe and America. The fame of Ostrovskii is quite overshadowed there by that of Chekhov (q.v.), but the old saying notwithstanding, he *has* been appreciated in his own country.

O'Sullivan, Owen Roe

(Eoghan Ruadh O Súilleabháin, Irish, 1748-84).

Is perhaps the best known Gaelic poet of the 18th

c. He was born near Killarney of a peasant family, and had a gay spirit and a heart for laughter in spite of the misery of Ireland in his time. He received a good education and opened a school when he was only eighteen, but the enterprise failed through his own fault, and the rest of his short life was spent in wandering adventure. He served in the British navy and took part in Rodney's victory over the French in the West Indies in 1782. After his discharge, he again opened a school near his birthplace, but again he failed. He died in misery in 1784. The hope of the Jacobites is his favorite theme; 19 of his extant poems are in *aisling-* form. His mastery of rhythm and rhyme is comparable to that of O'Rahilly.

Otfried Von Weissenburg

Frankish poet (ninth century).

A monk of the Weissenburg monastery in Alsace, a disciple of Hrabanus Maurus. Wrote in the East Frankish dialect that was later to develop into the German language; he is the first German poet known by name. Completed, about 868, a "Book of Gospels," which tells the story of Christ from the Gospels.

Ouida

English novelist (1839-1908).

Pen name of Louise de la Ramee, from her childish pronunciation of her given name. Born in Bury Saint Edmunds, died in Viareggio, Italy. Her 44 novels made her a perennial Victorian best-seller, and movie makers still find them a gold mine. Her "Under Two Flags" (1867) put the French Foreign Legion on the literary map.

Ovid

Roman poet (43 B.C.-17 or 18 A.D.).

Full name: Publius Ovidius Naso. Born at Sulmona in Central Italy; died at Tomi, a town about whose exact location there is no agreement among scholars, though it probably lay on the Romanian shore of the Black Sea. Member of a family of Roman "knights" (i.e., upper middle class); studied law and worked for a while in Roman government service. Left it to devote himself fully to writing. His brilliant poetry, with its strong erotic themes and overtones, became a favorite reading of Rome's golden and gilded youth. In 8 A.D. he was banished to Tomi at the order of Emperor Augustus. Scholars disagree as to the reasons behind the Emperor's decision. The two that are most frequently given are Augustus' disapproval of the immorality of Ovid's verse, and a scandalous affair of the poet with a woman belonging to the Emperor's family and household. Whatever the reason, Ovid had a very bad time in his desolate place of exile, though he put it to good poetic use. Chief works: "Medea," "The Heroines," "The Art of Love," "Remedies Against Love," "Metamorphoses," "Fasti," "Tristia," "Epistles From the Black Sea."

P

Pa Chin

Chinese writer (born 1905).

Real name: Li Fei-kan. Born in Cheng-tu. Went to Paris to study biology, but returned after a year (1927) to devote himself to writing. Best-known to Western readers by his short story "The Dog" (1936) which looks at man from the dog's point of view and finds him wanting.

Palamas, Kostes

(Greek, 1859-1942).

Is the foremost poet of modern Greece. A man of philosophic and intellectual bent, he has introduced many divergent influences into Greek poetry, but has maintained an individual lyric note. Throughout his entire life, he has worked consistently to show the continuity and unity of the Greek spirit in all its manifestations in the ancient, Byzantine, and modern worlds. His success can be judged by the imitators whom he has inspired and the followers whom he has influenced. He can be read as the best indication of the heights to which modern Greek literature may well aspire.

Panaferov, Fedor Ivanovich

Russian writer (born 1896).

Wrote a novel in four volumes on the Five Year Plan called "Bruski" (1931-37) which was widely praised for its enthusiasm and severely criticized, even by Gorki, for its bad craftsmanship. One of the pioneers of "socialist realism."

Panova, Vera Fedorovna

Russian novelist (born 1905).

Her novels give a remarkably realistic view of life in the Soviet Union, while fully maintaining the author's loyalty towards the Communist regime (one of her novels received the Stalin Prize). "The Train" (1947) told the story of a war-time hospital train; "The Seasons," published during the "thaw" gave an unvarnished account of family life in a small Soviet town.

Papini, Giovanni

Italian philosopher and writer (1881-1959).

Born and died in Florence. Professor of literature at Bologna University, later a professional writer. Papini has been one of Italy's most successful modern writers and his success has been world-wide. His writing is polished, in the Florentine tradition, and his books tend to produce sensations, literary and otherwise, by means fair or foul. His adaptability to the changing tastes of the Italian public—and politics—made the Italians nickname him "Papini the Chameleon." Even after his spectacular conversion to Catholicism (1919-20) put an end to his rabid atheist outbursts, he managed to write in the fifties "The Devil" which was widely condemned by Catholics for its pro-Devil slant, and was banned in Franco Spain. Other books: "The Twilight of Philosophers" (1907), "A Finished Man" (autobiography, 1912), "The Story of Christ" (1920), "Saint Augustine" (1929), "Gog" (1930), "The Living Dante" (1933), "My Italy" (1939), "Letters of Pope Celestine VI to Mankind" (1947).

Paracelsus, Philippus

Swiss scientist and adventurer (1493-1541).

Real name: Theophilus Bombastus Von Hohenheim. Born in Einsiedeln, Switzerland; died in Salzburg, Austria. Paracelsus was a strange mixture of genius, adventurer, and charlatan. He investigated the techniques of mining and the diseases of miners in Tyrolean mines, was forced to break off his university studies because he defied all academic traditions, practiced medicine without a medical degree in a wandering life that led him to various places in Switzerland and Germany until he ended at Salzburg. Paracelsus wrote a good deal on astrology, theology, mysticism, as well as on the practices of chemistry and medicine. His chief works include "The Great Miracle-Medicine" (1537), "The Book Paragranum," and "The Book Paramirum." They are written in style that gave birth to the adjective "bombastic." In his own time, Paracelsus was decried as a charlatan by the powers that be and the intellectuals with vested interests in their theories; but the people made of him a legendary figure of an adventurer who performed miraculous cures. Within the last fifty years science has made its amends to Paracelsus, who is now generally viewed as a chief founder of modern chemistry and medicine.

Parini, Giuseppe
Italian poet (1729-1799).

Born in Bosisio, died in Milan. A country boy who came to Milan, was educated in Barnabite schools and became a priest. Tutor with various noble families, from 1769 professor of eloquence in the Palatine schools. A city administrator under the French occupation, was dismissed from his post because of his austere morality and uncompromising patriotism. His "Odes" (1757-95) are Horatian. His long poem "The Day," in four parts (1763-1801), describes in minute detail the morning, noon, evening and night of an effete Milanese nobleman. It is a powerful attack on the prerogatives based on blood and a defense of the dignity of man, of labor and of family life.

Parker, Dorothy
American poet (born 1893).

Born Dorothy Rothschild in West End, New Jersey; took her first husband's name. Journalist and Theater critic, worked for the "New Yorker" magazine, and became one of the most prominent writers in the "New Yorker" manner. Her writing is exceedingly sharp, her wit is biting, and her sympathies are with underdogs of all kinds. Chief works: "Enough Rope" (1927), "Sunset Gun" (1928), "Laments for the Living" (1930), "Death and Taxes" (1931), "Not So Deep as a Well" (1936), "Here Lies" (1939).

Parkman, Francis
American historian (1823-1893).

Born in Boston, died in Jamaica Plain, Mass. Historian of the struggle between France and England over the control of the North American continent, in "Pioneers of France in the New World" (1865); "Montcalm and Wolfe" (1884); and "A Half Century of Conflict" (1892). Also wrote "The California and Oregon Trail" (1849) after a 1700 mile trip on horseback. Parkman preserved for his countrymen a past that he saw vanishing.

Parmenides
Greek philosopher (born about 540 B.C.).

Born in Elea, Southern Italy; founded the Eleatic school. Disciple of Xenophanes and of the Pythagoreans. Embodied his philosophy in a didactic poem, "Nature," of which only fragments are extant. Plato (q.v.) named a dialogue after him.

Pascal, Blaise
French philosopher and religious writer (1623-1662).

Born at Clermont-Ferrand in the Auvergne; died in Paris. Was a mathematical child prodigy: Completed an original treatise on conical sections at the age of 16, solved several problems involving the quadrature of cycloids, contributed to the development of the calculus and of the theory of probability. Went through a serious religious crisis in his early thirties, which made him give up his scientific work in order to devote himself to the religious life. In the great theological controversy on the doctrines of Jansenius, Pascal took the austere and puritanical Jansenist view which was ultimately condemned by the Catholic Church. Pascal came under the influence of his ultra-devout sister Jacqueline and joined the Jansenist religious community of Port Royal in 1655. His "Letters to a Provincial" (1655 *et seq.*) were an exceedingly bitter attack on the lax morality of the Jesuits who had taken up the cudgels against the Jansenists. His chief work of that period is, however, the "Pensées," a collection of some 1,500 fragments and aphorisms, collected by the Jansenists and published by them eight years after Pascal's death. It is now certain that the Jansenists "edited" the "Pensées" and censored them in their own interest. None the less, Pascal's book, even in its present mutilated form, is a classic of religion and philosophy. Pascal's view of man would be today described as existentialist: Man is "cast" into the world, and is surrounded by perils from which only the grace of God can save him. From a scientist, Pascal turned into a violent opponent of science: He opposed Descartes' "spirit of geometry" in the name of "the spirit of finesse" (subtlety). Today, however, his greatness is admitted by both sides to the controversy between science and religion.

Pasternak, Boris Leonidovich
Russian poet and novelist (1890-1960).

Born in Moscow, son of a Jewish painter and book illustrator. Started writing under the influence of the symbolist school. His poetry is primarily lyrical. It incudes "My Sister, Life" (1917) and "Spektorsky," an autobiography in verse. Had a difficult time in the Stalin era, being accused of excessive individualism. He published occasional volumes of verse, but was mostly busy with translations. The storm did not break loose until his novel "Doctor Zhivago," which expressed some critical views of the Revolution while accepting it as inevitable, was published in Italy and was awarded the Nobel Prize for 1958. Pasternak was forced to reject the prize, but remained in Russia and was not seriousy molested. Died of Cancer.

Pater, Walter
English writer and critic (1839-1894).

Born in Shadwell, died in Oxford. Studied in Oxford and remained there to teach. Exercised a strong influence on the writers of the closing 19th century by his preaching of the aesthetic values of "art for art's sake" and "experience as an end in itself." While Pater himself was inspired by the ideals of Plato and of the Renaissance, his followers tended towards glittering aestheticism and moral decadence. Wrote: "Studies in the History of the Renaissance" (1873); "Plato and Platonism" (1893) and a novel, "Marius the Epicurean" (1885).

Patmore, Coventry
English poet (1823-1896).

Born in Woodford, died in Lymington. Assistant in the printed books department of the British Museum, converted to Roman Catholicism. Married three times he wrote poems celebrating domestic love and connubial bliss, gathered in "The Angel in the House" (1862). After his conversion, turned to religious subjects in "Unknown Eros" (1877). Tends to be charming but superficial.

Paton, Alan

South African novelist (born 1903).

Born in Pietermaritzburg. His "Cry, the Beloved Country" (1948) has done much to present to the world the plight of the African population of the Union. Paton started the Liberal Party to oppose the South African government's proclaimed policy of "apartheid" (segregation of races).

Peacock, Thomas Love

English writer (1785-1866).

Born in Weymouth, died in Halliford. Friend of Shelley and his circle but his "The Four Ages of Poetry" (1820) provoked Shelley into writing his "Defence of Poetry." His novels, like "Headlong Hall" (1816) and "Nightmare Abbey" (1818) abound in dialogues and were largely written from conversations that Peacock overheard and noted. His verse is often in ironical and satirical vein.

Peguy, Charles

French writer (1873-1914).

Born in Orleans, killed in the Battle of the Marne. Self-educated, he became a pupil of Bergson. At the age of 25 started the "Cahiers de la Quinzaine," a magazine responsible for the discovery of many important French writers. Peguy himself was an ardent Catholic of a very democratic variety. He glorified Joan of Arc in his poems and defended Dreyfus (in "Our Youth").

Pellico, Silvio

Italian writer (1789-1854).

Born in Saluzzo; died in Turin. Son of a minor Italian poet, he developed romantic and patriotic views that made him a champion of Italian national unity against Austria which was its chief enemy. Became a European celebrity, met Byron, Madame de Stael, the Schlegels, etc. Lived in Milan, then under Austrian rule. The Austrian authorities forbade the staging of his play "Eufemio di Messina" and prohibited in 1819 the newspaper "Il Conciliatore" which he founded. In 1822 he was condemned to death for alleged membership in a secret nationalist society, the Carbonari. The Death sentence was commuted to twenty years' imprisonment, and he was put under strict confinement at the fortress of Spielberg in Moravia. Despite abominable treatment, he wrote two tragedies there. He received amnesty in 1830 and went to live in Turin, capital of the Kingdom of Sardinia that was the greatest hope of Italian nationalists. He was broken in health and spirits, but published in 1832 "My Prisons," a European bestseller and a classic of the Risorgimento. The horrors of our time, on much more gigantic scale, make the book less impressive to the contemporary reader.

Penn, William

English essayist and lawgiver (1644-1718).

Born in London; died near Reading. Son of Admiral Sir William Penn, the conqueror of Jamaica and one of the few prominent Englishmen to make personal profit out of both the Civil Wars and the Restoration. As a young man Penn became a Quaker and suffered a number of imprisonments for his views. He became one of the chief Quaker propagandists and wrote scores of religious books and tracts; of these the only one still much read is "No Cross, No Crown" (1682). In 1693 he proposed a "League of Nations" in his Essay Towards the Present and Future Peace of Europe." His best-known work is a collection of aphorisms, "Fruits of Solitude" (Part I, 1693; Part II, 1702), written while he was waiting out the aftermath of the Revolution of 1688. Penn was a personal friend

362

of James II and was Quakerism's representative at Court after the Restoration. From Charles II he received proprietorship of Pennsylvania in settlement of debts owed to his father by the crown. He advertised the new province throughout Europe as a refuge for the oppressed of whatever belief, thus helping create one of the noblest aspects of the American tradition. But his greatest contribution is his "Frame of Government" for Pennsylvania, in which he gathered together all the most enlightened ideas of his time into a flexible and lasting constitution. It is one of the main sources of the liberalism and humanism that was later written into the Declaration of Independence and the Federal Constitution.

Pepys, Samuel
English diarist (1633-1703).

Born and died in London. Worked for the Admiralty, did much to make the British navy the most powerful on the seven seas. In literature he lives for his "Diary" which covers the years from 1659-1669 and was written in a private shorthand. It remained unpublished until the 19th century (1825) but it has ever since enchanted its readers by its revelations of 17th century England, of life in London and of the character of Pepys himsef.

Percy, Thomas
English anthologist (1729-1811).

Born in Bridgnorth, England; died in Dromore, Ireland. A clergyman of the Church of England, he became royal chaplain in 1769 and bishop of Dromore in 1782. His own poetry is of slight interest, but his translations from the Icelandic are an important landmark in the appreciation of Northern literature. But it was his collection and publication of the "Reliques of Ancient English Poetry" (1765) that is a landmark of European literature and of early romanticism.

"Percy's Reliques," as it is generally called, inspired many other collectors and had a decisive influence on the work of men like Coleridge, Scott, Herder, and Goethe.

Pereda, Jose Maria de

Spanish novelist (1833-1906).

Born in Polanco, Santander, died in Santander. The last of 22 children of a wealthy and noble family. Studied at the artillery school, but soon returned to the family manor where his family made him an allowance that permitted him to become a professional writer. Pereda is at his best in novels of his native region, the Montana, whose men and nature he knew inside out: "Scenes from the Montana" (1862); "Sotileza" (1884) and "The Heights Above" (1896), his masterpiece. The results are less happy when he tries to preach his ultra-conservative ideas, as in "Don Gonzalo Gonzalez de la Gonzalera" (1878). His ultra-conservatism did not prevent him from becoming a close friend of Galdos whose ideas were anything but conservative. Pereda is an excellent stylist.

Peretz, Yitzhok Leibush

Yiddish writer (1852-1915).

Born in Zamosc, died in Warsaw. Started writing in Hebrew, but soon turned to Yiddish. A lawyer by profession, was barred from practicing it after 10 years by the Tsarist authorities, and spent the last 25 years of his life as official of the Jewish community in Warsaw. He tried to combine the best of the Jewish tradition—including Hassidism—with the best of the new. Wrote; "Pictures from a Provincial Journey" (1894), poems and plays.

Perrault, Charles

French writer and architect (1628-1703).

Born and died in Paris. Influential in various ways

in the reign of Louis XIV and certainly not the least of its glories. Controller of the king's buildings, had much to do with making the Louvre and Versailles the great monuments of Louis' reign. In charge of the French Academy, he introduced secret balloting in the election of new members. His poem on "The Century of Louis the Great" (1697) started the "Quarrel of the Ancients and the Moderns" in which the respective merits of classical antiquity and 17th century France were argued with much heat but little light. But Perrault's greatest though much disputed title to glory are his fairy tales which include "Cinderella." They were published in the name of his son Pierre and are sometimes ascribed to him.

Persius
Roman poet (34-62).

Full name: Aulus Persius Flaccus. Born in Volterra, Tuscany; died in Rome. A good friend of Lucan (q.v.), shared his indignation at the decline in Roman manners and morals. Persius was attracted by Stoic philosophy. His six "Satires," published by a friend, were among the favorite reading material of the middle ages.

Pestalozzi, Johann Heinrich
Swiss pedagogue and writer (1746-1827).

Born in Zurich; died in Brugg, Switzerland. Established in 1775 a school for poor children on his estate at Iferten, in which he tried to apply the educational principles developed by Jean-Jacques Rousseau (q.v.) in his "Emile." Although the school failed after five years, the experience proved valuable to him. Taught at and directed various schools in Switzerland where he applied his concrete approach to education, with material objects used to develop powers of observation and reasoning. These principles were later applied

throughout the world. Pestalozzi has his place in literature because he used a number of novels—some of
them very successful—to expound his pedagogical
views. They include "The Evening Hour of a Hermit"
(1780), "Lienhard und Gertrud" (1781-5), "Christoph
and Else" (1782), "How Gertrud Teaches Her Children" (1801), "The Mother's Book" (1803). He also
wrote an autobiography, "My Life's Fate" (1826).

Petöfi, Alexander

Hungarian poet (1823-1849).

Real name: Alexander Petrovic. He changed the
Serbian name of his father into its Hungarian equivalent as an expression of his Hungarian nationalism.
Born at Kiskoeroes in Southern Hungary; presumed to
have been killed in the battle of Segesvar in Tran-
sylvania, although his body was never found. Spent a
wild youth as actor, student, and soldier. His poetic
talents found a warm and unselfish sponsor in an
older poet, Michael Voeresmarty (q.v.), then at the
height of his fame. From 1844 started publishing a
series of books that made him Hungary's national poet,
a position he still occupies. A violent nationalist, he
supported the Hungarian Revolution of 1848-9 and
died in its defense. Petöfi excelled in prose, drama, and
poetry, but particularly in the latter. The main themes
of his verse are love and patriotism nor can any clear
line of distinction be drawn between—as can only be
expected of a violent romantic like Petöfi. He expressed the fiery side of the Hungarian character in
love, war, and writing. Chief works: "Poems" (1844-5),
"Janos the Hero" (1845), "The Tiger and the Hyena"
(1846), "Clouds" (1846), "Collected Poems" (1847).

Petrarca, Francesco (Petrarch)

Italian writer (1304-1374).

Born in Arezzo; died in Arquà near Padua. Educated at Avignon in Southern France, then the residence of the Popes. Studied law at Montpellier and Bologna, but left it to devote himself to the study of classics. Assumed minor ecclesiastical orders in 1326 and lived at Avignon, working for the Pope and for Cardinal Colonna. It was at Avignon that he met, in 1327, "Laura," the great inspiration of his poetry. She is traditionally identified with Laure de Noues, wife of Hugues de Sade of Avignon. After a visit to Rome in 1337, he retired to Vaucluse in the wilderness near Avignon. Was attracted by the movement to bring the Pope back from Avignon to Rome, with its Italian nationalist hopes. Went to Rome again in 1341 to be crowned as Poet Laureate, a revival of the classical ceremony. Went back to Avignon, stayed there till 1353, when he settled in Milan. The Visconti duke of that city entrusted him with diplomatic missions and acted as his patron. He also became friendly with Bocaccio (q.v.). Petrarch was prolific writer and his writings, both in Latin and Italian, make him a key figure of both Italian and world literature. He is best known as a lyrical poet who wrote the "Rime" and the "Canzoniere" to Laura. The sonnets and odes that he wrote for her have been ever since admired and widely imitated. Petrarch's "Platonic" love started another important trend. He is a significant pioneer of humanism: In addition to reviving Plato, he was one of the first Westerners to be interested in the revival of the classical Greek language, which he attempted to study. Roman revivalism and nascent Italian nationalism inspired his Latin epic "Africa," greatly admired by Mussolini. Petrarch was also an important literary critic, while his poems and his stay at Vaucluse are among the first manifestations of the modern Western approach to nature. He loved wild nature and was the first recorded Alpinist. Petrarch stood on the borderline between the Middle Ages and the Renaissance; he belonged to both, and his importance has transcended both.

Petrescu, Cesar

Roumanian writer (born 1892).

Born at Cotarni near Jassi in Moldavia. Journalist and novelist: He represents the revolt against city life and industrialization and the nostalgia for a simpler and patriarchal rural life. Progress is for him a tragedy, not a matter for rejoicing. His two best novels are "Calea Victoriei" (1930), the name of Bucharest's "Broadway" and "Black Gold" (1934) about the Roumanian oil fields.

Petronius

Roman writer (died 66).

Full name: Titus Petronius Arbiter. Died in Rome. Served as proconsul in Bithynia (Asia Minor), came back to Rome to serve as director of entertainment at Nero's court. Tacitus called him "The Arbiter of Elegance." Wrote the "Satyricon," a picaresque and satyrical romance which has survived only in fragments. The most famous of these is "The Feast of Trimalchio," a devastating account of a banquet given by the vulgar parvenu Trimalchio. Petronius was denounced to Nero as a conspirator and he committed suicide in the traditional Roman manner by opening his veins.

Petrovic, Petar II

Montenegrine poet (1831-1851).

Born in Njegushi, died in Cetinje. Became prince-bishop of Montenegro at the age of 17, fought against the Turks and introduced educational and other reforms. He raised the traditional folk poetry of his people to the level of high art in his "Mountain Garland" (1847) which bears the mark of influences ranging from Milton to Dante. Its ostensible subject is a massacre of pro-Turkish Montenegrins by their more indomitable brethren; but it rises from this local theme, beautifully documented, to loftiest debates on the clash between good and evil and the motives of human action. So topical is his poem that his countryman Milovan Djilas not only constantly refers to it but writes his biography in the jail to which Tito confined him.

Phaedrus
Roman writer (first part of First Century A.D.).

A Macedonian slave of the emperor Augustus who freed him. Lived on into the reigns of Tiberius and Caligula. Adapted the fables of Aesop into Latin verse about 35 A.D. A later prose version survived and was very popular in the middle ages, when the author was known as "Romulus." Of the original, only fragments survive. Influenced later writers of fables, especially La Fontaine (q.v.).

Philo of Alexandria
Jewish philosopher (1st century A.D.).

Lived in Alexandria in the first half of the first century. Headed a delegation of Jews to the emperor Caligula in 40 A.D. which successfully asked him not to demand divine honors from the Jews. His own writings reconcile Greek philosophy, notably that of Plato, with the teachings of Judaism. Their allegorical interpretations much influenced the Fathers of the Church.

Piccolomini, Enea Silvio de
Italian writer (1405-1469).

Born at Corsignano near Siena, of famous Sienese family; died in Ancona. Studied at Siena, moved to Basel (1431-35) and to the court of Emperor Frederick III of Germany (1442-47). Returned to Siena as bishop in 1449, became cardinal in 1456, and Pope

(Pius II, a name which he took in memory of Vergil's "Pious Aeneas"). A well-educated humanist, crowned "poet laureate" in 1442, patron of learning and literature. Best known for his letters and for his Latin novel "Lucretia and Euryalus" (1444) describing the tragic love affair of his friend, the German chancellor Kasper Schlick, with a married woman.

Pico della Mirandola, Count Giovanni

Italian humanist (1463-1494).

Born in Mirandola; died in Florence. Came to Florence and became a protegé of Lorenzo the Magnificent (q.v.). Studied Hebrew (including the Kabbala) and Arabic. Posted publicly in Rome in 1486 a list of 900 theses on all kinds of subjects—logic, ethics, theology, mathematics, cabalistic lore, physics, etc.—which he proposed to defend publicly against any opponent. Was accused of heresy by Pope Innocent VIII (was cleared by his more liberal-minded successor Alexander VI) and was reconverted to orthodoxy by Savonarola (q.v.). Died—as he lived—in the Renaissance style, of poison administered to him by his secretary. His works, written in Latin, including "Concordance Between Plato and Aristotle" and "On Human Dignity," are read today only by scholars and what most people know of Pico is only Voltaire's malicious epigram that "he wrote about all things that can be written about and a few others."

Pilnyak, Boris

Russian writer (1894-after 1938).

Pen name of Boris Andreyevich Wogau. Born in Mazhaysk. Fought in the Civil War. His "Naked Year" (1922) was a powerful and uncomfortably truthful account of the starving Volga region. Pilnyak welcomed the Revolution as an elemental renewal of Russian life; but, like so many others, he could not accept the rise of Stalinist bureaucracy. He tried to make up for it by writing a good novel on the Five Year Plan, "The Volga Flows into the Caspian Sea" (1930), but perished in the great Purges.

Pilpay

(Sanskrit, dates unknown).

Legendary fabulist, known through an ancient Sanskrit collection called *Panchatantra*. Translated into Pahlavi about 550, thereafter into Arabic. Versions also exist in Mongol, Malay and Afghan languages.

Pindar

Greek poet (about 516 B.C.-after 448 B.C.).

Born in Kynoskephalae near Thebes; died in Argos. Member of an old and noble Boeotian family. Last and greatest representative of Greek traditional lyric poetry. His poems were accompanied by instrumental music and sung by a choir. They are pervaded by religious, mythological, and archaic aristocratic views. Among his extant poems are forty-four Odes of Victory, which celebrate victories in the great Greek games, especially those held at Olympia; paeans of praise sung to Zeus and Apollo; choral dithyrambs sung to Dionysus; processional songs; choral songs for maidens; choral dance songs; laudatory odes; Festive Songs; dirges.

Pinski, David

(Yiddish, b. 1872).

Dramatist and story-teller. Born in Mogiloff on the Dnieper, he studied in Vienna and Berlin, simultaneously making his literary debut with stories of the life of the working man, as a contributor to Peretz' *Yomtov Bletlekh* (*Holiday Leaves*). Since 1899 in America, where he plays a prominent role in the ranks of Labor Zionism (former editor of the daily *Di Tsayt, Time*). He wrote historical romances; later, novels of Jewish life in America. His main accomplishment is in the field of the drama; beginning with family drama and realistic conflicts (*Yankel der Shmid, Yankel the Blacksmith*) and comedy (*Der Oyster, The Treasure*), he changed at about 1914 in the direction of symbolism and abstractionism. A number of his dramas have been translated into English: *Three Plays* (1918), *Ten Plays* (1919), *The Treasure* (1920), *King David and His Wives* (1923), *The Final Balance* (1926).

Pirandello, Luigi

Italian dramatist (1867-1936).

Born in Agrigento, Sicily; died in Rome. Lecturer on Italian literature in Rome from 1897 to 1922. Wrote poetry, short stories, and novels of some merit, but it was drama that finally proved his true literary vocation. Started his own theater in 1925. Was honored by the Fascist regime, to whom he gave a vocal allegiance tempered by intimate doubts. Became member of the Italian Academy in 1929; received Nobel Prize in 1934. Travelled in Europe and United States (1923-1935). Pirandello was one of the luminaries of modern European drama. The chief influences on him were his Sicilian background, the Italian grotesque tradition, and the modern age of anxiety. Many of his plays turn on the problems of identity and ask the question "what is man?" both in general and as regards the hero of the play. Chief works: "Love Without Love" (1894), "Blacks and Whites" (1904), "The Late Mattia Pascal" (1904), and the plays "Six Characters in Search of an Author" (1918, perhaps his greatest success), "Henry IV" (1922), "The Clothed and the Naked" (1923), "Somebody, Nobody, A Hundred Thousand" (1926), "When One Is Somebody" (1933).

Piron, Alexis

French writer (1689-1773).

Born in Dijon, died in Paris. Wrote plays of which the comedy "Metromania" (1738) was best, witty epigrams and salacious poetry. Was elected to the French Academy but his election was vetoed because his pornographic writings offended, of all people, King Louis XV. Great enemy of Voltaire and Rousseau, whom he covered with ridicule whenever they exposed themselves to it—which was fairly often.

Platen, August

German writer (1796-1835).

Full name: August Count Von Platen-Hallermuende. Born at Ansbach in Bavaria; died at Syracuse in Sicily. Lyrical and dramatic poet, also prose writer. Represents a classicist reaction to the prevailing romanticism, although he wrote some popular romances, e.g., "The Tomb in the Busento River," in a romantic vein. Influenced by oriental literature. Works include "Ghazals" (1821-4), "Plays" (two volumes, 1824-8), "Sonnets From Venice" (1825), "The League of Cambrai" (1833), "The Abbasids" (an epic, 1834).

Plato

Greek philosopher (427-437 B.C.).

Real name: Aristocles. Born and died in Athens. Member of a rich and powerful family, was called "Plato" because of his broad shoulders. Learned philosophy from Socrates, but also consorted with the Pythagoreans and had contacts with adherents of other philosophical schools. After the death of Socrates, Plato moved to Megara and then spent several years traveling in Egypt, Cyrene, and Southern Italy. About 390 B.C. was in Sicily at the court of the tyrant Dionysius of Syracuse. Fell out of favor with Dionysius, and the tyrant handed him over to a Spartan envoy, who sold him as a slave. Returned to Athens permanently in 387, started a school of philosophy in the grove of Academos—hence "the Academy," which lasted for over nine centuries and was closed only by the Byzantine emperor Justinian in 529 because it was the last bulwark of Hellenic paganism. Plato's most distinguished pupil was Aristotle (q.v.), whose teachings radically differed from those of his master. Plato's own teachings are enshrined in the form of dialogues—a throwback to Socrates' question and answer method, and opposed to Aristotle's treatises. It is still, however, a matter of dispute whether the Socrates of Plato's dialogues was anything like the Socrates of actual life. It would seem that all of Plato's works have been preserved, though critics doubt the authenticity of some of the material attributed to him, e.g. some of his letters. Plato's chief works are "The Republic" and "The Laws," on the ideal state; "Symposium," on ideal love; "Timaeus," on cosmogony; "Phaedrus," directed against the rhetoricians; "The Apology," purporting to give Socrates' defense at his trial; "Phaedo," on the immortality of the soul, given as a record of Socrates' last conversation before his execution. The other dialogues are "Charmides," "Cratylas," "Critias," "Crito," "Enthydemus," "Euthyphro," "Georgias," "Ion," "Laches," "Lesser Hippias," "Lysis," "Menexenus," "Meno," "Parmenides," "Philebus," "Politicus," "Protagoras," "Sophist," "Theaetetus." For all the progress that Western philosophy has made, it is still rooted in the works of Plato and Aristotle. The influence of Plato has been mainly thrown on the side of idealism in thinking and conservatism, if not reaction, in politics.

Plautus, Titus Macchius

Roman playwright (about 244 B.C.-184 B.C.).

Born in Sarsina in Umbria (Central Italy); died in

Rome. Translated, or rather, adapted Greek comedies for the Roman state. The plot and characters became Roman rather than Greek in his hands. His language and humor were those of the Roman people and the patrician society spurned his plays. This did not prevent them from staying alive, till our own time, being played at schools—in a Jesuit tradition continued, e.g. at English public schools—and influencing some of the world's greatest dramatists including Shakespeare, Molière, and Kleist. Of his 130 plays twenty-one are preserved, some of them incomplete: "Amphitryon," "The Gold Donkeys," "The Story of the Pot," "Bacchides," "Casina," "The Captives," "The Box," "The Corn Worm," "Epidicus," "Menaechmi," "The Merchant," "The Ghost," "The Boastful Soldier," "The Carthaginian," "Pseudolus," "The Persian," "The Dew," "Stichus," "Trinummus" or "The Three-penny Play," "The Truculent," "The Suitcase."

Plievier, Theodore
German novelist (1892-1956).

Born in Berlin; died in Wallhausen on Lake Constance. Wrote successful pro-Communist and anti-monarchist novels "The Emperor's Coolie" (1929), and "The Emperor Went—The Generals Remained" (1932). Emigrated to Moscow in 1932, fled spectacularly to the West in 1947. Wrote novels of World War II, including "Stalingrad" (1945), "Moscow" (1952), "Berlin" (1954).

Pliny the Elder
Roman scholar (23-79 A.D.)

Full name: Gaius Plinius Secundus. Born at Como (Northern Italy); died near Pompeii. Came to Rome as a youth; became government official and favorite of the Emperors Vespasian and Titus who entrusted him with high offices. Served in Africa, Germany, and Spain. An encyclopedic mind, he was distinguished in history, rhetoric, natural science, military tactics, etc. He died while watching the famous explosion of Vesuvius, carrying out his official duties and acting as a scientific observer. He was in command of the fleet sent to supply relief to the menaced cities of Pompeii, Herculaneum, and Stabiae, and was seeking to observe the eruption at first hand and from close quarters. Of his numerous writings only the "Natural History," in thirty-seven books, has been preserved. Its name is misleading to a modern reader: It is rather an encyclopedia of the knowledge of his time—a book that no single man could competently write today. It preserved for us the names of many classical writers and artists who would otherwise have been lost to us; and it included, in the case of the writers, samples of their works.

Pliny the Younger

Roman epistolary writer (61 or 62-about 114 A.D.).

Full name: Gaius Plinius Caecilius Secundus, nephew and adopted son of Pliny the Elder (q.v.). Born in Como. Entered government service, was governor of Bithynia, and of Pontica, now Northern Turkey. He lacked his uncle's universality of talents; he was a well-educated man and a somewhat mediocre writer, whose greatest virtues were the traditional Roman ones. Two sets of his letters are important: his correspondence with the historian Tacitus about his uncle's death at Pompeii, and the letters he exchanged with Trajan on the treatment of Christians in Bithynia. The latter letters are important evidence about early Christianity and the high quality of Trajan's administration: the emperor's refusal to act on anonymous denunciations is all the more creditable to him in view of modern practices to the contrary. But Pliny's eulogy of his emperor, much admired at one time, is too fulsome for modern taste.

Plotinus

Greek philosopher (about 204-270).

Born at Lycopolis (Egypt), of Roman parentage; died at Minturnae in Campania (Italy). Studied philosophy under Ammonius Saccas, taught philosophy in Rome from 224. His system is called neo-Platonism, is based primarily on Plato (q.v.); but Plotinus, the last creative philosopher of classical antiquity, systematized Plato's teachings and made innovations of his own, especially in aesthetics and metaphysics. His philosophy, edited and published in six volumes of "Enneads" by his disciple Porphyrius, was used as an intellectual weapon by the last defenders of paganism against Christianity; but it was, in turn, absorbed by Christianity and strongly influenced some of the Church Fathers.

Plutarch

Greek biographer (about 40-50-after 120).

Born in Chaeronea in Boeotia; died in Delphi. Educated in Athens, then lived in Alexandria and Rome. Trajan named him consul, Hadrian appointed him governor of Greece. A man of broad education and pronounced moral views, Plutarch's chief aim as a critic was to counteract the corruption of his time by moral and historical examples. This he did in the "Moralia," a collection of ethical, religious, political, and literary tales with a moral, and in the "Parallel Lives" of great Greeks and Romans of which twenty-three "double lives" are preserved. Plutarch did not intend to write history, and he is not to be taken seriously as a historian—he mixes legend and fact with a total lack of concern. But he achieved magnificently his purpose of providing historical moral examples not only for his time, but for all succeeding eras. His influence in Europe reached its peak during the Renaissance, as Shakespeare bears witness. It lasted long enough to affect Goethe and Beethoven and even to-day, though dimmed, it is by no means extinct.

Po Chu-I
Chinese poet (772-846).

Real name: Po Lo-tien. Born in Hsincheng, Honan Province (North China); died in Loyang, then the capital. Passed the Imperial Examinations in 800, member of Hanlin Academy in 807. Was involved in the tangled and troubled politics of the late T'ang dynasty; was in and out of imperial favor. Served as governor of Hangchow and Soochow and as chief magistrate of Loyang. His poetry is lyrical, occasional (often addressed to friends), and political. He had strong sympathies with the underdog and used folk-tunes and words of the common language. Nor did he hesitate to attack the "sacred cows" of Chinese culture, including Lao Tse (q.v.), of whom he wrote: "Lao Tse says, 'Silence is better than words.' Why then did he, to prove this point, write a book of 10,000 words?"

Poe, Edgar Allan
(U. S. A., 1809-49).

Erratic and tragically hyper-sensitive genius who was born in Boston of actor parents and educated in England and the South, did much of his creative work while a journalist in Philadelphia and New York. Defining *The Poetic Principle* (1848; pub. 1850) as "the rhythmical creation of beauty . . . an elevating excitement of the soul," he inspired through theory and practice especially the French *symbolistes* and later Anglo-American imagists. A master of prose tales of terror, sensuous beauty and ratiocination, he marked out valuable artistic "laws" of unity and effect for the short story. And he practically established the frequent personal crotchets of his own "tomahawk" method. His persistent romantic attempts to unite imagination and reason culminated in a puzzling prose-poem called *Eureka* (1849).

Poliziano, Angelo

Italian poet (1454-1494).

Real name: Angelo Ambrogini, but took his name from his birthplace, Montepulciano. Studied in Florence under the best tutors of the day; showed very early an extraordinary promise. Protégé of Lorenzo the Magnificent, tutor of his son Piero. Clashed with Lorenzo's wife, Clarice Orsini, and temporarily moved to Mantua to serve the Gonzagas (1479-80), but returned to Florence where Lorenzo appointed him professor of classical eloquence. Poliziano is one of the most representative writers of the Florentine Renaissance. Of his work, his Greek and Latin epigrams and his Italian pastoral poem "Orpheus" (1480) and verses celebrating the beauty of Simonetta Vespucci are among the best mirrors of their time.

Polo, Marco

Italian travel writer (1254-1325).

Born and died in Venice. Member of a prominent merchant family. Spent twenty-five years (1271-1295) on an epochmaking trip to China, where he spent a number of years in the service of the Mongol Emperor Kublai Khan. Among the things he brought home were several Chinese recipes, including one for spaghetti. Three years after his return (1290), he was captured by the Genoese in a naval battle and spent a year in a Genoese prison. It was there that he dictated in French, to his fellow prisoner Rustichello da Pisa —an Italian adapter of French romances—what became known as "The Book of Marco Polo." It was this book that first used the word "million" and gave its author the nickname of "Marco Millions." It has become a perennial classic of travel literature, and accompanied Columbus on his journey to emulate Marco Polo's exploits and to discover a new route to the riches of Asia.

Polybius

Greek historian (about 205 B.C.-about 125 B.C.).

Born and died at Megalopolis in Arcadia (Peloponnesus). A leader of the Achaean League, he was taken to Rome in 168 as one of a thousand political hostages. In Rome he became friendly with the younger Scipio and his hellenizing circle. He accompanied Scipio on his campaigns and witnessed the destruction of Carthage and of Corinth. He then devoted himself to the writing of his "History" in forty books, of which five are preserved complete and the others in extracts or summaries. Polybius wrote the history of the Romano-Greek world which culminated in the Roman conquest of the world or of that part of it that was known to classical antiquity. Polybius is a "historian's historian." His style, though good, is not brilliant. He excels in documentation and in historical analysis. He devised the first cyclical theory of history and is the "father" of similar theories elaborated by Vico, Spengler, and Toynbee.

Pontoppidan, Henrik

Danish novelist (1857-1943).

Born at Frederica in Jutland; died in Charlottenlund. Started as teacher at an elementary school, soon turned to literature. Shared the 1917 Nobel Prize with Karl Gjellerup (q.v.). Pontoppidan was a realistic and naturalistic writer and a sharp critic of his land and times. Novels include "Chronicles" (1890), "The Blessed Land" (1891-95, three volumes), "Hans Kvaest and Melusine" (1907), "The Empire of Death" (1912-15, five volumes).

Pope, Alexander

English writer (1688-1724).

Born in London; died in Twickenham, then a village, now absorbed in London. Son of a Roman Catholic linen draper, educated by private tutors because his religion barred him from attending public schools. Undermined his health by overstudy; developed physical deformity through a severe illness at the age of 12. A man of precocious literary talents, he wrote at 12 a tragedy based on the "Iliad" and a polished Ode on Solitude. Between 14 and 15 he composed an epic of 4,000 verses on classical models. At 16, his poetry attracted the attention of Wycherley his "Essay on Criticism," which came out in favor of the classical unities of time, place, and action; won Addison's (q.v.) praise seven years later. In 1712, he made his reputation with the reading public by his brilliant mock-heroic poem, "The Rape of the Lock." Worked together with Swift on the "Memoirs of Martin Scriblerus" (1721) and the "Miscellanies" (1727-32). After translating the "Iliad" and the "Odyssey," he attacked the critics in the "Dunciad" (1728-42), and expressed his philosophical views in the "Essay on Man" (1733). He spent the last twenty-five years in retirement at a villa in Twickenham, where he had withdrawn with his mother. He still indulged, however, in political attacks and lambasted Walpole and his policy. Pope is the chief glory of the English Augustan Age. He took his classicism mainly from Seventeenth Century France, Anglicized it and transmitted it to eighteenth century Europe.

Porter, Katherine Anne
American writer (born 1894).

Born in Indian Creek, Texas. Has specialized in short stories, of which she has written many but published few; for she is determined to publish only material that is up to her own high standards. Her special strength is psychological penetration. Published work includes: "Flowering Judas" (1930) and "The Leaning Tower" (1944), "Ship of Fools" (1961).

Pound, Ezra Loomis

American poet and critic (born 1885).

Born in Hailey, Idaho. Educated at Hamilton College and Pennsylvania University. Traveled widely in Europe and settled on the Italian Riviera in 1924. He returned there after a spell of internment in an insane asylum following his treasonable activities in World War II. Pound not only broadcast in favor of Fascism, but even sank so low as to gloat over the Nazi extermination of the Jews. Beneath contempt as a man, he is important as critic, translator, and poet. He translated a good deal from Chinese, Japanese, Provençal, Spanish, etc., wrote critical tracts, e.q. "Polite Essays" (1936) and "Guide to Kulchur" (1938), and a great many poems, including a long series of "Cantos" (from 1925) which, while fairly incomprehensible to the normal reader, exercised on Anglo-American poetry an influence comparable only to that of T. S. Eliot (q.v.).

Prevert, Jacques

French poet (born 1900).

Born in 1900 in Neuilly-sur-Seine (now absorbed by Paris). Published his lyrical poems for some time without attracting any attention; suddenly gained a broad audience when his collected poems were published in 1945 under the title "Paroles." This made Prevert the most-read poet of postwar France, whose influence has since spread all over the world. Prevert's strength lies mainly in his imagination; his technique was strongly influenced by surrealism. Prevert has won another and even more widespread fame as writer of movie scripts. He is responsible for the scripts of some of the great international successes of the French film, including "Quai des Brumes," "The Children of Paradise," "The Visitors of the Evening," etc.

Prévost, Abbé

French novelist (1697-1763).

Full name: Antoine François Prévost d'Exiles. Born in Hesdin (Northeast France); died in Courteil (Northeast of Paris). Entered the Benedictine Order in 1721, left it because his sensuous nature made monastic life unbearable. Became secretary to the Duc of Conti. Translated Richardson's novels and wrote sentimental stories of his own under their influence, e.g. "Cleveland or English Philosophy" (1731-38) and "The Dean of Killerin" (1735-40). His one book that counts is, however, a very different piece of work, "Manon Lescaut," the story of the love of the Chevalier Des Grieux for the prostitute Manon, a psychological novel on the lines inaugurated in France by Madame de Lafayette (q.v.) and harking back to the "Tristan" theme.

Prévost, Marcel

French novelist (1862-1941).

Born in Paris; died in Vianne, Lot-et-Garonne. Worked as engineer in the tobacco industry. Founded the literary magazine "Revue de France" and wrote a number of elegant psychological novels, mostly on problems of sex and marriage. These novels were much appreciated at the time but seem dated today. They include "A Woman's Autumn," (1893), "Letters From Women" (three volumes, 1892-97), "His Mistress and I" (1936), "Monsieur and Madame Moloch" (1937), etc.

Priestly, John Boynton

English writer and critic (born 1894).

Born in Bradford, Yorkshire. Has described the Yorkshire of his youth in his comedy "When We are Married," one of the mainstays of English amateur dramatics. Has written novels, e.g. "The Good Companions" (1929) and "Angel Pavement" (1930), and plays like "Laburnum Grove" (1930) that are English to the very marrow. In World War II his weekly radio talks came as close as possible to commenting on the events from the point of view of the mythical "man in the street."

Propertius
Roman poet (about 50 B.C.-about 15 B.C.).

Full name: Sextus Aurelius Propertius. Born near Assisi; died in Rome. Educated in the capital, became member of Maecenas' circle and friend of Ovid and Vergil. His reputation is highest as an elegiac poet, but the subject of his four preserved books of poems of some 4,000 verses varies from the amatory (addressed to his mistress Cynthia), through the patriotic to the exaltation of woman as wife and mother in the Cornelia elegy that strongly affected Goethe.

Proust, Marcel
French novelist (1871-1922).

Born and died in Paris. Son of a doctor of French peasant stock and of a Jewish mother from Alsace. His literary talents became apparent in his schooldays, and so did his morbidly unusual sensitivity. While Proust moved freely in French society in his twenties and early thirties, he was forced by asthma to shun increasingly the company of his fellow men and to devote himself to literature in a room whose walls were lined with cork to exclude the noises and distractions of the outside world. It was under these conditions that he composed his masterpiece, a collection of novels published from 1913 through 1927 under the general title of "Remembrances of Things Past." The individual titles are "Swann's Way" (1913-17), "Within a Budding Grove" (1918), "Guermantes' Way" (1921), "Sodom and Gomorrah" (1921), "The Captive" (1926), "The Sweet Cheat Gone" (1927). In addition he wrote "Pleasures and Days" (1896), "Pastiches and Miscellanea" (1919), and "Jean Santeuil," the first essay of his great masterpiece, recently discovered and published. Proust's reputation stands with that of "Remembrance of Things Past." He was honored by his literary peers in his lifetime, when "Within a Budding Grove" was awarded the Goncourt Prize. But official recognition, French and international, escaped him—he was not elected to the French Academy and was not awarded the Nobel Prize. These omissions in no way effect Proust's status as one of the great novelists of our century and of all times. C. K. M. Scott-Moncrieff's translations have made his novels accessible to Anglo-Saxon readers and they have had a formative influence that is world wide. His work shows the influence not only of the great masters of the French novel, but also of Freud and Bergson, though Proust himself denied the Bergsonian influence and he was influenced perhaps more by the French predecessors of Freud (Janet and Charcot) rather than by Freud himself. But above all, Proust's work bears the mark of his own personality: that of a chronicler of a world of French aristocracy that is about to wilt after its last flowering, a chronicler whose sensitivity, like that of Montaigne (q.v.), was abnormally sharpened by his mixed Franco-Jewish ancestry.

Prudentius

Roman poet (348-after 405).

Full name: Aurelius Prudentius Clemens. Born in Calagurris (now Calahora in Aragon); died in Rome. An ardent Christian, he held office under the emperor Theodosius the Great, who finally outlawed paganism. But he left his official post to devote himself first to writing and then to religious life. He died in retirement in a monastery. Prudentius is generally considered the greatest Christian poet of classical antiquity; his Latin has a Roman polish and a Spanish fervor. He wrote, "Cathemerinon," including twelve devotional hymns; "Psychomachia," on virtue and vice struggling for the soul of a Christian; "Peri Stephanon," on the first martyr and in praise of other martyrs; "Hamartigenia," on the origin of evil, and "Apotheosis," a defense of the doctrine of the divinity of Christ.

Pulci, Luigi or Lodovico
Italian poet (1432-1484).

Born in Florence, died in Padua. Patronized by the Medici, including Lorenzo. His "Morgante the Giant" (1460-70) took the theme of Charlemagne from the popular storytellers and turned it into literature, thus preparing the 16th century poems on Roland.

Pushkin, Alexander Sergeyevich
Russian writer (1799-1837).

Born in Moscow; died in Saint Petersburg. Pushkin's great-grandfather was an Ethiopian slave of Peter the Great and he was very conscious and proud of his ancestry. On his father's side, member of aristocratic Russian family. Received excellent Western-style education, but his literary work also bears the mark of the popular Russian tale, told him by his beloved nurse, Irina Rodionova. Worked in Ministry of Foreign Affairs after 1817; but his official career—which he did not take too seriously—was checkered. His early poems, strongly influenced by Byron and the German romanticists, expressed ultra-democratic views—especially the "Ode to Liberty" (1820), which earned him a period of exile in South Russia (Bessarabia and the Caucasus) and temporary dismissal from service. His involvement with the Dekabrist liberal conspirators against Tsar Nicholas I endangered his position and even his life, but the Tsar satisfied himself with warning Pushkin and acting personally as his censor. Pushkin at first chafed at his fate, and tried in vain to obtain permission to leave Russia. Later he accepted his situation—at least outwardly—but he could not abide the punishment of his friends, attacks from jealous scribblers, a general lack of understanding of his work, and (for all his writing glorifying tsars like Peter the Great) the atmosphere of Russia as ruled by Nicholas I, the "gendarme of Europe" and "emperor-rod." Accusations of infidelity rumored against his beautiful and insipid wife, whom he adored, proved the last straw. He fought a duel against d'Anthès, the chief of the rumormongers and a person despicable on all counts, and was killed by him. His death was suicide as well as murder. With Pushkin, modern Russian literature starts. As Hertzen put it, "Peter the Great issued a challenge to Russia, and Russia replied by producing Pushkin." Russia's "classical" literature stems from him by personal and direct contact, as in the cases of Gogol and Lermontov, or more indirectly, as with Dostoyevski and Tolstoy. Pushkin brought the Russian literary language to a perfection never attained before or since. He excelled in all the literary genres, and while both a classicist and a romantic, he cannot be contained by either of these categories. If his outside reputation is not equal to his stature in Russia, this is due less to his literary failures than to the language barrier which has made his work—and especially his poetry—all but untranslatable. Chief works: "Ruslan and Ludmila" (1820); "The Prisoner of the Caucasus" (1822); "Boris Godunov" (1825); "The Fountain of Rakchisarac" (1827); "The Gypsies" (1827); "Poltava" (1829); "Eugene Onegin" (the "novel in verse" that is his masterpiece, 1832); "The Copper Horseman" (1833), "The Pugachev Rebellion" (1834), "The Queen of Spades" (1834), "The Captain's Daughter" (1836).

Q

Quasimodo, Salvatore

Italian writer (born 1901).

Born in Syracuse, Sicily. Started by writing short lyrics on Sicilian themes. Fascism and war broadened his outlook and his "Day after Day" (1947) and "Life is not a Dream" (1949) protest against man's inhumanity to man. Was awarded the Nobel Prize for literature in 1959.

Quintilian

Roman orator and writer (about 35-about 95).

Full name: Marcus Fabius Quintilianus. Born in Calagurris (Northeast Spain); died in Rome. The emperor Vespasian called him to Rome to occupy the first public chair of rhetorics. After twenty years' occupancy of that chair he retired to become tutor of the grand-nephew of the emperor Domitian. Toward the end of his life, he summed up his pedagogical experiences in "The Twelve Books of Oratory." He gives in it, in addition to the matter indicated in the title, a description of the Roman educational system and an outline of Graeco-Roman literature. Quintilian was a staunch classicist and a great admirer of Cicero. His influence was paramount among the Latinists of the European Renaissance and Baroque.

R

Raabe, Wilhelm

German novelist (1831-1910).

Born in Eschershausen near Brunswick; died in Brunswick. Studied philosophy in Berlin, published his first literary work while still a student. He retired to Brunswick in 1870. Raabe is one of the most important German Realists and a humorist in the tradition of Jean Paul. Both are essentially chroniclers of the small German city of pre-Bismarck Germany. But unlike Richter (q.v.), Raabe is practically unappreciated outside Germany. Works include: "Chronicles of the Sperlingsgasse" (1856), "Our Lord's Chancery" (1862), "The Hunger Pastor" (1864), "German Nobility" (1880), "The Lugan Monastery" (1894).

Rabelais, François

French satirist (1493 or 1494-1553).

Born in La Devinière near Chinon, in the Touraine; died in Paris. Had a long and varied career as a monk, first Franciscan, then Benedictine; spent fifteen years (1509-1524) at Cordelier convent of Fontenay-le-Comte. Then left the monastic life and became a secular priest. After several years of wandering, studied medicine at Montpellier and practiced it at Lyons. There followed several years of wandering in France and Italy until he settled for two years at a parish in Meudon (1550-52). He edited various medical treatises, now mercifully forgotten, but his fame rests securely on the two novels "Gargantua" and "Pantagruel" (5 volumes, 1532-52 and 1564) which he published under an anagram of his name. "Alcofribas Nasier." The adventures of two giants, father and son, that gave the books their names, also gave us the adjective "Rabelaisian"; he stood between the Middle Ages and the Renaissance and he made it quite clear where his sympathies were. His satire hit monks, priests, doctors, politicians, intellectuals, with complete impartiality, but he hailed the new and condemned the unnatural restrictions that the Age of Faith had imposed on him. His own ideal was the "Abbey of Theleme," with the motto "Do What You Will" engraved over its door. But Rabelais' laughter, though often savage, had a healing quality as well, and "Gargantua" and "Pantagruel" are among the most loved books of all times. Nor is there any doubt that the "Gallic" character of their broad humor has contributed to their lasting popularity.

Racine, Jean

French dramatist (1639-1699).

Born in La Ferté-Milon near Soissons; died in Paris. Became a writer after studying theology; attracted the attention of the Court by an ode on the marriage of Louis XIV. Became friendly with Boileau, La Fontaine, and Molière, but was dissatisfied with the way in which Molière's company presented his first two plays and engaged a rival company for the following ones. Was highly honored at court, became member of the Academy in 1673, and was given honorary posts at court. However, he lost the King's favor by a petition on behalf of the tax-burdened people of France, and spent his last years in retirement and subject to attacks. He wrote no plays in the last ten years of his life because he came under the influence of Jansenism and considered the theatre sinful. Racine made Corneille's heroic figures human and brought the French classical drama to perfection. Perhaps his two outstanding achievements are his exceedingly subtle language and his insight into feminine psychology. Wrote "The Thebaid" (1664), "Alexander" (1665), "Andromache" (1667), "The Pleaders" (1668), "Britannicus" (1669), "Iphigenia" (1674), "Berenice" (1670), "Bajazet" (1672), "Mithridates" (1673), "Iphigenia" (1674), "Phedra" (1677), "Esther" (1669), "Athalia" (1690), "History of Port Royal" (published posthumously).

Radiguet, Raymond
French writer (1903-1923).

Born in Parc-de-Saint Maure; died in Paris. Son of a cartoonist, came to Paris at the age of 15 and attracted the friendship and patronage of Jean Cocteau (q.v.). In addition to two volumes of poetry, published two novels, "Le Diable au Corps" (The Devil in the Body, 1923), and the "Ball of the Count of Orgel" (posthumous, 1924). These novels, especially the former, show a psychological realism and a maturity hard to imagine in a young man of Radiguet's age in a country other than France. "Le Diable au Corps" seems to be certain of a place as a minor literary classic.

Radishchev, Alexander Nikolayevich
Russian novelist (1749-1802).

Born in Saratov province, died in Saint Petersburg. Wrote an "Ode to Liberty" and a novel "A Journey from Saint Petersburg to Moscow" (1790), a merciless attack on Tsarist autocracy and the degradations of serfdom which inaugurated the vein of social protest that is one of the roots of the "Russian novel." Radishchev paid dearly for his pioneering humanitarianism. Catherine II condemned him to death. The punishment was commuted to exile in Siberia from which he was freed by Catherine's successor Paul. But his spirit was broken and he committed suicide.

Raimund, Ferdinand

Austrian poet and dramatist (1790-1836).

Born in Vienna; died in Pottenstein. Apprentice to a confectioner, became actor and finally a dramatist who carried to perfection the popular Viennese comedy. His plays are rich in humor and imagination but also reveal the deep pessimism that made him end his life by suicide. Chief works: "The Maker of Barometers on the Magic Island" (1823), "King of Alps and Enemy of Men" (1828), "The Spendthrift" (1834).

Ramsay, Allan

Scottish poet (1686-1758).

Born in Leadhills, died in Edinburgh. Went to Edinburgh as apprentice to a wig-maker in 1700. Opened a bookshop and started Scotland's first circulating library. Worked hard to acquaint his countrymen with their literary heritage, both popular and learned. Collected folk-songs and wrote songs that became folk-songs. His pastoral comedy "The Gentle Shepherd" (1725) has been successfully revived at the Edinburgh Festival.

Ransom, John Crowe

American poet (born 1888).

Born in Pulaski, Tennessee. Was chief founder of the group of "Fugitives," poets associated with Vanderbilt University where he studied. The "Fugitives" took it upon themselves to preserve and restore the values of the Agrarian South. In addition to his poems, e.g. "Grace After Meat" (1924), Ransom performed this task in biting critical essays.

Rashi

Jewish religious writer (1040-1115).

Abbreviation of his real name: Rabbi Sholomo ben Izhak. Born and died at Troyes in the Champagne. Studied at Worms and Mainz and started a Talmudic academy at Troyes. Wrote commentaries on the Bible and the Talmud that became standard in orthodox Jewish circles. The French glosses which he scattered through both commentaries are important linguistic documents. Rashi also wrote some excellent liturgical poetry.

Raspe, Rudolf Erich

German adventurer and writer (1737-1794).

Archaeologist and mineralogist, whose "Baron Muenchhausen's Narrative of His Marvellous Travels and Campaigns in Russia" (1785) is the backbone of the Muenchhausen book of adventures. His own exploits rival those of the "Lying Baron." A professor of archeology and curator of the museum at Kassel, he was charged with stealing and selling medals and had to flee to England (1775). There he masqueraded as a mining expert and swindled Sir John Sinclair of considerable sums by claiming to find gold and silver on his estate. Sir Walter Scott used him for the character of Douster-Swivel in his "Antiquary." His authorship of the Muenchhausen stories was not revealed until 1824.

Reisen, Abraham

(Yiddish, b. 1876).

Popular poet and writer of short stories. Born in a small town in White Russia into a family of more than mean literary ability—his father wrote Hebrew poetry, his sister Sarah is a poetess and storyteller and a younger brother Zalmen is a linguist and a student of literature. He published his first poem at the age of 16 in Peretz's *Yidishe Bibliothek,* and toward the end of the century began writing stories in *Der Yid.* In 1900 he published a miscellany (*Twentieth Century*) in which he defends the use of Yiddish. Settled in America in 1914. In 1928, toured the U. S. S. R., where he was given an enthusiastic reception. His influence is manifest in a number of Russian Yiddish writers.

Remarque, Erich Maria

German novelist (born 1898) .

His real name is given as Remark or Kramer. Born in Osnabrueck. Fought in World War I, became world-famous with his pacifist novel "All Quiet on the Western Front," published in 1928 after it had been rejected by a formidable number of publishers.

Renan, Ernest

French writer (1823-1892) .

Born in Treguier in Brittany, died in Paris. Intended for the priesthood, but gave up his theological studies under the influence of rationalism and the "higher criticism" of the Bible. Taught at the College de France from 1862 and was elected to the French Academy in 1876. Travelled widely in Italy, Greece, Syria and Palestine. His "Future of Science" (1848) and even more his "Life of Jesus" (1863) were much read and their influence was world-wide. His nostalgic "Recollections of My Youth" (1883) and "My Sister Henrietta" (1895) were popular with a public that did not necessarily care for his more prominent books.

Retif de la Bretonne, Nicolas de Monte

French novelist (1734-1806).

Also known as "Restif de la Bretonne." Born at Saci near Auxerre (Burgundy) ; died in Paris. Led an unsettled, adventurous, and amorous life, which provided him with the themes of his novels, which were unusually voluminous. They earned him the nicknames of "Rousseau of the Gutter" and "Voltaire of the Chambermaids" and include "The Pornographer" (1769), "The Perverted Peasant" (1776), "The Perverted Peasant Woman or the Perils of the City" (1779), "Contemporary Adventures of the Prettiest Woman of Our Time" (1780's, 42 volumes), "Monsieur Nicolas or the Human Heart Unveiled" (1794-7, 16 volumes).

Retz, Cardinal de

French writer (1614-1679).

Real name: Francois Paul de Gondi. Born in Montmirail, died in Paris. Became priest in 1643 and cardinal in 1651. Took prominent part in the Fronde and had to abandon the archbishopric of Paris after Louis XIV assumed personal power. In retirement, wrote his famous "Memoirs" (published 1717) much admired for their style but not for their veracity.

Reuchlin, Johannes

German humanist (1455-1522).

Born in Pforzheim; died in Bad Liebenzell. Granduncle and teacher of Melanchthon (q.v.). Entered the service of Duke Eberhard of Wurttemberg in 1481, later served the Swabian League (1510-6). Taught Greek and Hebrew at Ingolstadt and Tubingen Universities. He championed the modern pronunciation of Greek, named "Reuchlian" after him. His violent controversy with the obscurantist Dominicans of Cologne led to the publication of the "Epistles of Obscure Men," a classic of humanism. Works include: The first modern Hebrew grammar, published in Latin (1506); an edition of seven penitential psalms (1512); the Latin satirical comedies "Sergius" (1497); cabalistic works including "On the Miraculous Word" (1494) and "On the Cabalistic Art" (1517); etc.

Reuter, Fritz

German writer (1810-1874).

Born in Stavenhagen in Mecklenburg; died in Eisenach. A man of radical ideas in his youth, he was arrested in 1833 and condemned to death for alleged treasonable activities. King Frederick William III of Prussia commuted the sentence to thirty years' imprisonment. Liberated after several painful years in jail, he led a wandering and adventurous life. Published "Laeuschen und Rimels" in his local Low German dialect in 1853. This proved such a success that he turned to literature and became the classical writer in the "Plattdeutsch" (Low German) dialect, to which he gave the dignity of a literary language. His chief works, "From the French Days" (1859) and "From My Prison Days" (1862), are marked by vigor, realism, and wry humor. They are still read throughout Germany.

Reymont, Wladyslaw

Polish novelist (1868-1925).

Also known as "Rejmont." Born in Kobiele Wielkie (near Radom in Central Poland); died in Warsaw. After several years' work as a railway employee, left his job to devote himself to literature. Of peasant origin himself, his novels offer an epic picture of the Polish peasant moving to the city under the pressure of industrialization. The two stages are presented in "The Peasants" (1904-1910, 4 volumes named after the four seasons) and "The Promised Land" (1899), an earlier work which gives a penetrating and unflattering description of the industrial town of Lodz. Reymont received the 1924 Nobel Prize by a fluke: It had been unofficially given to an Italian writer who could not accept it because he was unacceptable to his government, and the Polish ambassador in Stockholm used this chance to supply the members of the jury with copies of the excellent German translation of Reymont's masterpiece. None the less the prize was richly deserved. Reymont's sympathies were of the right: as a nationalist he resented the Jews and the Germans who dominated the Polish town of Lodz. But in the "Peasants" the resentment is overcome and disappears in a classical picture of peasant life, not only in Poland but anywhere.

Rice, Elmer
American playwright (born 1892).

Born in New York. His "Street Scene" (1929) and "Adding Machine" (1923) express, in an expressionistic language, the author's pessimism about modern civilization as exemplified by life in a city block or business office.

Richardson, Samuel
English novelist (1689-1761).

Born in Derbyshire; died in London. Went to London, set up a printshop and became printer of journals of the House of Commons, and King's Printer (1760) by purchasing the patent. Famous for his three novels in letter form: "Pamela, or Virtue Rewarded" (1740), an interminable defense of her virtue by a maidservant, "Clarissa Harlowe, or the History of a Young Lady" (1747-8, 7 volumes), and "Sir Charles Grandison" (1753), which sets out the ideal of a Christian gentleman. Richardson was phenomenally popular in his time. His novels of bourgeois sentimentality are a landmark in European literary history. Among the men he influenced were Rousseau, Diderot, and Goethe, and there is a belated echo of his popularity in Pushkin's "Onegin," whose heroine Tatiana "loved Richardson." The novels would make unbearable reading matter to the sophisticated reader of today, but a cheap reprint might well prove them still to the popular taste.

Richter, Jean Paul Friedrich
German writer (1763-1825) .

Generally known by his pen name "Jean Paul." Born in Wunsiedel (Central Germany) ; died in Paris. Had a difficult youth, became teacher in an elementary school, later managed to squeeze a living from his writings. Started as a classicist, veered to romanticism. His novels are fantastic and psychological, with a wise and deep humor. They were much read at the time and had a European influence. They represented—and still represent—the other face of Germany, the very opposite of Bismarck's "blood and iron." Chief works: "The Life of the Gay Schoolmaster Maria Wuz in Auenthal" (1793) , "The Invisible Lodge" (1793), "Life of Quintus Fixlein, Drawn From Fifteen Card Boxes" (1796) , "Flowers, Fruits and Thorns of Marriage, Death and Wedding of the Poor Lawyer F. S. Siebenkaes" (1796 et seq.), "Titan" (1800-03) , "Doctor Katzenberg's Journey to the Watering Place" (1809).

Riley, James Whitcomb
American poet (1849-1916) .

Born in Greenfield, Indiana, died in Indianapolis. Started writing poems in a homey Hoosier vernacular after earning his living as sign painter, actor and musician. His "Old Swimmin'-Hole" (1883) gave him national fame.

Rilke, Rainer Maria
Austrian poet (1875-1926).

Born in Prague; died in Muzot Castle, Switzerland. Member of a Carinthian noble family. Sent to a cadet school at 10. Studied at Munich, Vienna, and Berlin Universities. From 1902, led a wandering life in Paris (where he was secretary to the sculptor Auguste Rodin) , Italy, Scandinavia, Russia, Austria, and

Switzerland, staying mostly at the houses of patrons and patronesses. This life was broken by an unhappy spell of soldiering in the Austrian army in World War I. He died a death befitting a poet, of blood poisoning from the thorn of a rose he picked for his hostess. Rilke is one of the greatest, if not the greatest, German lyric poets of the Twentieth Century, and there is certainly no other who enjoys anything like his reputation right now, both at home and abroad. His strongest points are his musical language, his fine sensitivity, and his mystical understanding of men and objects. These are balanced by wooliness, preciosity, and the kind of desperate nostalgia that made W. H. Hudson baptize him "The Santa Claus of Loneliness," and which constitutes his chief appeal to the West German literary audiences today. Chief works: "Life and Songs" (1894), "Advent" (1897), "Song of the Life and Death of Ensign Christopher Rilke" (1906), "The Book of Pictures" (1902), "The Book of Hours" (1905), "New Poems" (1909), "Notebooks of Malte Brigge" (1909), "Life of Mary" (1913), "The Return of the Prodigal Son" (1918), "Sonnets to Orpheus" (1922), "Duino Elegies" (1923).

Rimbaud, Arthur

French poet (1854-1891).

Born in Charleville (Northeast France); died in Marseilles. At 17, was invited by Verlaine, who admired his poetry, to come to Paris. Lived with Verlaine in intimate friendship until they quarrelled. Rimbaud was wounded by Verlaine on this occasion. His poetic vein had given out by the time he was 20; tired by alcoholic and other excesses, he left France at 23 and went to Ethiopia. He settled in Harrar where he established himself as a merchant. According to some sources, he also engaged in the slave trade. Overcome by sickness and feeling the approach of death, he left for Europe and died, lonely and deserted, in Marseilles. Rimbaud is (with Verlaine) a figure that divides French (and general) literature into two periods—before and after him. He broke the mold of classical French literature and inaugurated the era of symbolism and, later, surrealism. Prompted by his poetic genius and his youthful revolt against all restraint and tradition, whether literary, religious, or political, he flashed across the European literary scene; the effort proved too much for him. Chief works: "A Season in Hell" (1873), "The Sleeper of the Valley," "The Drunken Ship," and "Illuminations" (published 1886, and including the famous "Sonnet of Vowels").

Rivarol, Antoine

French writer (1753-1801).

Called himself Count. Born in Bagnols, died in Berlin. Brilliant wit and epigrammatist, exiled by the French Revolution to a Germany which he did not cherish. Wrote "The Cabbage and the Turnip" (1782) and "Discourse on the Universality of the French Language" (1782) which contains his famous saying "What is not clear, is not French," less true now than in his day.

Rivas, Duke of

Spanish writer (1791-1865).

Full name: Angel Perez de Saavedra, Duke of Rivas. Born in Cordoba; died in Madrid. Grew up in the turmoil of the Napoleonic War. Showed his sympathies with the liberal movement which gave Spain the Constitution of 1812, in his "Political Essays" (1813). Fought against the despotism of Ferdinand VII and was condemned to death in 1823. He escaped this fate by fleeing to England. There he expressed his sadness over the fate of his native land in the patriotic epic "Florinda." More importantly, he discovered in England the romantic movement, which he was to introduce—belatedly—to Spain. He returned to that country in 1834 when the liberals returned to power after Ferdinand's death. He celebrated his return with another patriotic epic "The Exposed Moor" (1834). Became premier under the liberal regime, which he also served as Spanish ambassador to France, Naples, and Tuscany. He continued to write—dramas, romances, lyrical poetry—but his pioneering literary role was over.

Rivera, José Eustasio

Colombian novelist (1889-1928).

Born in Neiva, died in New York. His novel "The Vortex" (1924) created a sensation by its tremendous vision of the tropical forest which draws into its maw the oppressed Indian rubber workers and the city traders who exploit them. It has since become appreciated as the great novel of tropical America.

Rizal, José

Philippine writer (1861-1896).

Born in Calamba, shot in Manila by Spaniards. Devoted his life to the cause of Philippine independence from Spain. For this purpose he conspired and plotted a rebellion and wrote two novels, "Noli Me Tangere" (1886, published in Berlin) and "Filibusterism" (1891, published in Ghent, Belgium). These novels are still the national novels of the Philippines although he wrote them in Spanish, a language that is now all but dead in the islands.

Robinson, Edward Arlington

American poet (1869-1935).

Born in Head Tide, Maine; died in New York. Moved to New York City in 1897, but remained practically unknown till the 1920's, when general literary tastes caught up with his own. He became famous through his long narrative poems, often based on Arthurian motifs; but he is at his best perhaps in his tender, humorous, and yet basically tragic lyrics. Chief works: "The Torrent and the Night Before" (1896), "The Children of the Night" (1897), "The Town Down the River" (1910), "The Man Against the Sky" (1916), "Merlin" (1917), "Lancelot" (1920), "The Man Who Died Twice" (1924), "Tristram" (1927), "Sonnets" (1928), "The Glory of the Nightingales" (1930), "Nicodemus" (1932), "King Jasper" (1935).

Rodenbach, George

Belgian writer (1855-1898).

Born in Tournai; died in Paris. Leading figure of the French-language literary revival in Belgium. Brought up in the Flemish towns of Ghent and Bruges, which provided the scene for his rather morbid literary work. Of the symbolist school. Chief works: "The Reign of Silence" (poems, 1891), "Bruges the Dead" (novel, 1892, his masterpiece), "The Bell Ringer" (poems, 1897).

Rojas, Fernando de

Spanish writer (about 1475-1538 or 1541).

Born at Puebula de Montalban in the province of Toledo; died at Talavera. Little is known about him beyond the facts of his Jewish origin and his term of service as mayor of Talavera. He is generally considered the author of the "Tragicomedy of Calixto and Melibea," generally known as "The Celestina," a novel in dialogue form which is a fountainhead of both Spanish and European novel and drama. Highly praised in its day, especially by Cervantes, it suffered an eclipse of reputation which was broken only in our day, when its true merits were perceived. Rojas' great achievement lies in his freeing literature from all kinds of fictions—religious, humanist, idealistic—and in his presenting men and women as realistically as art will permit.

Rojas Zorrilla, Francisco de
Spanish dramatist (1607-1648).

Born in Toledo; died in Madrid. Studied in Salamanca, moved to Madrid. Wrote some seventy plays under the influence of Calderon, some of which, like "Garcia del Castanar" and "Below the King—Nobody," have become part of the classical Spanish repertoire and have exercised a strong influence on the French classical theatre of Corneille, Scarron, and Lesage (q.v.).

Rolland, Romain
French writer (1866-1944).

Born at Clamecy (Nievre); died at Vezelay. Professor of History of Music at the Sorbonne; gave up the post in 1912 to devote himself exclusively to writing, following the great success of his novel in ten volumes about a contemporary musician of genius (1904-12), which won him the prize awarded by the French Academy (1913) and the Nobel Prize (1915). Rolland was essentially a neoromantic with high humanitarian ideals which made him oppose both rational Classicism and Rousseauan sentimentality. His political sympathies gradually veered to the left, but his motivation lay in pacifism and humanitarianism, which made him take up a position "above the struggle" in World War I, rather than in any sympathy with the growing left-wing totalitarianism. Among his great achievements are his biographies of great men whom he "humanized" and thus made accessible to the average reader. Works include also "The Theater of the (French) Revolution" (1898-1902), "Beethoven" (1903), "Michelangelo" (1908), "Musi-

403

cians of Yesterday" (1908), "Musicians of Today" (1908), "Haendel" (1910), "Tolstoy" (1911), "Colas Breugnon" (1913-4, a historical novel), "Gandhi" (1923), "Goethe and Beethoven" (1932), "Companions on the Way" (1936).

Romains, Jules

French novelist (born 1885).

Real name: Louis Farigoule. Born in Saint Julien Chapteuil (Haute Loire). Studied in Paris. Schoolteacher in provincial towns. Became professional writer; member of French Academy in 1946. Exponent of doctrine of "unanimism," according to which the unifying principles of human groups are more important, in literary treatment, than personal peculiarities. In practice, an advocate of democracy, peace, and humanism. Wrote, in addition to a series of novels grouped together under the general title of "Men of Good Will" (1932-47), "The Soul of Men" (1904), "Unanimous Life" (1908), "Somebody Died" (1911), "Odes and Prayers" (1913), "Dr. Knock" (a satire on doctors, 1923), "The Dictator" (1926), "The White Man" (1937), "Salsette Discovers America" (1942).

Ronsard, Pierre de

French poet (1521-1585).

Born in the castle of La Poissonière near Vendome; died in Tours. A page at the courts of Charles, Duke of Orleans, third son of King Francis I, and of James IV of Scotland. Suffered an accident at 18 which made him deaf and caused him to withdraw from court life. He devoted himself to study and writing. In 1550, he formed the "Pleiad," an association of seven poets devoted to the revival of French poetry and to making it supplant the Latin, Greek, and Italian poetry which dominated French literary life. This polemic purpose did not prevent him and other members of the "Pleiad" from incorporating into their writings some of the best features of the writers whom they wanted to supplant. Ronsard returned to court after the accession of Charles IX, whose favorite he was. He left the court again at Charles' death in 1574 and retired to the Loire country. Ronsard's genius is primarily lyrical. His long and labored attempts at producing a national epic, the "Franciad," were crowned by conspicuous failure. But this failure was more than redeemed by his "Odes" (1550-3), "Loves" (1552-60), "Hymns" (1555-6), "Eclogues" (1560-7), and "Sonnets for Hélène" (1568-74), which made him the father of modern French lyrical poetry. Ronsard was a classicist; his great strength lies in his language, his style, and in his restrained sentiments. But he was also a Frenchman, and this shows most clearly in his love poetry.

Rosegger, Peter
Austrian writer (1843-1918).

Born at Alpe in Styria; died at Krieglach in Styria. Son of peasants, apprenticed to a tailor because his parents thought him too weak for farm work. Became a journeyman, wandered from farm to farm, and wrote poems between spells of tailoring work. He published a collection of these in 1870, and found himself famous. He founded a literary magazine in Graz, the Capital, and wrote a series of novels of Styrian peasant's life, of which the "Notes of a Forest Teacher" (1875) is the most famous. Rosegger's writings are remarkable documents of Austrian peasant life.

Rosenfeld, Morris
(Yiddish, 1862-1923).

First prominent Yiddish poet in America. Born in a village in the district of Suwalki, he began at

15 to write poetry under the influence of the folk poets Eliakum Zunser and Michael Gordon, and the Haskalah poet, Abraham Goldfaden. Leaving Russia in 1882, he lived for a while in Amsterdam and in London, settling in New York in 1886. In 1889, his first collection of poetry, *The Bell,* appeared, followed by *Di Blumen-Kete (The Garland),* and *The Book of Poems* (trans. Leo Wiener, *Songs from the Ghetto;* 1898). Meanwhile Rosenfeld earned his livelihood as a tailor in a sweatshop. Later he was on the staff of several Yiddish periodicals. His poems excel in realistic directness and frequently in detailed pathos, fresh and impassioned.

Rossetti, Christina
English poet (1830-1894).

Born and died in London. Sister of Dante Gabriel Rossetti (q.v.), published her first verse in the Preraphaelite magazine "The Germ." Her verse, especially "Goblin Market" (1864), has weathered better than her brother's.

Rossetti, Dante Gabriel
English poet and painter (1828-1882).

Born in London; died in Birchington-on-Sea. Son of Gabriel Rossetti, a Neapolitan political exile who settled in London. His talents matured at an early age: He wrote his best poem, "The Blessed Damozel," at 18, and founded the Preraphaelite school of painting (with Hunt, Millais, etc.) at 20. Leading figure of a circle that included Swinburne, Ruskin, Burne-Jones, and William Morris. Wrote also: "The Portrait," "The Choice," and "Dante and His Circle" (1861-74). His popularity barely survived the Victorian Age, whose "preraphaelite" aspects he so ably expressed.

Rostand, Edmond

French dramatist (1868-1918).

Born in Marseilles; died in Paris. His dramas in verse opposed the then prevailing naturalism both in spirit and in letter. His vivid imagination and excellent style contributed to their great popular success. Chief works: "The Faraway Princess" (1895), "Cyrano de Bergerac" (1898), "The Eaglet" (1900), "Chanticler" (1910).

Rousseau, Jean Jacques

French-Swiss writer and philosopher (1712-1778).

Born in Geneva; died in Ermenonville (France). Son of a watchmaker, ran away to Savoy, became lover of Mme. de Warens who supported him for ten years (1731-41) with intervals during which he wandered away from her. From 1741 he lived mostly in Paris. It was there that he met his wife, who bore him five children—all of whom he placed in a foundlings' home. He earned a living as a copyist of music and as a hack writer, e.g., for the "Great Encyclopedia." He became suddenly famous in 1750, when he answered the prize question of the Dijon Academy, "Did the Re-establishment of Arts and Sciences Contribute to the Purification of Morals," with a resounding "no," which asserted the superiority of the "noble savage" to civilized man. Established by Mme. D'Epinay in a country cottage, he wrote there a novel in letters, "Juliette or the New Heloise," which ushered in the age of sentimentalism (1761). In the following year he published "The Social Contract," a treatise of political science, which had much to do with the coming of the French Revolution and with the courses it took, and "Emile," a landmark of "progressive education." The latter book was burned by the public hangman in Paris and Rousseau had to take refuge in

Switzerland and England for five years (1762-67). His last years were taken up with the writing of his autobiographical "Confessions" (published posthumously 1781-88). Rousseau is unquestionably one of the men who made the modern age, though this title to glory may well be a back-handed compliment. His modern admirers, like Lewis Mumford, would not have convinced a man like his contemporary, Voltaire, who told Rousseau that his philosophy made him feel like walking on all fours.

Rueckert, Friedrich

German writer (1788-1866).

Born in Schweinfurt; died in Neusess near Coburg. Professor of Oriental languages, lyrical poet and translator. Sympathetic to German nationalism but in a mild and middle-class way. Chief works: "Armored Sonnets" (1814), "Love Spring" (1823), "Oriental Tales" (1837).

Ruiz, Juan

Spanish poet (died about 1350).

Probably born in Alcala de Henares, became archpriest of Hita, a title by which he is generally known. Although he is now considered one of the greatest Spanish poets, he was all but unknown to his contemporaries and his "Book of Good Love" contains most of the little we know about his life. It is a poetic miscellany drawn from many sources but what makes its greatness is the unadorned tale of the life and loves of its author with his adventures which foreshadow those of Don Juan and Don Quixote.

Ruiz de Alarcon, Juan

Spanish dramatist (1581-1639).

Born in Taxco (Mexico), emigrated to Spain in 1600. His comedies are classical in form and are marked by imagination and psychological insights, partly derived from his deformity (he was a hunchback). Chief works: "The Suspicious Turk" and "Examination of Husbands."

Rumi, Jalal ud Din
Persian poet (1206-1273).

Born in Balkh, died in Konia. A sufi mystic, disciple of the weird and mysterious Shams-i-Tabrizi, founded the order of dancing dervishes called the Mowlavi and became Persia's greatest mystic poet. His "Masnavi" in six books is a collection of anecdotes, precepts and reflections intended to teach the sufi doctrine. His odes, dedicated to his master Shams-i-Tabrizi, are better poetry than the "Masnavi" but are less appreciated by the Persians.

Runeberg, Johan Ludvig
Finnish writer (1804-1877).

Born in Jacobstad; died in Borga. Wrote in Swedish, his mother tongue, but became Finland's first national poet by his Finnish patriotism. Taught the classical languages in Helsinki and Borga. Chief works: "Poems" (1830-43), "The Elk Hunters" (1832), "Hanna" (1836), "Christmas Eve" (1861), "Nadejda" (1851), "King Fjalar" (1844), "Ensign Stahl's Tales" (1848-50), "King of Salamis" (1860). Runeberg wrote the text of the Finnish national anthem, "Our Country."

Runes, Dagobert D.,
Born 1902 in a Balkan village.

Went west as a boy; pursued the study of philosophy at the University of Vienna, where he received his Doctorate. After graduation he left for the States, dedicating himself to study and writing in the field of Social Philosophy. Among his many works, some of which have become standard in the field, are: Dictionary of Philosophy; Dictionary of Thought; Pictorial History of Philosophy; On the Nature of

Man; Of God, the Devil and the Jews; Pictorial History of Despotism.

Runyon, Damon
American writer (1880-1946).

Born in Manhattan, Kansas, died in New York. A columnist, specializing in sport and underworld stories, spiced with the slang of the milieu he described. They include: "Guys and Dolls" (1932) and "Take It Easy" (1938).

Ruskin, John
English writer and critic (1819-1900).

Born in London, died in Brantwood in the Lake District. Son of a rich wine merchant, was educated at Oxford. His independent fortune permitted him a great deal of traveling. Ruskin revolted against much of Victorian England but was, nonetheless, one of its typical products, even in his revolt. He was a critic of both art and society. In art he championed Turner against Whistler and the primitives against the masters of the Renaissance. He condemned the social evils of industrialism in the name of medieval craftsmanship. His writings, in a style much influenced by the Bible, include: "Modern Painters" (1843); "The Seven Lamps of Architecture" (1849); "The Stones of Venice" (1851-53) and "Unto This Last" (1862).

Russell, Bertrand
English philosopher and writer (born 1872).

Born in Trelleck. Philosopher and mathematician, whose "Principia Mathematica," written with A. N. Whitehead, (1910-13) revolutionized our logical concepts. Also essayist who often expresses unpopular views on anything from marriage—which made him lose a teaching post in New York—to atomic disarmament. Received the Nobel Prize in 1950.

Ruteboeuf

French poet (second half of the 13th century).

Probably came from the Champagne, lived in Paris under Saint Louis. Employed by a number of patrons who may have included the King himself, his satirical verse spared no authority in church and state and thus started an enduring French literary tradition.

Rydberg, Abraham Victor

Swedish writer (1828-1895).

Born in Joenkoeping, died in Stockholm. Journalist, became professor of art in history at Stockholm University. His works are marked by an academic humanism and his interest in Northern mythology. Chief works: "Roman Tales of Saints Peter and Paul" (1874), "Poems" (1882-91), "Prometheus and Ahasuerus" (1877), "Faust and Faustian Studies" (1876).

S

Sa'adi

Persian poet (1194-about 1285).

Full name: Muslih-al-Din Sheikh Sa'adi. Born and died at Shiraz. Traveled extensively in the countries between India and Morocco (1226-56) then returned to his native city where he was patronized by its Sultans. Sa'adi is ethical rather than religious, and his moralizing is not without a touch of Macchiavellianism. Humor is his strong point, especially in his "Gulistan," a miscellany in rhymed prose. The "Bustan" (1257), a didactic poem with mystical tendencies, is his poetic masterpiece.

Saadiah Gaon

Jewish religious writer (892-942).

Born in Dilaz, Egypt, died in Sura. Appointed director (*gaon*) of the Talmudic college of Sura in Iraq. Translated the Old Testament into Arabic, wrote the first Hebrew dictionary and grammar (partly preserved), theological treatises, an autobiography and liturgical poems called *piyutim*. Strong defender of orthodox Judaism against the rationalist trends of his time.

Sacchetti, Franco

(ca. 1330-1400).

Was one of the figures approaching major importance in late 14th c. Italian literature. He is remembered chiefly for his poetry, especially gracious ballads and madrigals, and for his *novelle*. These are preserved in a collection of 223, out of 300 originally written. They are artless rather than studied in their narrative technique, and do not show either the psychological insight, or the mastery of prose style that characterizes Boccaccio's tales. They are still notable, however, for their natural and spontaneous style, their humor, and their realistic portrayal of 14th c. bourgeois existence.

Sacher-Masoch, Leopold Von
Austrian writer (1836-1895).

Born in Galicia (now Poland, then Austria) of Jewish parentage, wrote in German. Wrote a four-volume novel, "The Testament of Cain" (1870-7), which today is as forgotten as "The Messalina of Vienna" (1874), "Stories of Polish Jews" (1886), etc. But his name lives on in that of the sexual perversion which he described in "Venus in Furs."

Sachs, Hans
German writer (1494-1576).

Born and died in Nuremberg. After several years at a Latin school, was apprenticed to a shoemaker. During his journeyman years started to write poetry and songs in the "Meistersinger" style, the bourgeois art form that replaced in Germany the aristocratic "Minnesang." Appeared at the court of Emperor Maximilian I to recite his poems. He became an early adherent of Luther, and to him devoted his best-known piece of work, the song on "The Wittenberg Nightingale" (1523). Sachs' output was enormous—some 4,000 poems and songs, 1,700 stories and tales, 200 dramatic works. He was formed by humanism, the Reformation, and the bourgeois world in which he grew up, and his works mirror all these with a realism which may be at times pedestrian, but is often spiced with humor. Forgotten after his death, he was rediscovered by Goethe. Richard Wagner set him a musical monument in his "Meistersingers of Nuremberg," in which "The Wittenberg Nightingale" is incorporated as a popular chorale.

Sade, Marquis de
French writer (1740-1814).

Full name: Donatien Alphonse François, Count de Sade (he only assumed the title of Marquis). Born in Paris; died in Charenton Insane Asylum near Paris. Army officer until 1768. Sentenced to death by default at Aix for a sexual offense in 1772. Was reprieved but continued to indulge in the excesses associated with his name and spent thirty years in prison. He embodied his views—and his experiences—in books like "Justine, or the Misfortunes of Virtue" (1791) and "Juliette, or the Pleasures of Vice" (1798). He enjoyed two periods of popularity: in his own day, for carrying the eighteenth century's individualism and libertinism to their disgusting extremes, and in our own day, when a "Sade revival" caused a new literary flurry first in Paris and then in the circles influenced by Paris. This made "the divine Marquis" one of the patron saints of existentialism.

Sagan, Françoise
French novelist (born 1935)

Pen name of Françoise Quoirez. Born in Paris, of well-to-do middle class family. Startled the world with her "Bonjour Tristesse" (1955) written at 17 or 18 with astonishing maturity in style and treatment of characters. Has become the spokesman of the disillusioned young, has been herself astonished by her success, which she calls "a sociological phenomenon." Has written more novels, a ballet and a play, "Castle in Sweden" (1960). Her writing is, for all its precocious modernity, in the tradition of her two favorite novelists, Stendhal and Proust.

Sainte-Beuve, Charles Augustin

French literary critic (1804-1869).

Born in Boulogne, died in Paris. Friend of Victor Hugo, broke with him after falling in love with his wife, Adele. Moved from liberalism to acceptance and championship of Napoleon III. Wrote poetry and a novel, "Lust" (1834), with strangely modern overtones, but is important for his literary criticisms, the "Monday Talks" which he started in 1851 and published in the most influential Paris newspapers. His psychological and aesthetic penetration enabled him to overcome his strong personal prejudices which he himself called "my poisons."

Saint-Exupery, Antoine de

French writer (1900-1944).

Born at Lyons; died over the Mediterranean when his plane was shot down. Member of a noble family, became a professional pilot. Flew passenger and transport planes between France, Africa, and America for various air lines. Fought in French Air Force in 1939-40, joined the Free French Air Force after the debacle, following an adventurous flight from occupied France to the United States via Portugal. Saint-Exupery wrote a simple but effective prose in the classical French style, whose musical resources permitted him to express his passionate and emotional nature. He was one of the first writers to conquer for literature the realm of the air and of the men who fly in it. The other, more tender, side of his nature showed itself more rarely, but was charmingly revealed in "The Little Prince," already a classic children's book. His outlook recalled, in many ways, the existentialism that Sartre made popular after Saint-Exupery's death. Chief works: "Mail to the South" (1928), "Night Flight" (1931), "Wind, Sand, and Stars" (1938), "Flight to

Arras" (1942), "The Little Prince" (1943), "Letter to a Hostage" (1943).

Saint-John Perse

(Alexis Saint-Léger Léger, French, 1887-   ).

Elegant poet and diplomat. Born in Guadeloupe, went to Paris for education. Entered the Foreign Service, working closely with Briand. Came to America when Nazis took France. Painter of rich and unusual images, especially admired by poets and intellectuals. Most famous work, *Anabasis,* has been translated by T. S. Eliot.

Saint-Simon, Louis de Rouvroy, Duke of

French writer (1675-1755).

Born in Versailles; died in Paris. Professional soldier, served in army of Louis XIV and distinguished himself at Namur and Neerwinden. Frequented the courts of Louis XIV and Louis XV after retiring from the army after refusing the promotions due to him because he felt he was slighted. Member of Council of Regency for the infant Louis XV and ambassador to Madrid (1721). Retired to write his famous "Memoirs," a pitiless critique of the court of Louis XIV and its society by an aristocrat who despised it as absolutist and "bourgeois." His style and psychological penetration are in the best French tradition. The monarchy forbade publication of the "Memoirs"; they circulated in manuscript until they were published in the late 1820's under the pressure of public opinion and as propaganda—of the bourgeois, not the aristocrats—against the absolutism of Charles X. It was this publication that confirmed the status of the "Memoirs" as one of the classic documents of the "Age of Louis XIV."

Salacrou, Armand

French playwright (born 1895).

Born in Rouen. Studied medicine, law, and philosophy. Secretary of a Paris theater, wrote his first play in 1924, "The Breaker of Dishes," which was an instant success. Salacrou is one of the best craftsmen of the modern French theater, equally at home in realistic and fantastic plays. Wrote "The Bridge of Europe" (1927), "A Laughable Story" (1931), "Nights of Anger" (1946), "Why Not I" (1951), etc.

Sallust

Roman historian (86-35 B.C.).

Full name: Gaius Sallustius Crispus. Born in Amiternum in the Sabine country (now Abruzzi, Central Italy); died in Rome. A strong partisan of Caesar, who appointed him quaestor (49) and praetor. Accompanied Caesar on his African campaign against the partisans of Pompey, whom he defeated at Thapsus (46). Caesar finally appointed him governor of Numidia (North Africa), a post in which he amassed a great fortune. He returned to Rome and devoted himself to the study and writing of history. His chief surviving works are "The War of Jugurtha" and "The Conspiracy of Catiline"; of his "History of the Roman Republic" only fragments have survived. Sallust is a good rather than a great historian. He is important as a source, and his easy and simple style have made his works an ideal introduction to Latin prose for school children for over twenty centuries.

Salomon Ibn Adret

Spanish Jewish theologian (about 1235-about 1310).

Born and died in Barcelona, where he was a rabbi. He was greatly respected by the Jews not only of Spain but of the neighboring countries, who sent legal queries to the "Rabbi of Spain," as he was called. Some 6,000 of his "Responses" have survived and are a valuable source.

417

Saltykov-Shchedrin, Mikhail Evgrafovich

Russian novelist (1826-1889).

Born Mikhail Evgrafovich Saltykov, used the pen name of "N. Shchedrin." He is now generally referred to as above. Born at Spas-Ugol in Tver (now Kalinin) province in Central Russia; died in Saint Petersburg. An official in the War Ministry, exiled to Vyatka (1847-55) after publishing novel "A Complicated Story." Returned to imperial favor after death of Nicholas I. Alexander II made him governor of Ryazan province, later of Tver. Became publisher of "Patriotic Notes," but his works "Provincial Sketches" (1856), "Satires in Prose" (1863), "The Golovyevs" (1880), and above all, "The Story of a Town," a parody of Russian history, are among the most bitter satires ever penned. They are among the classics of Russian literature—the favorite reading of Lenin and Stalin, among others —but, as is the case with so many other Russian classics, they have so far proved too Russian for Western tastes.

Sand, George

French writer (1804-1876).

Real name; Aurore Dupin; married Baron Casimir Dudevant (1822). Born in Paris; died at her country home in Nohant. Her husband separated from her when she started a literary and erotic liaison with Jules Sandeau (1831), from whose name she took her pen name. To earn her living, started miniature painting, then writing. It was in collaboration with Sandeau that she wrote her first novel, "The White Rose" (1832). She left Sandeau for Alfred de Musset (q.v.) and a string of other affairs, the most famous with Chopin. A strong feminist, she shocked her bourgeois contemporaries by wearing trousers and smoking cigars, but earned the respect and friendship of men like Liszt, Balzac, and Delacroix. Her novels propagated socialist and feminist ideas, especially the demand for divorce. They include "Indiana" (1832), "Valentine" (1832), "Lelia" (1833), "Mauprat" (1837), "Spiridion" (1839), "The Countess of Rudolstadt" (1843-5), "The French Journeyman" (1840), "Consuelo" (1842-3), "The Devil's Swamp" (1846), "François le Champi" (1849), "The Marriage of Victorin" (1851).

Sandburg, Carl
American writer (1878).

Born in Galesburg, Illinois. Son of a Swedish immigrant, roved the Middle West between odd jobs in small towns. His poetry sings of the prairie and the city, notably of Chicago—"hog butcher to the world"—in a language that is folksy and earthy. His folk biography of Lincoln (1926-39) was written from material collected in thirty years' research.

Saneatsu Mushakoji
(Japanese, 1885-   ).

Modern Japanese dramatist, noted for unconventional ideological plots. Embarked on impressive literary career after leaving school. Influenced by European dramatists: Ibsen, Maeterlinck, Tolstoy. Authored several novels, books of essays, and many plays. Plays known in translation: *A Family Affair, The Sister*.

Sannazaro, Jacopo
Italian poet (1457-1530).

Born and died in Naples. A man of broad humanist education, he wrote in both Latin and Italian. His pastoral romance "Arcadia" (1501), twelve poems with prose interludes, opened the way for the pastoral novel and drama which held the stage during the two succeeding centuries. His Latin epigram on Lucrezia Borgia, which calls her "the daughter, wife and daughter-in-law of Pope Alexander VI," reveals another and less idyllic side of his character.

Santillana, Inigo Lopez de Mendoza, Marquis of
Spanish poet (1398-1458).

Born in Carrion de los Condes. Took a prominent part in the wars and civil wars of his time. Had Homer, Vergil and Seneca translated for him and tried to naturalize the sonnet and Italian meters in Spain, without any conspicuous success. Of his own writings, the most read are the *Serranillas,* poems in which he relates his encounters with mountain girls.

Sappho
Greek poetess (about 620-about 565 B.C.).

Born on the island of Lesbos of an aristocratic family; died by throwing herself from the Leucadian rock because of unrequited love for young Phaon, according to a traditional story which is generally, though not universally, accepted. Married to Kerkolas, by whom she had a child. After his death, gathered around her a circle of young girls whom she taught literature and with whom she engaged in the kind of love that is associated with the name of her native island. Highly esteemed in classical antiquity, she was compared to Homer, and Plato called her "The Tenth Muse." Her poetry, originally in nine books, fell almost entirely victim to the ferocious hatred of the Byzantine church: Only a few complete poems and some fragments remain, supplemented of late by finds among the Egyptian papyri. Even these pitiful remnants show—especially in love poems and descriptions of nature—that classical antiquity was more right in its judgment of her than the Byzantine Church.

Sarbiewski, Maciel
Polish poet in Latin (1595-1640).

Born in Sarbiewo, died in Warsaw. Teacher at Jesuit

schools, his odes written in the style of Horace and Pindar earned him the title of "Christian Horace." Sarbiewski was the last European poet of any standing to write Latin poetry that was generally read: there were 58 editions of his works between 1625 and 1892.

Sardou, Victorien

French playwright (1831-1908).

Born and died in Paris. Journalist who became the most popular playwright of his time, both in France and abroad. His comedies are primarily entertainment. They are not only brilliantly put together but also show at their best the spirit of Paris and the author's wit. Chief works: "The First Arms of Figaro" (1859), "Fly's Feet" (1860), "Let Us Divorce" (1880), "Feodora" (1882), "Tosca" (1887), "Madame Sans Gêne" (1893), "The Affair of the Fish" (1907).

Sarmiento, Domingo Faustino

Argentine writer and politician (1811-1890).

Born in El Carrascal, died in Asuncion, Paraguay. Fought against the dictatorship of Rosas, was exiled in Chile and Uruguay. After the defeat of Rosas, became president and introduced many useful reforms, particularly in education. Of his very voluminous writings, two deserve special notice: "Facundo" (1845) which under cover of a biography of Juan Facundo Quiroga, a provincial imitator of Rosas, presents a classical examination of "civilization and barbarism" in the Argentine; and "Provincial Memories" (1850) a remarkable account of life, men, and society in an Andean backwater.

Sarojini Najdu

(Indian, 1879-1949).

Gifted English language lyricist of Indian themes. One of first Indians to achieve mastery of English verse. A woman who married out of her caste, and later became President of the Indian National Congress. Principal volumes: *The Golden Threshold, The Bird of Time, The Broken Wing.*

Saroyan, William
American writer (born 1908).

Born in Fresno, California, of Armenian parents. Won great success in the thirties with his short stories which were chaotic and ecstatic hymns about life, mostly in praise of it, e.g. "The Man on the Flying Trapeze and Other Stories" (1934). Later turned playwright with "My Heart Is in the Highland" (1940), other whimsical and symbolic plays.

Sarpi, Fra Paolo
Italian historian (1552-1623).

Born and died in Venice. Changed his name from "Peter" to "Paul" when he took Holy Orders. His "History of the Council of Trent" (1619) is more than a mere history: it mirrors the strong personality and prejudices of its author who defended the claims of his native Venice against all comers, including the Pope.

Sartre, Jean-Paul
French philosopher and writer (born 1905).

Born in Paris, of family with Norman roots and Protestant connections (his mother is related to Albert Schweitzer). Spent his childhood at La Rochelle, then moved to Paris where he studied philosophy and graduated first on the list. He taught philosophy at Laon and Le Havre, and had an interlude at the French Institute in Berlin, where he became acquainted with the German philosophy derived from Kierkegaard, which led him to found the philosophy of existentialism. After returning to France, he wrote his first novel, "Nausea" (1938), which attracted the attention of the critics, and short stories published as "The Wall" (1939). During the war, Sartre took part in the Resistance and developed his philosophical and literary talents. In those days, his existentialism was a call to human dignity and "engagement" to fight against tyranny; in the post-war years it came to stand, without Sartre's seeming to notice it, for the exact opposite: a justification for self-pity and inertia in the face of events over which the individual feels he has no control. It is too early to determine Sartre's stature as philosopher and writer, but it can already be said that no future historian will be able to interpret the mid-Twentieth Century without taking him and his influence into account. Works include: the philosophical treatises "Being and Nothingness" (1943) and "Existentialism Is a Humanism" (1946); four novels grouped together as "The Roads of Liberty" (1945 ss.), "The Age of Reason," "The Reprieve," "Death in the Soul," and "The Last Chance"; the plays "The Flies" (1943), "The Respectful Prostitute" (1946), "Dirty Hands" (1948), "The Prisoners of Altona" (1959).

Savonarola, Girolamo

Italian preacher (1442-1498).

Born in Ferrara; died in Florence. Became a Dominican in 1475, was named in 1491 prior of the Dominican cloister of San Marco in Florence. From there he engaged in his passionate campaign against the sins of the city, among which he included the Renaissance in all its aspects, and the Medici, whom his followers deprived of power. When he also attacked the sins of the Vatican, as personified by Pope Alexander VI, he was excommunicated, seized, tortured, hanged, and burned. His sermons, letters, and poems have earned him a place in Italian literature.

Saxo Grammaticus

(?1150-1220).

The father of Danish literature. His book *Gesta Danorum* became a constant informative and inspirational source of literary productions through many centuries, and became a fountain of Danish nationalism. It contains the story of Hamlet.

Scarron, Paul

French writer (1610-1660).

Born and died in Paris. Entered the service of the bishop of Le Mans in 1633, became paralytic in 1638, and married in 1652 Françoise d'Aubigné who took care of him in the last eight years of his life. (Later she became mistress and morganatic wife of Louis XIV as Madame de Maintenon.) Scarron was a humorist and a satirist who tried most of the literary genres. His wit is of the Gallic variety, and is spiced with a considerable dose of realism. His masterpiece is the "Comic Novel" (1651-7), describing the wandering life of provincial acting troupes. He dedicated his epic "Typhon" (1644) to Cardinal Mazarin, and when the latter failed to make a suitable response, retorted with a satirical "Mazarinad" (1651). Scarron also wrote comedies on the Spanish model and a travesty of Vergil.

Scheffel, Joseph Victor Von

German writer (1826-1886).

Generally known as Victor Scheffel. Born and died in Karlsruhe. Wrote as a later day romantic in a popular vein. His songs in praise of Germany's glories were widely sung, e.g. "Old Heidelberg" and "When the Romans Became Impudent." Also wrote "The Trumpeter of Saeckingen" (1854), a poem that is a perennial feature of German schoolbooks, and "Ekkehard" (1862), a historical novel.

424

Schendel, Arthur Van
Dutch novelist (1874-1946).

Born in Batavia (now Jakarta) in the Dutch East Indies (now Indonesia); died in Amsterdam. Started as a romantic novelist of the Italian Renaissance, went through a phase of Dutch nationalism, and ended as a classical humanist. Chief works: "A Wanderer in Love" (1906), "A Wanderer Lost" (1907), "The Frigate 'Johanna Maria'" (1930), "A Dutch Drama" (1935), "The Rich Man" (1936), "The Gray Bird" (1937), "A Play of Nature" (1942).

Schenkendorf, Max Von
German poet (1783-1817).

Born in Tilsit (East Prussia, now Russia); died in Koblenz. Paralyzed in his right arm in consequence of a duel; fought nonetheless against Napoleon in 1813-4. His songs, of a flaming patriotism, include the famous (or notorious) "Watch on the Rhine."

Schiller, Friedrich Von
German writer (1759-1805).

Born in Marbach on the Neckar (Southwest Germany); died in Weimar. Son of a military surgeon, was sent to Military Academy at Stuttgart in 1773, after frequenting Latin School. The Academy, which mirrored the despotic spirit of Duke Karl Eugen of Württemberg, was not to the liking of the young cadet, who secretly read Rousseau, Lessing, and Shakespeare, and who was preparing a play, "The Robbers," that was among other things a hymn of hate against princely absolutism. He became regimental surgeon in Stuttgart but was arrested after "The Robbers" was first presented at Mannheim (1782), and forbidden by the duke to write any more comedies. Schiller completed another "comedy," "The Conspiracy of Fiesco" (1782), and fled from Stuttgart. He wrote another attack on despotism, "Intrigue and Love" (1783), and worked as theater director in Mannheim for a while, until Duke Karl August of Weimar, a very different spirit from Karl Eugen, called him to his court. There he wrote "Don Carlos" (1787), in which his love of freedom found a less stormy and more mature expression. He met Goethe in 1788, who, after an initial coolness, became his great and lifelong friend. In 1789 Schiller became professor of history at Jena. In 1804 his life's work was crowned by the homage paid to him in Berlin by Queen Louise of Prussia and the leading spirits of the Prussian capital. He died of tuberculosis. Schiller's literary activity in his Weimar years progressed from a stormy romanticism to a classical humanism, not unlike that of his friend Goethe, who has overshadowed his fame outside Germany. Among his chief creative works, in addition to those already named and his lyrical poems, are "History of the Dutch Revolution" (1788), "History of the Thirty Years' war" (1791-3), "Wallenstein" (a trilogy, 1800), "Mary Stuart" (1801), "The Maid of Orleans" (1802), "The Bride of Messina" (1803), "William Tell" (1804), "Demetrius" (an unfinished play, 1805). In addition to his creative work, Schiller was an important critic and theoretician of aesthetics. The worldwide celebration of the 200th anniversary of his birth, in 1959, re-emphasized his classical stature.

Schlegel, August Wilhelm Von
German writer (1767-1845).

Born in Hanover, died in Bonn. Brother of Friedrich Schlegel (q.v.). Studied theology and philology at Göttingen, became tutor in Amsterdam, later at Jena. There he met Schiller, who became his close friend, and founded with his brother the magazine "Athenaeum" which became an early champion of romanticism. Later he moved to Berlin and Vienna. Accompanied Madame de Stael (q.v.) on her tour of France, Germany, Italy, and Scandinavia. Fled to London in 1812 before Napoleon's onslaught. From 1818 professor at Bonn. Schlegel excelled as philosopher, philologist, and, most of all, as translator. His translations of Shakespeare (from 1798), continued by Dorothea Tieck and Count Wolf Baudissin, made Shakespeare a German as well as an English classic. His interest in drama also bore fruit in translations from the classical Spanish theater, in his Vienna lectures "On Dramatic Art and Literature" (1809-11), and in a tragedy "Ion" (1803).

Schlegel, Dorothea

German writer (1783-1839).

Born Dorothea Mendelssohn, daughter of German Jewish philosopher Moses Mendelssohn. Married (1) the banker Simon Veit; (2) in 1804, the writer Friedrich Von Schlegel (q.v.). Born in Berlin; died in Frankfurt. After her second marriage, conducted an important literary salon in Vienna, later in Frankfurt. Translated Madame de Stael's "Corinne" and wrote several romantic novels, "Florentin" (1801), "Lother and Maller" (1805), "Merlin the Enchanter" (1811).

Schlegel, Friedrich Von

German writer (1772-1829).

Born in Hanover; died in Dresden. Brother of August Wilhelm Schlegel (q.v.). After some years in Berlin became lecturer in Jena (1801), where he worked with Dorothea Veit, who later became his wife. Both were converted there to Roman Catholicism in 1808. In that year, Schlegel moved to Vienna, where he occupied important posts at the court of Emperor Francis I. Like his brother, he was a romanticist, and, again like his brother, he was a better philosopher, philologist, and translator than a creative writer. His own creative work—the novel "Lucinda" (1799) and the play "Alarcos" (1802)—are overshadowed by the essay "On the Language and Wisdom of the Indians" (1808), a landmark in the growth of European understanding of the East; by his "History of Ancient and Modern Literature" (1815), his "Philosophy of Life" (1828), and his "Philosophy of History" (1829).

Schleiermacher, Friedrich Daniel
German theologian (1768-1834).

Born in Breslau (now Wroclaw, Poland), died in Berlin. Brought up as a Moravian brother, he broke away from the sect in 1786 and studied theology and philosophy at Halle. Became professor at Halle and Berlin. A prominent romanticist, he was a friend of the Schlegels. His "On Religion" (1799), a much read book, defends religion in the romantic manner as an essentially personal matter—"the poetry of the soul."

Schnitzler, Arthur
Austrian writer (1862-1931).

Born and died in Vienna. Of Jewish middle-class family; studied medicine and practiced it from 1885. Gave up medicine to become full-time writer after his first literary successes. He wrote under the influence of Flaubert, Maupassant, and French impressionism, but his works mirror Vienna at the turn of the century in a very Austrian way. He was a member of the "Young Vienna" literary circle and a frequenter of Viennese salons. His chief interest was the psychology of love; he was one of the first writers to use the achievements of the Vienna school of psychoanalysis. His style is excellent. Schnitzler's works have not yet "dated" and he is likely to survive as a minor classic. Interest in him has been revived lately through several films based on his writing, especially on "La Ronde." Chief works: "Anatole" (1893), "A Love Affair" (1896), "The Green Cockatoo" (1899), "La Ronde" (1903), "Young Mendarus" (1910), "Lieutenant Gustl" (1901),

"Casanova's Return" (1918), "Miss Elsa" (1924),
"Dream and Fate" (1931).

Schopenhauer, Arthur

German philosopher (1788-1860).

Born in Danzig (now Gdansk, Poland); died in
Frankfurt. Grew up in Hamburg, because his father
left Danzig as a protest against the Prussian occupation of the city in 1793. After his father's suicide, left
Hamburg to study at Göttingen, Berlin (under Fichte),
and Jena. Became a lecturer at Berlin University, retired from the post in 1831 and moved to Frankfurt to
devote himself to his writings. His philosophy combines German idealism with Eastern (especially Indian) influences into a most pessimistic skepticism,
which exercised a profound influence on Europe's
spiritual development—one of its literary precipita-
tions can be seen in Thomas Mann's "Buddenbrooks."
This was largely due to Schopenhauer's literary charms
—he was entirely devoid of any personal charms, and
his violent misogynism was appropriate in one of the
ugliest men ever born. Chief works: "The World as
Will and Idea" (1819), "On Will in Nature" (1838),
"The Two Basic Problems of Ethics" (1841), "Parerga
and Paralipomena" (1851).

Schreiner, Olive

South African novelist (1855-1920).

Born on Wittebergen Mission Station in Cape Province, died in Capetown. Her "Story of a South African
Farm" (1883) put South Africa on the English literary
map. Its strength lay in the description of the landscape and the author's sympathy with the lowly and
oppressed.

Schurer, Fedde

(Frisian, b. 1898) .

Is the most widely read poet of the Young Frisian

Movement. He has stood nearer to the people than any other of the Young Frisian poets, whose art has often been too intellectual and individualistic. Schurer's inspired verse may be called genuine national art. It is graceful, spontaneous, and direct, reaching its greatest heights in the religious and the national. Many of his spirited patriotic poems have become the battle hymns of the nationalists. His poems are collected in *Verse*, 1925, *On Wings of Song*, 1930, *With Every Wind*, 1936, and *Voices From Two Shores*, 1940. Schurer has also written some short stories, a few plays, and *Samson*, a Biblical drama in verse.

Scott, Sir Walter

Scottish novelist and poet (1771-1832).

Born in Edinburgh; died in Abbotsford. Member of old Scottish family, whose main line are the Dukes of Buccleugh; it was one of his ancestors, a 16th century Sir Walter Scott, whose life inspired him to write "The Lay of the Last Minstrel." As a boy Scott devoured ballads, romances, and chapbooks; learned French and Italian to read the medieval romances, Dante, and Ariosto. Studied law at Edinburgh, was called to the bar in 1792. Became sheriff of Selkirk in 1799 and a principal clerk to the court of session in 1812. But he had meanwhile started a literary career that was soon to absorb him completely. After publishing anonymously or under a variety of pen names translations from Goethe and Bürger and some ballads of his own, he brought out his first two important works: "Minstrelsy of the Scottish Border" (3 volumes, 1802-05), and "The Lay of the Last Minstrel" (1805). He started to write the historical novel "Waverley" that initiated the main line of his literary activity and entered into a partnership with the publisher John Ballantyne, that later brought him much sorrow.

For twenty years or so, he was at the pinnacle of his literary fame and financial prosperity: these were the years marked by the publication of "Marmion" (1808); "The Lady of the Lake" (1810); "Waverley" (1814); "The Lord of the Isles," "Guy Mannering," and "The Antiquary" (all in 1815); "The Black Dwarf" and "Old Mortality" (1816); "Rob Roy" (1817); "The Heart of Midlothian" and "The Bride of Lammermoor" (1818); "Ivanhoe" (1819); "Kenilworth" (1821); "Quentin Durward" (1823); etc. He was also editor of the influential "Quarterly Review" (from 1809) and was offered in 1813 the post of Poet Laureate, which he declined in favor of Southey. Then disaster struck. In 1826, he became involved in the failure of two publishing houses, Ballantyne and Co. and Constable and Co.; and also lost his dearly beloved wife. It was then that Scott proved that he not only wrote about chivalry, but was the soul of chivalry. He assumed personal responsibility for the debts of the two firms, and drove himself to an early death by writing at an incredible speed a series of potboiling books, none of them up to the literary standard of his earlier work. Even a number of apoplectic strokes in 1830 failed to stop his pen, though it sent him on a Mediterranean cruise in a last vain effort to regain his health. He came home to Abbotsford to die. The outstanding balance of his debts was paid through the disposal of copyrights of his books. A grateful nation buried him, with its other heroes, in Dryburgh Abbey. It is difficult to grasp today the influence that Scott once wielded. He created the modern form of the historical novel; he made Europe conscious of its history as no historian did. He restored to European consciousness the Age of Chivalry that Burke had mourned. Beyond the Atlantic, his admirers were inspired by his picture of chivalry to remold the image of the American South into a false though fatally attractive form, that had much to do with the coming of the Civil War and its still-continuing aftermath. But today, Scott, though still read by school children the world over, is no longer a living influence—possibly because the Age of Chivalry is now really gone.

Scribe, Eugene
French dramatist (1791-1861).

Born and died in Paris. A skillful dramatic writer, he supplemented his skills with those of his forty-eight collaborators to produce some 400 plays and 60 operatic libretti, most of which proved popular successes. Scribe had wit and a sure "nose" for what the public wanted, but today he is dated. Chief works: "Bertrand and Raton" (1833), "A Glass of Water" (1840), "Adrienne Lecouvreur" (with Legouvé, 1851).

Scudery, Georges de
French writer (1601-1667).

Born in Le Havre; died in Paris. Like his sister Madeleine (q.v.), he opposed the men who became the classics of the "Age of Louis XIV," in the name of the more precious standards of the literary salons, especially of the Hotel Rambouillet. Scudery, primarily a dramatist, opposed Corneille. When he wrote an epic poem, "Alaric or Rome Vanquished" (1654), he drew the withering scorn of Boileau.

Scudery, Madeleine de
French writer (1607-1701).

Born in Le Havre; died in Paris. Sister of Georges de Scudery (q.v.), for whom she kept house. She also conducted one of the most important literary salons of Paris. Her own novels, which earned her the nickname of "Sappho," were long and very romantic "romans a clef," i.e., stories about well-known people of her time, suitably camouflaged. Contemporaries read these novels for their allusions; today they are quite dead. Wrote "Ibrahim or the Illustrious Pasha" (1641), "Artamene of the Great Cyrus" (1648-53, in ten volumes, her chief work), "Illustrious Women" (1654-5), "Clelia" (1654-61), "Almahide" (1660-3), "The Promenade of Versailles" (1669), "Conversations" (1680-8).

Sealsfield, Charles
Austrian-American writer (1793-1864).

Real name: Karl Anton Postl. Born in Poppitz (Moravia, now Czechoslovakia); died in Solothurn (Switzerland). Educated for the priesthood but fled from the Jesuit seminary of which he was undergoing the novitiate, before consecration. He assumed the name "Charles Sealsfield" and his true identity was discovered only after his death. Traveled in the United States (1823-6, 1827-32) and became an American citizen. He retained his U. S. citizenship after settling in Switzerland. He had a great success in Europe in his day with his novels, modeled after Cooper (q.v.), of the "Wild West." Chief works: "Tokeah, or the Wild Rose" (1828), "The United States" (1828), "Pictures of Life in the Western Hemisphere" (1834-7), "The Cabin Book on National Characteristics" (1841), "North and South" (1842-3).

Se'ami
Japanese dramatist (1363-1443).

Son of Kan'ami (died 1384). Together with his father created the *noh*, the classical drama of Japan. Together they wrote some 250 *noh* plays. Some of his treatises on the technique of drama and acting were discovered recently.

Sei Shonagon
Japanese writer (966-1013).

Entered the service of Empress Sadako in 991. Her "Pillow Book," a prose miscellany, gives a very feminine account of the years 1000-1013. Some of it is a diary, some is written in essay form. She is believed to have died a nun.

Senancour, Etienne Pivert de
French novelist (1770-1846).

Born in Paris, died in Saint Cloud. Fled to Switzerland during the French Revolution, returned to Paris in 1804 and earned his living as a hack journalist. His novel written in form of letters, "Obermann" (1804), is the best of the French sentimental novels inspired by Goethe's "Werther."

Seneca, Lucius Annaeus
Generally known as "Seneca the Younger." Second son of Seneca the Elder (q.v.). Studied law in Rome, became a famous lawyer and official who rose to the posts of quaestor and senator. Banished to Corsica in 41 A.D. at the instigation of Empress Messalina, who objected to his ethical and moral teachings. Recalled in 49 A.D. to become tutor to young Domitius, who became the Emperor Nero five years later. For the next two years, Seneca was Nero's favorite and exercised a very strong influence in the government of the Empire. But he lost Nero's favor in 62 A.D. He was accused of taking part in the "Conspiracy of Piso" against Nero and committed suicide at the Emperor's order. Seneca is Rome's most important literary figure in the transition from the Golden Age of Vergil, Horace, and Ovid to the Silver Age of Tacitus. His tragedies, e.g., "Hercules in Fury," "Medea," "Phaedra," "Oedipus," were revived during the Renaissance and had a great formative influence on the birth of modern European drama. Even more important were his philosophical treatises like "On Anger," "On Consolation," "On the Brevity of Life," "On Leisure," and "On Peace of Soul." They express a stoic philosophy and ethic which Seneca did not always practice in his life, e.g.

434

he engaged in black market operations in grain in time of famine and was not above indulging in corruption on a considerable scale. But his ethical teachings were more followed than his unethical practices. He was very popular in the Middle Ages, and he was at one time generally regarded as a Christian.

Seneca, Marcus or Lucius Annaeus
Roman rhetorician (about 54 B.C.-39 A.D.).

Born in Cordoba, Spain. Known as "Seneca the Elder." Wrote ten volumes of "Controversies," i.e., imaginary legal cases and methods of presenting them; "Persuasions," and a historical work now lost.

Serafimovich, Alexander Popov
Russian writer (1863-1949).

Born at the Cossack "stanitsa" (village) of Nizhna Kurmoyarskaya on the Don. Studied in Saint Petersburg, where he became a friend and disciple of Alexander Ulyanov, the older brother of Lenin who was executed in 1887 because of his involvement in an attempt on the life of Tsar Alexander III. It was then that he started writing his first short stories. In 1890 he returned to his home village. He became an ardent Socialist, later a fanatical Communist. He hailed the Revolution of 1905 with "A City in the Steppe" (1905), and that of 1917 with "The Iron Stream," a novel on the birth of the Red Army from scattered groups of partisans and revolutionaries welded into an iron discipline. This is generally considered one of the masterpieces of socialist realism and has been a perennial best-seller in Russia. Serafimovich was—not surprisingly—Stalin's favorite writer, and a town was named after him. Although translated into most western languages, and vigorously peddled from Moscow, "The Iron Stream" remains practically unknown this side of the Iron Curtain.

Sergeiev- Tsenskii, Sergei Nikolayevich

Russian novelist (1876-1945).

Born in Tumbovsk, Central Russia. Started writing at a time when Russian literature veered from naturalism to symbolism. He was at first influenced by the latter but soon forsook it for a more positivistic realism, which made him one of the most respected writers of the Soviet Union. His fame is based on a trilogy of novels, "Valia," describing the Russian intelligentsia in the two decades preceding the Revolution. He wrote it during World War I, while working as a cowherd in the Crimea. He also wrote short stories.

Sevigné, Madame de

French writer (1626-1696).

Maiden name: Marie de Rabutin-Chantal, married the Marquis de Sevigné. Born in Paris, died in Grignan. Granddaughter of Jeanne de Chantal, friend of Saint Francis de Sales (q.v.) and herself canonized. Her marriage, not very satisfactory, ended with her husband's death in a duel (1651). Has a place in French literature through her lively and intelligent letters, of which some 1500 are preserved. Most of them were written to her daughter Françoise-Marguerite who married the Count of Grignan and lived with him in the Provence, of which he was lieutenant-governor. The literary public was more aware of the value of the letters than their immediate recipient, whose response to her mother's outpourings was definitely on the cool side.

Shaftesbury, Earl of

English philosopher (1671-1713).

Full name: Anthony Ashley Cooper, Earl of Shaftesbury. Born in London; died in Naples. After a Grand Tour of Holland, France, Italy, and Germany, went back to England and was elected to the House of Com-

mons in 1695. His philosophy is, in the main, a neo-
platonist aestheticism, presented in the polished language of the Augustan Age. It has considerable influence in Europe, especially Germany, where Shaftesbury's disciples included Herder and Goethe. Chief
work: "Characteristicks of Men, Manners, Opinions,
and Times" (1711-4).

Shakespeare, William

English playwright and poet (1564-1616).

Born and died in Stratford on Avon, Warwickshire.
His father, John, was a glovemaker and dealer in farm
produce. William went to Stratford Grammar School
and helped in his father's business. In 1582 he married
Ann Hathaway; he was 18 and she 26. The marriage
was not a happy one; she gave him three children and
he, in his will, gave her his "second-best bed." In 1585,
he went to London as actor-playwright. Established
himself at the Globe Theater; became member of the
Chamberlain's Players (King's Players in 1603). He
prospered financially, purchased property in Stratford,
and obtained a grant of family arms for his father.
Retired to Stratford, but continued to visit London.
These few facts are about all that is known of his life,
incredible as this may seem today for a man who is
incontestably the world's greatest dramatist and, in the
judgment of many, the greatest lyric poet of the Elizabethan Age. But although his genius was recognized
by some contemporaries, e.g. Ben Jonson and Francis
Meres, who compared him to Seneca and Plautus—high
praise indeed during the Renaissance—it remained for
posterity to perceive his true merits. These trium-
phantly survived the sneers of a Voltaire, who called
him "A barbarian of genius," the prudishness of Dr.
Bowdler who "bowdlerized" him. But there has remained about his life and his genius an element of
deep mystery, that the ridiculous theories ascribing

his plays to Francis Bacon or Queen Elizabeth merely illustrate, but do not even begin to elucidate. Perhaps the most powerful factor of Shakespeare's dramatic and lyrical genius is its incredible range, embracing deepest tragedy and shallowest farce, the tenderest sensitivities and the cruellest passions, but never losing the common touch of humanity. He has not only his fellow-writers but all of mankind in his debt. Wrote: the poems "Venus and Adonis" (1593), "The Rape of Lucrece" (1594), and the "Sonnets" (a sequence of 154, 1609); and the plays (dates are approximate) "Henry VI" (in three parts, 1590-92), "Comedy of Errors" (1591-92), "Two Gentlemen of Verona" (1592), "Richard III" (1592-93), "Titus Andronicus" (1593), "Love's Labor Lost" (1594); "King John" (1594), "Romeo and Juliet" (1594-95), "Richard II" (1595), "A Midsummer Night's Dream" (1595), "Taming of the Shrew" (1596), "Merchant of Venice" (1596), "Henry IV" (two parts, 1597-98), "Much Ado About Nothing" (1598-99), "Henry V" (1599), "Julius Caesar" (1599-1600), "As You Like It" (1599-1600), "Merry Wives of Windsor" (1599-1600), "Hamlet" (1600-01), "Twelfth Night" (1601), "Troilus and Cressida" (1602), "All's Well That Ends Well" (1602), "Measure for Measure" (1604), "Othello" (1604), "King Lear" (1605-06), "Macbeth" (1605-06), "Anthony and Cleopatra" (1607), "Timon of Athens" (1608), "Pericles" (1608), "Coriolanus" (1608-09), "Cymbeline" (1610), "A Winter's Tale" (1611), "The Tempest" (1611), "Henry VIII" (1612-13), "Two Noble Kinsmen" (1612-13).

Shaw, George Bernard

Anglo-Irish playwright (1856-1950).

Born in Dublin; died in Ayot Saint Lawrence, Hertfordshire, England. Son of an impoverished but genteel Anglo-Irish family; went to London to become a writer in 1876. Did not gain any appreciable success for almost twenty years. His five novels were rejected by all publishers to whom he submitted them and proved flops when they were at last published after "G.B.S." had become a famous dramatist. Still, he did manage to earn a living as a music and drama critic, who championed Wagner and Ibsen. Another of his early interests was Fabian socialism. This he expounded in books like "Fabianism and the Empire" (1900) and "The Intelligent Woman's Guide to Socialism and Capitalism" (1928); but in practice he was not above some harmless though noisy flirting with totalitarianism of both right and left. But Shaw's reputation stands or falls with his plays, which shocked contemporaries with their "advanced" and "shocking" views—and paradoxes. In the last few years of his life and after his death, Shaw's reputation slumped somewhat, but this may be merely the prelude to a revival. His plays are, for all their stagecraft, Shavian monologues delivered through a number of characters, and the appeal of the dramatist is primarily the appeal of the man. Chief plays: "Widower's Houses" (1893), "Mrs. Warren's Profession" (1894), "Candida" (1895), "The Man of Destiny" (1898), "You Never Can Tell" (1898), "Caesar and Cleopatra" (1901), "John Bull's Other Island" (1902), "Man and Superman" (1903), "The Doctor's Dilemma" (1906), "Getting Married" (1912), "Androcles and the Lion" (1912), "Heartbreak House" (1917), "Back to Methuselah" (1921), "Saint Joan" (1923), "The Apple Cart" (1929), "Too True to Be Good" (1932), "Geneva" (1938), "In Good King Charles' Golden Days" (1939).

Shaw, Irwin

American writer (born 1913).

Born in Brooklyn, graduated from Brooklyn College. Wrote plays before the war, e.g. "Bury the Dead"

(1936), "Siege" (1938), "The Gentle People" (1938), "Sailor off the Bremen" (1939). Also published novels and short stories, but only became real success after World War II, in which he fought, with such best-sellers as "The Young Lions" and "Lucy Crown."

Shelley, Mary
English writer (1797-1851).

Born and died in London. Daughter of the anarchist William Godwin and the feminist Mary Wollstonecraft. Married Percy Bysshe Shelley (q.v.); won her own niche in literature with "Frankenstein" (1818), a novel about a monster that destroys its scientist-creator, which has since spawned a crop of bad novels and worse films, and on another level has become a key folk-myth of the Technological Age.

Shelley, Percy Bysshe
English poet (1792-1822).

Born in Warnham, Sussex; died of drowning in the Gulf of Spezia, Italy. Studied at Eton and Oxford. Was expelled from Oxford with his friend Thomas Hogg, for circulating a pamphlet "The Necessity of Atheism." English public opinion was outraged and, in one sense, has not yet recovered from the outrage. The pressure in his lifetime was such that the government deprived him of the right to educate his children by his first wife, Harriet, and he had, in the end, to abandon England and live abroad. He kept on shocking his countrymen by espousing the cause of the Irish nationalists, by becoming a disciple of the anarchist William Godwin, and by marrying Godwin's daughter Mary after Harriet's suicide. Nor did his becoming a friend of Byron help him in this respect. In 1818 he left England for good and settled in Italy. He was lost in a storm sailing back from a visit to Leigh Hunt in Pisa; his body was washed ashore and burned on a funeral pyre, in classical Greek style. Shelley's reputation as a poet has never quite been as high in England as on the continent of Europe; but he did become a hero to some of his contemporaries after his death. With all his faults, he remains one of the glories of English romanticism. Chief works: "Queen Mab" (1813), "Revolt of Islam" (1817), "Prometheus Unbound" (1818), "The Cenci" (1822), "The Masque of Anarchy" (1819), "Ode to the West Wind" (1819), "The Skylark" (1820), "Epipsychidion" (1821), "Hellas" (1821).

Shen Tsung-Wen

(Chinese, 1902-   ) .

Prolific Chinese novelist and critic. Had military rather than conventional academic background. Edited *Ta-kung pao* literary supplement. Author of some 60 novels, volumes of stories and other works.

Sheridan, Richard Brinsley

Anglo-Irish playwright (1751-1816).

Born in Dublin; died in London. Studied in Oxford, eloped to France with Elizabeth Ann Linley. Came back to England to settle in London and to write a series of plays that are the last epigones of the Restoration Comedy: "The Rivals" (1775), "The Duenna" (1755), "The School for Scandal" (1777), "The Trip to Scarborough" (1777), and "The Critic" (1779). Became manager of the Drury Lane Theatre in London (1776), was ruined financially when his theater burned down in 1809. Meanwhile he started on a political career as Whig M.P., and rose to be Secretary of the Treasury and Under Secretary for Foreign Affairs. He also won fame as one of the best parliamentary orators of his time, and, indeed, of all time. Among his classic speeches are those he made opposing the war against the American colonies and proposing the impeachment of Warren Hastings. Buried at Westminster Abbey.

441

Sherwood, Robert Emmet
American writer (1896-1955)

Born in New Rochelle, N. Y. Best-known for his plays, the pacifist "Idiot's Delight" (1936), the biographical "Abe Lincoln in Illinois" (1939), and the topical "There Shall Be No Night" (1941), condemning Russia's invasion of Finland. Was chief writer of President Roosevelt's speeches.

Shevchenko, Taras
Ukrainian poet (1814-1861).

Born in Morinsty, died in Saint Petersburg. Born a serf, came to Saint Petersburg after a very unhappy childhood as apprentice to a craftsman. His artistic talents were revealed by accident and a number of Russian intellectuals, including the poet Zhukovski and the painter Bryullov, bought his freedom and enabled him to enter the Academy of Art in 1838. Discovered his poetic gifts while studying painting. His first and most important book of poems, "Kobzar" (the traditional Ukrainian bard) appeared in 1840. Other verses, which expressed his own and his people's hopes and sufferings, followed. Nicholas I had him arrested in 1847 and sent as a common soldier to the Urals, forbidding him to write or paint. He returned in 1858, broken in body but not in spirit. Russians and Ukrainians acclaimed him as national poet of the Ukraine.

Shin Nai-An
(Chinese, *ca.* 1290-1365).

Traditional author of *All Men Are Brothers,* one of four or five masterpieces of Chinese fiction. Written in the fourteenth century, improved and embellished during two succeeding centuries, receiving its final form. The novel is based on a cycle of stories about a band of outlaws.

442

Shneor, Zalman

(Hebrew; Yiddish; b. 1887 in Shklov, Russia).

The son of a jewelry merchant, ran away from home at the age of 13, and remained a rebellious spirit in his literary work as in his life. His poetry, as well as his prose both in Hebrew and in Yiddish, is marked by great vigor and individuality. He is almost always concerned with universal subjects, and the problems that torment his soul. He is a realist, laying bare the sordid life around him. In his novels, he loves to portray rough and vigorous characters. Shneor traveled extensively, living in Odessa, Warsaw, Berlin, Paris, and since 1940 in New York.

Sholem Aleichem

Yiddish writer (1859-1916).

Pen name of Sholem Rabinovich. Born in the Poltava district, Ukraine, died in New York. Became a village rabbi at 21, gave up his post after two years to devote himself to writing. Moved to Kiev, later to Switzerland and New York. A humorist who "laughs in order not to cry," he was a genuine humanitarian. His stories, especially "Menachem Mendel" and "Tevye the Milkman" are an epitaph on the Jewish world of Eastern Europe, now gone forever. Sholem Aleichem is still widely—and nostalgically—read. Some of his sayings became folk proverbs, e.g. "if you have money, you are beautiful, you are clever, and you can even sing."

Sholokhov, Mikhail Alexandrovich

Russian writer (born 1905).

Born in Veshenskaya on the Don, member of a Cossack family. The fighting of the Revolution, through which he lived as a boy, provided the theme of his most important work, the trilogy "And Quiet Flows the Don" (1925-35), "Virgin Soil Upturned" (1932-33), and "The Don Flows Home to the Sea" (1937). The trilogy made Sholokhov the last representative, together with Boris Pasternak (q.v.), the last upholder, of the traditions of the great Russian novel. He viewed the Revolution and the Counter-Revolution in historical perspective and not, Stalinist fashion, in black and white. His prestige, his refusal to engage in literary politics, and—it is said—the admiration of Stalin himself, kept him out of trouble during the purges. He has remained in his modest home in a Cossack "Stanitsa" (village), from which he occasionally emerges to take trips to Moscow and abroad. His independent attitude has won him respect inside and outside the Soviet Union. His other writings include "The Lapis Lazuli Steppe," "The Mortal Enemy," "The Family Man," and "They Fought for Their Country," a novel of World War II.

Sidney, Sir Philip

English poet (1554-1586).

Born in Penshurst, Kent; died in Arnhem (Holland). After studies at Oxford and Cambridge, and a European Grand Tour, fought in Ireland (1576-7). Upon return to London met Edmund Spenser (q.v.), who became his great friend and wrote "To Astrophel" for him after his untimely death. Became member of the "Areopagus," a group interested in writing English verse in classical meters. Wrote in 1578 a masque "Lady of May" with which his uncle, the Earl of Leicester, entertained Queen Elizabeth I. After losing the Queen's favor for opposing her proposed marriage to the Duke of Alençon, he retired to his sister's country home at Wilton. There he wrote his euphuistic pastoral poem "Arcadia" (1580-1), in the first place to amuse his sister. Fell in love with Penelope Devereux, wrote 100 sonnets and 11 songs for her, later published as "Astrophel and Stella." When a Puritan named Gorson attacked poetry, Sidney replied vigorously with his "Defense of Poesie." Though married to Frances Walsingham, continued to write verses to Penelope Devereux. Tried to join Drake's expedition, was sent instead to Holland with Leicester and died of wounds received at the battle of Zutphen. Sidney, a good poet and a great gentleman, is one of the glories of England's first Elizabethan Age.

Sienkiewicz, Henryk
Polish novelist (1846-1916).

Born in Vola Okrzejska (East Poland, now Russia); died in Vevey (Switzerland). Studied history in Warsaw, traveled in Europe, America, Africa, and Near East, and wrote journalistic accounts of them. An ardent Polish patriot, he died of overwork and overstrain in taking care of Polish prisoners of war in World War I. His stature as a novelist is more secure abroad, where he is known mainly, if not entirely, by his Nobel Prize winning novel on the early Christians, "Quo Vadis" (published 1896, Nobel Prize 1905), than in his own homeland. Polish opinion is still sharply divided about him. The right praises his historical—"With Fire and Sword" (1886), "The Flood" (1886), "Mister Wolodyjowski" (1884-8), and "The Knights of the Cross" (1900)—while the left resents his conservative and religious criticism of modern "decadence" in his novels of contemporary life, "The Polaniecki Family" (1893) and "Without Dogma" (1902). The consensus seems to be, however, that Sienkiewicz's merits are extra-literary rather than literary.

Sillanpaeae, Frans Eemil
Finnish writer (born 1888).

Born in Haemeenkyroe in Southwest Finland, studied natural sciences at Helsinki University. His novels are lyrical in tone and deal with Finnish country life.

He tends toward a northern "nature mysticism." Won Nobel Prize in 1939. Chief works: "The Pious Poverty" (1919), "Fallen Asleep While Young" (1931), "A Man's Way" (1932), "People in a Summer's Night" (1934).

Silone, Ignazio
Italian writer (born 1900).

Born in Pescina dei Marsi, Abruzzi. Bitterly opposed to Fascism, he was one of the founders of the Italian Communist Party in 1921. He left the party nine years later, completely disillusioned. His "Fontamara" (1930), published in exile, is a sardonic denunciation of Fascism. His novels made him famous abroad, but he was practically unknown in Italy until he returned there following Mussolini's defeat. He has since returned to the Christianity of his childhood and youth.

Silva, Jose Asuncion
Colombian poet (1865-1896).

Born and died in Bogota. Lived an unhappy life, bitterly resenting his isolation in a country outside the main currents of world culture, died by his own hand. Much influenced by French contemporaries, he was one of the chief talents of the "modernist" school that revolutionized Spanish and Spanish-American poetry. Some of his poems, like the "Nocturnes" are in the subtle tradition of Baudelaire; others, reflecting his native background, are satirical in intent and popular in tone.

Simonides
Greek poet (556-468 B.C.).

Born on the island of Ceos; died in Syracuse. Resided at the courts of Hipparchos of Athens (till 514 B.C.), of various tyrants of Thessaly and finally of Hiero of Syracuse. His poetic output was very varied and exercised a strong influence on Alexandrian and

Roman literature. It included odes, elegies, dirges, epigrams, and hymns to the gods. Only fragments have been preserved but every school child knows—or knew —his epitaph on the 300 Spartans, led by King Leonidas, who died defending the pass of Thermopylae against the Persians.

Simonov, Konstantin Mikhailovich
Russian writer (born 1915).

Leaped to fame in World War II, with his poignant love poems and his Stalingrad novel "Days and Nights" (1944). Since then he has lived on his wartime reputation and on the privileges as "official" writer that it earned him.

Sinclair, Upton
American novelist (born 1878).

Born in Baltimore, of a Southern family ruined by the Civil War. Educated at City College, New York. Started politically as a defender of the "Lost Cause" of the South—his first novel published was to be on the Battle of Manassas. But he soon veered to a Socialism which has become somewhat less radical in the course of the years, but has remained steadfast and highly personal. His career as socialist politician was marked by several unsuccessful candidacies for government offices, culminating in the "End Poverty in California" (EPIC) 1934 campaign for the governorship of that state. He founded the American Civil Liberties Union in California and never shifted from his basic defense of the rights of the underdog. He gained fame by a series of expose-type novels, some of which, especially "The Jungle" (1901, an attack on the Chicago meat-packing plants), had a good deal to do with inciting remedial legislation. "The Jungle" was followed by "The Money Changers" (1908), "King Coal" (1917), "The Brass Check" (1919), "The Goose-Step—A Study of American Education" (1923), "Oil"

(1927), "Boston" (1928), "The Way Out" (1933). In 1940, he started a series of novels, now running to eight, about the adventures of an American secret agent, "Lanny Budd."

Singer, J. J.
(Yiddish, 1893-1944).

One of the outstanding Yiddish novelists of the *interbellum* period. Son of a Rabbi in a small town in Poland, he surreptitiously read the secular literature in Yiddish and in Hebrew. He wrote a long naturalistic novel, which won him a large reading public. His novels are highly naturalistic, presenting striking and usually negative characters from different Jewish strata against a broad background. Popular in English translation are *The Sinner; The Brothers Ashkenazi; East of Eden.*

Sitwell, Edith
English poetess (born 1887).

Born in Scarborough, Yorkshire. Her father, Sir George Sitwell, was a noted English eccentric; her two brothers, Sir Osbert (born 1892) and Sacheverell (born 1897) are well-known men of letters. Her poetry moved from fanciful through realistic to reflective without losing its brilliant imagery and verbal felicity. It includes: "Clown's Houses" (1918); "The Wooden Pegasus" (1920) and "Elegy for Dead Fashion" (1926).

Sjoeberg, Birger
Swedish novelist (1885-1929).

Born in Vaenersborg; died in Vaxjoe. Became a journalist in Stockholm, but retired in 1926 to live in a small town. His novels deal with small-town life, at first romantically and humorously, but later more and more tragically and pessimistically. Chief works: "Frieda's Book" (1922), "The Broken Quartet"

(1924), "Crisis and Wreaths" (1926), "Frieda's Second Book" (1929).

Skelton, John

English poet (about 1460-1529).

Became court poet of Henry VII in 1488, later tutor of future Henry VIII, whom he served as king. His poems were official panegyrics of both kings, but he made strong attacks on Cardinal Wolsey. His verses were published posthumously and include "Magnificence" and "Philip Sparrow." They are on the borderline between medieval and modern literature.

Slowacki, Juljusz

Polish poet (1809-1849).

Born in Krzemieniec Podolski (now Ukraine); died in Paris. Son of a university professor, entered government service in Warsaw (1829). Greeted enthusiastically the Polish rising of 1830, had to leave Poland after its defeat by the Russians next year. He spent the rest of his life wandering in Germany, England, Switzerland, and the Middle East; but finally settled in Paris. Slowacki was with Mickiewicz and Krazinski (q.v.), one of the "Three Greats" of Polish romanticism. He excels in his language, which reached artistic and poetic heights not attained before and rarely since. But his unrestrained emotionalism and imagination lack the high seriousness of Mickiewicz and the polish of Krasinski. Chief works: "Jan Bielecki" (1830); "The Arab" (1830), "Lambro" (1832), "Poems" (1832-3), "Kordian" (1833), "Balladyna" (1839), "Mazepa" (1840), "The Spirit King" (1841).

Smollett, Tobias

Scottish novelist (1727-1771).

Born in Dalquhurn, died in Leghorn, Italy. Studied at Glasgow University, became a doctor and settled in England until ill-health drove him abroad. Was much influenced by European literary currents—he translated Voltaire and Cervantes—but his humor and wit remained insular. He is at his best in picaresque novels in which the savagery of the Spanish originals is softened by the gentler English touch. They include; "Roderick Random" (1748) and "Peregrine Pickle" (1751).

Socrates

Greek philosopher (about 470-399 B.C.).

Born and died in Athens. Son of a sculptor and a midwife. First active as sculptor, then turned to philosophy. Attacked the Sophists and created Greek philosophy as we know it through his "Socratic" questionings. Fought in the Peloponnesian War and saved the life of Alcibiades, Athenian commander at the battle of Potideia (424). Alcibiades became his friend and adherent, together with Plato, Xenophon, and many others. Socrates was condemned to death by the democratic government of Athens after the end of the Peloponnesian War for alleged godlessness and corrupting of youth, actually because his role as "gadfly of Athens" and his friendships with aristocrats like the three men named above could not be stomached by the men who ruled the city. Socrates refused to recant or to save his life by escaping from jail and died by the traditional Athenian death of the hemlock cup. He left no writing but his place in world literature is secure not only through the literary portraits drawn by his disciples Plato and Xenophon but also by his immense influence on writers of all countries and times.

Sologub, Fjodor

Russian writer (1863-1927).

Real name: Fyodor Kusmich Teternikov. Born and died in Saint Petersburg. Born of a poor family, became teacher at a provincial school, rose to be inspector of elementary schools in Saint Petersburg. His poetry, of the symbolist school, is marked by pessimism and fear of death. He also wrote short stories and translated foreign classics, especially Kleist. Chief works: "Heavy Dreams" (1896), "The Goad of Death" (1904), "The Little Demon" (1905), "A Book of Tales" (1905), "The Charm of Death" (1908), "The Mad Tear" (1916).

Solomos, Dionysios
Greek poet (1798-1857).

Born on the island of Zante, died on Corfu. Was educated in Italy and started writing in Italian. But the politician Trikoupes persuaded him to switch to the spoken tongue of Greece and he became the first great modern Greek poet. He tried all literary genres. Best-known for his "Hymn to Liberty," his ode on the death of Byron, and his play "Lambros."

Solon
Greek writer and lawgiver (about 640-about 599 B.C.).

Born and died in Athens. Member of aristocratic family, but his legislative reforms were in the direction of democracy and he was forced into a ten years' exile by the aristocratic faction. Solon was also a philosopher —one of the "Seven Sages of Greece"—and a poet. His poems, highly esteemed in antiquity, were mostly didactic and elegiac. The most famous was his elegy on the loss of Salamis to Athens' traditional enemy Megara. Its recital launched Solon's political career.

Soloviev, Vladimir Sergeyevich
Russian philosopher and poet (1853-1900).

Born in Moscow; died in Uzkoye near Moscow. Taught philosophy at Moscow and Saint Petersburg Universities. Had to give up his university post because he protested against the execution of the murderers of

Tsar Alexander II. Became leading champion of the reconciliation of the Greek Orthodox and Roman Catholic churches; became Roman Catholic in 1896. His philosophy was a Platonizing and aestheticizing mysticism; his lyrical poetry belongs to the symbolist school. Chief works: "The Crisis of Western Philosophy" (1874); "Of God-Man" (1877-81); "The Spiritual Foundations of Life" (1882-84); "History of Theocracy" (1888); "Russia and the Universal church" (1886); "The Justification of the Good" (1897); "War, Progress, and the End of History" (1900); The Talks" (1900).

Somadeva

(Sanskrit, 11th Century).

Legendary Kashmir Brahmin. Little known of his life. His celebrated collection of stories, *The Ocean of the Streams of Story,* is based on a still earlier collection.

Sophocles

Greek dramatist (about 497-about 406 B.C.).

Born in Colonos near Athens; died in Athens. Took part in parade to celebrate the Athenian victory of Salamis (480). His place in the history of the Greek drama is indicated by two dates—468, when he defeated Aeschylus for the tragedy prize, and 441, when he was defeated by Euripides. In the course of his long life he wrote 123 plays of which 111 are known by name. Only seven of them are preserved: "Oedipus Rex"; "Oedipus at Colonus"; "Ajax"; "Electra"; "Antigone"; "Philoctetes"; and "The Trachinian Women." Their perfection makes the loss of the others even more deplorable. Sophocles introduced important changes in dramatic technique; he added the third actor and reduced the role of the chorus. His outlook is between that of Aeschylus, in whom the gods dominate man, and of Euripides, in whom man

452

stands alone with the gods only symbols. Sophocles' man is ruled by ethical law rather than blind fate, and his tragedy comes from within rather than from without. The language of the plays is Attic Greek in its classical apogee.

Southey, Robert

English poet (1774-1843).

Born in Bristol, died in Keswick. Studied at Oxford where he met Coleridge and shared his enthusiasms. Together with Coleridge and Wordsworth headed the school of "Lake Poets" which consecrated the victory of romanticism in English letters. Settled at Keswick in the Lake District to support a large family. Started as a political hothead and a metrical experimenter but became a conventional poet who took the world as it was and found it good. His shorter ballads like "Battle of Blenheim" and "Bishop Hatto" belong to the first vein, his "Vision of Judgment" (1821) in praise of George III, in whose name he became poet laureate, to the second. It was savagely attacked by Byron in a poem of the same name. Voluminous prose writer and correspondent.

Spee, Friedrich Von

German poet (1591-1635).

Born in Kaiserwoerth near Dusseldorf; died in Trier. Entered the Jesuit order in 1610, taught at Paderborn, Cologne, and Trier. Fought against the contemporary mania of witchcraft trials, after acting as confessor to 200 victims of whose innocence he was convinced. His poems, among the best of the Baroque age, are imbued with mysticism. Chief works: "Criminal Caution" (against witchcraft trials, in Latin, 1633); "The Trusty Nightingale" (lyrics, 1639).

Spender, Stephen

English poet (born 1909).

Born in London. One of "modern poets" of the

thirties who tried to renew English poetry by imbuing it with social consciousness and writing it in the language of the day. Since then, he has become quieter and more restrained. Wrote: "Twenty Poems" (1930); "Poems from Spain" (1939); "The Still Centre" (1939) etc.

Spengler, Oswald

German historian (1880-1936).

Born in Blankenburg; died in Munich. Became world famous by his philosophy of history, "The Decline of the West" (2 volumes, 1919 and 1922), from which Toynbee's work stems. His thesis is that civilizations are born, grow, decay, and die like organisms. Also wrote "Prussianism and Socialism" (1920); "Man and Technics" (1931), which expressed critical views of Western Man and made the Nazis favorably inclined to him. He seems, however, to have sharply condemned the Hitler regime in his last years, though the evidence is not conclusive.

Spenser, Edmund

English poet (1552-1599).

Born and died in London. Educated at Cambridge. Became a protege of Sir Philip Sidney (q.v.), to whom he dedicated his "Shepherd's Calendar," twelve eclogues (1579) which are generally considered the first major work of Elizabethan literature. Accompanied Lord Grey de Wilton, the Viceroy, to Ireland, serving as his secretary. Spent a number of years there, and received an estate in County Cork including Kilcolman Castle, confiscated from the Irish rebel, the Earl of Desmond. Wrote there "To Astrophel" (1586), an elegy on the death of Sidney, and started on his allegorical poem "The Faery Queen" (1590-96) which glorified England, Elizabeth I, Protestantism, and Puritanism, in a refined and polished language. Also wrote love poems for Elizabeth Boyle, whom he married in 1594; and a "View of the Present State of Ireland" (1596), a strong plea for the English conquest and rule of Ireland, a book which the Irish nationalists have not forgotten nor forgiven. While he served as sheriff of Cork (1598), Kilcolman Castle was attacked by the Irish and burned. Spenser's youngest child and manuscripts (including perhaps parts of the "Faery Queen") were lost in the fire, and the poet barely saved his wife and other children. He died shortly afterward and was buried in Westminster Abbey, near Chaucer. Spenser was the greatest lyricist of the Elizabethan age and deserved his name of "the poet's poet" for his technical innovations, including the "Spenserian stanza."

Spinoza, Benedict

Jewish philosopher (1632-1677).

Real name: Baruch Spinoza; used "Benedict" in his writings. Born in Amsterdam; died in the Hague. Descendant of a Portuguese-Jewish family, forcibly converted to Christianity in the 15th Century and returned to Judaism in the more tolerant atmosphere of Holland. Received careful humanistic education, but exercised at first his father's profession as lens grinder. His pantheistic philosophy led to a conflict with the Jewish community of Amsterdam which found his mixture of Cartesianism and mysticism contrary to the tenets of the Jewish religion. Spinoza was excommunicated in 1656, after which date he was no longer considered a Jew. His fame was in eclipse for a century or so after his death but it was rescued by the enthusiasm of Herder and Goethe. His works, written in Latin, include: "Theologico-Political Treatise" (1670); "Ethics Proved by Means of Geometry" (1674); "Posthumous Works" (1677).

Spitteler, Karl

Swiss novelist (1845-1924).

Born in Liesthal near Basel; died in Luzern. Studied law and theology, became a teacher, then a writer. A narrative writer in the Swiss realistic tradition, but with epical and mystical overtones. Won Nobel Prize in 1919. Wrote "Prometheus and Epimetheus" (1880-81); "The Butterfly" (1889); "Conrad the Lieutenant" (1898); "Laughing Truths" (1898); "Olympian Spring" (4 volumes, 1900-1908); "Imago" (1906); "Prometheus the Sufferer" (1924).

Ssü-K'ung t'u

(Chinese, 837-908).

Scholarly pedantic stylist. Like many another Chinese poet, gave up an official career to write in retirement. His work shows great erudition rather than originality. Most famous: a 24 stanza poem, *Êrh-shih-ssu shih-p'in*.

Ssu-ma Ch'ien

Chinese historian (145-86 B.C.).

Born in Lung Men. In his youth travelled in central and eastern China visiting historical sites and preparing himself for his career as official in charge of calendar and historical records, a post in which he succeeded his father, Ssu-ma T'an, in 108. Aroused the emperor's anger by defending a personal friend, general Li Ling, who was defeated and taken prisoner by barbarians. Was given the choice of death or castration, chose the latter in order to be able to complete his "Historical Records," the first connected history of China. He inaugurated the Chinese historical tradition, being both China's Herodotus and Thucydides. His assertion that "one can govern well by simply doing one's duty and acting rationally" is still topical in China—and elsewhere.

Stael, Germaine de
French writer and critic (1766-1817).

Maiden name; Germaine Necker. Born and died in Paris. Of Swiss origin, daughter of banker who was financial adviser to Louis XVI. In 1786 married Baron de Stael Holstein, the Swedish minister to France. Started writing under the influence of Rousseau. Won fame with "Of Literature Considered in Relation With Social Institutions" (1800), a critical attack on classical formalism and revolutionary materialism. Exiled by Napoleon, did not return to France until after his fall. Wrote two novels, "Delphine" (1802) and "Corinne" (1817), much read in her days, and "On Germany" (1810), a classical account of the country and a plea for romanticism, by which her reputation stands today.

Steele, Sir Richard
English essayist (1672-1729).

Born in Dublin, died in Llangunnor. Educated in England (Charterhouse and Oxford), served in the British army and was knighted for political services in 1715. Founded "The Tatler" in 1709, edited "The Spectator" with Addison (q.v.) from 1711. Wrote essays for both. Steele was a moralist, but of the 18th century variety. Good manners and good taste were to him inseparable from good ethical principles.

Stein, Gertrude
American writer (1874-1946).

Born in Allegheny, Penna., died in Paris. Studied psychology under William James (q.v.) at Radcliffe and medicine at Johns Hopkins. The family settled in San Francisco but she moved on to Paris where she met and acted as patron to painters then unknown and now world-famous, like Picasso and Matisse. Her "Three Lives" (1909) was an experimental novel

457

that influenced younger writers. Her writing moved from experimentation to incomprehensibility, which had, however, no serious effect on her popularity. In her last years, she was a celebrity in her own right and a Paris landmark for American tourists. Her humor tended towards the impish and she wrote her life story as "The Autobiography of Alice B. Toklas" (1933), her constant companion.

Steinbeck, John

American novelist (born 1902).

Born in Salinas, California. Educated at Stanford University. Started writing under the influence of his first wife; achieved his first success with "Tortilla Flat" (1935), a story of California "characters." But he did his best work under the influence of the social doctrines of Roosevelt's New Deal: "In Dubious Battle" (1936), "Of Mice and Men" (1937), and "The Grapes of Wrath" (1940), describing the plight of various kinds of underdog. There has been a falling off of his literary powers in his work published in the forties and fifties. At its best, as in "Cannery Row" (1945), it represents new variations on old themes; at its worst, it sinks into bathos. Nobel Prize 1962.

Stendhal

French novelist (1783-1842).

Real name: Henri Beyle; took his pen name from a town, now a railroad junction, in North Germany, whose charm he was alone in seeing. Born in Grenoble; died in Paris. Brought up by parents who failed to understand him, amid the turmoil of the French Revolution. Entered the French army under Napoleon, took part in the Russian campaign, and rose to high rank. Was therefore out of favor under the Restoration; earned his living with his pen, writing popular biographies of Haydn (1814), and Rossini

(1824), romantic novels like "Armance" (1823), and deep studies like "Of Love" (1822) that sold exactly seventeen copies in his lifetime. The July monarchy made him French consul in Trieste (1830) and transferred him to Civitavecchia a year later. His superiors refused to transfer him, and he remained in that dismal town, an exile in fact yet not in name. From it he ventured occasionally on trips to Paris and Rome. Stendhal was a lonely man, who brooded on his misfortunes and those of his country, but he also loved Italy—he wanted to be buried as "Arrigo Beyle, Milanese"—and in his two great novels, "The Red and the Black" (1830) and "The Charterhouse of Parma" (1839), he combined the methods of French and Italian realism, while embodying the psychological insights of romanticism and of his own long and checkered quest for love. He became one of the founders of the modern novel as well as a precursor of modern depth psychology. Men like Balzac and Victor Hugo, to their great credit, recognized his genius, although their talents and expression were so different from his. But they were exceptions, and Stendhal died a forgotten man. He was rescued from oblivion by men like Taine and Nietzsche and the equally devoted labors of less known critics and admirers. Today, his towering position in French and European letters is quite unaffected by changes in literary fashions and styles.

Sterne, Laurence

English novelist (1713-1768).

Born in Clonmel, County Tipperary, died in London. Son of an English officer stationed in Ireland, was educated at a school in Halifax and at Cambridge. Became an Anglican parson in Sutton and Coxwold; it was in the latter place that he wrote his "Tristram Shandy" (1760-67), a novel which blends humor, eccentricity, pruriency and sentimentality in a very personal mixture. Critics have found in it affinities ranging from Rabelais to Joyce. A trip to France inspired him to write his "Sentimental Journey" (1768) which enhanced his fame.

Stevens, Wallace
American poet (1879-1955)

Born in Reading, Pa. Educated at Harvard, became lawyer and insurance executive at Hartford, Conn. His poems are musical and abound in happy images. They include: "Harmonium" (1923); "Ideas of Order" (1935) and "The Man with the Blue Guitar" (1937).

Stevenson, Robert Louis
Scotish novelist and poet (1850-1894).

Often referred to by his initials "R. L. S." Born in Edinburgh; died in Vailima (Samoa). Grandson of Robert Stevenson, the famous engineer and builder of lighthouses. Studied first engineering, then law. Started literary career as essayist. He described his unconventional travels in Europe in "An Inland Voyage" (1878) and "Travels With a Donkey in the Cevennes" (1879). Spent a couple of years in the United States, then returned to Scotland where he wrote his best-remembered tales, including "New Arabian Nights" (1882), "Treasure Island" (1882), and "Dr. Jekyll and Mr. Hyde" (1886). Ill health, with which he was afflicted from his childhood, drove him to a voluntary exile in the Pacific islands; he finally settled in Samoa where the Samoans made him an honorary chief under the name of "Tusitala," meaning "Teller of Tales." His later works include "The Master of Ballantrae" (1889), "Weir of Hermiston" (his last novel, left unfinished), and "The South Seas." Stevenson was enormously popular in his lifetime; some of his work has dated by now but his tales of adventure and fantasy have remained ever fresh. Still popular are his poems for children, "A Child's Garden of Verses"; and his short poem "Requiem," which was used as his epitaph, has become immortal.

Stifter, Adalbert
Austrian writer (1805-1868).

Born in Oberplan, a village in the Boehmerwald mountains; died in Linz. Studied at Vienna University. Worked as tutor in prominent Austrian families; he tried to become a teacher in government schools, but did not appear at the oral examination, though he had passed the written test, and therefore had to continue as private tutor. Started writing in his middle thirties, and soon acquired his reputation as the greatest Austrian narrative writer of the 19th Century. An unfortunate family life and the death of close relatives turned him into a recluse and he finally committed suicide in a fit of insanity. His writings, mostly dealing with his part of Austria and full of deep psychological insights, include "The High Forest" (1842), "Abdias" (1845), "Late Summer" (1857), "Witiko" (1865-67).

Storm, Theodor
German writer (1817-1888).

Born in Husum; died in Hademarschen. Lawyer, later judge in his native town. A master of style in his short stories; a realist in his descriptions of his Schleswig landscape and in his analyses of human characted. Works include "Lake Immensee" (1849), "Pole Poppenspaeler" (1873-74), "Renate" (1877-78).

Strachey, Lytton
English biographer and critic (1880-1932).

Born in London, died near Hungerford. After

writing some excellent critical studies of French and English literary figures, he found his true vocation in biography. Identified in the popular mind as "debunker," notably of the Victorian greats; he himself was more concerned with making biography a work of art. Wrote: "Eminent Victorians" (1918); "Elizabeth and Essex" (1928) etc.

Strindberg, August

Swedish writer (1849-1912).

Born and died in Stockholm. Brought up in very poor circumstances in a Stockholm slum. Strindberg was a fighter against social injustice. He worked as teacher, tutor, actor, journalist, and librarian, until he could earn his living as a writer. Became the first novelist of Stockholm life in "The Red Room" (1879). He delved into moral issues in his first play "Master Olaf" (1872), the story of a seeker of truth. Although he wrote other novels and short stories, his literary vocation was the drama. His plays tackle two series of problems: his interpretation of great figures of Swedish history, e.g. "Gustavus Adolphus" (1900), "Erik XIV" (1901), "Charles XII" (1902); and the relations between men and women, on which he took, aggressively the part of man. This was partly, at least, due to his unfortunate experiences with women, which included four marriages. But another part of Strindberg's motivation was his reaction against women's emancipation generally, of which he took an exceedingly dim view. He was particularly incensed at what he regarded as Ibsen's unfair advocacy of women's rights. Strindberg found it difficult to become accepted by his countrymen in his lifetime; his life was punctuated by crises of all kinds. It was largely through the German expressionists, who hailed him as one of their masters, that he gained final recognition at home and abroad.

Sturluson, Snorri

Icelandic historian (1178-1241).

His father was a minor chieftain, his mother came from a family with literary associations. He was one of the richest and most powerful men of his day, deeply involved in politics and the relation between Iceland and its suzerain, the king of Norway. He was killed at the order of king Haakon, following long and sordid intrigues. Snorri is the greatest figure of the medieval Scandinavian culture. His poems and sagas are the culmination of the old Norse tradition. His "Heimskringla," the history of the kings of Norway, is a prime historical source, with many anticipations of modern historical methods e.g. the use of literary and archeological sources.

Sudermann, Hermann

German novelist and dramatist (1857-1928).

Born at Matziken (East Prussia); died in Berlin. As a writer moved from naturalism to realism in his descriptions of town and country. Was very popular in his day; now tends to be dated. Wrote: "Frau Sorge" (1887), "Honor" (1889), "Homeland" (1893), "Lithuanian Stories" (1917), etc.

Suetonius

Roman historian (about 70- about 140).

Born and died in Rome. Taught rhetorics, then entered government serivce. Accompanied the young Pliny (q.v.) to Bithynia in 112; became private secretary to Emperor Hadrian (119-121) but was dismissed in disgrace. Apart from fragments, only his "Lives of the Caesars" from Julius Caesar to Domitian are preserved. Suetonius was more a gossip writer than a historian, but he provided European literature with valuable examples of historical biography.

Sully- Prudhomme

French poet and critic (1839-1907).

Full name: Rene Francois Sully Prudhomme. Born in Paris; died at Chatenay Castle near Paris. Took part in Franco-Prussian War of 1870-71. His poems, classically perfect in form, often give voice to a deep underlying pessimism. He was awarded the first Nobel Prize for Literature in 1901. Works include "Stanzas and Poems" (1865), "The Trials," (1866), "The Solitudes" (1868), "Impressions of the War" (1872), "Destinies" (1872), "Expression in Fine Arts" (1884), "Happiness" (1888), "What Do I Know" (1896), "Poetic Testament" (1901), "True Religion According to Pascal" (1905), "The Psychology of Free Will" (1907).

Sun Hsi-Chen

(Chinese, 1906-   ).

Novelist popular among Chinese youth. Admired for his stories of rural life. Most widely known books: *Beaten Gold, Woman of the Night,* and a war trilogy: *The Field of War, War,* and *After War.*

Sun Tzu

Chinese writer traditionally ascribed to 6th century B.C.

Name given to Sun Wu who wrote the classic Chinese treatise on military affairs. The scholars hold divergent theories as to his personality—some hold that there were two authors—and dates. But there is no doubt that the book was a classic for over 2000 years, and has been used by every Chinese general, all the way to Chiang Kai-shek and Mao Tse-tung. The Japanese militarists held it in equally high esteem, and no less than four English translations appeared within three years of Pearl Harbor.

Surtees, Robert

Engish writer (1803-1864).

Novelist and writer on sports. Published "The Horseman's Manual" (1831) and a series of novels on fox hunting that still have their place in any country gentleman's library. Their hero is the sporting cockney grocer, John Jorrocks. They include: "Jorrocks' Jaunts and Jollities" (1838), "Handley Cross" (1854), "Hillingdon Hall" (1845).

Suso or Seuse, Heinrich

German mystic (1300-1366).

Real name: Heinrich Berg. Born in Ueberlingen on Lake Constance; died in Ulm. Studied at Cologne under Eckhart, became a mystic under his influence. A Dominican monk, wandered through Swabia as an itinerant preacher (about 1335-48), finally settled in Ulm. His religious mysticism is emotional, and not without erotic overtones. Wrote in German: "Autobiography," "The Booklet of Eternal Wisdom," and "The Booklet of Truth," which he combined in a Latin translation as "Exemplaris." Suso is, with Eckhart, a classical German mystic.

Su Tung P'o

Chinese poet (1036-1101).

Also known as Su Shih. Born in Mei-shan, died in Ch'ang-chou. An important public official, was strongly opposed to the revolutionary reforms of Wang An-shih, who had him banished. Returned to court after Wang's fall, but suffered another exile when his followers returned to power. Su is also famous as painter and calligrapher. His poetry is remarkable for its wide range and its use of the vernacular—he made a point of reading his poems to an old peasant woman to make sure of their intelligibility. It is no less delicate and polished for that.

Svevo, Italo
Italian novelist (1861-1928).

Born in Trieste, died in Motta di Livenza. A businessman, who wrote novels on the side. James Joyce (q.v.) who was his friend and taught him English, may well have learned something from him, as his novels are psychological studies on the lines later made familiar by Proust. Wrote: "A Life" (1893); "Senility" (1898) and "The Confessions of Zeno" (published 1923, his masterpiece).

Swedenborg, Emanuel
Swedish mystic and scientist (1688-1772).

Born in Stockholm; died in London. Like Pascal, he was a distinguished scientist before he became a mystic. He excelled as a mining and military engineer and was ennobled in 1719 by Queen Ulrika Eleonora for his services to the Swedish state. Wrote a number of scientific treatises. But science gradually lost its attractions to him and he devoted himself more and more to mysticism, theology, and theosophy, his "Divine Love and Wisdom." His followers, the Swedenborgians, maintain to this day the church he founded. Swedenborg's ideas were not only influential on the cultural life of Europe in his time; they also had a great influence on later figures, including Balzac, William Blake and Henry and William James.

Swift, Jonathan
Anglo-Irish writer (1667-1745).

Born and died in Dublin. Cousin of John Dryden (q.v.). Came to England in 1668, was secretary to Sir William Temple. Returned to Ireland and took orders (1694), but soon returned to England and Sir William Temple's household in Surrey. It was there that he supervised the education of Esther Johnson, who became his "Stella." The patronage of Temple, a prominent Whig, helped him greatly in 1702-10, which he spent between London and Dublin, at home in the literary and political coteries of both. In 1710 he switched his loyalties from Whigs to Tories, for whom he wrote witty pamphlets, including the very popular "The Conduct of the Allies" (1711), which helped to earn him his post as Dean of Saint Patrick's, two years later. Queen Anne's death brought the Whigs back to power and Swift became more and more bitter and disillusioned. The devotion of two women, "Vanessa" (Esther Vanhomrih) who followed him to Ireland, and "Stella" (Esther Johnson) to whom he addressed his "Journal" (from 1710) and whom he may have married, failed to cure his bile. His championship of the Anglo-Irish against the Whigs in "The Drapier Letters" (1724) and of the Irish against the Anglo-Irish in the savage "Modest Proposal" (1729), i.e., to eat Irish children as a remedy against overpopulation, show that politics had lost all charms for him. The book by which he lives today, "Gulliver's Travels" (1726), has had the sad fate of being bowdlerized and "castrated" into a children's book, a fate that might have made the sardonic author exclaim "I told you so." But the humanity of Swift has withstood not only the passage of the years but even his own expressed preference for horses as the masters of men. Not even the bestiality of the Yahoos could prevail against it. Today, Swift is still read and commented upon, and the many mysteries of his life are as tempting to his biographers today as they were two centuries ago.

Swinburne, Algernon Charles

English poet (1837-1909).

Born and died in London. Influenced by both romanticism and classicism, the latter via Italy, which he knew at first hand, and through the Greek drama.

A friend of the Rossettis and of William Morris, he spent the last thirty years of his life in the house of Theodore Watts-Dunton in Putney. His poetic genius first won wider recognition with "Atlanta in Calydon" (1865), modelled on the classical Greek drama. His "Poems" and "Ballads" (1866 and 1886) shocked the Victorians by their advocacy of political republicanism and sexual license. Swinburne's writing pioneered trends which came to the fore in the 1890's with Wilde, Beardsley, etc.

Synge, John Millington

Irish dramatist (1871-1909).

Born and died in Dublin. Of an Anglo-Irish family from County Wicklow, studied at Trinity College, Dublin. Travelled in Germany and France, pursuing his interests in music, literature and natural history. In Paris he met W. B. Yeats who persuaded him to go to the Aran islands where the old Irish culture and language had survived all but intact. Synge went and was inspired to write plays that were produced in the Abbey Theater and made him Ireland's national dramatist—against all kinds of vocal opposition, political, reigious and moral. Died of cancer. Wrote "Riders to the Sea" (1904); "Playboy of the Western World" (his much-contested masterpiece, 1907); "Deirdre of the Sorrows" (1909).

T

Tacitus

Roman historian (about 55-about 122).

Full name: Publius Cornelius Tacitus. His birth-place is not known, but some authorities favor Southern Gaul; the place and circumstances of his death are also unknown. Tacitus came from a good Roman family, in which the great traditions of the Roman Republic were alive and their passing was re-gretted. He served Domitian, whose despotism he despised, as quaestor (78) and praetor (88). Nerva, who tried to revive the old Roman ways, made him consul. Tacitus first earned his reputation as orator. In 98, he inaugurated his career as a writer with three books: "Dialogue on the Orators," which deplores the decline of Roman oratory from the days of Cicero; "The Life and Habits of Julius Agricola," a life of his father-in-law, the Roman commander who made his famous expedition to Northern Scotland, situated for the Romans at the end of their known world; and "On the Original Location, Customs, and Peoples of the Germans," generally known as "Germania." This is a landmark of history, geography, and even more important, of European "sensibility." Tacitus compares the vigorous barbarians of the German forest with the decadent inhabitants of metropolitan Rome, but he is by no means blind to the faults and vices of his "noble savages," nor to the virtues of the Romans. Later on, he wrote two large historical works, the "Histories," of which the first four and one-half volumes are preserved out of a total of twelve, and the "Annals" from the death of Augustus; books one to six and eleven to sixteen are preserved. Tacitus is the greatest of Roman historians and among the greatest of all historians. With Thucydides (q.v.) he molded the writing of European and world history. His two main strengths are his psychological penetration and his incomparable, though difficult, style, peppered with epigrams that are still alive. e.g., "They made a desert and called it peace."

Tagore, Rabindranath

Indian writer (1861-1941).

The original form of his family name in Bengali is "Thakur." Born in Calcutta; died at Shantiniketan ("The Abode of Peace"). Born of a family of Bengali Brahmins, many of whose members were prominent in the great revival of arts and letters in Calcutta at the turn of the century. Tagore himself was a painter and composer as well as a writer; he was equally at home in England, but returned home without practising it. He became engulfed in the growth of Indian nationalism and was particularly concerned with education. He founded a school in the village of Shantiniketan that grew into the international university of Visva-Bharati. In 1913 he was awarded the Nobel Prize for literature, the first and so far the only Asian to be so distinguished. He obtained it on the strength of an English translation of his Bengali poem "Gitanjali." Among the European writers impressed by his work was W. B. Yeats. He used the prize money to support his school. His position as one of India's great national figures became accentuated when he resigned his knighthood in 1919 as a protest against the massacre of Amritsar. The journeys he made to Europe and Russia in his late years showed that he was a great figure of world as well as of Indian culture.

Works include: "Mashi" (1918) and "Broken Ties" (1925), short stories; "The Home and the World" (1919), a novel; "Gitanjali" (1912), "The Gardener" (1913), and "The Crescent Moon" (1913), poems; "The Post Office" (1914) and "Red Oleander" (1924), plays; "Nationalism" (1917), an essay of political interpretation.

Taha Hussein
Egyptian writer and educator (born 1889).

Born near Maghagha. Son of peasants, he became blind as a child. Went to Al Azhar University at the age of 13. Later studied in Paris. Became professor of Arabic literature at Cairo University in 1925, rector of Alexandria University in 1912. Foremost humanist of 20th century Egypt. His novels deal romantically with the past and symbolically with the present. His two-part autobiography, "An Egyptian Childhood" and "The Stream of Days," is available in English.

Taine, Hippolyte
French writer and critic (1828-1893).

Born in Vouziers in the Ardennes; died in Paris. Contributed to the important Paris journals and became professor of aesthetics at the Beaux-Arts in 1868. His books of history and literary criticism mirror the age of positivism. Chief works: "History of English Literature" (1864), "The Philosophy of Art" (1865), "The Origins of Contemporary France" (1875-93).

T'ao Ch'ien
(Chinese, 372-427).

Profoundly influential rustic poet of China. After brief official career, retired to live rural life. His prose poem, *Kuei-ch'ü-lai tz'u* (*Returning to Live on the Farm*), and shorter lyric poems are known to all Chinese school children. Simplicity of his life and work earned him reputation as "the most harmonious product of Chinese culture."

Tao Yuan-ming

Chinese poet (372-427).

Born and died in Shang-ching, Kiangsu province. Was a public official for several years but hated the ceremonial and the enforced humility towards superiors which it involved. Gave up his magistracy after he threw away the heavy official robe that he was going to put on to welcome a visiting big-wig, exclaiming: "I will not bow to anyone for the sake of five pecks of rice." He retired to a quiet life in the country, where he wrote his most famous poem, "Returning Home." His poetry is marked by simplicity and spontaneity. Prose works include the autobiographical "Gentleman of the Five Willows."

Tasso, Torquato

Italian poet (1544-1595).

Born in Sorrento; died in Rome. Educated by the Jesuits in Naples, became a protege of the Este and Gonzaga families and spent most of his life at their courts of Ferrara and Mantua. His father, Bernardo, had also been a poet and writer of novels of chivalry, including an "Amadis." Torquato followed in his footsteps with infinitely more talent, to become the greatest writer of the Italian Counter-Reformation. He made his reputation with the Carolingian epic "Rinaldo" (i.e., Roland, 1562) and the pastoral poem "Aminta" (1573) ; he reached the height of his powers and reputation in the religious epic "Jerusalem Liberated" (1575). The rest of his writing was anti-climactic, especially another epic, "Jerusalem Conquered" (1593). Tasso was an exceedingly sensitive man, tortured by doubts and fears. He spent seven years in a mental institution and was released only through the intervention of the Gonzagas. He also spent years in wandering. He suffered from delusions and a persecution complex, but also from the natural resentments of a poet conscious of his great talents who has to rely on the patronage of princes whom he considers his mental inferiors and who is exposed to the petty jealousies and hatreds prevailing at princely courts. Goethe, whose position at Weimar, while infinitely more favorable, was not without certain parallels to that of Tasso, was attracted to the Italian's life and character and wrote a play about him.

Tate, Allen

American poet (born 1899).

Born in Winchester, Ky. One of the southern regionalists who founded the "Fugitive" movement. His "Ode for the Confederate Dead" is its program. Also wrote biographies of Stonewall Jackson (1928) and Jefferson Davis (1929).

Tauler, Johannes

German mystic (about 1300-1361).

Born and died in Strasbourg. Pupil of Eckhart (q.v.). A Dominican monk who lived as a wandering preacher and became known as the "Illuminated Doctor." His sermons and some spurious works attributed to him were influential among German romanticists.

Taylor, Edward

American poet (about 1645-1729).

Born in England; died in Westfield, Massachusetts, after sixty years there as pastor and physician. Studied at Harvard. Taylor is now regarded by many critics as the best American poet prior to Poe. His poetry consists wholly of devotional verse, mostly written in connection with his celebrating the Puritan communion service. It is based on themes from the Bible, especially the Song of Solomon, and on homely subjects (e.g., "Housewifery"); its theology is that of an orthodox Puritan. Yet it expresses an intense personal mysticism generally thought to be alien to the Orthodox Puritan tradition. Even more anomalously, stylistically it belongs in the "metaphysical" tradition of John Donne and other high-church writers whose literary methods were despised by the Puritans. At Taylor's request his poetry was left unpublished by his heirs, and it was unknown until 1937.

Tegner, Esaias
Swedish poet (1782-1846).

Born in Kyrkerud, died in Oestrabo. Son of clergyman, he became professor at Lund and bishop of the official Lutheran church. His politics veered from a youthful liberalism to a stubborn conservatism. Tegner was much affected by the romantic renascence of old Scandinavian themes to which he contributed powerfully with his "Svea" (1811) and "The Frithjof Saga" (1825). But he maintained an independent attitude between classicists and romanticists, was attacked from both sides and retaliated against both. His output is very varied and includes love songs, philosophical poems, essays etc.

Tennyson, Alfred Lord
English poet (1809-1892).

Born in Somersby, Lincolnshire; died in Aldworth, Sussex. Son of a country clergyman, he studied theology at Cambridge, where he joined an influential undergraduate society, "The Apostles." While in Cambridge he published, with his brother Charles, "Poems by Two Brothers" (1827). Left Cambridge in 1831 without a degree. Travelled with his friend Arthur Henry Hallam, his sister's fiancé, on the Rhine; was deeply moved by Hallam's death in 1832.

Wrote "In Memoriam" (not published till 1850) for him. His poetical career was not, at first, crowned with any great success. His "Poems" (1832) was brutally treated in the "Quarterly Review" although it contained poems that were very popular later, e.g., "The Lady of Shalott" and "The Palace of Art." Then success came with the "Poems" of 1842 that included "Morte d'Arthur," "Locksley Hall," and "Break, Break, Break"; He became the acknowledged bard of the Victorian Age. He maintained and enhanced his reputation with "In Memoriam," "Ode on the Death of the Duke of Wellington," (1852), "The Charge of the Light Brigade" (1854), "Maud" (1855), and "Idylls of the King" (1859-85). Full official patronage came with the peerage, the poet laureateship, visits to Queen Victoria, and burial at Westminster Abbey. The 1890's put Tennyson out of fashion; in the first part of the 20th Century his name became the byword of "Victorianism" in the pejorative sense. Of late, men like W. H. Auden have tried to rehabilitate him by stressing his technical achievements; but form, however perfected, cannot quite overcome an essential hollowness of content.

Terence

Roman playwright (after 201 B.C.-159 B.C.).

Full name: Publius Terentius Afer. Born in Carthage; died in Greece. Was taken to Rome as slave of a senator, was well-treated and eventually freed. Like Plautus (q.v.), adapted Greek comedies, mostly of Menander (q.v.), to Roman tastes. However, he catered rather to the taste of reputable Roman society. His influence, transmitted through such agencies as Jesuit schools, has lasted well into the modern age. Among the European playwrights indebted to him are Hrotsvitha Von Gandersheim, Holberg, and Molière.

Tertullian

Roman theologian (about 150-about 220).

Full name: Quintus Septimus Florens Tertullianus. Born and died in Carthage. Became converted to Christianity and devoted himself to its defense against Roman persecution and internal schisms. Chief founder of Latin theological language in writings like "Apologeticus," "A Defense of Christianity Against the Persecution of Septimus Severus," "To the Martyrs," "On Baptism," "On the Soul," etc. A passionate and "African" nature—it was he who said "I believe *because* it is absurd"—he succumbed in 207 to the Montanist heresy which was founded on enthusiasm.

Tevfik Fikret

(Turkish, 1867-1915).

Was one of the most popular poets of this century, and famous as the editor of the weekly journal *Serveti Funun* during the New Literature (Edebiyatī Jedide) period. He created a new language of poetry, and made new rules for rhyme on the principle that rhyme is intended for the ear rather than the eye. Whereas the older poetry made each verse a unit in meaning, Fikret made the sentiment run through the whole poem or at least several verses. He also introduced the sonnet. His great work is the collection of poems called *Rubabi Shikeste* (*The Broken Lute*). One of his famous poems, *Sis* (*Mist*), was directed against the despotic rule of Abdul Hamid. In recent years his fame has suffered, partly due to the presence in his poems of many unusual Persian and Arabic words, thus putting him out of tune with the present-day tendency toward Turkification.

Thackeray, William Makepeace

English novelist (1811-1863).

Born in Calcutta, India; died in London. His father

476

was an official of the East India Company, who sent him home to school at the age of 6. From school he went to Cambridge, where his circle of friends included Tennyson and Fitzgerald. Became a barrister, but gave up law for journalism. Met Goethe on a journey to Germany in 1831. His novels are primarily concerned with man as a social animal, and his chief field of interest in indicated in the title of his first important work, "The Book of Snobs" (1846-47). Far superior to his contemporary Dickens as a stylist, his reputation is today below that of his rival because he did not probe nearly so deeply. Chief novels: "Vanity Fair" (1847-48); "Our Street" (1848); "Dr. Birch and His Young Friends" (1849); "Pendennis" (1848-50); "Henry Esmond" (1852).

Theocritus

Greek poet (early 3rd century B.C.).

Born in Syracuse; date and place of death not known. Frequented courts of Hiero II of Syracuse and Ptolemy II of Egypt. His thirty preserved idylls created the vein of bucolic poetry expressing the nostalgia of the inhabitant of the big city—Syracuse was a metropolis of a million people—for the simple pastoral life of "Arcadia."

Theophrastus

Greek philosopher and writer (372-287 B.C.).

Born in Eresos on the island of Lesbos; died in Athens. A pupil of Aristotle, whom he succeeded as head of the Peripatetic School. An expert botanist, wrote two botanical treatises; but his fame rests on his "Characters" (after 319 B.C.), which offer thirty standard specimens of human character—the flatterer, the grumbler, etc.—which inspired many literary imitators, e.g., La Bruyere—and the scientific study of psychology.

Theresa of Avila, Saint

Spanish mystic (1515-1582).

Born in Avila; died in Alba de Tornices. Became a Carmelite nun, as "Teresa de Jesus," in 1534; founded the reformed (discalced) Carmelite order in 1562. She had her troubles with the Inquisition in her lifetime because of her indomitable will to sweep away the abuses that had crept into her order in the course of centuries. Moreover—as has been discovered recently by two Carmelities—she had some Jewish ancestry on her father's side. She was canonized in 1622. Her writings, published posthumously, include "The Way to Perfection," "The Book of Her Life," "The Interior Castle." St. Theresa's mysticism is of a homely variety, in the British sense of that adjective, as shown in her saying "The Lord wanders among the cooking pots." Her strong personality exercises a great attraction on today's neurotic age, as witnessed by numerous biographies and interpretations.

Thomas a Kempis

Dutch religious writer (about 1380-1471).

Born in Kempen in the Rhineland. Studied at the chapter school in Deventer and joined the monastery of the canons regular at Saint Agnietenberg near Zwolle. He was ordained priest in 1413 or 1414. Although he wrote religious poetry, biographies and a number of tracts, he lives by his "Imitation of Christ," a guide to an ascetic and mystical religious life that was the most-read book in Christendom after the Bible. The authorship of the book has been a very controversial matter for a long time but there seems to be little doubt about it now.

Thomas Aquinas, Saint

Italian theologian (about 1226-1274).

Born at the family castle of Roccasecca at Aquino

near Naples; died at the Fossanova monastery near Rome. Became a Dominican in 1243, student in Paris and in Cologne (under Albertus Magnus). Established a theological school at Cologne (till 1252). After nine years (1252-61) at the Saint Jacques monastery in Paris, returned to Italy. He was canonized in 1325, proclaimed doctor of the Church in 1567, and patron of Catholic Schools in 1880. His theology is now the official theology of the Roman Catholic Church, a position which it did not occupy in his life-time. Saint Thomas' great task was to reconcile Christian belief with the Aristotelian heritage, then newly rediscovered through Aristotle's Arab commentators and Jewish translators. These sources in no way diminish the magnitude of his achievement. Chief works, written in voluminous Latin: "Summa Against the Gentiles" (1259-64) and "Summa of Theology" (1265-73).

Thomas of Celano, Saint

Italian religious writer in Latin (about 1200-about 1255).

Born in Celano. Became a Franciscan in his teens, served as provincial in Germany. Was commissioned by Pope Gregory IX to write an "Official" life of Saint Francis, which he did in his "First Legend." Generally considered the author of the hymn "Dies Irae" (Day Of Wrath) which is part of the Roman Catholic Mass for the Dead.

Thomas, Dylan

Welsh poet in English (1914-1955).

Born in Swansea, died in New York. His poetry abounds in unusual images and striking rhythms. Also wrote stories, including "Portrait of the Artist as a Young Dog" (1940) and radio plays, e.g. "Under Milkwood." But even more important than his writing was his personality. To a whole generation of young Americans, Thomas has become the very archetype of the poet, especially of the poet damned and doomed. The Thomas cult has greatly benefited from the records of his poetry readings.

Thompson, Francis

English poet (1859-1907).

Born in Preston, Lancashire; died in London. Started to study medicine in Manchester, but gave it up. Lived in utmost poverty in London, working in a bootmaker's shop. Fell prey to opium. He was saved from degradation by the poets Wilfred and Alice Meynell, to whom he sent his poems and who took care of him, and by his conversion to Roman Catholicism. His poetry is melancholy, lyrical, and symbolist, and is highly valued today. Works: "Poems" (1893); "Sister Songs" (1895); "New Poems" (1893); and a posthumous life of Loyola.

Thomson, James

British poet (1700-1748).

Born in Ednam, Scotland; died in Richmond, now part of London. Came to London in 1725, became a prominent member of its literary life, and managed to obtain a pension that permitted him to devote himself to writing. Important as author of the narrative poem "The Season" (1726-30), which foreshadowed the romantic attitude toward nature; and of the text of "Rule, Britannia."

Thoreau, Henry David

American writer and philosopher (1817-1862).

Born and died in Concord, Mass. Of French-Scottish Quaker origin. Graduated from Harvard (1837), taught school at Concord for a while; also worked as a surveyor. Lived in Emerson's house and associated with the Transcendentalists. Retired for two years (1845-47) to a hut which he built by Walden pond, as an experiment in simple living. He spent the rest of his life in his father's house, and was in frequent trouble with the authorities because of nonconformity and his refusal to pay taxes that helped support slavery. His two chief works are "Walden" (1854) and the essay on "Civil Disobedience" (1849). Unknown in his own lifetime beyond a small circle of friends, his reputation and influence have now spread far beyond his native land. Tolstoy and Gandhi are among those who acknowledge his influence.

Thucydides
Greek historian (about 465-about 400 B.C.)

Born in Athens; place of death unknown. During Peloponnesian War commanded an expedition sent out from Athens to relieve Amphipolis, but which failed to prevent its capture by King Brasidas of Sparta (424). He then went into exile for twenty years (423-403) during which time he wrote his "History of the Peloponnesian War" (which breaks off in 411, but is preserved in full). Thucydides can well claim title as the first scientific historian, though he is by no means contemptible as an artist—his style is excellent and his speeches are set pieces. Nor does his strong moral attitude obtrude itself on his judgments of people and events. Tacitus was among his admirers and imitators.

Tibullus
Roman poet (about 60 B.C.-19 A.D.).

Full name: Albius Tibius Tibullus. Little is known of his life, but he is known to have been a friend of Horace and a protege of Maecenas. Four books of "Elegies" are preserved singing nostalgically in classical Latin of love and rural life. Two of his books are, however, of doubtful authenticity.

Tieck, Ludwig

German writer (1773-1853).

Born and died in Berlin. Prominent as writer, theatrical director, and critic and pioneer of romanticism in Germany. His plays are hardly ever played today, but children still enjoy his Tales, including the immortal "Puss in Boots."

Timmermans, Felix

Flemish writer (1886-1947).

Born and died in Lier near Antwerp. One of the chief figures of the Flemish Renaissance; painter and illustrator as well as writer. Although born in a small town, he glorified in his books the Flemish peasant in his earthy joys and mystical longings, very much in the spirit of Breughel's paintings. Chief works: "Pallieter" (1916); "Little Jesus in Flanders" (1917); "Peasant Balm" (1935).

Ting Ling

Chinese writer (born 1907).

Real name: Chiang Ping-chih. Born in Li-ling. One of the earliest adherents to Communism, she welcomed its rise to power enthusiastically in her novel "The Sun over the Sangan River." For reasons unknown here, she fell foul of the Peking government and was reported working as floorsweeper at the Writers Club, in punishment for her literary and political sins.

Tiruvalluvar

Tamil poet (date unknown).

A weaver in Southeast India, his life has been placed by scholars in all the centuries of the first millennium A.D., the second being a recent favorite. Reputed author of "The Holy Kurral," a collection of 1300 moral maxims that is the most popular religious book of that area.

Tiutchev, Fyodor Ivanovich

Russian poet (1803-1873).

Born in Ustug near Orel; died in Tsarskoye Selo near Saint Petersburg. In diplomatic service (1822-37); attached to Russian legations at Munich and Turin; from 1848 worked as censor in Saint Petersburg. His lyrics are highly regarded today; in his own day, he was more famous for his exaltation of Russia as savior of Europe from the specter of revolution. These views, expressed in a French pamphlet, "Russia and the Revolution" (1849), won him the admiration of Dostoyevski.

Toller, Ernst

German Jewish dramatist (1893-1939).

Born in Samochin, died in New York. Took part in the abortive German Revolution after World War I, remained a Communist to the end. Wrote expressionist plays, including "The Mass Man" (1921); "The Machine-Wreckers" (1922) and "Hinkemann" (1924). Hitler drove him into exile and suicide.

Tolstoy, Count Alexei Konstantinovich

Russian writer (1817-1875).

Born and died in Saint Petersburg. An eccentric member of the family that produced a number of great writers. Together with the two Zhemchuzhnikov brothers published the poems and biography of an imaginary poet, "Kuzma Prutkov" which satirizes the kind of poetry that official Russia enjoyed—and wrote. His "History of the Russian State" is a brilliant parody of Karamzin's history. Was particularly interested in "Ivan the Terrible" (1866); "Tsar Fedor" (1868) and "Tsar Boris" (1870) as well as a novel "The Silver Prince" about a rebel against Ivan. He confessed that he often dropped the historical source and banged his fist on the table in rage not because Russia produced an Ivan the Terrible but because she did not oppose him.

Tolstoy, Alexei Nikolayevich
Russian novelist (1882-1945).

Born in Nikolayev; died in Moscow. A relative of Leo Tolstoy (q.v.). Went into exile in 1917 but came back in 1923 and placed his talents unreservedly at the disposal of the regime. Chief works: "The Death of Danton" (1919); "The Childhood of Nikita" (1922); "Peter the Great" (1930).

Tolstoy, Count Lev Nikolayevich
Russian writer (1828-1910).

Born on the family property of Yasnaya Polyana in Central Russia; died in Astapovo. Born of a noble and much ramified family. Left an orphan; was brought up by relatives. Studied mathematics and law at Kazan University, did not finish his studies. Became officer and served in the Caucasus campaigns and in the Crimean War. It was this experience that first turned him to writing. He started with an autobiographical sketch, "Childhood" (1852); but it was "The Comrades" (1854) and "Sebastopol" (1855) that made him known as a writer of talent and promise. Alexander III asked him to retire from the army and devote himself to writing. Tolstoy travelled in Europe, then retired to the parental estate when he devoted himself to the welfare of his peasants and married Sophia Beers, who made him an extremely unsuitable but very challenging wife. It was in the years following the marriage that Tolstoy wrote his two most inspired books, "War and Peace" (1864-69), which is to many people *the* Russian novel, and "Anna Karenina" (1873-76), whose position is not very far behind. Tolstoy then underwent a deep spiritual crisis which made him denounce official Orthodox

Christianity and start a brand of his own, based on the Sermon of the Mount and having as its chief tenet nonresistance to evil. Tolstoy remained faithful to this belief until his death, it affected his life with its continuous renunciations of property and family ties, and it made his later writings propaganda for his morality. The Kreutzer Sonata (1889), a plea for sexual abstinence; "Resurrection" (1899-1900), the story of the spiritual regeneration of a simple peasant girl; "What Is Art?" (1896), an essay with the thesis that art is wicked and that Shakespeare, to take one example, is less valuable to humanity than a pair of shoes. But Tolstoy's personal eccentricities and even his follies never affected his stature as a writer and as a man. He denounced the art of writing but practiced it in the very denunciation; he proclaimed nonresistance to evil but won the admiration of Russia and the world by his courageous protest against the brutal repressions practiced by the Tsarist police. Even the Communists thought it wiser to enshrine him rather than to attack him.

Trissino, Giangiorgio

Italian poet and dramatist (1478-1550).

Born in Vicenza, died in Rome. He influenced the literary course of the Italian Renaissance by his strong Hellenist tendency. Wrote an epic poem, "Italy Liberated from the Goths" (1547-48) with all of Homer's tricks of style but none of his poetic genius. More important and lasting was his "Sophonisbe" (1524), the first Renaissance tragedy on a Greek model.

Trollope, Anthony

English novelist (1815-1882).

Born and died in London. A civil servant employed by the Post Office, wrote his novels at a regular rate of 1000 words an hour from 4 A.M. till breakfast time. His reputation survived, though not untarnished, his confession in his "Autobiography" that he wrote for two main reasons: vanity and money. Invented a county, "Barsetshire" people with literary characters of a kind that would appeal for a Victorian amateur of light reading with a touch of clerical whimsy. The "Barsetshire" novels include "The Warden" (1855) and "Barchester Towers" (1857).

Trotsky, Lev Davidovich

Russian politican and writer (1879-1940).

Real name: Bronstein. Born in Janovka, Ukraine, died in Coyoacan, Mexico. Of Jewish origin, took prominent part in the Revolution. Murdered at the order of Stalin. Important for literature by his volume of criticism, "Literature and the Revolution" (1923) and by the protection which he offered, in spite of his rabid Communism, to non-Communist writers willing to accept the regime, whom he baptized "fellow-travellers."

Ts'ao Hsueh-ch'in

Chinese novelist (about 1715-1763).

Born in Nanking, died in Peking. Son of rich family that inherited the office of supervisor of the imperial textile factory at Nanking. But in 1728 they lost the imperial favor and all their property was confiscated. Only a small house was returned to them, and the family moved there to live in great poverty. The misfortunes of the family no doubt inspired him to write "The Dream of the Red Chamber" (first printed in 1792, with additional chapters by Kao Wu, who also wrote the preface). This is the story of the fall of a great family, centering upon the love of the heir and his consumptive cousin. Ts'ao himself did not think much of it. He said: "I have come to the end of a long and dusty road and I find myself a complete and utter failure." Posterity did not endorse his verdict. The novel, which added refinement of style to the vernacular language, is generally considered the artistic peak of the traditional Chinese novel.

Tschernichowsky, Saul

Jewish poet (1875-1943).

Born in Mikhailovka on the Crimea, died in Tel Aviv. Educated at Russian schools and Swiss and German universities. Physician in Russia, and since 1931 in Palestine, wrote in Hebrew. His poetry, including "Idylls" sings of the joy of living with marked pagan accents which made his readers bestow upon him the names of "The Hellene" and "The Heathen." But if he loved the Greek gods, he was equally fond of biblical themes and Jewish history. Excellent translator of Homeric and other epics.

Tu Fu

Chinese poet (712-770).

Born in Kung-hsien, died near T'an-chou. Failed to pass the official examinations in 735 and did not succeed until 22 years later. Travelled a good deal all over China. Met Li Po (q.v.) and was much impressed by him, but his poetry was not much affected by the meeting. He actually had a greater influence on his immediate contemporaries than Li Po and was a more typical poet of the T'ang era; but Li is generally considered the greater poet. Tu's verses are more intellectual, less narrowly personal. He had a strong social conscience and was much distressed by the people's sufferings during the disastrous rebellion of An Lu-shan. He yearned for peace and opposed militarism.

Turgenyev, Ivan Sergeyevich

Russian novelist (1818-1883).

Born in Orel; died in Bougival near Paris. Son of a

landowning family; accepted a minor government post in 1840, but soon devoted himself to writing. An inheritance enabled him to live mostly abroad after 1850. In Paris, he became a great center of attraction, the friend of men like Flaubert and Henry James, as well as the generally accepted spokesman for Russia. But Turgenyev, who started with a condemnation of Russian reality that was all the more effective because of the artistic restraint with which it was expressed, became increasingly sceptical and "Hamletic" about the possibilities of reform, let alone revolution. His analytical studies of the reformers and revolutionaries condemn their inhumanities and their nihilism, but cannot suggest what values to put in their place. Nor did Turgenyev put much faith in the values of old Russia. He therefore became an increasingly lonely and isolated figure, and the admiration of foreigners could not compensate him for his loss of touch with Russia. Turgenyev was the best Russian stylist between Pushkin and Chekhov. He was at one time the chief representative in the West of the "Russian novel"; but his reputation sank when the West started whoring after the strange gods of Dostoyevski. Works include: "Notes of a Sportsman" (1852); "Rudin" (1856); "A Nest of Gentlefolk" (1858); "On the Eve" (1860); "Fathers and Sons" (1862); "Smoke (1867); "Virgin Soil" (1877).

Twain, Mark

American writer (1835-1910).

Real name: Samuel Langhorne Clemens. Born in Florida, Missouri; died in Reading, Connecticut. Spent his childhood and adolescence (1839-53) in Hannibal, Missouri, a riverside town on the shores of the Mississippi. Had an adventurous youth as journeyman printer (1847-55), Mississippi pilot (1857-61), prospector and newspaper reporter in Nevada (1861-2).

Started writing under pen name of "Mark Twain" (a term meaning a depth of two fathoms) previously used by another Mississippi pilot, Isaiah Sellers, in articles published in the New Orleans "Daily Picayune." Went to California in 1864, published in 1865 his first great success, "The Jumping Frog of Calaveras County," which, together with other sketches, came out in book form two years later. "The Jumping Frog" gave literary form to Western frontier humor. Twain meanwhile started on another successful career as a lecturer. He went on a cruise to the Mediterranean, that included a pilgrimage to the Holy Land, and published his impressions in "An Innocent Abroad" (1869), a scathing account of old and decrepit Europe as viewed by a young and brash American. The next twenty years saw the peak of his literary activity. It was then that he published "Life on the Mississippi" (1883), the literary record of his pilot days, "The Gilded Age" (1873, with Charles Dudley Warner), a bitter account of the corruption under Grant's administration, which gave the era one of its names; "A Connecticut Yankee in King Arthur's Court" (1889), a historical fantasy that would now be called "Science fiction"; and, above all, two novels based on his Hannibal days, "The Adventures of Tom Sawyer" (1876) and "The Adventures of Huckleberry Finn" (1885). The latter, in particular, is generally regarded as Twain's best work; to many critics it is *the* American novel. After 1889 Twain wrote a good deal without reaching his best; except perhaps in some of the bitter and misanthropic writings of his last years, e.g. "Pudd'nhead Wilson" (1893), "The Man Who Corrupted Hadleyburg" (1900), "Personal Recollections of Joan of Arc" (1896), and "Eve's Diary" (1906). The reasons were many: failure of the Webster publishing house in which he was financially involved, disastrous investments in his inventions, his marriage to a genteel

489

woman who tried to "smooth out" his roughness, disappointment in his children, etc. These constituted what Van Wyck Brooks called "The Ordeal of Mark Twain," but Twain succumbed to it only after he had given his best.

Tynyanov, Yuri Nikolayevich
Russian novelist (1894-1944).

Wrote excellent historical novels on Pushkin and his circle: "Kukhlya" (1925), on Pushkin's friend Kuchelbecker; "The Death of Vazir Mukhtar" (1929), on Griboyedov (q.v.); "Pushkin" (1936-37), not up to the level of the other two. Tynyanov was a leading "formalist," but managed to survive the purges and to die a natural death.

Tzara, Tristan
Roumanian poet in French (born 1896).

Born in Moineste, Roumania. Founded in 1916 the "dada" movement in Zurich, wrote its manifestoes. Dadaism represents the final stage of linguistic and literary disintegration. It led to the surrealist experiments of the twenties. Tzara himself gave up his dadaist brainchild and started to write poems of great lyrical beauty in ordinary language.

U

Uhland, Ludwig

German poet (1787-1862).

Born and died in Tübingen. Lawyer by training; became professor of German literature at Tübingen University. A lyricist and story teller in a sincere, though rather shallow, Swabian popular vein. Chief works: "Poems" (1815), "Patriotic Poems" (1817), "Ernst, Duke of Swabia" (1818).

Ulfilas

Gothic writer (about 311-381).

His Gothic name "Wulfila" was Grecized into "Ulfilas." Born in Cappadocia or according to other authorities, in Constantinople. Consecrated bishop at the Synod of Antioch (341) and became missionary to the Visigoths. He translated the Bible from Greek into Visigothic and invented a Gothic alphabet for this purpose. He did not translate the Books of Kings because he felt that the Goths were bloodthirsty enough without any additional stimulation. His translation has survived in part in a magnificent manuscript called "Codex Argenteus," now preserved at Uppsala in Sweden.

Unamuno, Miguel de

Spanish philosopher and writer (1864-1936).

Born in Bilbao; died in Salamanca. Became professor of Greek at Salamanca in 1891. As rector (1901-14, 1930-36) did much to restore the university to its former glory. Started as a novelist, with a novel of the Cartist War, "Peace in War" (1897), that took him twelve years to write. He lavished less care on his later novels. He was also a leading Spanish poet; e.g., in his "Christ of Velazquez," and an essayist ("Essays," published 1916-18 in several volumes, with other collections to follow). But his chief title to fame is his interpretation of the fate of Spain and of humanity in books like "About *Casticismo* (i.e., nativism)," "The Life of Don Quixote and Sancho" (1905), "On the Tragic Sense of Life" (1913), "The Agony of Christianity" (1925). Unamuno owes much to foreign influences—he was a classicist and learned Danish to read Kierkegaard in the original several decades before Sartre discovered him. But his deepest insights come from his fundamental Spanishness. He excelled in presenting—and preserving—the traditional Spanish values, in the modern context. He died in bitter disillusionment with the military rebellion of 1936. He had welcomed it at first, but was put under house arrest after a speech on Columbus Day 1936 in which he openly denounced the inhumanity of fascism.

Undset, Sigrid

Norwegian novelist (1882-1949).

Born in Kalundborg (Denmark); died in Lillehammer. Worked in an office, until the success of her first novel, "Mrs. Martha Oulie," freed her from drudgery. Obtained a government grant which enabled her to travel to Rome. She became a Roman Catholic. Her novels, which won her the Nobel Prize in 1928, are mostly historical but always deeply concerned with the fate and role of women. She spent the war years in the United States (1940-45). Chief works: "Christine Lavransdatter" (1920-22), "Three Sisters" (1927), "Olav Audunsson in Haestvicken" (1925), "The Steadfast Wife" (1936).

Ungaretti, Giuseppe

Italian poet (born 1888).

Born in Alexandria (Egypt). Influenced at first by French symbolism and Italian futurism; returned to the great traditions of Italian lyrical poetry. Wrote: "The Buried Harbor" (1916), "The Sense of Time" (1933), "Translations of Foreign Verse" (1933), etc.

Urfe, Honoré d'

French writer (1567-1625).

Born in Marseille, died in Villefranche-sur-Mer. Of noble origin, related to the duke of Savoy, spent much time in his service. Wrote religious verse, but is remembered for his immensely long and immensely popular pastoral novel "Astrea" (1607-1627), completed and published after his death by his secretary Baro. Much influenced by Spanish and Italian models, its French popularity was enhanced by its setting in a mythical and druidical Gaul.

V

Valera, Cipriano de

Spanish religious writer (1532-after 1602).

Born in Seville, died in England. A Spanish monk who became a Protestant and emigrated to England. From there he issued a manifesto "To all the faithful of the Spanish Nation" (1597). He made a masterly translation of the New Testament and also translated Calvin's "Institutes."

Valera, Juan

Spanish novelist (1824-1905).

Born in Cabre in Andalusia; died in Madrid. A diplomat with private means, he wrote novels although, as he put it, "the money that I got for my books wouldn't buy a single dress for my wife." Valera, a psychological realist and a witty ironist, is at his best in "Pepita Jimenez" (1874).

Valery, Paul

French poet and essayist (1871-1945).

Born at Sète in Southwest France; died in Paris. Started writing as a student, but "An Introduction to the Method of Leonardo da Vinci" (1895) and "The Evening with M. Teste" were followed by a silence of over twenty years. His later writings, which brought him into the front rank of French letters, include: "The Young Parque" (1917), "The Crisis of the Spirit" (1919), "The Cemetery by the Sea" (1920), "On the Crisis of Intelligence" (1920), "To Rainer Maria Rilke" (1926), "Degas, Dance and Design" (1937), "Narcissus" (1891-1938), "The Freedom of the Spirit" (1939). Valery was in the French rationalist tradition —above all, he hated stupidity.

Valla, Lorenzo

Italian humanist (1407-1457).

Born and died in Rome. Had a chair of rhetoric at Pavia, had to leave it when he attacked the authority of Bartolo, the much venerated jurist. Served under Alfonso of Aragon in Naples; while there published his "Dialectics" (1439) in which he attacked Aristotle's dialectics. Returned to Rome, where he launched his most famous attack: "On the Donation of Constantine" (1440) which conclusively proved that Constantine's alleged gift of Rome to the Popes was an eighth century forgery. But Valla was more than the greatest critical mind of the Italian Renaissance: his treatise "On the Elegance of the Latin Tongue" (1444) did much to restore Latin from its medieval corruptions to something like its pristine purity.

Valle-Inclan, Ramon Maria del

Spanish writer (1869-1936).

Born in Puebla de Caraminal, died in Santiago de Compostela. A figure even more fantastic than the heroes of his own novels. Started as a decadent, developed into a witty and burlesque satirist. His four "Sonatas" (1902-05) named after the four seasons, established his fame. His "Tirano Banderas" is a brilliant but much-resented portrait of the military ruler of an imaginary, but all too realistic, "banana republic." His "Esperpentos" created a new form of play, based on the significant distortion of reality. It was characteristic of him that, a traditionalist at heart, he gave his enthusiastic support to the Spanish Republic.

Valmiki

Hindu poet (about 4th century B.C.).

A Brahmin from Oudh in the central Ganges Valley who, according to Hindu tradition, wrote the epic "Ramayana" on the exploits of Rama. He was said to have been inspired by Brahma, chief god of the Hindu Pantheon.

Vasari, Giorgio

Italian biographer (1511-1574).

Born in Arezzo, died in Florence. Came to Florence at 13 to study under Michelangelo. Became a facile painter, patronized by the Medici and the Popes. His frescoes are to be found all over Italy; but he did infinitely more for art with his "Lives of the Most Excellent Painters, Sculptors and Architects" (two editions, 1550 and 1568). This book, which he wrote at the suggestion of the historian Giovio and Cardinal Allesandro Farnese, is our most important source for the lives of Renaissance artists. Vasari's own views, in particular his belief that art should represent nature realistically and that it reached its climax with Michelangelo, occasionally interfere with historical truth, but not too often.

Vercors

French novelist (born 1902).

Real name: Jean Bruller. Born in Paris. Electrical engineer, painter, and engraver. Founded, during the German occupation, the "Editions de Minuit" (the Midnight Publishers), the secret publishing house of the resistance movement. He took his pen name from a mountainous district of Eastern France which was one of the great centers of the "Resistance." His "Silence of the Sea" (1942), a story about a Nazi officer billeted on a French family, was widely read during the war in France and abroad. Since the war, Vercors has been active in preserving the values for which the war-time resisters to Nazism and Petainism had stood.

Verga, Giovanni
Italian novelist (1840-1922).

Born and died in Catania. His books, dealing mostly with his native Sicily, started in the romantic vein, with descriptions of the native landscape and customs. But Verga soon became a masterly analyst of Sicilian society and a champion of "Verismo" or realism. He was insufficiently appreciated in his lifetime; his fame, both in Italy and abroad, is largely posthumous. Chief works: "Country Life" (1880), "The Malavoglia" (1881), "Rural Tales" (1883, includes "Cavalleria Rusticana"), "Maestro Don Gesualdo" (1888).

Verhaeren, Emile
Belgian writer (1855-1916).

Born in Saint-Amand near Antwerp; died in Rouen (France), to which he had fled from the German invasion of Belgium. Of Flemish origin, he wrote in French. A leader of the "Young Belgium" symbolist school. Started from naturalism, moved into a despairing mysticism, and finished by praising technical progress and the big cities that he had violently condemned before. Chief works: "The Evenings" (1888), "The Illusory Villages" (1895), "The Tentacular Cities" (1896), "All Flanders" (1904-11, in five volumes).

Verlaine, Paul
French poet (1844-1896).

Born in Metz; died in Paris. Brought up in a bourgeois family, seemed set for a solid middle-class life with a government post and a respectable wife. Gave it all up to lead a vagabond life with the young Rimbaud (q.v.), traveling in France, Belgium, and England. The friendship with Rimbaud, by which mod-

497

ern symbolist poetry was started, ended with a quarrel. Verlaine fired several shots at Rimbaud and was condemned to one and one-half years in prison, although Rimbaud refused to testify against him. After he left jail, he spent most of his time in taverns and hospitals. His despair and remorse ennobled his poetry and breathed humanity into what would have been cold, parnassian verse. Chief works: "Saturnian Poems" (1886), "Les Fêtes Galantes" (1869), "The Good Song" (1870), "Songs Without Words" (1874), "Then and Now" (1884), "Loves" (1888), "My Prisons" (1893), "Death" (1895).

Verne, Jules

French novelist (1828-1905).

Born at Nantes; died in Amiens. Started as playwright and feuilletonist but soon found his true vocation in adventure stories and what is today called science-fiction. He foresaw many of the technical achievements of the 20th century; and his books are still read by old and young, to say nothing of Hollywood scriptwriters. Chief works: "Five Weeks in a Balloon" (1863), "Journey to the Center of the Earth" (1864), "From the Earth to the Moon" (1866), "Around the Moon" (1869), "20,000 Leagues Under the Sea" (1869), "Around the World in Eighty Days" (1873).

Vicente, Gil

Portuguese playwright (about 1470-about 1540).

Born and died in Lisbon. May be identical with the goldsmith of that name. Founded the Portuguese drama, but wrote also in Spanish. His plays were performed at court. They mingle Renaissance ideas with the feelings of the Portuguese country people. Chief works: "Autos (i.e., plays) of Hell, Purgatory, and Paradise," "Auto of the Soul," "The Poor Nobleman."

498

Vico, Giambattista
Italian philosopher (1668-1744).

Born and died in Naples. Son of a poor bookseller, largely self-taught. Took a law degree while working as a tutor. Became professor at Naples University in 1698, but the salary was miserably small and his life was full of privations. Charles III rescued him from drudgery by making him the Historiographer Royal in 1735. Vico was a voluminous writer. He wrote books on history, law, philosophy, art, etc. and a good deal of poetry. His system is enshrined in his "New Science" (two versions, 1725 and 1730). His "Autobiography" (1725) tells the story of his struggles. Vico is one of the seminal minds of modern Europe: he was the pioneer of historicism, aestheticism and romanticism. His influence was posthumous. Hamann, Hegel, Michelet and Marx built upon his work, Croce finally proclaimed his greatness.

Vigny, Count Alfred de
French writer (1797-1863).

Born at the family castle of Loches in the Touraine; died in Paris. Officer in the French army (1814-28); retired after an accident. Excelled in all literary genres and was comparatively little-affected by the all-prevailing romanticism. His aristocratic sensitivity and disdain made him a classicist and a predecessor of the Parnassians. Wrote: "Poems" (1822), "Poems, Ancient and Modern" (1826), "Cinq Mars" (historical novel, 1826), "Chatterton" (a play, 1835), "Military Grandeur and Servitude" (1835).

Villehardouin, Geoffroy de
French chronicler (died about 1212).

Knight of Champagne, about whose life little is known. He was an influential adviser to the leaders of the Fourth Crusade, was granted lands in Macedonia, and appears to have remained in that country. He left a voluminous account of events between 1198 and 1207, aristocratic in style, probably an attempt to justify the diversion of the crusading armies to Constantinople which they captured in 1204. "The Conquest of Constantinople" is written in clear, terse prose, and reveals Villehardouin as the first great master of the French language.

Villiers de l'Isle-Adam, Philippe
French writer (1838-1889).

Born in Saint Brieuc, died in Paris. Of a noble Breton family, spent a dreamy youth at the family home. Most of his adult life was spent in Paris in bitter poverty which did not, however, make him lose his pride. His "Cruel Tales" (1883-89) are in the vein explored by Hoffmann, Poe, and Baudelaire. Also wrote a poetic drama "Axel" (1890) which defends the right of superior minds to refuse to come to terms with the realities of the outside world.

Villon, François
French poet (1431-after 1463).

Real name perhaps François de Montcorbier, or Des Loges. Born of poor family, was adopted by Guillaume de Villon, and took his name. Grew up in a period of foreign and civil wars, when life was cheap. Got into trouble with the law while still a student, and had to flee from Paris. The last mention of his name is in a document commuting his death sentence for knifing a man. But Villon's verse mingles the wildest and the tenderest of sentiments, and his deep religious faith and love for his mother remained quite unaffected by the vicissitudes of his life. In spite of princely patronage in his day, it was only posterity that recognized in him the greatest French poet of the middle ages. Wrote: "The Small Testament" (1454) and "The Great Testament" (1461).

Vladimir, Monomakh

Russian writer (reigned 1113-1125).

Prince of Kiev, one of the best rulers of his time. Highly educated, spoke six languages. His famous "Testament" is more than its name implies: it is actually a full autobiography, written as a cautionary tale for his children.

Voeresmarty, Michael

Hungarian poet (1800-1855).

Born in Kapolnasnyek; died in Budapest. Member of the "Aurora" circles of poets started by the Kisfaludy brothers (q.v.). But he reacted somewhat against their romanticism in the direction of classical style and form. Wrote dramas, lyrical verse, and epigrams, but his chief claim to fame is the epic "Zalan's Flight" (1824). His poem "Szozat" became a national anthem.

Voltaire

French writer and philosopher (1694-1778).

Pen name of François Marie Arouet. Born and died in Paris. Educated by the Jesuits; started early to write satires which earned him a beating from the servants of an enraged nobleman and a couple of terms in the Bastille. Released in 1726 on condition of leaving France, he went to England. There he spent three years (until 1729) and was deeply impressed by political freedom and religious tolerance, but also by moral hypocrisy and abominable food. His "English Letters" (1734) are a landmark in Europe's appreciation of England. They caused an uproar that made Voltaire retire to Cirey Castle in Lorraine (1734-49) where he lived with Mme. Du Chatelet. After her death, he accepted an invitation from Frederick the Great of Prussia, but they soon quarreled. Voltaire left Berlin in 1753 and Frederick took a somewhat undignified revenge by having Voltaire painted as a monkey on a wallpaper in his palace of Sans Souci. Voltaire spent his last twenty years at Ferney near Geneva. He had become the chief figure of the Enlightenment and Europe's political and religious conscience, though he never lost his pettishness and sneering disposition. Nor was he free from inconsistencies: He defended religious freedom in the case of Calas, a man executed for heresy, yet denied it to the Jews. As a writer, Voltaire is the most prominent figure of the 18th century in France and—therefore—in Europe. He excelled as a playwright: "Oedipus" (1718), "Brutus" (1730), "Zaire" (1736), "Alzire" (1736), "Mohammed" (1741), and "Merope"; as a satirical and philosophical novelist: "Zadig" (1747) and "Candide" (1759); as a poet in the "Henriade" (1723) and "The Maid" (i.e., of Orleans, 1755); as a historian: "The History of Charles XII" (1736), "The Age of Louis XIV" (1757), and "Essay on Customs" (1756); as a philosopher in "The Philosophical Dictionary" (1764).

Vondel, Joost Van den
Dutch writer (1587-1679).

Born in Cologne, Germany, died in Amsterdam. Born of Mennonite parents who had to flee from Antwerp to Amsterdam. Vondel became a Mennonite deacon, but was converted to Roman Catholicism in 1640. He was the greatest writer of Holland's Golden Age, but his literary achievements can hardly be placed in the same category as the works of the great Dutch painters. He is at his best in pastoral poems and in dramas like "The Pasha" (1612) and "Jephta" (1659). According to his wish, he was borne to his grave by fourteen poets.

Voss, Johann Heinrich

German poet (1751-1826).

Born in Sommersdorf (Mecklenburg); died in Heidelberg. An idyllic poet, leading spirit of the group of poets of the "Göttingen Grove." Perhaps more valuable than his own poetry—"Louise" (1795) and "Idylls" (1801)—are his translations, especially that of the Odysseus (1781).

W

Wace, Robert
French chronicler (about 1100-1175).

Born on the island of Jersey, brought up at Caen
in Normandy. Patronized by Henry II of England,
who made him a canon of Bayeux in 1158. Wrote a
history of the Normans ("Rou") and one of the Bri-
tons ("Brut") which were important source books for
medieval poets. His "Brut," in particular contains the
first mention of the Arthurian Round Table in literature.

Waller, Edmund
English poet (1606-1687).

Born in Coleshill, died in Beaconsfield. Had a long
and checkered political career as an ardent champion
of the Parliament. Acknowledged in the 18th century
as the creator of the neo-classical style of English
poetry. Some of his poems, e.g. "Go, Lovely Rose," are
still read, but the bulk of it is justly forgotten.

Walpole, Horace
English writer (1717-1797).

Born and died in London. Fourth son of Sir Robert
Walpole, long-time prime minister. Became Earl of
Oxford, but retired from politics to his neo-Gothic
castle "Strawberry Hill" near London. A precursor of
romanticism in two books of horror: "The Castle of
Otranto" (1764, a novel) and "The Mysterious Mother"
(1768). His "Letters" (about 2,700) are a charming
and important document of the history of his time.

504

Walpole, Sir Hugh

English novelist (1884-1941).

Born in Auckland, New Zealand; died in London. His novels, immensely popular at the time, are not likely to last, with the possible exception of the series called "The Herries Chronicle" (1925-1939), a family tale.

Walther von der Vogelweide

German poet (1170-1227 to 1230).

Believed to have been born in the Tyrol and died in Würzburg. Educated at the Babenberg court of Austria and studied poetry under the troubadour Reimar the Old. He spent most of his life at the courts of German emperors and princes. A staunch supporter of the Hohenstaufen emperors against the Popes and the Guelphs, whom the Papacy supported, in his political "Sayings" and religious poems like "The Song of the Cross." But it was not these, but pure lyrics and love songs, e.g. "Under the Linden Trees" that make him the greatest poet of medieval Germany.

Wang Wei

(Chinese, *ca.* 700-760).

Leading Sung landscape painter. Also devout Buddhist as well as successful politician. Su Shih said of him: "There is painting in his poetry and poetry in his painting." Noted for his four-line *chueh-chu* poems.

Warren, Robert Penn

American writer (born 1905).

Born in Guthrie, Kentucky. Youngest of the group of southern agrarians who founded "The Fugitive." Poet, critic and playwright. His novel, "All the King's Men" (1946) won the Pulitzer Prize. It is a powerful study of a Louisiana dictator that is unmistakably modeled on Huey Long, with a thorough examination of the forces that brought about his rise and fall.

Washington, Booker T.

American Negro educator and writer (1856-1915).

Born in Hale's Ford, Va., died in Tuskegee, Ala. Born a slave, he educated himself and devoted his life to educating his race. The Tuskegee Institute is his monument. Wrote "Up from Slavery" (1901), an autobiography of the inspirational type that has been translated into many languages.

Wassermann, Jakob

German novelist (1873-1934).

Born in Fuerth, of Jewish origin, died in Alt-Aussee. Won an international reputation with novels that often dealt with strange characters and situations. Wrote: "The Jews of Zirndorf" (1897); "Caspar Hauser" (1908); "The Maurizius Case" (1928), etc.

Waugh, Evelyn

English novelist (born 1903).

Born in London. Studied at Oxford, became converted to Roman Catholicism, officer in World War II. His novels are often satirical and sometimes devotional and include: "Decline and Fall" (1928), "Scoop" (1938), "The Loved One" (1948), and "Brideshead Revisited" (1954).

Wedekind, Frank

German dramatist (1864-1918).

Born in Hanover, died in Munich. One of the founders of the expressionist drama, with bohemian and anti-bourgeois overtones. Only one of his plays, "Spring's Awakening" (1891) is still played.

Wells, Herbert George

English writer (1866-1946).

Born in Bromley, Kent, now part of London; died

in London. Began as a science teacher, became a journalist. "H. G.," as he was generally known, wrote very popular novels of what is now called science fiction, and books popularizing science. A staunch materialist, rationalist, and pacifist, he lived to see the ruin of his ideals in World War II. His last book was called, characteristically, "Mind at the End of Its Tether" (1944). Time will tell how much of his work will remain significant. It includes: "The Time Machine" (1895), "The Invisible Man" (1897), "The First Man in the Moon" (1901), "Kipps" (1905), "A Short History of the World" (1922); "The Work, Wealth, and Happiness of Mankind" (1932).

Welty, Eudora
American novelist (born 1909).

Born in Jackson, Mississippi. Her novels and short stories deal with the more exotic and grotesque aspects of life in the Deep South. They include: "The Robber Bridegroom" (1942) and "Delta Wedding" (1946).

Werfel, Franz
Austrian writer (1890-1945).

Born in Prague; died in Beverly Hills, California. Worked at first as a publisher's reader. An expressionist poet who became a novelist with books like "Not the Murderer But the Victim Is Guilty" (1920), "Paul Among the Jews" (1928), and "The Forty Days of Musa Dagh" (about the Armenian massacres, 1933). Had an adventurous and hair-raising escape from the Nazis which he attributed to Saint Bernadette. He became a Catholic convert and wrote "The Song of Bernadette" (1941), which made him world-famous.

Wergeland, Henrik
Norwegian writer (1808-1845).

Born in Kristiansand, died in Oslo. Son of a clergyman who dabbled in politics, studied theology at Oslo

University. His radical views prevented him from obtaining preferment until 1840, when the King appointed him as archivist. He had to earn a living by journalism and a life full of privations made him a victim of tuberculosis. Wergeland was primarily a lyrical poet in the high romantic vein that made him the author of the Norwegian national anthem. He also wrote plays and a constitutional history of Norway. He is still Norway's national poet.

Werner, Zacharias
German writer (1768-1823).

Born in Koenigsberg (East Prussia); died in Vienna. Studied law at Koenigsberg University, did not complete his course, and, after a short spell as a civil servant, lived a wandering life. After a spectacular conversion to Catholicism he became a priest in 1813. A dramatist, he excelled in the "tragedy of fate." His masterpiece is "February 24" (1815), in which all possible things—and a few impossible ones—happen on that day.

Wharton, Edith
American novelist (1862-1937).

Born Edith Newbold Jones in New York, died in Saint-Brice-sous-Foret, France. Friend and disciple of Henry James (q.v.). Her background of New York society upbringing gave a ring of truth to her ironical novel "The Age of Innocence" (1920). She is best known, however, for a grim New England tragedy, "Ethan Frome" (1911).

Whitman, Walt
American poet (1819-1892).

Born in West Hills on Long Island, N. Y., of Dutch and Quaker parentage; died in Camden, N. J. After working as office boy, printer's devil, schoolmaster, and typesetter, started his journalistic career as editor of the Brooklyn "Eagle" (1846-48); continued it in New Orleans and elsewhere. His poetic career began when he published the first edition of his masterpiece, "Leaves of Grass," in 1855 (other revised and enlarged editions till 1891-92). Served as a hospital nurse in Washington during the Civil War (1862-64); became a clerk in the Department of the Interior but was summarily dismissed a year later (1865) by the Secretary of the Interior who objected to his poetry. Obtained another clerk's post at the Attorney General's office, kept it for eight years (1865-73), until he was stricken with paralysis and retired to Camden. His work also includes "Drum Taps" (1865), "A Passage to India" (1871), "Two Rivulets" (1876), "November Boughs" (1888), and "Goodbye, My Fancy" (1891). Whitman's poetry was influenced by the Bible, Shakespeare, Ossian, Scott, and Dante, among others; and by childhood memories of the powerful, hypnotic preaching of the Quaker schismatic Elias Hicks; all this he merged into an unmistakably individual and American style. His verse is dithyrambic in style ("Whitmanesque"), unconventional in its opinions and feelings, and varies in quality. This was partly why recognition of its merits came slowly and at first from abroad. But he was not wholly unappreciated in his lifetime. Emerson, to his lasting credit, encouraged Whitman and strove to gain recognition for him.

Whittier, John Greenleaf
American poet (1807-1892).

Born in Haverhill, Mass., died in Hampton Falls, N. H. Grew up on the Massachusetts farm of his Quaker parents, which he later described in his most famous poem, "Snowbound" (1866). Received a scanty education and edited country newspapers. His pamphlet "Justice and Expediency" (1833) announced his anti-slavery stand, which he maintained uncompromisingly through all the dark days ahead. He wrote political and religious poems as well as ballads in the salty New England style.

Wieland, Christoph Martin

German writer and philosopher (1733-1813).

Born in Oberholzheim; died in Weimar. Taught philosophy at Erfurt, became tutor of the heir to the throne of the Duchy of Saxony-Weimar and moved to its capital. Wieland was at his best as a satirist, in the 18th century style; but his "Story of Agathon" (two volumes, 1766-67) was an important model for the German "novel of education and growth" describing the development of a man, a genre cultivated by Goethe and Mann among many others. Other works include: "Don Silvio de Rosalva" (1764), "The Abderites" (1774), "Oberon" (1780).

Wilde, Oscar

Anglo-Irish writer (1854-1900).

Born in Dublin; died in Paris. Studied at Trinity College, Dublin, and moved to Oxford, because as Provost Mahaffy put it, "he wasn't clever enough for Trinity College, Dublin." Wilde spent most of his life disproving Mahaffy's stricture. He became an aesthete who delighted in "shocking the bourgeois" in England and America, where he lectured in 1892. He walked down Piccadilly in London holding a lily in his hand and told the American customs officer that he had nothing to declare but his genius. Wilde was at his most brilliant in his comedies, sparkling with wit and paradox: "Lady Windermere's Fan" (1892), "A Woman of No Importance" (1893), "An Ideal Husband" (1895), and "The Importance of Being Earnest" (1899), which are still played and have been made into movies. He also wrote a "Salome" (1894) which was produced in French with Sara Bernhardt in the lead and was later made into an opera by Richard Strauss. Some of his short stories, collected in "The Happy Prince and Other Stories" (1888) show him at his most charming. But the more serious side of his aestheticism showed itself in "The Picture of Dorian Gray," with its premonitions of doom. Doom duly came to Wilde with a trial for homosexuality, in which he fell victim to a prudery that objected as much to his manners as to his morals. A two-year prison term chastened him and produced the heart-rending "Ballad of Reading Jail" (1895-97). His last years were spent in poverty and despair in Paris.

Wilder, Thornton

American novelist and playwright (born 1897).

Born in Madison, Wisconsin. His father was U.S. consul in China, and young Wilder lived there for several years. Studied in the United States and at the American Academy in Rome. Taught English at the Lawrenceville Academy and the University of Chicago in the twenties and thirties. Started on his literary career with a successful novel, "Cabala" (1925). His fiction also includes "The Bridge of San Luis Rey" (1927), which won the Pulitzer Prize, as did his play "The Skin of Our Teeth" (1942). Wilder's greatest stage success was "Our Town" (1938), a play conceived in the American spirit of the New Deal that is a standby of little theaters and dramatic societies.

Williams, Tennessee

American playwright (born 1914).

Real name: Thomas Lanier Williams. Born in Columbus, Miss. His plays, now played on the world's stages, use symbolism—often of the weirdest and most sexual variety—to point up the contrast between reality and illusion. Their outlook on life is as grim as could be and it is significant in this respect that Wil-

liams himself has expressed the fear that psychoanalysis may make him view life more cheerfully and
dry up the sources of his creativity. Plays include:
"The Glass Menagerie" (1946), "A Streetcar Named
Desire" (1947), "The Rose Tattoo" (1950).

Williams, William Carlos

American poet (born 1883).

Born in Rutherford, New Jersey. Studied medicine
at the universities of Leipzig and Pennsylvania, has
practiced it in his native town since 1905. His poetry
is characterized by sharp observation and colloquial
language. Best-known for his long poem, "Paterson"
(1946).

Winckelmann, Johann Joachim

German critic (1717-1768).

Born in Stendal, North Germany, died in Trieste,
killed in a mysterious tavern brawl. Tutor and librarian, became converted to Roman Catholicism in 1754,
and went to Rome a year later. The Vatican employed
him as librarian and art custodian, and he was able to
visit Florence, Naples, and Pompeii. Winckelmann's
researches helped to found the science of art history;
they revolutionized our aesthetic conceptions and our
views of classical antiquity. Winckelmann was an
idealist. His classicism inspired men like Goethe and
was not seriously challenged until Nietzsche developed
his dichotomy of "Dionysian" and "Apollonian."
Winckelmann's chief works are "Thoughts on the
Imitation of Greek Works in Painting and Sculpture"
(1755) and "History of Classical Art" (1767).

Wolfe, Thomas

American novelist (1900-1938).

Born in Asheville, N. C., died in Baltimore. Studied
at the University of North Carolina and at Harvard,
where he took drama courses. Taught English at New

York University (1924-30). Was freed from teaching by the success of his first novel, "Look Homeward, Angel" (1929), followed by a number of others, including "Of Time and the River" (1935), "The Web and the Rock" (published 1939) and "You Can't Go Home Again" (1940), as well as short stories. He made a number of trips to Europe, especially to Germany, the home of some of his ancestors. He remained, nonetheless, one of the most American of writers, for good and for bad, and this is the foundation of his enduring popularity in his native land as well as in Europe. The epic sweep of his story is matched by the shapelessness of his form, which makes his writings look like fragments of a single novel that has neither beginning nor end. Wolfe owed a good deal to his editor, Maxwell Perkins. To his credit, he acknowledged his debt to Perkins even after the breach between them, caused by envious writers who claimed that Perkins actually "wrote" Wolfe's novels rather than just edited them.

Wolfram Von Eschenbach

German medieval poet (about 1170-about 1220).

Born and died in Eschenbach in Franconia. Forced by poverty to seek the patronage of princes, wandered from one princely court to another. His patrons often furnished the themes of his works. The most illustrious of them was the Landgrave Hermann of Thuringia, at whose court he met Walther Von der Vogelweide. This is the factual foundation of the legends of the "Poets' War at Wartburg Castle." Wolfram was a great epic and lyric poet. The inspiration of his lyrics, especially the "Day Songs" and "Love Songs" is personal and German. The theme of his chief epic "Parsifal" is French; he used the model provided by Chrestien de Troyes (q.v.). But he pervaded it with Teutonic depth and a very personal moral earnestness, and it was his "Parsifal," not Chrestien's, that inspired Wagner's opera. Wolfram also wrote epical fragments on the Arthurian theme of Titurel and an unfinished epic on the medieval William of Orange, whom he presented as a model of knightly virtues.

Woolf, Virginia

English novelist (1882-1941).

Born Virginia Stephen, daughter of the critic Sir Leslie Stephen, died by suicide in the Ouse river, Sussex. Married Leonard Woolf, one of the leading British socialists and critic of the colonial system. Her novels are weak in plot and strong in psychology and use the "stream-of-consciousness" technique. They include: "Mrs. Dalloway" (1925), "Orlando" (1928), and "Between the Acts" (1941).

Woolman, John

American essayist and abolitionist (1720-1772).

Born on the banks of the Rancocas in New Jersey; died in York, England, of smallpox, while on a preaching tour. A Quaker whose life is generally regarded as the purest example of the Quaker variety of saintliness. He worked as a tailor and orchardist, branched out as a merchant and prospered, then abandoned this business because he was accumulating more "outward cumber" than he needed to live comfortably: Poverty, he felt, was due to the selfishness of those who are not poor, and he embodied this view in his essay "A Word of Caution and Remembrance to the Rich" which was reprinted a century and a half later as a socialist tract by the Fabian Society. But his life work was in the cause of abolition of Negro slavery, to which end he traveled and preached extensively, and wrote a two-part essay "Considerations on the Keeping of Negroes" (Part I, 1754; Part II, 1762). His primary emphasis was not on the enslaved Negro but on the spiritual dangers of being a slaveholder, and his method relied on personal persuasion and example rather than exhortation. He lived to see slaveholding completely wiped out among Quakers, and perhaps more than any other man deserves the title of Father of American Abolitionism. Today he is chiefly known for his posthumous "Journal" (1774), a spiritual autobiography remarkable for its gentle, serene spirit, its pure, subdued style, and the magnanimity of the views it expresses. It is the noblest specimen of a genre of Quaker journals written to convert non-Quakers and provide an example for Quaker children; as such it was heavily "edited" by the Quaker Overseers of the Press, and Woolman's original version was not published until 1950.

Wordsworth, William

English poet (1770-1850).

Born in Cockermouth, Cumberland, died in his Rydal Mount property in the Lake District. Studied in Cambridge. Traveled in France and Switzerland in 1791. Sympathized at first with the French Revolution; was later horrified by its excesses. Had an affair with Marie Anne Vallon, who bore him a daughter. She is the "Annette" of his poems. A walking tour in the Swiss Alps inspired him to write "Descriptive Sketches" (1793). Was deeply disillusioned and a prey to pessimism for several years after his return to England. His spirits were lifted by the devotion of his sister Dorothy, his constant companion, his friendship with Coleridge (q.v.) and the great success of their first literary venture, the "Lyrical Ballads" (1798-1805), which inaugurated fully-fledged English romanticism and is one of the landmarks of English literature. Wordsworth's chief contribution was his "Lines composed a few miles above Tintern Abbey." His statements on the functions and techniques of poetry caused a furor among his contemporaries. Went to Germany in 1798-99, lived in Goslar, and started there a spiritual autobiography in verse, "The Prelude," which was not published until after his death. In 1799 settled in the Lake District, where he acquired Rydal Mount on Grasmere in 1813. The beauties of the Lake District inspired some of his best poetry which, in turn, made the Lakes one of England's most popular beauty spots. His later views are marked by increased conservatism and decreased poetic powers. He became Poet Laureate in 1843.

Wright, Richard
American Negro novelist (born 1908).

Born in Natchez, Miss. Moved northwards to Chicago, later New York. Embraced Communism but was soon disillusioned with it. His "Native Son" (1940) added a new, existentialist, dimension to the American Negro novel. "Twelve Million Black Voices" (1941) was a folk history of the Negro, with emphasis on his sufferings; "Black Boy" (1945) —his own poignant and bitter autobiography. Has lived in Paris since the war because, as he puts it "there is more freedom in a Paris back street than in the whole United States of America." For all that, he himself has remained clearly and unmistakably American, and his writing shows no appreciable impact of France or any other country but America.

Wyatt, Sir Thomas
English poet (1503-1542).

Was ambassador of Henry VIII to Italy (1526), France (1528-32) and Spain (1537-39). Derived his poetical innovations, including the English Petrarcan sonnet, from what he learned on his travels. His own best poems treat love in a most un-Petrarcan manner: their sentiments are robust and they are written in short meters designed for songs accompanied by the lute.

Wyclif, John

English religious reformer (1320-1384).

Born near Richmond, Yorkshire. Attacked the abuses of church and state of the England of his day, which were many and bad. Advocated a return to the Bible and the early, uncorrupted Christianity; rejected transubstantiation and the mediating power of the priest between man and God. To spread his views, translated the Bible into English and sent out "poor preachers" to teach the people. His followers were called Lollards.

X

Xenophon
Greek historian (about 435-about 355 B.C.) .

Born in Athens, died in Corinth. A pupil of Socrates. Joined a Greek expedition to Persia organized by Cyrus the Younger to overthrow his brother, king Artaxerxes II. After Cyrus' defeat and death at Cunaxa (401) , he led 10,000 Greek soldiers in an adventurous retreat to the Black Sea. His pro-Spartan views and activities led to his exile from Athens. He lived at Olympia, later moved to Corinth. Xenophon's numerous works reveal a man of action rather than a man of letters; but their value is by no means only documentary. Socrates is the hero of his "Memorabilia" and "Symposium." His "Hellenica" continues the Greek history of Thucydides. Cyrus the Younger inspired the "Cyropedia," a historical novel rather than history. Xenophon also wrote treatises on horsemanship and economics. But he gained immortality not with either of these but with the "Anabasis"; the heart-stirring and epic account of the Retreat of the Ten Thousand.

Y

Yamanoe No Okura

(Japanese, 659-733). Moralist and philosopher. One of the best poets from the *Manyōshū* anthology. Notable for his sympathy for the suffering poor and for children. Pursued a diplomatic career.

Yeats, William Butler

Irish poet (1865-1939).

Born in Sandymount near Dublin, died in Cap Martin on the French Rivera. Spent his boyhood in the wild countryside of County Sligo which left a permanent imprint on his mind and on his verse. His first writings show the mark of the "Celtic Revival," notably the "Wanderings of Oisin" (1889). But Yeats was also in the mainstream of English letters, beginning with his early friendships with William Morris, W. E. Henley and Arthur Symons, and although he chose the Irish nationality and became a Senator of the Irish Free State, there was nothing provincial about his Irishness. He took a prominent part in the great Irish cultural revival of the turn of the century. The title of his book of essays "The Celtic Twilight" (1893) became proverbial. For the nascent Irish theater he wrote plays in verse—"The Countess Kathleen" (1892) and "The Land of the Heart's Desire" (1894) —and in prose—"Cathleen in Houlihan" (1902) ; "The Hour Glass" (1904) etc. He was also a leading spirit behind the Abbey Theater and induced J. M. Synge (q.v.) to come home to Ireland and to become a playwright. But for all these varied activities Yeats remained primarily a poet. His poetry grew from a youthful "embroidered" style into an austere maturity in works like "The Wild Swans at Coole" (1917) and "The Tower" (1927). He was much aided in this transition by Ezra Pound (q.v.) who changed his emphasis from the abstract to the concrete. Yeats' politics were those of a poet. He hailed the heroic failure of the Irish Easter Rising of 1916 in one of his most moving poems; he grew weary of the small and petty minds that came to govern independent Ireland and gave vent to some pro-Fascist utterances. He was also an adherent of spiritualism and published in "A Vision" (1926) opinions that were purportedly transmitted to his wife by supernatural powers. Yeats was moved by a despair over the catastrophic decline of the values of Western civilization. His international stature was sanctioned by the Nobel Prize he received in 1923.

Yuan Mei

Chinese writer (1716-1798).

Born in Hangchow, died in Nanking. A civil servant, was fortunate to retire at 32. His house and garden became a gathering place for male and female disciples. He advocated "natural genius" in literature, asked that poetry must have free form, expression and choice of subject—the same things that the romanticists were demanding in Europe at that time. However, the classicist tradition that Yuan Mei was attacking was infinitely stronger. He excelled as poet, essayist and letter writer.

Yunus Emre or Emer

Turkish poet (died 1320).

Lived in Anatolia, but travelled in Syria and Persia and met Rumi (q.v.) and other mystics. His poems preach mysticism in a very pure Turkish and in the traditional Turkish syllabic meter. He was very popular in his day: seven villages in Anatolia claim to possess his tomb. He was then forgotten until revived in the 19th century as part of the renascence of old Turkish cultural traditions against the Arab and Persian.

Z

Zamyatin, Evgenii Ivanovich

Russian novelist (1884-1939).

Born in Lebedyan, died in France. Wrote satires in which he spared neither his native Russia nor England, a country in which he lived several years. Got into hot water with the Soviet authorities over his novel "We," a Soviet forecast of 1984. He wrote it as early as 1920, and Orwell read it in English translation. Zamyatin had to publish it abroad (1924-29), and was permitted to leave Russia in 1931.

Zhukovsky, Vasily Andreyevich

Russian poet (1783-1852).

Born in Tula, died in Baden-Baden, Germany. Illegitimate son of a Russian landowner and a Turkish slave girl. Received a good education. Translated a good deal from German and English, including Gray's "Elegy," as well as the Homeric epics. These translations are perhaps more important for the sudden flowering of Russian letters than his own writings, which tend to be sentimental and popular in vein. His best-known poem is "Svetlana." Zhukovsky prepared the coming of Pushkin; to his great credit he hailed him as a master and was a prominent member of his circle. In dealings with his fellow writers he displayed a good will and generosity as admirable as they were rare.

Zola, Emile

French novelist (1840-1902).

Born and died in Paris. Son of an Italian father and a French mother. Spent his youth in the Southern French town of Aix-en-Provence, failed in his studies, and moved to Paris. Was employed at the Hachette bookstore, passed through some very difficult years until he gained a reputation as journalist and art critic. In the latter capacity he was one of the few champions of Cezanne, a friend from his Aix days. In literature he advocated an extreme naturalism which meant, in practice, meticulously accurate descriptions of the less pleasant aspects of human nature and denunciation of social evils. Leon Daudet sneered at him as "the Victor Hugo of the public toilet" but Zola's views had a worldwide resonance especially as presented in his novels. He followed some early successes, especially "Therese Raquin" (1867) with a series of 20 novels published under the collective title of "The Rougon Macquarts," including "The Belly of Paris" (1873); "The Slaughterhouse" (1877); "Nana" (1880, the classical novel of prostitution) "The Joy of Living" (1884); "Germinal" (1885); "The Debacle" (1892). Zola wanted to do for the Paris of the Third Empire what Balzac's "Human Comedy" did for the Paris of the July Monarchy and, within the limitations of his talents, he succeeded. He grew flabby with success, but was roused from his apathy by the Dreyfus affair. His defense of Dreyfus, in "I Accuse" (1898) earned him a term of exile in England and a place among the heroes of humanitarianism. He died of a mysterious poisoning with fumes from his stove.

Zoroaster

Persian religious leader (6th century B.C.).

His historicity has been doubted, but is now generally accepted. He founded a new religion, named

523

after him and based on the duality of good and evil. He is also supposed to have written the sacred book of his religion, called "Avesta," or at least some parts of it, the poems called "Gathas." Zoroaster's great personality inspired Westerners as well as Persians, notably Nietzsche.

Zorrilla, Jose
Spanish dramatist (1817-1893).

Born in Valladolid, died in Madrid. Studied law, but abandoned his studies to escape from his father. Travelled in France and Mexico. One of the most popular writers of Spanish Romanticism, was solemnly invested with the poet's crown in 1889. Today his reputation is at a low ebb, and only one of his numerous works survives, his "Don Juan Tenorio," a sentimental and watered-down dramatization of the Don Juan theme that is played every year in Spanish theaters in the first week of November.

Zoshchenko, Mikhail Mikhailovich
Russian writer (born 1895).

Born in Poltava. Wrote short stories like "The Woman Who Could Not Read," "The Electric Bulb" and "The Wonderful Dog" which treated the petty misfortunes of Soviet life with sardonic humor. Was singled out for attack by Zhdanov in 1947 as "individualist" and "cosmopolitan," tried to redeem himself with a novel about the war-time exploits of partisans and has remained more or less silent since.

Zuckmayer, Carl
German playwright (born 1896).

Born in Nackenheim in the Rhenish part of Hesse. Started as a poet, with anarchist sentiments. Gained popularity with "The Gay Vineyard" (1925), echoing the spirit of his native region. His democratic views made him dramatize the story of "The Captain of Koepenick" (1931) and emigrate to Switzerland and the United States when Hitler came to power. His "Devil's General" (1947), based on the case of a personal friend, General Udet, is one of the best treatments of the human issues that confronted the Germans through the victory of Nazism.

Zweig, Arnold

German novelist (born 1887).

Born at Glogau in Silesia, of Jewish origin. Served in World War I, which provided the setting for his two best-known novels "The Case of Sergeant Grisha" (1927) and "Education before Verdun" (1935), in which the horrors and dehumanization of war are denounced. Zweig spent the Hitler years in Palestine, where he settled accounts with the Nazis in a novel, "The Axe of Wandsbeck," about a butcher whom the Nazis turn into executioner. He now lives in East Germany.

Zweig, Stefan

Austrian writer (1881-1942).

Born in Vienna, died in Petropolis (Brazil). Member of a cultured Jewish family of the upper middle class, grew up in Vienna under the shadow of Sigmund Freud. His writing is at its best in its style and its psychological penetrations, e.g. in "Amok" (1923): "The Impatience of the Heart" (1938) and numerous biographical studies of Balzac, Fouche, Marie Antoinette, Erasmus etc. Hitler drove him to despair and exile; but when he finally committed suicide it was because he realized that his world was, in the title of his autobiography, "A World of Yesterday."

Zwingli, Ulrich

Swiss theologian (1484-1531).

Born in Wildhaus near Toggenburg, died in the

battle of Kappel. Became a priest and accompanied as such the mercenary troops that fought in the battles of Novara (1513) and Marignano (1515) in Italy. Returned home and received in 1519 an appointment to the Great Minister of Zurich. It was there that he preached his own brand of the Reformation, milder and more humane than that of Luther. Zwingli defended it in his "Of True and False Religion" (1525) and in theological debates with Luther. He was killed as chaplain of the Zurich troops fighting against the Catholic cantons.